Legends of the Security Services Industry

The global contract security market now totals over $200 billion, with the number of private security officers exceeding that of public law enforcement officers. But this wasn't always the case.

Legends of the Security Services Industry: Profiles in Leadership presents the unique stories of 15 industry legends, who transformed the industry from early private detective and small night watch companies into large-scale contract security companies. The large-scale companies include, but are not limited to, Pinkerton, Burns International, The Wackenhut Corporation, Guardsmark, Wells Fargo, and U.S. Security Associates; as well as today's leading security companies, Allied Universal, Securitas, G4S, Prosegur, and GardaWorld.

The book begins in the nineteenth century, with early U.S. legendary detectives: Allan Pinkerton and William Burns. Then, the book focuses largely from the mid-twentieth century to the present, where successive generations of legends built large-scale contract security companies which competed with, and then acquired, those formed by the early legends. Part II legends George Wackenhut, Ira Lipman, and Tom Wathen; Part III legends, Charles Schneider, Kenneth W. Oringer, William Whitmore, Jr., and Albert Berger; and Part IV, Scandinavian legends Jørgen Philip-Sørensen, Lars Nørby Johansen, and Thomas Berglund, all developed major security companies. Part V includes current global security leaders Helena Revoredo Gut, Stephan Crétier, and Steve Jones. Part VI reviews the timelines and successful leadership of these legendary leaders, with a look at the future of the industry.

The legends' personal stories contain colorful insight into how they capitalized on the industry's explosive growth. While each generation of legends faced unique social and competitive landscapes, their personal stories illustrate how they respectively succeeded. Their leadership and management prowess enabled them to achieve great success, as they displayed vision and achieved their goals through grit, determination, hard work, charisma, organizational skills, and calculated risk-taking.

Each chapter has been extensively researched and includes firsthand accounts based on interviews with living legends, colleagues, and family of deceased legends. Personal, company and signature event photos add further color to the moving narrative. Their stories are not only highly interesting, but also provide a framework for current leaders, and the next generation of entrepreneurs, on how to build and lead large-scale security service companies.

With a Foreword from Robert D. McCrie, PhD, longtime John Jay Professor and editor of the renowned industry publication *The Security Letter*.

Legends of the Security Services Industry

Profiles in Leadership

Keith Oringer
and
Michael Hymanson

CRC Press
Taylor & Francis Group
Boca Raton London New York

CRC Press is an imprint of the
Taylor & Francis Group, an **informa** business

First edition published 2025
by CRC Press
2385 NW Executive Center Drive, Suite 320, Boca Raton FL 33431

and by CRC Press
4 Park Square, Milton Park, Abingdon, Oxon, OX14 4RN

CRC Press is an imprint of Taylor & Francis Group, LLC

ISBN: 978-1-032-25904-8 (hbk)
ISBN: 978-1-032-25905-5 (pbk)
ISBN: 978-1-003-28556-4 (ebk)

DOI: 10.4324/9781003285564

Typeset in Sabon
by SPi Technologies India Pvt Ltd (Straive)

Dedicated to the memory of our beloved parents, Kenneth and Cecile Oringer, and Harry and Selma Hymanson.

"First say to yourself what you would be; and then do what you have to do."

Epictetus

Contents

Foreword   xvi

Preface   xix

Acknowledgments   xxi

About the Authors   xxiv

Introduction   1

How We Understand Security Services Today   2

The Growth of the Security Services Industry   3

How This Book Is Organized   5

Notes   7

PART I   THE EARLY LEGENDS

Chapter 1   Allan Pinkerton: America's First Great
            Detective   11

Early Life and Career   12

The Pinkerton Agency Grows   14

   Service during the Civil War   15

   Notable Hires: Kate Warne and George H. Bangs   15

   The Reno Gang   18

   The Express Companies: Pony Express, Wells Fargo   19

Key Business Innovations: The Pinkerton Code and the
Rogues' Gallery   20

Pinkerton's Later Life   21

   Violence in the Pennsylvania Coal Fields: The Molly
   Maguires   21

   Allan Pinkerton's Death and Company Succession   23

After Allan Pinkerton: The Homestead Strike and the
Anti-Pinkerton Act   23

    The Pinkerton Dynasty   24

    A Series of Ownership Changes   25

    Legacy   25

Notes   27

Chapter 2   **William J. Burns: Showman and Master
Investigator**   **31**

Early Life and Career   31

    Developing Theatrical Talent and Curiosity about
    People   31

    A Gift for Conversation and Getting Confessions   33

    Breaking the Brockway Counterfeiting Ring   33

    Conducting Land Fraud Investigations for the U.S.
    Department of the Interior   34

    Burns, Heney, and the San Francisco
    Corruption Cases   35

Founding of the Burns Namesake Agency   36

    Showtime: The 1910 *Los Angeles Times* Bombing   36

    Setbacks: 1913 Leo Frank Case, 1920 Wall Street
    Bombing   38

Bureau of Investigations Appointment and
Teapot Dome   40

The Burns Dynasty   42

    The Last Generation: George E. B. King   43

    Acquisition by Borg-Warner   43

    Legacy   43

Notes   45

PART II   NEW LEGENDS TAKE ON THE OLD GUARD

Chapter 3   **George R. Wackenhut: "Know-How and
Know-Whom"**   **49**

Early Life: Diving for the Ball   49

    Military Service, Pearl Harbor, and Marriage   52

    Teacher and Coach, Always Looking Ahead   56

    An FBI Stint Primes George for a Security Career   57

The Wackenhut Corporation Becomes an
Industry Power   58

    Organic Growth and Diversification at the
    Wackenhut Company   59

    Controversy and Notoriety   61

    Group 4 Falck Acquires the Company   64

Legacy   66

Notes   68

Chapter 4   **Ira A. Lipman: Principles and Profits**   **71**

Early Life and Career   71

    The Insider at Central High School in Little Rock   73

    Foundational Values   75

    Finding a Career Direction: Custom Security
    Services   75

Founding of Guardsmark   76

    Setting High Professional Standards   77

    Key Events Shape Guardsmark   79

    The Family Faces Adversity   81

Guardsmark Moves On   82

A Legacy of Philanthropy, Humanitarian, and Industry
Awards   82

    Endowments   83

    Humanitarianism   83

    Awards and Honors   83

    Authored Books and Articles   83

Reflections on a Legendary Career   84

Notes   86

Chapter 5   **Thomas W. Wathen: No Fear of Flying**   **88**

Early Life   88

    A Passion for Aerospace and Security   91

    Gone West   91

Growing CPP   92

    Understanding Risk Profiles—His Own and
    His Customers'   92

    Organic Growth   94

Storm Clouds 94

    A Challenging Acquisition 94

    Help from a Friend 95

    The GM Deal and a Change in Operational Leadership 96

Winds of Change 96

    Securitas Acquires Pinkerton 97

Legacy 97

Notes 100

PART III   A NEW WAVE OF COMPETITORS IN A GOLDEN ERA

Chapter 6   Charles R. Schneider: Engineering Success   107

Early Life and Education 107

    Service in the U.S. Navy 109

    Building Skills with People and Processes 111

Launching a Security Career at Baker Industries 111

    Borg-Warner Acquires Baker Industries 112

    Borg-Warner Acquires Burns International Security 113

    Mentors Help Chuck Succeed as a Leader 114

    Departure from Borg-Warner 115

Chuck Co-Founds U.S. Security Associates 116

    Implementing Systems and Controls for Operating Efficiency 117

    Right Partners, Right People 118

    Innovative Programs; Certifications and Awards 119

    Employee Morale and Company Growth 120

    U.S. Security Associates Acquired 121

Reflections on a Legendary Career 122

Notes 124

Chapter 7   Kenneth W. Oringer: The Artful Closer   126

Early Life and Career 126

    Law Degree, Military Service, and Marriage 127

    Breaking into Accounting, Tax, and Finance 128

Developing Financial Acumen   128

Searching, Then Finding a Security Career at Baker
Industries   130

Teaming Up with Systems Engineering Expert
Chuck Schneider   132

A Season of Change   133

Planting Seeds for U.S. Security Associates   134

Expansive Acquisitions and Successive Investors   136

Goldman Sachs Private Equity Takes a Majority
Stake in U.S. Security   140

Acquisition by Allied Universal   140

Reflections on a Legendary Career   141

Notes   143

Chapter 8   William C. Whitmore Jr.: A Steady Hand   144

Early Life and Career   144

Key Role as SpectaGuard Expands   146

Becoming a National Company Leader   148

Bill Leads Allied Security under New Ownership   149

AlliedBarton Attracts High-Profile Investors   150

AlliedBarton and Universal Services Merge   153

Legacy   153

Notes   156

Chapter 9   Albert J. Berger: The Right Formulas   159

Early Life and Education   159

A Mentor and Higher Education   161

Military Service and a Chemical Industry Career   161

Career in the Security Services Industry   162

A Chance Meeting   162

A Consequential Role at CPP and Pinkerton   162

At Gryphon Partners, CEO for SpectaGuard, and
Allied Security   163

MacAndrews and Forbes Buys Allied,
Acquires Barton   164

Mission Focused Management   166

Legacy and Charitable Work   167

Notes   169

PART IV   SCANDINAVIANS BUILD GLOBAL
COMPANIES

Chapter 10   Jørgen Philip-Sørensen: Traversing the Globe   175

Family Roots in the Security and Cleaning Industry   177

Erik Philip-Sørensen's Acquisitions Set the Stage for
Sons Jørgen and Sven   178

Jørgen's Early Life   178

Learning the Security Business the Hard Way   179

A Family Rift   180

Building Group 4 Globally   180

A Key Sponsorship   184

Integrating Security and Technology   184

Facing Obstacles   185

Major Mergers and Acquisitions   186

Legacy   186

Memorial Service Family Address by
Mark Philip-Sørensen   188

Notes   190

Chapter 11   Lars Nørby Johansen: Gaining Trust through
Solutions   193

Early Life   193

Leaving Academia for the Private Sector   194

Growing Falck's Security Company   195

Going Public and Accelerating Acquisitions   196

Two Legends Merge Their Firms   197

Group 4 Falck Acquires Wackenhut Corporation   198

Group 4 Falck Acquires Securicor, Falck Is Demerged   200

Lars Exits Group 4 Securicor   202

Legacy   204

Notes   206

Chapter 12   Thomas F. Berglund: Success by Lifting Others   209

Early Life and Education   210

From Government Service to Private Industry   211

Berglund's Security Industry Career at Securitas AB   213

Leading Securitas in the Tradition of Integrity,
Vigilance, and Helpfulness   214

Securitas Becomes the Leading Security Services
Company Worldwide   216

Reflections on a Legendary Career   220

Notes   224

PART V   TODAY'S GLOBAL SECURITY LEADERS

Chapter 13   Helena Revoredo Gut: Resilience and Vision   229

Early Life and Education   232

Prosegur Is Founded and Family Settles in Spain   233

Helena Steps Up to Run Prosegur   234

Prosegur's Global Expansion and Resilience   235

Expansion into the U.S. Market   236

Navigating Loss, Recession, and the Pandemic   236

A Successful Family Enterprise   238

Civic, Charitable, and Professional Endeavors   239

Notes   242

Chapter 14   Stephan Crétier: The Disruptor   244

Early Life in Canada   244

Lessons Learned from Baseball and College   245

Transition to the Security Industry   246

Building GardaWorld   247

Managing through the Financial Crisis of 2008   249

Garda Goes Private, Global Growth Continues   250

Garda Expands in U.S. Presence and Forms
New Divisions   251

The Battle for G4S   254

Garda Emerges Strong from the Pandemic   254

Garda's Rise as a Global Security Company   256

A Focused and Inspired Leader   257

Service and Awards   258

Notes   260

Chapter 15   Steve Jones: Up Tempo   263
              Early Life and Mentors   264
                  A Real-World Struggle   266
                  Fortune 500 Job Experience   267
              A Meteoric Security Career Begins   267
                  Quick Action after the 9/11 Attacks   269
                  Calculated Risks to Attain National Status   269
                  Advancing with Integrated Security   270
              Entering the New York Market   270
                  A Prized Acquisition   271
                  Universal Merges with AlliedBarton   272
                  The Acquisition Spree Continues   272
              Allied Universal Becomes the World's Largest Security
              Company   273
              Testaments   274
              Interview with Steve Jones   275
              Legacy   277
              Notes   279

PART VI   CONCLUSIONS: DYNAMIC PEOPLE,
           COMPANIES, AND TIMES

Chapter 16   Forward Momentum   285
              What Happened to the Legends and Their Companies   285
              Past Experiences Formed Strong Leaders   297
              Shared Attributes, Traits, and Values Promoted
              Success   298
              Unique Personalities, Leadership, and
              Management Styles   299
              Luck, Fate, and Enhancing Your Chance of Success   300
              Notes   302

Chapter 17   Opportunities for Future Leaders in the
              Security Services Industry   303
              Factors in the Growth of the Security Industry   303
              Investments in Technology Accelerate   305

Opportunities for Entrepreneurs   307

    Build from a Base and Leverage Relationships   307

    Have a Vision, a Plan and Execute   308

    Manage Risk   308

    Watch Your Cash Flow and Do Not Depend on Any
    One Customer   309

    Gain Traction, Expand, and Lead the Team   309

Management Opportunities in the Security Industry   310

Security Remains a Vital Service in a Challenging
Environment   311

Notes   312

Bibliography   314

Index   333

Foreword

"Are we safe?" Or "Are our assets safe?" Answers to these simple but inextricably profound questions provide the existential raison d'être of contemporary security services businesses in North America and elsewhere. Civilization mandates security. This is not really a debatable proposition. Without security, human well-being, the accumulation of capital to provide for growth, and the ability to creativity flourish for human betterment are all imperiled.

From earliest organized society, providing security—that is, the condition of being safe, secure, and out of harm's reach—has been an ongoing duty—indeed the *primary duty*—of those who govern. In the modern democratic era, this concept evolved in a way that created special opportunity for the private sector. The growth of cities and the expansion of maritime commerce created new security requirements. Protection was needed for commercial entities, factories, and storage facilities, as well as for packet ships with their precious cargoes resting at harborside. In Great Britain, by the nineteenth century, factory owners and ship captains or investors routinely hired watchmen, installed primitive alarms, and trained guard dogs to protect their people and property.

But as an organized economic activity, the origins of this type of enterprise—guarding—occurred far from the storage houses and docks of London. Serendipitously, the location of this new form of protection was Chicago. Rapid industrial growth in the mid-1800s had arrived in the United States, a period often termed the New Industrial Revolution. This exciting time was also one where progress had its perils. Railroads crossed the country, yet occasionally trains would be stopped en route and robbed. A few rail personnel themselves were thieves. Theft within the United States Postal Service was a concern. Also, no federal agency issued banknotes, so individual banks, insurance companies, and private businesses would issue their own "legal tender" as banknotes which could too easily be counterfeited. This offense often flourished with impunity, a nonviolent crime that attacked the reliability of business operations.

An unlikely pioneer emerged who was to create a new industry. Allan Pinkerton was an entrepreneur, a barrel maker working in Kane County, Illinois. When he learned that counterfeit banknotes were circulating in his area, the righteous Pinkerton tricked the crook and had him arrested. The sheriff in much more populous Cook County (Chicago) also had problems with counterfeit banknotes being passed there and threatening commerce. He entreated Pinkerton to become his first investigator, in fact the first working for any criminal justice agency in the United States. But the canny incipient sheriff's detective drove a bargain: he would work for the sheriff on a case-by-case basis and would maintain his independence, being free to take assignments from other police agencies and private industry, should there be any. This public investigator (and his growing band of operators) would become the first organized private detective agency, "the eye that never sleeps" in their parlance.

An offer from a consortium of railroads in 1855 provided significant recurring revenues ($10,000 per year) that permitted the business to expand.[1] Soon the Pinkertons developed a reputation for fearlessness, originality, honesty, and perseverance. They made important arrests in both the private and public sectors. You will read more about this security pioneer and "the Pinks" in a few pages. Allan Pinkerton's original services were investigations and consultations. With the Civil War, he offered his growing resources to Lincoln's government, briefly providing personal protection to Lincoln and then creating an important spy ring to aid the North. Their work is considered the precursor to the Secret Service.[2] Following the end of the war, industry expanded and Allan and his two sons were busy investigating a surge of railroad thefts. The now seasoned businessmen also had added a new service: guarding.

Revenues from armed and unarmed security personnel services soon surpassed that of investigations. A biographer of Allan Pinkerton writes, "Incredibly, at one point in its history, the Pinkerton organization employed more personnel than the standing army of the United States."[3] Guarding had become a critically important business and, in the decades to follow, it would only grow larger—an agency to make people feel safe, a force to deter crime and maintain order, and a service as the true first responders when an emergency or untoward event occurs.

Today contract security guard personnel is the largest single component based on expenditures and personnel for the category of protection services, products, and systems. Global manned guarding for 2022 is estimated at $201.2 billion.[4] In North America alone, there are over 8,000 entities providing guarding service with the top three companies accounting for $21 billion in revenues. These are fascinating enterprises. The ease-of-entry for this commercial endeavor remains uncomplicated: just get and keep the contract. But what then?

In *Legends of the Security Services Industry: Profiles in Leadership*, you will encounter 15 profiles of "legends," many with amazing and often candid stories of their founding and development of the foremost private sector security businesses of their day. Through their exemplary and extraordinary leadership skills, the 14 men and one woman profiled—hailing from the United States, Canada, Europe, and South America—turned smaller guard and investigative companies into large-scale security guard and patrol services. This book will reveal how the four leading global security companies were formed, and how they are coupled today with extensive consulting and security technology divisions.

The passionate compilers and editors of this volume couldn't be more appropriate for the task they have undertaken. Keith Oringer and Michael Hymanson were "born into" the contract security guard industry, being sons of principals of security guard businesses, and they have spent much of their careers in it. Both are well known; indeed, this exceptional book could only be realized by persons possessing deep knowledge of the industry and be trusted by many of those "legends" profiled to share candid facts and opinions of their businesses and the particular developmental trek they have taken.

Legends of the Security Services Industry: Profiles in Leadership includes much that can inform and entertain diverse audiences. It will provide good reading for anyone interested in knowing about the gestation of the contract security industry and how some enterprises rose above their competitors. Would-be and successful entrepreneurs will glean how service businesses evolved historically and especially during the recent past. Then again, the retired law enforcement officer who dreams of becoming a security guard company operator had better pay attention to these pages. Finally, educators and their students in criminal justice, management and entrepreneurial studies, and security management will ascertain how private security services hold a critical role in making and keeping clients—and larger society—safe.

Robert McCrie, PhD, CPP
Professor of Security Management
John Jay College of Criminal Justice/CUNY

NOTES

1 Robert McCrie, "Allan Pinkerton (August 25, 1819–July 1, 1884): Founder of the Security Services Industry." *Journal of Applied Security Research* 5 (2010): 1–10.
2 Jay Bonansinga, *Pinkerton's War: The Civil War's Greatest Spy and the Birth of the U.S. Secret Service.* (Guilford, CT: Lyons Press, 2012).
3 Bonansinga, 248.
4 Global Industry Analysts, Inc., "Manned Guarding Services—Global Strategic Business Report," November, 2023.

Preface

As longtime security service industry owners and executives, the authors, Keith Oringer, and Michael Hymanson, initially became acquainted as mutual members of business and industry associations. Ten years later in 2006, U.S. Security Associates, a company cofounded by Keith's father, Kenneth W. Oringer, and where Keith was employed, acquired Michael's company, Pan American Investigation Service. Keith served as the New York Metro business unit president into 2014 and then founded Security ProAdvisors in 2015. Michael continued to work for U.S. Security into 2018, and the authors remained in touch before collaborating on *Legends of the Security Services Industry: Profiles in Leadership*.

When Keith became aware that no previous book examined the lives of multiple industry legends who created or developed the great security companies, he approached Michael about authoring a book that would contain their stories. Ideas for the book project began to take shape, and encouraged by a mutual acquaintance, Robert D. McCrie, PhD—a professor at John Jay College of Criminal Justice and author of various industry publications—we put together an outline to seek a book publisher. When the publisher gave us the green light to proceed, research began, as did the arrangement of interviews with living legends, relatives of deceased legends, and persons familiar with the legends.

Because we had sought to delve into the early lives and personalities of the legend's interviews proved to be a key to accomplishing this vision. From these we were able to develop interesting background stories to present to readers, in addition to facts about their business careers, and information about their impact on the trajectory of their respective companies. In the process, we learned and discovered much about the individuals profiled in the book. The authors formed new acquaintances through speaking and working with some of the legends, their family members, and associates. We developed an appreciation for the legends' hard work, perseverance, leadership, and management skills that went into the creation of their large-scale security companies. Their stories inspired us, and our interest in and respect for them grew as the book progressed.

During the project, which has taken over two years to come to fruition, much has happened. Keith's father, Ken, who is one of the legends
profiled in the book, passed away; as did Donald Walker, a well-known
industry executive whom we interviewed. We believe each recognized the
importance of their contribution to the book, and we regret that they did
not survive to see the work published. For those legends profiled who are
still alive, and for those individuals who contributed to our work, along
with our readers: we hope that you will join us in our interest and fascination with the stories included here. For people who were instrumental
in building great security service companies that we did not profile, we
trust that you will understand that we did not intentionally overlook
anyone but chose to focus on the 15 legends in the book. To each reader
of our book—enjoy!

Acknowledgments

The authors would like to thank, recognize, and acknowledge the legends, family members, colleagues, and industry executives below who participated and gave their time to the authors for our project. Without their contributions, the book would not have come to fruition. The order in which we present the names below is based on the chapter order in which the legends appear.

Richard R. "Rick" Wackenhut, son of the late legend, George R. Wackenhut, who is profiled in Chapter 3, gave significant support and time to our project through several interviews and by providing us with photos and other information. His personal account was informed by his career and senior executive positions at the Wackenhut Corp.

Gustave K. "Gus" Lipman, son of the late legend, Ira A. Lipman, profiled in Chapter 4, was interviewed by the authors and provided us with several photos. Like Rick Wackenhut, Gus's insights were also enhanced through his career and senior executive positions at his family-owned security company, Guardsmark.

Susan Wathen, the youngest sister of the late legend, Thomas W. Wathen, who is profiled in Chapter 5, participated enthusiastically in our interview. Her contributions and colorful family stories resonated with the authors. Donald W. Walker, a renowned senior security executive, was interviewed by the authors about his time working with Thomas. Despite being in ill health, Don generously gave his time to speak with us. He passed away on October 13, 2022.

Charles R. "Chuck" Schneider, profiled in Chapter 6, spoke with the authors on several occasions and provided us with valuable personal and business insight into the security industry and his management style. He also provided the authors with photos, and an audio recording about his naval experience, highlights of which are contained in the chapter. The authors had the pleasure of working for Chuck Schneider, as well as Kenneth W. Oringer (see below) during their respective employment at U.S. Security Associates. Keith Oringer also worked at Baker Industries, during the time Chuck and Ken were there as well.

Kenneth W. "Ken" Oringer, profiled in Chapter 7, is the father of author Keith Oringer. He passed away on September 28, 2022. Ken was interviewed formally and informally many times during the project. He provided photos, materials, and much information. His insights, wit, and wisdom will forever be remembered.

Alton Harvey, Denman Brown, Mark Reed, and John Harford worked in executive or management positions at U.S. Security Associates and provided us with their reflections on the leadership and management styles of Chuck Schneider and Ken Oringer for Chapters 7 and 8.

David I. Buckman, a senior executive at Allied Universal, provided his time and insight into the management skill of William C. "Bill" Whitmore Jr., who is profiled in Chapter 8. David was hired by Bill and worked alongside him while at AlliedBarton, and Allied Universal.

Albert J. "Al" Berger, profiled in Chapter 9, was interviewed for several hours by the authors on June 12 and August 14, 2023. In addition to providing information on his career, he commented on working alongside both Tom Wathen, Chapter 5 and Bill Whitmore, Chapter 8.

Ron Rabena, Chief Client Officer at Allied Universal, was the Senior Vice President of Operations, SpectaGuard when Al Berger and Gryphon Partners acquired SpectaGuard. He shared his thoughts on Al's leadership and management with the authors, and provided photos for this chapter as well as for Chapter 8.

Without question, the cooperation we received from Waldemar Schmidt, a noted Danish businessman, author, and educator, cannot be minimized. Waldemar was interviewed and provided us with much information on Jørgen Philip-Sørensen and his family, for Chapter 10. He also facilitated our interview with and provided information on Lars Nørby Johansen, Chapter 11; he likewise provided comments on Thomas F. Berglund, Chapter 12. Chris Holliday also provided the authors with information on Jørgen. Lars Nørby Johansen, and Thomas F. Berglund, profiled respectively in Chapters 11 and 12, were interviewed and provided us with photos as well. They were witty, congenial, and brilliant, as well as enthusiastic in their support of our book. For Chapter 12 we also thank Tony Sabatino, Chief Executive Officer of Securitas Critical Infrastructure Services, Inc., for providing comments on Thomas Berglund, as well as photos.

Helena Revoredo Gut, profiled in Chapter 13, provided the authors with written responses to submitted questions; and her devoted and brilliant son Christian Gut, the CEO of Prosegur Compañía de Seguridad, S.A., was interviewed and provided us with photos. We also recognize Jaime Ron Alpañes, Director—Office of the Chief Executive Officer at Prosegur, for his assistance in arranging interviews and providing photos and information from Helena and Christian Gut.

Ashish Karandikar, a partner at Apax, a firm that invested in GardaWorld, and Jean-Michel Filiatrault, a senior executive at GardaWorld, provided the authors with their insights on the management and leadership style of Stephan Crétier, profiled in Chapter 14. Stephan's interview with the authors was marked by his enthusiasm as an owner-operator of one of the world's foremost security services company. We are deeply grateful to Stephan for his help in facilitating our interview with Christian Gut. Both men have a deep respect and friendship for each other. In addition, we acknowledge Isabelle Panelli, Vice President, Office of the CEO at GardaWorld, for arranging our interview with Stephan Crétier and for providing photos.

For Chapter 15, profiling Steve Jones, we thank Steve for participating in an interview. We acknowledge Allied Universal executives Justin Nagy, President, Central Region and John Harford, VP of Corporate Development, for their comments on Steve's leadership. We also thank Lori D. Olin, VP Communications at Allied Universal, for her assistance in setting up the interview with Steve and for providing photos.

The following people provided technical and logistical support to the authors. Their knowledge and skills enabled the authors to better understand the intricacies involved in completing the manuscript, and this book. We would not have been able to execute the project without their help. Professor Robert D. McCrie, PhD, assisted the authors in getting our work started and provided ongoing assistance with the book. His industry knowledge and educational acumen are deeply appreciated, as is his work on the book Foreword. Susan Herman of Rhuby Editorial provided ongoing critical, technical, and creative assistance. Maureen G. Nowak, Maureen G. Nowak Photography, arranged and helped select photos for presentation by the authors to the publisher. Maureen also was the photographer for the photos of the authors. Photos of the authors were taken at 100 Summit Lake Drive in Valhalla, New York, through the courtesy of Reckson Associates Realty executives, John D. Barnes and Will Overlock. We also thank Harriet E. Donnelly of e5 Marketing Inc., who designed and created several tables contained in the book. Lastly, we thank Mark Listewnik, Senior Editor, Forensic Science/Homeland Security at Taylor & Francis, who collaborated with the authors from inception, through publication.

About the Authors

FIGURE 0.1 Authors Michael Hymanson (left) and Keith Oringer (right). (Maureen G. Nowak Photography)

Keith Oringer has a distinguished career in the security industry and currently serves as president of Security ProAdvisors, which he founded in 2015. The company is a leading brokerage, advisory and consulting firm to the industry, completing many significant acquisition transactions representing sellers. Keith is the publisher of *The Security Advisor* and has authored articles for that magazine, *Security Magazine*, and several others. He is a frequent speaker at industry associations, including NASCO (National Association of Security Companies), and a member of ASIS International. Keith obtained a BS in Accounting from SUNY Binghamton, an MBA in Finance from Pace University, and became a CPA. He began his business career at KPMG in accounting and then as a senior financial analyst at Merrill Lynch, and then W.R. Grace. In 1991, Keith began his security industry career in operational roles at Wells Fargo Guard Services (formerly a division of Borg Warner Protective Services). In 1994, Keith joined U.S. Security Associates, which was cofounded by his father Kenneth W. Oringer, as its third employee. In 2014, Keith left the firm as a business unit president, and shareholder, having played a key role as the company became a leading national security company with over 46,000 employees and $1.2 billion in revenue.

Michael Hymanson is a career security services industry professional, currently providing consulting, writing, and research services for select industry clients. After graduating from Cornell University with a BS in Industrial & Labor Relations, he began his security career in 1974, at Pan American Investigation Service, Inc. He became a licensed private investigator, president, and owner of the company until U.S. Security Associates acquired the company in 2006. From 2006 until 2018, he held regional operating and sales positions at U.S. Security Associates, including time as the company qualifying officer and licensee for New York State. Michael is a Board-Certified Protection Professional (CPP®) and has conducted security consulting services to Fortune 500 companies, and many major organizations and institutions. Michael is a long-time member of ASIS International and Associated Licensed Detectives of New York State, where he served as president, chairman, and treasurer. He has authored articles for *Hotel Business Review*, *Security Director Magazine*, and other trade publications.

Introduction

The "legends" profiled herein include highly successful founders and leaders of the dominant security services companies in the United States and Europe from the mid-nineteenth century until today. We have focused primarily on legends who built companies that rose to prominence as leading suppliers of contract security guard services, although most of the companies have or continue to provide additional physical and investigative security services.

Providing security is a noble task. Everyone has a need to feel and be protected. In reading this book we hope you will come to appreciate the significance of the industry and through a look at the legends' lives gather some insights that will help you identify patterns in the twists and turns that characterize your own unique life and career path. While the legends were all highly successful in business, we also hope that by highlighting certain pieces of their personal stories, it will inspire you to reflect on how to apply the skills and resources you have to pursue happiness and improve your lot and the lives of those around you. In their own ways, we believe the legends whose stories we share each demonstrate a core value: that there is no sense in working hard and achieving success without a personally rewarding outcome.

The early legends in the United States, Allan Pinkerton and William J. Burns, initially built companies starting as detective (investigative) agencies; their companies evolved to become primarily security guard companies. Every legend that followed founded or directed contract security service companies, with components that primarily consisted of security guard services, and in varying degrees cash-in-transit (armored car) services, consulting and investigations, alarm monitoring, and, later in the twentieth century, integrated security technology. In Europe, the legends profiled built global companies that originated as security guard companies, referred to at the time as "night watch" companies. The Philip-Sørensen family largely influenced the development of these companies into global leaders. An exception was Danish security company Falck, which began as a fire safety and rescue (ambulance service) company.

DOI: 10.4324/9781003285564-1

While volumes have been written about some of the legends, we provide a concise narrative that highlights milestones in their lives and careers, and the leadership methods and personal traits that made them successful. To bring color and context to their stories, the authors interviewed several of these leaders, or their descendants, as well as several of their colleagues.

While we do trace key events about the companies our legends founded or led, our intent is to provide an interesting narrative that goes beyond a recitation of historical facts. The book examines the times and places each leader inhabited, and some specific dilemmas that they faced in business and in life.

The security services industry has gone through a lot of change—the technology alone has been transformative. What haven't changed are the human qualities and methods deployed that made the individuals profiled effective leaders and managers. Their character strengths and personal skills are enduring. For building out different areas of the security services industry, and for founding and leading successful companies, they can indeed be considered legends; however, they are not so legendary that their successes can never be repeated. There is much we can learn from them. Thus, our hope with this book is that its readers can extrapolate from the stories a path and set of goals for which they themselves can aim.

We expect that some of our readers will be at the beginning of a career in the industry, perhaps enrolled in graduate courses or even a professional certificate program in security management, criminal justice, or cybersecurity. Others may be seasoned security guard managers or leaders who are transitioning from law enforcement or the military into the security services field. We would be pleased if we also reached readers who are interested, or are involved, in fields beyond criminal justice, since there are universal threads between the mindset and daily habits of successful leaders past and present in any industry. We hope to assist you to recognize and develop those attributes in yourself and those whom you may mentor.

HOW WE UNDERSTAND SECURITY SERVICES TODAY

Security and investigative services have always been devoted to the detection and recovery of assets in response to crime, and to the protection of assets through deterrence methods, such as manned guarding. How these functions and services are performed has changed significantly over time. The stand-alone guard or escort, once equipped with basic weaponry, is today a trained security officer who, assisted through artificial intelligence and physical enhancements, is not only able to deter but also able to predict crime before it has even occurred. Investigations originally served to solve crimes, recover stolen assets, and locate criminals to bring them to justice. Investigations are now a diversified suite of services utilizing advanced biological tools, information technology, and other techniques to solve crime and thwart large-scale cybercrimes. Yesterday's detective and guard agencies have evolved into today's integrated security service firms, designed to contain risk against multiple threats which can cause large-scale devastation to persons, companies, systems, and governments.

THE GROWTH OF THE SECURITY SERVICES INDUSTRY

Little is known about the size of the security services market during the period when the early legends founded their agencies; much more can be determined for the period from the 1950s to present. Yet, while the overall growth of the private security services industry worldwide during the period from 1950 to present is clear, an exact measurement of growth is more difficult due to varied definitions within the industry itself, information calculated by different organizations, as well as a lack of data for some time periods.

What we do know is that the size of the overall security services market today is staggering, and that the period of greatest growth started in Europe in the 1970s, reaching its peak during the 1980s in both Europe and the United States. This is significant because the legends profiled who started their businesses in the 1950s and 1960s thrived in a less robust market and were still able to compete with the earliest security dynasties. Those that came along during or after the boom times had the benefit of a rapidly expanding or larger market, but faced more competition as there were additional large firms in the industry. Each legend prospered by growing their firm organically and through acquisitions, based on their preferred growth models and strategies.

Growth in security industry revenue is a helpful indicator for understanding just how much the security industry has grown. Varying sources placed sales of all security equipment and services in the United States at just over $511 million in 1958, with contract guard services alone reaching over $5 billion in the 1980s.[1] Those numbers are dwarfed, though, in comparison with the security market today. "By 2015, more than 40 countries—including the United States, China, Canada, Australia, and the United Kingdom—had more workers hired to protect specific people, places, and things than police officers. The global market for private security services, which include private guarding, surveillance and armed transport, was worth an estimated $180 billion".[2] As of 2019, the size of the security services market including guarding, alarm, cash-in-transit service, and integration services reached approximately $76 billion in North America, $39 billion in Western Europe, and $6 billion in Eastern

Europe.[3] The book will illustrate that investment in the security services industry increasingly caught attention and financing from major financial institutions.

The number of security guards employed also illustrates the dramatic growth of the industry, especially during the boom periods. From 1980 to 2010 in the United States, total security industry employment and within contract firms increased about 80 percent, with much of the growth occurring during the 1980s. Sources place the number of U.S. contract guards from just fewer than 400,000 in 1980, to about 600,000 in 1990, and with in-house guards included, from 600,000 in 1980, to about 950,000 by 1990.[4] Total security employment then leveled off through 2020, ranging up to a high of about 1.1 million.[5]

The number of service firms in the United States, as measured by multiple sources, ranged from approximately 4,000 firms in 1967, to between 8,000 and 10,000 from 1980 to 1990, and then to as high as 14,000 firms between 2005 and 2010. While approximately 80 percent of contract firms employed one to nine employees, 70 percent of the employees of contract firms were employed by firms with 100 or more employees.[6] The success of the legends profiled in this book is remarkable considering the number of firms and company owners and leaders they competed against.

Industry sales in Britain were reported to have grown from under £5 million in 1950 to about £55 million in 1970 and from approximately £357 million in 1981 to over £800 million in 1987. Precise numbers for total security employment in Britain are unavailable, but it is certain that between 1970 and 1992, the number expanded significantly.[7] In Britain, 232,000 private guards were employed in 2015, compared with 151,000 police.[8]

As of 2019, in the European Union (EU), the private security sector is made up of almost 60,000 companies, together employing around 1.5 million workers. In terms of company size, the sector is dominated by small businesses with four in five companies employing only 0–9 workers. However, in terms of both employment and turnover, in the security guard and cash-in-transit service sectors, a substantial part is provided by large companies, notably G4S and Securitas. "Employment in the sector has been stable over the past few years. In absolute numbers, the sector is largest in Germany, the UK, Spain, Romania and Poland. Together, these countries make up about 68% of the EU's total private security workforce." Particular features of the sector are its low share of female workers (around 20 percent) and low union density.[9]

Some factors cited for the growth of private security include increased awareness of the effectiveness of private security, declining rates of public expenditure for law enforcement, rising fear of crime, and increases in workplace crime.[10] The authors also believe that the "fear factor" can be attributed to the rise and reporting of particularly violent crimes worldwide, and significant transitional periods and events, including the 1960s social unrest in the United States, the rise of mass shooting incidents, and several large-scale terrorist attacks such as the following:

- The Iran hostage crisis in 1979
- The Lockerbie bombing in 1988
- The World Trade Center bombing in 1993
- The Oklahoma City bombing in 1995
- The events of September 11, 2001
- The Madrid train bombing in 2004
- The 2008 Mumbai Hilton attack

During the past several years, the "global pandemic, natural disasters, accidental catastrophes, civil unrest, insider threats, economic downturns, supply chain disruptions, and cyberattacks has had a major impact on the security management field."[11] The manner in which enterprises handle such threats, more generally termed Enterprise Security Risk Management (ESRM), has led to a heightened recognition of the importance security plays in predicting and containing evolving and increasing risks.

While no one can predict the exact form the next wave of security threats will take, what is certain is that the industry will continue to grow and will keep presenting opportunities for those seeking to become a success, or even a legend, themselves.

HOW THIS BOOK IS ORGANIZED

Our narrative starts with the early leaders and ends with the companies and persons engaged today in high-level and comprehensive security services. Some of the names survive, but the companies today bear little resemblance to the early agencies.

Part I begins with Allan Pinkerton and William J. Burns, legendary detectives who built the earliest national security companies largely as investigative firms with a protection component. Their descendants would manage the namesake companies for decades, during which time their primary business would evolve into security guard agencies. These industry pioneers, starting with Pinkerton in the mid-nineteenth century and Burns in the late nineteenth century, operated in eras quite different from the legends that followed, as will be reflected in their respective stories.

Part II introduces the reader to the legends who founded or led the earliest major competitor security services agencies for the Pinkerton and Burns agencies. George R. Wackenhut founded his powerhouse namesake company in 1954; Ira A. Lipman founded hugely successful Guardsmark in 1963; and Thomas W. Wathen, starting in 1964, transformed CPP (known as California Plant Protection in that state) into the largest domestic U.S. security company at the time when CPP acquired Pinkerton in 1988. Each legend and company would take a different path to attain significant success in the security services industry.

Part III contains the stories of legendary businessmen who would found or lead companies that provided the next wave of competition in the domestic U.S. security industry. First, we consider Charles R. (Chuck) Schneider, and Kenneth W. Oringer, who met first at Baker Industries which had been acquired by conglomerate Borg-Warner Corporation, operating largely under the Wells Fargo name. Borg-Warner later acquired Burns International and sold the rights to the Wells Fargo name back to Wells Fargo Bank. Schneider and Oringer would co-found U.S. Security Associates in 1993 as a startup and transform the company into the fourth largest security company in less than 20 years. The careers of William C. Whitmore Jr. and Albert J. (Al) Berger are also contained in Part III, and it charts how they transformed SpectaGuard, a regional security company, into a domestic security industry leader operating as Allied Security, and then AlliedBarton. AlliedBarton and U.S. Security became the largest wholly U.S.-owned security guard companies and would compete against the largest global companies, Securitas and Group 4 Falck, after these companies entered the U.S. market in 1999, and 2002 respectively.

Part IV is devoted to three Scandinavian legends who led European global security companies starting in the latter half of the twentieth century. They include Sweden-born Jørgen Philip-Sørensen, who was instrumental in leading U.K.-based Group 4, and Denmark-born Lars Nørby Johansen, who led Copenhagen-based Falck. The companies merged to first form Group 4 Falck, which subsequently acquired U.S.-based Wackenhut Corp., and then London-based Securicor, to form Group 4 Securicor. Group 4 Securicor was later known as G4S. G4S and Sweden-based Securitas would, until 2021, compete for the title of world's largest global security company. Swedish legend Thomas F. Berglund is profiled next, as he substantially increased Securitas revenues during his tenure, which included the acquisition by Securitas of Pinkerton's in 1999, and Burns International in 2000.

Part V highlights three legends of the industry who founded or led global security companies that continue to compete today. The legends include Argentina-born Helena Revoredo Gut, who became a director and then president and chairman at Madrid-based Prosegur, after the tragic accidental death of her husband, Herberto Gut, the company founder. Also profiled is Stephan Crétier, a Canadian who in 1995 founded, owned and led Canada-based global security giant GardaWorld. The final legend profiled is Steve Jones, who starting in 1996 would spectacularly transform a $12 million Southern California–based security firm, Universal Protection Service, into the world's leading security services company, which through acquisition became Allied Universal. That company today is the world's third largest employer, with revenues exceeding $20 billion.

Part VI reviews the character attributes that shaped each legend's unique style as well as the common threads in the leadership and management skills they deployed. We believe readers can glean many lessons from the legends, and from those lessons develop insight into how to succeed across many industries, notably service industries that are labor intensive. We also provide a look at where tomorrow's leaders can find significant opportunity in the dynamic security services industry.

The legends' success and achievements are remarkable when one considers tens of thousands of industry competitors. From the many are the few legends and companies that achieved levels of success that most only dream about. We trust you will enjoy their stories and that the insights contained herein will help contribute to your success.

NOTES

1   Les Johnston, *The Rebirth of Private Policing* (London: Routledge, 1992), 79.
2   Claire Provost, "The Industry of Inequality: Why the World Is Obsessed with Private Security," *The Guardian*, May 12, 2017, https://www.theguardian.com/inequality/2017/may/12/industry-of-inequality-why-world-is-obsessed-with-private-security
3   The Freedonia Group, *Global Security Services*, 2022.
4   Kevin Strom, et al., *The Private Security Industry: A Review of the Definitions, Available Data Sources, and Paths Moving Forward*, Bureau of Justice Statistics, 2010, 31–4, https://www.ojp.gov/pdffiles1/bjs/grants/232781.pdf
5   U.S. Bureau of Labor Statistics, *Occupational Employment and Wage Statistics*, 2021, https://www.bls.gov/oes/tables.htm
6   Strom et al., *The Private Security Industry*, 31–4.
7   Johnston, *The Rebirth of Private Policing*, 73–4.
8   Provost, "The Industry of Inequality."
9   Anna-Karin Gustafsson and Peter Kerckhofs, *Representativeness of the European Social Partner Organisations: Private Security Sector* (Dublin, Ireland, 2019), https://www.eurofound.europa.eu/publications/report/2019/representativeness-of-the-european-social-partner-organisations-private-security-sector
10 Strom et al., *The Private Security Industry*, 31.
11 Kevin E. Peterson, *The State of Security Management: A Baseline Phenomenological and Empirical Study*, 2022, https://www.asisonline.org/publications--resources/the-state-of-security-management/

PART I

The Early Legends

Allan Pinkerton and William J. Burns are the only leaders profiled in the book who were born in the nineteenth century. Both were legendary detectives who parlayed their investigative skills to achieve fame prior to their establishment of namesake agencies. These agencies would become the first dominant U.S.-based national security agencies, providing extensive investigative and protective services.

Pinkerton was the earliest industry pioneer, and his career spanned the days of the Wild West and Civil War. Burns was born 41 years after Pinkerton and would not establish his renowned namesake firm until early in the twentieth century. The United States was, by then, an industrial power, with significant socioeconomic development having taken place.

While Pinkerton and Burns came from dissimilar backgrounds, they shared many qualities and abilities that would enable them to form enduring companies that would compete as security industry leaders for more than 100 years. They remain the most famous detectives in the security industry of the United States to this day, and their fame extends far beyond the nation's borders.

DOI: 10.4324/9781003285564-2

CHAPTER 1

Allan Pinkerton
America's First Great Detective

From an impoverished childhood, Allan Pinkerton rose to prominence and achieved extraordinary success, as the first and perhaps the most legendary detective in the history of the security service industry in the United States. The era that Pinkerton lived in was marked by westward territorial expansion, when communications and industry in the United States were in an early stage of formation. A visionary and an innovator, he was able to see and anticipate the areas of developing U.S. commerce and government where security services would be most urgently needed. He would capitalize on his personal skill in solving crimes and prosper by building a business that would meet the security needs of the nascent railroad, banking, and mining industries.

He created a security services dynasty while leading a life marked by incongruences between his ideals and business practices. Pinkerton's work, both against and on behalf of unionized labor, was an ongoing tension throughout his life, though the conflicts this tension produced ultimately led to positive developments that shaped both the security industry and U.S. labor policy. His work helping enslaved people get to freedom, and his fervent desire to establish moral codes of conduct in his life and business can be weighed against injustices his agents caused in the discharge of some of their protective and investigative duties.

Allan Pinkerton's leadership and management skills, as well as those of his descendants, enabled them to expand their business; the renowned company that bears his name was directly controlled by Allan and his descendants from its founding in 1850 until 1967. Until its acquisition by Securitas in 1999, the Pinkerton agency was at various times either the largest or second-largest domestic U.S. security company. The Pinkerton brand survives today as the risk management division of Securitas AB.[1]

DOI: 10.4324/9781003285564-3

EARLY LIFE AND CAREER

Allan Pinkerton was born in Glasgow, Scotland, on July 21, 1819, to William Pinkerton and Isabella McQueen. The family lived in a tenement in Glasgow's poor and crime-ridden Gorbals section. Growing up, Allan fought off countless diseases. After his father's death when Allan was a young boy, the family's poverty was such that Allan had to leave elementary school and go to work in a pattern-making shop, where he labored from dawn to dusk. He later left the pattern-making shop and apprenticed as a cooper. By 1838 he became devoted to Chartism, a revolutionary movement of labor agitators that was sweeping Great Britain, and from 1839 to 1842, Glasgow newspapers revealed that Pinkerton was a well-known figure among the Glasgow-based Chartists who favored physical force methods to advance their cause.[2]

On March 13, 1842, as he was getting married to Joan Carfrae, Pinkerton was warned that he would be arrested due to his political activity. The couple fled as their wedding ceremony was ending (Figure 1.1). They came first to Canada and then made their way to the Chicago area. A Scottish friend offered the destitute Pinkerton a job as a cooper, working for Lill's Brewing in Chicago, Illinois. He accepted the job and worked there for a few years before earning enough money to establish

FIGURE 1.1   An early picture of Allan and Joan Pinkerton.

(Source: Library of Congress.)

his own business. He set up a barrel shop in Dundee, a rural farming area about 40 miles from Chicago.[3]

Around this same time, he became interested in criminal detective work. While looking for trees to make barrels, "he stumbled upon a band of counterfeiters, watched them for some time, and informed the local sheriff, who arrested them."[4] After discovering the counterfeiting operation, he achieved some fame and was appointed deputy sheriff of Kane County, Illinois, in 1846. He ran for sheriff on the Abolitionist ticket, but lost the election after he was accused by a local pastor of being an atheist and selling alcohol. In 1847, he moved to Cook County, where he accepted a position as deputy sheriff. He resigned in 1850 due to political interference and was appointed as a special agent for the U.S. Post Office in Chicago. He investigated cases where mail with money and valuables went missing or were mishandled. He went undercover and, in one instance, became suspicious of a mail sorter who was later found to be related to the postmaster.

A subsequent search, conducted at the sorter's home, nearly failed after removal of floorboards did not reveal any contraband. Pinkerton then removed the backing from several wall hung paintings, revealing some of the missing bank bills. He obtained confessions and solved the case within three weeks. His thorough work exposed fraudulent issues within the postal service from which the organization would take months to recover.[5]

Moving to the Chicago area contributed heavily to Allan Pinkerton's later success because it was a hub of railroad and commercial activity and a major gateway to the expanding West. He transitioned from barrel maker to investigator in early adulthood and quickly capitalized on his first successes in the field. In 1850, he organized America's first national private detective agency, specializing in railway thefts. Its motto was "We never sleep," and its logo, a prominent, unblinking eye, came to be associated with all future private eyes (Figure 1.2).[6]

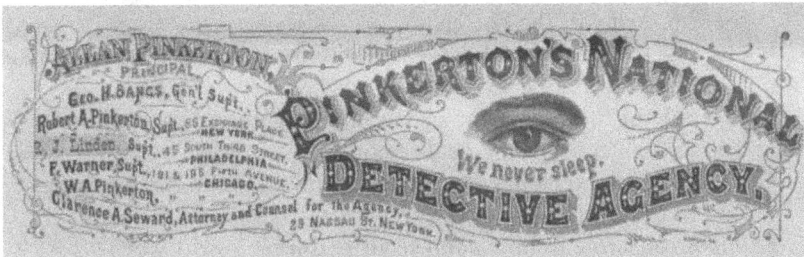

FIGURE 1.2   The Pinkerton logo.

THE PINKERTON AGENCY GROWS

Pinkerton's agency came to "fill the niche between the lack of rural law and the incompetence of corrupt urban law-enforcement organizations [with] a private police force that could move across local, county, and even state boundaries in the pursuit of criminals." When starting out, he hired five detectives, a secretary, and a few clerks.[7]

Railroad expansion provided Pinkerton's company with a major source of revenue over its first decades; the agency's first big contracts were with railroad companies. The Library of Congress Administrative File on Pinkerton's agency includes a copy of a contract signed in 1855 with the Illinois Central Railroad, whose legal counsel was Abraham Lincoln. Its director of security was George B. McClellan, who would play a role later in Pinkerton's story.[8]

The agreement was historic in American business, as it was the first time a railroad had contracted with a private security agency. Along with protecting the Illinois Central Railroad, the contract indicated that Pinkerton's agency also protected many other railroads, including the Michigan Central, Michigan Southern and Northern Indiana, Chicago and Galena Union, Chicago and Rock Island, Chicago, and Burlington & Quincy railroads.[9]

Once Pinkerton's agency was established, it had a role in many major cases and events in U.S. history. His exploits, and those of his agents, were reported on by newspapers throughout the country. Along with growing fame based on the successful resolution of cases, Allan Pinkerton would capitalize on the connections he made and exhibit an ability to tightly manage his business in an era of growing commerce.

The Library of Congress holds 63,000 items in its collection on Pinkerton's National Detective Agency, and these include records of its investigative methods, business principles and practices, and daily business activities, alongside reports on major cases and events. Among the collection are included records of:

- The establishment by Allan Pinkerton in 1861 of a security service to protect the president and provide military intelligence for the U.S. Army of the Potomac
- His role in detecting sabotage and espionage in the Washington, D.C. area during the Civil War
- The role of the Pinkerton agency in labor unrest and unionization in the Pennsylvania coal region
- Reports of Pinkerton agent James P. McParland in the investigation of the Molly Maguires
- Pinkerton's role in homeland security during World War I
- Cases involving notorious criminals including the Reno Gang, Herman Mudgett, Jesse James, and Butch Cassidy and the Sundance Kid

Service during the Civil War

Pinkerton was opposed to slavery, leading him to choose service in the Union cause. In spite of the Fugitive Slave Law of 1850, which made it a federal crime to assist runaway slaves, his home in Chicago was a station on the Underground Railroad. In January 1859, abolitionist leader John Brown stopped there while escorting 12 runaways on their journey north. Pinkerton raised $500 among his abolitionist friends for Brown's journey to Harper's Ferry.[10]

Pinkerton's contacts at the Illinois Central Railroad, Abraham Lincoln and George B. McClellan, would be consequential, leading to his fame as well as significant service to country and to the formation of what would become the United States Secret Service.

When newly appointed commander of the Union Army, General George B. McClellan, tasked Pinkerton to replace Secretary of State William H. Seward as head of counterintelligence during the Civil War, Confederate spies were busy obtaining information detrimental to the Union (Figure 1.3). As counterintelligence chief, Allan Pinkerton soon organized a "secret service" through which he and his detectives obtained military information from the Southern states during the war. He sent agents into Kentucky and West Virginia, and personally traveled under the pseudonym of Major E. J. Allen to conduct covert investigations in Tennessee, Georgia, and Mississippi.[11]

In 1861, while investigating a railway case, one of Pinkerton's agents uncovered an apparent assassination plot against Abraham Lincoln. It was believed that the conspirators intended to kill Lincoln in Baltimore during a stop along the way to his inauguration. Pinkerton warned Lincoln of the threat, and the president-elect's itinerary was changed so that he passed through the city secretly at night.

After McClellan was replaced as the commander of the Army of the Potomac in 1862, Pinkerton resumed management of his detective agency. He opened up new offices after the Civil War, in New York City in 1865 and in Philadelphia in 1866. As his business grew, Pinkerton drew public attention for his agency by producing a series of popular "true crime" stories.[12]

Notable Hires: Kate Warne and George H. Bangs

By hiring talented agents and managers, and utilizing his trusted sons in the business, Pinkerton was able to effectively develop and control his business. Two of his notable hires were Kate Warne, the first female detective in the United States, and George H. Bangs, a talented investigator and law enforcement officer who he had met during Civil War service. Both hires became legendary in their own right as a result of their work under Pinkerton (Figures 1.4a and b).

FIGURE 1.3   Figure of Pinkerton with Lincoln. Allan Pinkerton, President Abraham Lincoln, and Major General John A. McClernand. This photo and another very similar to it were taken not long after the Civil War's first battle on northern soil in Antietam, Maryland on October 3, 1862. In his role as head of Union Intelligence Services during the war, Pinkerton foiled an assassination attempt against Lincoln. His wartime work was critical in raising Pinkerton's profile and helping to bolster the reputation of his Pinkerton National Detective Agency, which pioneered the American private detective industry.

(Source: Library of Congress.)

(a)

(b)

FIGURE 1.4 (a) A close-up of a watercolor portrait of Kate Warne from 1866. (b) Photograph of a young George H. Bangs during the war. An operative with Pinkerton, he had a career in journalism, but changed paths and became a New York City policeman. In 1853 he was assigned to work at the Crystal Palace, where he was introduced to Allan Pinkerton. He soon began what would be a long and successful career with Pinkerton's National Detective Agency.

(a) (Credit: Chicago History Museum.)

In 1856, Pinkerton hired Kate Warne after she convinced him that she could uncover secrets in places where it was not possible for male agents to do so. She became friends with a thief's wife and was able to find out the location of stolen cash. She also went undercover as a fortuneteller and convinced another suspect to reveal information. But, her most famous case was the Baltimore Plot, where she helped stop an assassination plot against Abraham Lincoln. Warne worked with Pinkerton throughout the Civil War and served as his "right hand" until she passed away from pneumonia in 1868. She was buried in the Pinkerton family plot.[13]

George H. Bangs served as an agent under Pinkerton during the Civil War and provided information on the Confederacy. After the Civil War, Pinkerton hired Bangs to run his New York office, and he later became the General Superintendent of Pinkerton's offices in Philadelphia, Chicago, and New York. He was in charge of investigating the famous Adams Express robbery, in which the firm recovered nearly all of the approximately $600,000 stolen during a holdup on the Cos Cob Bridge in Connecticut. He also participated in uncovering plots by the notorious Molly Maguires against mine owners, strikebreakers, and the police during the Pennsylvania coal miner turmoil. Many of the gang members were subsequently executed.[14]

The Reno Gang

Security for the transport of money and the growth of railroads provided Pinkerton with many opportunities to provide security and investigative services, and his agents successfully handled many notorious cases. One of the early major cases that the agency was involved with centered on the Reno Gang. The Reno Gang, often credited with the first train robbery in America, were a gang of outlaws operating in the Indiana and Missouri countryside in the 1860s, stealing money from banks and county treasuries. At their peak, the Renos and their copycats stole nearly half a million dollars within two years. The gang's core consisted of four brothers—John, Frank, Simeon, and William Reno—alongside a cadre of counterfeiters, ruffians, and petty thieves. "While their crimes became legendary, the community's response proved equally legendary. Local sheriffs, Allan Pinkerton's men, Canadian detectives, and the Jackson County Vigilance Committee all strove to exact justice on the Renos and their accomplices."[15]

The Reno Gang were some of the first modern criminals in American history, using technology and organization to steal great fortunes with skill and ease. Law enforcement alone was unprepared to handle them, so Pinkerton was retained by their customer, Adams Express, and his agents foiled some of the gang's crimes. The U.S. Government retained Pinkerton to extradite Frank Reno and an associate from Canada. By 1868, the gang was effectively thwarted and the last of them were captured. A vigilante committee would take justice into its own hands. In 1868, within a span of six months, the committee lynched ten men of the Reno Gang, including three of the four brothers.[16]

The Express Companies: Pony Express, Wells Fargo

The express companies were originally founded in the 1840s as messenger services to locally transport money, documents, letters, and some freight by means of pony, horse driven coach, and truck (Figure 1.5). The original express companies transporting by horse and wagon become larger freight forwarding companies. They leased rail cars and transported money and freight from the end point of the railway to form a continual freight shipment process. With westward expansion, and the economic expansion of commerce and banking, growing industries required extensive private protection and investigative services as crime and lawlessness abounded—due in large part to the relative absence of organized public law enforcement agencies.

FIGURE 1.5 Wells Fargo & Company Express horse drawn wagon around the turn of the century.

The Wells Fargo Express, founded in California in 1845, was one of the main transport companies and the most famous of its time. It added value to communications and transportation by also including a banking function, which would boom during the Gold Rush. Along with other express companies, they employed Pinkerton agents and investigators even though they had their own agents.[17] Pinkerton, and later on William J. Burns and his agents (see Chapter 2), recovered huge sums of money from their successful investigations of theft and assisted their clients through the pursuit and prosecution of outlaws.

The evolution of the express companies may be viewed as a microcosm of the transformation of the country and economy, in addition to the type of protective and investigative services the agencies would provide from their inception to present day. The telegraph would largely replace the need for a Pony Express; horse-driven coaches and trucks used for freight and money transport would evolve into fully armored and motorized armored car companies.

In order to consolidate and speed transportation necessary in World War I, in 1918, "the Woodrow Wilson administration forced Wells Fargo Express and competitors to form the formally governed American Railway Express Company. After sixty-six years, from stagecoach to wagon to truck, Wells Fargo gave up its express business."[18] American Express acquired what was left of the gutted company (Wells Fargo Express), and a subsidiary of American Express operated the armored car business under the Wells Fargo name using the Pony Express logo.[19] Baker Industries and its successor company, Borg-Warner Security, acquired the license for their names from American Express in 1967, for use in their security guard and armored car divisions.[20] By 2001, as a result of a deal in 1999 between Borg-Warner and Wells Fargo Bank, Borg-Warner stopped using the Wells Fargo's trademark, service mark, and trade name.[21]

KEY BUSINESS INNOVATIONS: THE PINKERTON CODE AND THE ROGUES' GALLERY

Pinkerton sought to manage his company in an ethical way, although the conduct of his agents did not always lead to pristine outcomes. The Pinkerton Code of ethics required that his agents be honorable, and that they not work for criminal defendants or investigate jurors, union members, or public officials.[22] "In a day when many law enforcement officers openly associated with criminals and shared their illegal profits, the code of ethics Pinkerton drew up for his organization reflected the honesty and integrity of the man."[23]

Allan Pinkerton also "devised the first Rogues' Gallery—a compilation of descriptions, methods of operation, hiding places, and names of criminals and their associates. While the San Francisco Police Department may have started the practice about the same time, by 1858, New York City had a collection of about 450 ambrotypes (images on glass plates). This led to the practice of collecting and publicizing criminal mug shots which spread across the nation and the world."[24]

PINKERTON'S LATER LIFE

In 1868, Pinkerton's brother Robert died, and Allan suffered a massive stroke. According to one biographer:

> Although he eventually overcame much of the physical damage to his body, his writing and movements were permanently affected. The Chicago fire in 1871 destroyed the agency's offices, which housed most of Pinkerton's Civil War files, and much of the Rogues Gallery. Despite the setback, the business was rebuilt within the year. [...] By the 1870s, the adventures of Pinkerton and his agents had achieved some notoriety in the public consciousness, prompting him to begin writing books and novels about his life. Altogether, Pinkerton wrote eighteen books—five by himself and the rest with the help of a ghostwriter.[25]

Violence in the Pennsylvania Coal Fields: The Molly Maguires

The Pinkerton agents' role in the violent Pennsylvania coal country labor unrest demonstrated their prowess to protect the interests of their big business clients, and also ignited conflicts that damaged the agency's public image and internal relations. While they brought a murderous gang to justice, their work in subverting labor would later result in negative perceptions and heavy sanctions, leading eventually to the passage in 1893 of the Anti-Pinkerton Act.

The Molly Maguires were a secretive terrorist society and gang that waged an industrial war with coal and rail interests in rural Pennsylvania during in the mid-nineteenth century. In the 1870s, the country was in a depression and conditions in the mines for the workers were very bad. With violence increasing against business interests, in 1873 Franklin Gowen, president of the Reading Railroad which owned over 100,000 acres of land in Pennsylvania coal country, enlisted Pinkerton to infiltrate and bring down the gang. Pinkerton tasked an undercover agent named

FIGURE 1.6   The Molly Maguires. A drawing that appeared in Harper's
Magazine of the Molly Maguire men.

("**The Strike in the Coal Mines—Meeting of Molly Maguires." From
Harper's Weekly, January 31, 1874.**)

James McPartland with infiltrating the gang, under the alias James
McKenna (Figure 1.6).[26]
    The labor strikers in anthracite mining regions in Pennsylvania
were developing incendiary weapons and were committing murder and
"general fiendishness." Men were waylaid, mines fired by incendiaries,
and the lawless were attempting to enforce their own prices for labor.[27]
McPartland, the plant within the gang starting in April 1874, testified
against the gang members who were put on trial. His testimony led to
their conviction and subsequent execution.[28] On June 21, 1877, it was
reported that eleven men of the Molly Maguire gang were to be hanged
in Pottsville, Pennsylvania. They had for 14 years, beginning in 1862,
committed innumerable outrages, murders, and assassinations.[29]
    It appears that Pinkerton was not proud of the work his agents did to
squelch labor unrest. While Pinkerton's agency did investigate labor unrest,
and was involved in strikebreaking at mining operations and related industries, very little documentation of these activities is in the collection at the
Library of Congress. Records of such operations were returned to clients.[30]

Allan Pinkerton's Death and Company Succession

By this time, Pinkerton's health continued to decline and, up to his death in 1884, he became increasingly distraught over personal and business situations. It would seem to Pinkerton that the family, company, and his world that he was long able to control and influence were slipping away from him.

He became distraught when his daughter was "disobeying his stern rules," having fallen in love with William Chambers, whom she would later marry. He was also upset that some of those whom he most loved and trusted were either turning on him, or behaving in ways that challenged his authority and need for control and order. His sons began viewing him as archaic and old-fashioned. On the business side, he learned that his trusted long-time manager, George Bangs, had a drinking problem, and that there had been a scandal with some executives at the Chicago office stealing funds. The superintendent in the Philadelphia office, Benjamin Franklin, was pressuring him with salary demands, and some offices were balking at hiring female agents, which he had long championed.[31]

Despite Allan's declining health and other problems, he remained a resilient and persistent presence, continuing to support the Pinkerton agency. In the late 1870s, Pinkerton's made its debut outside the United States, employing their expertise in hunting international criminals who had robbed express cars, banks, and brokerage houses.[32]

On July 1, 1884, Allan Pinkerton passed away. One day later *The New York Times* reported on their front page that he was surrounded by his family when he died. His son William would continue to run the Western division, and his son Robert, as general superintendent, would be in charge of the Eastern offices. It was noted that "very few great crimes in the past 20 years in the U.S. were in the detection of which Pinkerton's agency did not have a hand," and that Allan Pinkerton was an active agent of the Underground Railroad and conscientious opponent of the fugitive slave law.[33]

AFTER ALLAN PINKERTON: THE HOMESTEAD STRIKE AND THE ANTI-PINKERTON ACT

Even with the success of Pinkerton's descendants, the agency would face a crisis due to their work on behalf of big business steel owners to infiltrate and thwart labor. The calamity of the 1892 Homestead Strike would result in the subsequent passage of the Anti-Pinkerton Act.

The skilled workers at the steel mills in Homestead, seven miles southeast of downtown Pittsburgh, were members of the Amalgamated Association of Iron and Steel Workers. They had bargained for and received exceptionally good wages and work rules. However, steel company owner Andrew Carnegie, along with management, was determined to lower production costs by breaking the union. The existing contract was ending and the company was not negotiating.

The company chairman, Henry Frick, hired Pinkerton's agency. A plot to sneak in 300 Pinkerton agents on river barges before dawn on July 6 was discovered, however, and word spread across town as they were arriving. Thousands of workers and their families rushed to the river to keep the agents out. Gunfire broke out between the men on the barge and the workers on land. The Pinkerton agents surrendered and came ashore, where they were beaten and cursed by the angry mob. Seven workers and three Pinkerton agents died in the battle.[34]

On March 3, 1893, Congress passed the so-called Anti-Pinkerton Act, stating, "an individual employed by the Pinkerton Detective Agency, or similar organization, may not be employed by the Government of the United States or the government of the District of Columbia."[35]

The act, however, would later not preclude security companies from providing security services to the federal government. Subsequent determinations were that the law was to be applied:

> when a guard service would provide a quasi-military armed force, but a company which provides guard or protective services does not thereby become a "quasi-military armed force" even though the company may be engaged in the business of providing general investigative or "detective services."[36]

The Pinkerton agency's role in the Homestead and other strikes, and the notoriety associated with the Anti-Pinkerton Act, was unfavorable. However, the Pinkerton agency survived the bad press, and their business of supplying security guard and investigative services would grow and prosper. Their business model would evolve away from labor-management disputes, instead rising to meet demand for security services for an expanding base of new commercial and industrial facilities including office buildings, hospitals, schools, residential communities, retail, utilities, and expanding transportation, warehouse, production, and manufacturing facilities.

The Pinkerton Dynasty

When Robert A. Pinkerton died in 1907, the agency had 2,000 employees, safeguarded 4,000 banks in the United States, and had branch offices operating throughout the country.[37]

Robert A. Pinkerton's son, Allan Pinkerton (1876–1930), would manage the New York office after his father's sudden death in 1907, continuing the agency partnership with his uncle, William, who remained head of the Chicago office. When William died in 1923, Allan Pinkerton incorporated the agency and became the sole family director. Allan's son, Robert A. Pinkerton II, succeeded him in 1930 and was the last of the family to direct the agency.[38] He was the fourth-generation Pinkerton to head the agency. During his tenure the company's revenues increased from $2 million to $71 million in 1966. He changed the name of the company to Pinkerton's Inc., from Pinkerton National Detective Agency, believing it better reflected the agency's business as a supplier of uniformed guards to many verticals.[39]

In 1967, Pinkerton's Inc. became a public company, and Edward J. Bednarz became the company president, the first non-family member to lead the company, which continued to grow.[40]

A Series of Ownership Changes

In 1983, the conglomerate American Brands Inc. acquired Pinkerton's Inc., "one of the biggest names in security services," for about $165 million.[41]

In 1988, CPP Security Service, a California-based company, acquired Pinkerton's from American Brands for an undisclosed price. The purchase of Pinkerton's doubled the number of CPP employees to 50,000, and it was expected to lift CPP's annual revenue from $250 million to about $650 million. The newly merged company would initially operate under the name CPP/Pinkerton and would vie with Borg-Warner's security guard unit as the biggest player in the $6 billion security guard market. CPP, known in California as California Plant Protection, was owned by its president, Thomas W. Wathen.[42] (Thomas Wathen is featured in Chapter 5.)

By 1990, Pinkerton's would go public again,[43] and, in 1999, Pinkerton's was acquired by Securitas AB. Securitas today operates Pinkerton's as its risk management arm, under the name Pinkerton Consulting & Investigations, Inc.[44]

Legacy

Allan Pinkerton was an accomplished investigator, the founder and leader of a highly successful firm that was the nation's first national security company, at a time when communication and transportation infrastructures were in an early stage of development.

FIGURE 1.7   Base of Pinkerton memorial, Graceland Cemetery, Chicago, Illinois. "A Friend to Honesty and a Foe to Crime."

(Used per CC 4.0 Share-Alike International; Author: Paul R. Burley.)

His company fulfilled a need in America at a critical juncture in the nation's history and development. Pinkerton's agents fulfilled their role with fidelity to those who employed them.[45]

He championed the rights of women to work in the security industry at a time when this was largely not accepted, and was an ardent abolitionist who opposed slavery. Yet, despite his early involvement with pro-labor causes, his agency participated in many labor-management disputes, hired by and aligned with protecting big business. Some disputes ended in violence and death. At the same time his agents were interceding in labor disputes, he developed a code of ethics for his company that included a prohibition on investigating union members.

He was a complex man, determined and compassionate. His father William was a jailer who died when Allan was about twelve, two years after suffering a severe beating from an inmate. He rose from abject poverty to a position of wealth and power, with an extraordinary ability to adapt to changing circumstances. The oldest son in his family, he sent money to his mother and his younger brother Robert, who would live with Allan until they died. His success in law enforcement was marked by an "unwillingness to compromise on his convictions about right and wrong," at a time when corruption was rampant. He was a hunter of criminals, yet interceded with judges and parole enforcement on behalf of his captives. His choice of career and causes represents many of the larger struggles that have marked social history in the United States: between police and criminal, abolitionist and slave owner, employer and striker. Allan Pinkerton had supreme self-confidence, and, at times, was a mysterious character with special insights. He was a spectacularly good judge of character, and though he lacked formal education, he combined intuition and observation to understand human nature. He was tenacious and had a willingness to stake his life or reputation on his conclusions, which made him a dynamic and forceful figure.[46]

The Pinkerton dynasty owes its start and much of its success to its founder. His investigative prowess and innovative techniques formed a basis for modern detective work. His name will always be associated with the security services industry (Figure 1.7).

NOTES

1 "Our Story," https://pinkerton.com/our-story/history
2 James D. Horan, *The Pinkertons: The Detective Dynasty That Made History* (New York: Crown Publishers, 1967), 2–5, 7–11.
3 Horan, *The Pinkertons*, 6–9.
4 Geri Walton, "Allan Pinkerton: Great American Detective and Spy," January 17, 2020, https://www.geriwalton.com/allan-pinkerton-great-american-detective-and-spy/

5 Robert McCrie, "Allan Pinkerton (August 25, 1819–July 1, 1884): Founder of the Security Services Industry," *Journal of Applied Security Research* 5, no. 4 (2010), https://doi.org/10.1080/193616 10.2010.510127

6 "Allan Pinkerton," National Park Service, updated July 31, 2020, https://www.nps.gov/people/allan-pinkerton.htm

7 Horan, *The Pinkertons*, 27.

8 "Pinkerton's National Detective Agency Records, 1853–1999: Finding Aid Scope and Content Note," Library of Congress, updated May 2021, https://findingaids.loc.gov/db/search/xq/searchMfer02. xq?_id=loc.mss.eadmss.ms003007&_faSection=overview&_ faSubsection=scopecontent&_dmdid=d13497e25

9 Horan, *The Pinkertons*, 31.

10 Jon McGinty, "Allan Pinkerton: America's First Private Eye," *Northwest Quarterly*, no. December 12, 2014. https://oldnorthwestterritory. northwestquarterly.com/2014/12/12/allan-pinkerton-americas- first-private-eye/

11 Frank J. Rafalko, "Chapter 2. The Civil War: Lack of a Centralized Direction," in *A Counterintelligence Reader: American Revolution to World War II, Volume 1*, Homeland Security Digital Library (Washington, DC: National Counterintelligence Center, 2001).

12 "Today in History—August 25: The Pinkertons," Library of Congress, 2021, https://www.loc.gov/item/today-in-history/august-25/

13 "Unsung Heroes: First Female Detective Kate Warne," updated March 27, 2020, https://pinkerton.com/our-insights/blog/ unsung-heroes-first-female-detective-kate-warne

14 "A Remarkable Detective; Work of the Late George Henry Bangs. Some of the Principal Cases Which He Successfully Conducted and the Thieves Whom He Captured," *New York Times*, September 15, 1883.

15 Justin Clark, "Outlaws, Pinkertons, and Vigilantes: The Reno Gang and its Enemies," Hoosier State Chronicles, November 30, 2017, https://blog.newspapers.library.in.gov/reno-gang/

16 Clark, "Outlaws, Pinkertons, and Vigilantes: The Reno Gang and Its Enemies."

17 Philip L. Fradkin, *Stagecoach: Wells Fargo and the American West* (New York: Free Press, 2003).

18 J. S. Holliday, "Foreword," in *Stagecoach: Wells Fargo and the American West* (New York: Free Press, 2003), xi–xii.

19 Fradkin, *Stagecoach*, 205.

20 Fradkin, *Stagecoach*, 214.

21 "Armed-Guard Company to Stop Using Wells Fargo's Name," May 5, 1999, https://www.americanbanker.com/news/armed- guard-company-to-stop-using-wells-fargos-name.

22 McCrie, "Allan Pinkerton (August 25, 1819–July 1, 1884): Founder of the Security Services Industry."

23 McGinty, "Allan Pinkerton: America's First Private Eye."

24 Harry Kyriakodis, "From Click to Clink: A History of Mug Shots in the Quaker City," *Hidden City: Exploring Philadelphia's Urban Landscape*, no. September 20, 2018, https://hiddencityphila.org/2018/09/from-click-to-clink-a-history-of-mug-shots-in-the-quaker-city/

25 McGinty, "Allan Pinkerton: America's First Private Eye."

26 Horan, *The Pinkertons*, 204–208.

27 "The Labor Strikes in the Anthacite Coal Regions in This State," *Somerset Herald* (Somerset, PA), March 3, 1875, https://guides.loc.gov/chronicling-america-molly-maguires/selected-articles

28 "The Molly Maguire Murder Trial," *The Columbian* (Bloomberg, PA), May 26, 1876, https://guides.loc.gov/chronicling-america-molly-maguires/selected-articles

29 "The Great Pennsylvania Execution," *New York Tribune*, June 21, 1877, https://guides.loc.gov/chronicling-america-molly-maguires/selected-articles

30 Pinkerton's Agency Records LOC Finding Aid.

31 Horan, *The Pinkertons*, 243–48.

32 Horan, *The Pinkertons*, 254.

33 "Allan Pinkerton's Death; the Career of the Great Detective Ended. Dying From the Result of an Accident—Winning Fame and Fortune From a Modest Beginning," *New York Times*, July 2, 1884, https://www.nytimes.com/1884/07/02/archives/allan-pinkertons-death-the-career-of-the-great-detective-endeddying.html

34 "Key Events in Labor History: 1892 Homestead Strike," https://aflcio.org/about/history/labor-history-events/1892-homestead-strike

35 Employment of Detective Agencies; Restrictions, 5 U.S.C. § 3108 Pub. L. No. 89–554 80 Stat. 416 (March 3, 1893, Rev. September 6, 1966).

36 "Comments Concerning the Anti-Pinkerton Act B-139965," March 16, 1980, Gao.gov/assets/b-139965.pdf

37 Pinkerton's Agency Records LOC Finding Aid.

38 Pinkerton's Agency Records LOC Finding Aid.

39 "Robert A. Pinkerton, Chairman of Detective Agency, Is Dead," *New York Times*, October 12, 1967, https://www.nytimes.com/1967/10/12/archives/robert-a-pinkerton-chairman-of-detective-agency-is-dead.html

40 "Non-Pinkerton Gets High Company Post," *New York Times*, August 8, 1967, Business & Finance, https://www.nytimes.com/1967/08/08/archives/nonpinkerton-gets-high-company-post.html

41 Tamar Lewin, "Pinkerton's Is Being Acquired," *New York Times*, December 8, 1982, D, https://www.nytimes.com/1982/12/08/business/pinkerton-s-is-being-acquired.html

42 "CPP Security Completes Acquisition of Pinkerton's," *Los Angeles Times*, January 26, 1988, https://www.latimes.com/archives/la-xpm-1988-01-26-fi-38676-story.html

43 Tom Petruno, "Investors Cast Watchful Eye on Initial Pinkerton Offering," *Los Angeles Times*, March 28, 1990, https://www.latimes.com/archives/la-xpm-1990-03-28-fi-352-story.html

44 Pinkerton Consulting and Investigations, Our Story.

45 Horan, *The Pinkertons*, 515–16.

46 Sue Chance, "Allan Pinkerton: A Psychobiographical Sketch," *American Imago* 42, no. 2 (1985).

CHAPTER 2

William J. Burns
Showman and Master Investigator

William J. Burns, like Pinkerton a few decades before him, was the most famous detective of his time. He was a colorful character, and his investigative skills were extraordinary. The cases he solved, both in public and private service, filled the newspapers of the day. Like Pinkerton, he capitalized on his successes in providing valuable information to government leaders and by delivering criminals to law enforcement, building his namesake agency on that foundation. While Burns had stronger family support than Pinkerton did in his early days, Burns can also be described as a self-made success in the sense that his natural talent for acting, and ability to converse easily with others, allowed him to uncover plots. These personal skills, combined with intuition and business sense, allowed Burns to found a company that eventually became a security services dynasty.

In 1909, at the age of 49, Burns seized the opportunity to provide extensive security and investigative services to an established banking industry; for the next 91 years, the Burns agency would compete against Pinkerton and numerous other companies (Figure 2.1).

EARLY LIFE AND CAREER

William John Burns was born in Baltimore, Maryland, in 1861. William was the son of Michael Burns and Bridget Trahey. The family moved to Columbus, Ohio, where William attended parochial schools and business college.[1]

Developing Theatrical Talent and Curiosity about People

William's parents were Irish immigrants who had left Ireland to escape the potato famine. Michael, who arrived in the United States in 1853 at the age of 12, was the poor son of a potato farmer. Michael had worked

FIGURE 2.1   A William J. Burns International Detective Agency Inc. guard badge.

hard and after years as a journeyman tailor and then junior partner opened his own shop in Columbus, Ohio. As a youth, William had a theatrical talent, was captain of his school debating club, and had early aspirations to be an actor. Michael, however, was determined for his son to have a more stable career and wanted William to go to law school. William took a business course after high school and then went to work at his father's now successful tailor shop.

Near the Columbus, Ohio tailor shop, a counterfeiter named Charles Ulrich set up an engraving business. William frequented Ulrich's shop and was fascinated with the colorful tales the con man would relate. Many years later, William would again run across Ulrich in the course of an investigation.

At age 17, William had the first big break in the start of his prolific investigative career. It came after his father was elected police commissioner. William started hanging around the police station, favoring the office of two detectives. He was taking part in some cases on an informal basis. After a series of six burglaries, William interviewed the victims and determined that the burglaries were likely the work of a local Columbus man. Each of the burglaries occurred when the victims were on trips which had been published in the society pages of the local newspaper. The clever teenage Burns provided the tip to the detectives, which led to their solving the crime.[2]

A Gift for Conversation and Getting Confessions

Burns married Anne Marie Ressler in 1881, and, in 1885, while still work-ing at the tailor shop and part-time as an unofficial detective, Burns was approached by Cyrus Huling, the Columbus prosecutor, to investigate the results of a local election that had surprised officials. Burns was enthused with the assignment believing the ballots might have been forged. He began his investigation by socializing with several guards from the local penitentiary. The guards related the story of a convict who had claimed he had forged the tally sheets in the prison hospital ward. Burns checked on the background files of prison employees at the ward and determined that a noted safe-cracker was working there for "Doc Montgomery." He con-vinced the man to confess. Then Burns remembered that one of the clerks for Robert Montgomery, the former prosecutor and brother of Doc, had quit just after the election. Checking police records, he determined the clerk named Chase was actually Algernon Granville of Chicago, a former inmate at the pen. He tracked Granville down and obtained his confes-sion implicating Robert Montgomery as the planner. After three trials, Montgomery avoided conviction, but the public was convinced Burns had solved the case.[3]

Not unlike Pinkerton, Burns had a knack for intuitive detective work, piecing together confessions alongside other types of evidence. Shortly after solving the election fraud case, and confident in his ability to suc-ceed in the field, he began working full-time as a private detective under the tutelage of Thomas Furlong, a local detective who ran a small agency that worked doggedly at taking clients away from Pinkerton. In 1889, after working on a series of cases for Furlong that took him all over the country, Burns submitted an application and was accepted for employ-ment with the U.S. Secret Service.

Soon after joining the U.S. Secret Service, Burns became a star detec-tive known equally for his ability to hunt down a clue and for his pen-chant for chasing after the limelight. Burns was not a braggart, but he enjoyed courting the public's admiration.[4]

Breaking the Brockway Counterfeiting Ring

In the 1890s the Secret Service had primary responsibility for investi-gating counterfeiting. William solved one such case with the help of his wife and the previously noted Charles Ulrich. In 1894, Ulrich was in Cincinnati and was believed to be planning to contact a big counterfeit-ing ring headed by a New York counterfeiter named William "Long Bill" Brockway. To avoid suspicion, William had his wife set up a surveillance hideout across the street from Ulrich's apartment flat. After months of surveillance, she told her husband that Ulrich was on his way out. Burns followed Ulrich to the train station and observed Ulrich purchasing a ticket. Burns asked the ticket agent if his "uncle," whom he described using Ulrich's features, had purchased two tickets to include one for him. The clerk told him no, there was only one purchased by the man for a trip to New York.

Burns boarded the train and managed to search Ulrich's suitcase which contained engraving tools and plates used in the counterfeiting process. He notified the agency, and when Ulrich telegraphed Brockway, agents arrested him. Burns convinced the agents to let him interview Ulrich, and he told Ulrich that he was the young red-headed boy who had enjoyed being regaled by Ulrich's stories in Columbus years ago. He convinced Ulrich, now a family man, to become an informant by letting him know that turning evidence would help him avoid a lengthy sentence. On the basis of Ulrich's testimony, Brockway was sentenced in 1895 to ten years in prison. Ulrich would live on, setting up a small engraving shop in Connecticut.[5] Secret Service chief William P. Hazen praised Burns for his surveillance work and success in planting Ulrich, and promoted him to full agent status.[6]

Conducting Land Fraud Investigations for the U.S. Department of the Interior

In 1898, Chief Hazen was replaced at the Secret Service by John Wilkie, who would send Burns on assignment to the Interior Department. It was not unusual at the time for agents to be assigned to another government agency. Secretary of the Interior Ethan Hitchcock was "staggered by the extent of corruption his agents were uncovering in the General Land Office" and needed someone with Burns' talent.[7] Burns had earned a reputation by now as superior investigator. The land fraud cases that Burns would work on were large in scale, spanned many years, and would further add to his reputation and fame.

The land fraud cases in Oregon and California centered on the Homestead Acts, a series of laws that provided for the sale of public land to proven settlers. Burns, along with Inspector Alfred A. Green, gathered information on speculators who filed fraudulent claims and bribed General Land Office officials to approve them. The speculators in some cases used fictitious names and, once their patents had been approved, sold the land to lumber and livestock companies for a profit. These fraudulent exchanges caused large tracts of valuable timber and grazing land to be stolen from the American public.

In 1903, grand juries in Washington, D.C. and Portland indicted several men along with their coconspirators. In 1904, Burns, and lead prosecuting attorney Francis J. Heney, persuaded Stephen Puter, who was convicted for land fraud, to cooperate in their investigation. Puter then implicated several prominent officials in his testimony and helped elicit confessions from coconspirators to substantiate his allegations. By the time the Portland grand jury concluded its term in 1905, it had indicted nearly 100 people, including the commissioner of the General Land Office, Binger Hermann, U.S. Senator John H. Mitchell, U.S. District Attorney John Hall, and Congressman John N. Williamson. Most were convicted.[8]

Burns, Heney, and the San Francisco Corruption Cases

In 1905, Freemont Older, a crusading editor for the San Francisco Chronicle, met with President Theodore Roosevelt to convince him to assign Burns and Heney to investigate large-scale corruption in San Francisco. Roosevelt, who prided himself in being an anti-corruption crusader, let Older know that he couldn't legally send federal agents to clean up one city, and Older said he would find private citizens to fund the endeavor. A bank president named Rudolph Spreckler funded the investigations allowing Burns and Heney to work on loan, privately from their government service. The investigations dragged on until 1911, at a cost of nearly $250,000.

While watching a crowd leaving a Union-Labor political meeting, Burns recognized a fugitive forger from ten years earlier named Roy Moritz Golden, who at this time was using the alias George M. Roy. He had Older create a phony news headline—"Prominent Businessman Exposed as Fugitive Felon"—and showed this to Roy. Roy was thus tricked and enlisted to offer bribes to several local politicians, who were caught taking the bribes. The locals told Abraham Ruef, an attorney and political power broker at the center of some corruption cases, that Burns "got us." Burns played on Ruef's vanity by convincing him that a guilty plea, after painting a sympathetic persona at trial, would create a sensation. Ruef plead guilty and received a 14-year sentence served at San Quentin. While several prominent, but corrupt, businessmen who were bribing the politicians evaded conviction, the extensive graft was exposed. Older would unsuccessfully lobby, to no avail, for Ruef's parole as he had become a cooperative witness against others and was the only one to receive a lengthy sentence.[9]

FOUNDING OF THE BURNS NAMESAKE AGENCY

While Burns did extensive and important work for the government, the pay was relatively low, and he realized that he could profit more himself by setting up his own agency. He would have a much later start than Pinkerton in going into private practice, but, once established, the agency would soon take off due to his reputation, contacts, and abilities.

In 1909, at the age of 48, Burns, along with William Sheridan, founded the Burns and Sheridan Agency. That same year, Burns signed a contract with the American Bankers Association (ABA) to provide guarding services to 11,000 member banks. This would prove to be the cornerstone contract for Burns and his agency, and the immediate growth would be exceptional, as Burns signed additional contracts with the National Retail Dry Goods Association and with various hotel chains. To fulfill the contractual obligations, he set up more than two dozen regional offices, and designated his son Raymond as the company secretary-treasurer as well as manager of the Chicago headquarters. In 1910, William Sheridan sold his interest in the agency, which was re-named the William J. Burns National Detective Agency.[10] Securing large contracts with multiple locations was a tremendous springboard for its growth.

Pinkerton, who had previously served the American Bankers Association, had pressed them for a contract at a higher price, believing that they had no competition. This attitude displeased the Association's executive leaders.[11] Moreover, Burns' reputation with bankers had been burnished by years of solving major cases, including the counterfeiting cases while he was at the Secret Service, which struck at the heart of the banking business. The fact that the Pinkerton agency did not renew this contract proved to be a tactical error on their part since it opened them to their first major competition. The competition between the Burns and Pinkerton agencies would last for the next 91 years.

Showtime: The 1910 *Los Angeles Times* Bombing

While William Burns had not yet appeared in any professional stage productions, the high-profile cases he took on earned him plenty of recognition in the press. One of his "good reviews" came as the result of his work on the infamous *Los Angeles Times* building bombing. On October 1, 1910, a bomb exploded at the *Los Angeles Times* building, resulting in the death of 20 employees (Figure 2.2). The *Times* declared the attack as the "Crime of the Century." Following the bombing, the city of Los Angeles hired the now private detective Burns to find the suspects. His work led to the arrest and subsequent conviction of brothers John J.

FIGURE 2.2   Photograph of the *Los Angeles Times* building, after the bombing disaster on October 1, 1910. The left section of the building is almost completely destroyed. Smoke can be seen rising from the destroyed section.

(Source: Los Angeles Times, Fair Use.)

and James B. McNamara (Figure 2.3). The brothers were trade unionists, defended by Clarence Darrow. Darrow lost the case when the brothers changed their pleas to guilty. James McNamara received a life sentence. John received 15 years.

Eighteen of the dead were buried next to a monument at Hollywood Memorial Park—now Hollywood Forever—and, for years, surviving employees attended remembrance ceremonies at the *Los Angeles Times* Bombing Memorial.[12]

"Burns was an early user of the dictograph, a device that enabled one to listen in on a phone conversation." One was discovered in the prison where suspects Ortie McManigal and the McNamara brothers spoke with their family and lawyers. That and evidence obtained caused Darrow to conclude the best he could do for the brothers was avoid their execution. Use of the dictograph enhanced Burns reputation which

FIGURE 2.3 A newspaper clipping from the San Francisco Call, April 24, 2011. The caption reads: "Wreck of the Los Angeles Times building, photographed on the morning after it was dynamited last October, and a portrait of Detective William J. Burns, who has cause the arrest of John J. and James W. McNamara and Ortie E. McManigal on the charge of complicity in the crime." Without question, this case single-handedly propelled Burns' name and reputation nationally.

"ultimately led to his appointment as head of the Justice Department Bureau of Investigation (later to be known as the FBI).[13]

The *Los Angeles Times* bombing case added to Burns fame. "Business was booming, and by 1913 the William J. Burns Detective Agency became the Burns International Detective Agency."[14]

Setbacks: 1913 Leo Frank Case, 1920 Wall Street Bombing

The Leo Frank case would be the first early setback for Burns. Burns spent more than a year conducting a private investigation into the 1913 murder of Mary Phagan, a 13-year-old factory worker who was supposedly strangled to death by Leo Frank, the factory's superintendent and a Jew from Brooklyn. Phagan's murder helped to revitalize the Ku Klux Klan (which was initially reborn as the Knights of Mary Phagan) and drew worldwide attention because of the subsequent horrific lynching of Frank by a mob. Burns doubted Frank's guilt, believing that there was scant evidence in the case and that it was based on the work of a competitor Pinkerton investigator, Henry Scott, who had no experience in murder investigations. Along with police Scott had obtained a statement from Jim Conley, a sweeper at the factory, that Frank was a pervert. Burns subsequently found a witness who produced sexually explicit letters that Conley had sent to her. When Burns provided this evidence, he was labeled a Jew lover and run out of town. Conley was later said to have confessed to the murder on his deathbed.[15]

The May 2, 1914, headline of the *Atlanta Constitution* reported that Burns was driven out of Georgia before he could sway the public's opinion on Frank's guilt in the case. This case, along with the Wall Street bombing in 1920, would begin to erode his reputation as a flawless detective.[16]

The Wall Street bombing on September 16, 1920, occurred at 12:01pm, during the lunch rush. A nondescript man drove a heavily loaded, horse-driven cart in front of the U.S. Assay Office, across from the J. P. Morgan building. The driver got down from the cart and disappeared into the crowd. Within minutes, the cart exploded into a hail of metal fragments.[17]

The explosion on the corner of Wall and Broad streets in New York City resulted in the deaths of 38 people, with hundreds more wounded (Figure 2.4). It was the deadliest terrorist attack in the United States,

FIGURE 2.4   A photograph of the 1920 Wall Street Bombing. As much as the *Los Angeles Times* case propelled Burns, the Wall Street Bombing would prove a disappointing and vexing mark on Burns' resume.

(Source: Library of Congress.)

until the Oklahoma City bombing in 1995. The subsequent investigation was conducted by the Bureau of Investigation (forerunner to the FBI), the New York City Police Department (NYPD), and the William J. Burns National Detective Agency.[18]

Burns' investigation began within an hour of the blast. He placed advertisements in various newspapers, offering a $50,000 reward for information leading to the identity of the perpetrators. While he did not disclose who retained him, it was believed at the time that a group of bankers had done so.[19]

The Bureau initially suspected followers of an infamous Italian anarchist, Luigi Galleani, who were allegedly involved in other similar bombings. Supporters of Galleani fled the country after the bombing. Over the next three years, any leads went cold, and the perpetrators were never sufficiently identified. While the Bureau's initial analysis of the evidence after the bombing led to a conclusion that a small group of Italian anarchists who fled the country were responsible for the crime, the case went unsolved and the mystery remained.[20]

BUREAU OF INVESTIGATIONS
APPOINTMENT AND TEAPOT DOME

Burns was friends with President Warren G. Harding's attorney general, Harry M. Daugherty, and on August 22, 1921, he was appointed Director of the Bureau of Investigation (Figure 2.5).[21]

Daugherty hired Burns, as there was a demand for an expert organizer to remake the agency for the protection of the American people. The plan was to consolidate various departments of the government under the direction of the Bureau. Burns began the establishment of a central Washington bureau of fingerprint records, which became an invaluable government resource. He set out to make the agency not only for the apprehension of criminals but also for the prevention of crime. He began to implement a vast upgrade of the agency through additional training programs, and the establishment of training centers for agents across the country.[22] Burns' exceptional work at the agency would unfortunately be cut short. He was caught in the fallout from what is widely known as the Teapot Dome scandal.

Teapot Dome was the largest scandal in the U.S. government since the administration of President Ulysses S. Grant. It became a permanent symbol of corruption in government and a darker side of the Roaring Twenties, and it was the first time in U.S. history that an officer in a president's cabinet would be convicted of a felony and serve a prison sentence.[23]

FIGURE 2.5   Burns as Director of the FBI.

(Source: Library of Congress.)

In early April 1922, Secretary of the Interior Albert Fall leased the U.S. Navy's emergency oil reserves in Teapot Dome, Wyoming, to Harry Sinclair's Mammoth Oil Company. The lease was exclusive with no competitive bidding and was secretly done in return for a kickback. Rumors of fraud first began when trucks with the Sinclair logo were noticed moving into the Teapot Dome area. The *Wall Street Journal* broke the story on April 14.

Burns became a casualty of the Teapot Dome affair after he sent his men to dig up dirt on Senator Burton K. Wheeler, a key player in the Senate investigation of Teapot. Burns did this at the request of his friend Harry M. Daugherty, who was later forced out of office. Daugherty's replacement, Harlan Fiske Stone, subsequently requested Burns' resignation. Burns complied, and June 14, 1924, was his last day as director.

The Teapot Dome scandal hung over Burns long after his resignation. He was also under attack for what was considered by some to be his relentless anti-union and anti-communist activities. Burns retired to Florida and went on to publish detective and mystery stories. He also made numerous film appearances until a year or so before he died. His life had come full circle; he was fulfilling his earlier aspirations to be an actor. While he believed as a youth that he was destined to be famous, his fame was earned through his investigative exploits and not the stage.[24]

While Sinclair, Albert Fall, and others were convicted, a conviction of William J. Burns was ultimately reversed due to a lack of sufficient evidence.[25]

THE BURNS DYNASTY

Soon after the Teapot Dome scandal, William would retire and his sons Raymond J. Burns and William S. Burns would take over the day-to-day operations of the agency. From its inception, the company prospered and, until it was acquired by Securitas in 2000, it was one of the largest providers of security services in the world. The company would have tens of thousands of security officers guarding many industrial and commercial facilities.

The sons had been active in the agency for over a decade, and, after World War I, expanded into guard services. While security for the banking industry would remain a major source of revenue for the firm, they expanded into additional verticals on a large scale. The opportunities for growth in the security business paralleled the growing strength and breadth of the U.S. economy.

When he was sent as the secretary-treasurer of the company to Chicago, to open and manage that office, Raymond was only 23 years old and had recently graduated from Ohio State University. He became president of the company in 1949. In 1959, Raymond celebrated 50 years as a private detective as well as the company's 50-year association with the American Bankers Association. He retired in 1970 from the Burns Company, where he had been named chairman of the board in 1955 and executive committee chairman in 1964.[26]

William Sherman Burns joined the Burns agency in 1914. He once told interviewers that while criminal investigations offered excitement and glamor, he became convinced after World War I that the real growth of the business would be in providing private personnel for industrial security. He was successful in selling industry on the concept of using professionally trained and supervised uniformed guards for plant security and was credited with transforming the company from a noted investigative agency into one of the world's most prestigious private security companies. He foresaw the need to improve techniques to cope with increasing crime, and he was a pioneer in developing electronic alarm systems.

"Sherm," as he was referred to, was involved primarily in the administrative end of the business, but he occasionally supervised major investigations. He became chairman of the security agency in 1964 when his son, D. Bruce Burns, succeeded him as president. In 1970, Sherm was elected chairman of the executive committee. Although he retired in 1971 to his ranch in Wyoming, he would continue with the Burns agency as a consultant and director.[27]

The Last Generation: George E. B. King

On May 4, 1978, George E. B. King, the 56-year-old grandson of William J. Burns, was elected chairman of the executive committee and chief executive officer of the Burns International Security Services, Inc. King began working with the company as a management trainee starting in 1952. By 1955, he was in charge of Burns' West Coast operations, which was reported to be among the company's most profitable and fastest-growing territories. King was said to be largely responsible for Burns' diversification into electronics and for establishing the company's nuclear power plant security program.[28]

Acquisition by Borg-Warner

King served as Chairman of Burns until 1981, and, in 1982, the Borg-Warner Corporation acquired Burns International Security "for $82.5 million. By this time, Burns had 36,000 employees and revenues of $240 million."[29] Five years later in 1987, Merrill Lynch Capital Partners would take Borg-Warner Company, including the Burns Security division, private.[30]

By 1993, saddled with debt, Borg-Warner split the automotive and security businesses into separate entities and each entity went public. Seven years later, on August 4, 2000, Burns International Security agreed to be acquired by rival Securitas AB for $457 million. Including the assumption of Burns debt, the transaction had a total value of $650 million. Burns had been struggling to keep fully staffed during a tight labor market, in an industry that was largely fragmented. Burns was, at the time, the leading U.S. guard company but held less than a 10 percent market share and was faced with a tough pricing environment. The addition of Burns, with its 58,000 employees, would give Securitas a total of about 210,000 employees, cementing its position at the time as the world's largest security company.[31]

Legacy

William J. Burns followed his early fascination with crime and law enforcement to become, in his day, the most famous detective in the United States. He built his reputation, and then his firm, upon the kudos earned from solving numerous sensational cases, small and large, which made headlines throughout his career. "Though he had no formal training on crime detection, his skill was probably a rare and highly perfected form of common sense, combined with dogged perseverance and what was almost certainly a photographic memory."[32]

When Burns founded the company that bore his name in 1909, he quickly secured the lucrative American Bankers Association contract away from Pinkerton. Several other large contracts, resulting in the expansion to many offices, propelled the company into a powerful firm in direct competition with the large and established Pinkerton agency.

A household name, his abilities as a detective culminated in his appointment as Director of the Bureau of Investigation (precursor to the FBI). There for a brief time, he was instrumental in transforming the agency by upgrading training of the agents and establishing a central records bureau. His reputation as a government agency director supplemented his fame as a private investigator, and founder of a large and powerful security services agency.

To compete with Pinkerton in the service of private industry, Burns and his firm provided security services that some considered anti-labor. Likewise, Burns' reputation would be tarnished by the Teapot Dome scandal. Neither issue seriously hampered the success of the company, which became a dynasty.

Burns' career spanned a time when the United States was rapidly expanding its industrial and commercial base. Sometimes called the Second Industrial Revolution, the early decades of the twentieth century were marked by the rapid scale-up of commerce and industry due to innovations

FIGURE 2.6   An older notice sign in front of a Burns-protected property.

such as mass production in manufacturing, the combustion engine, and the development of communications including telephones.[33] These developments created opportunity for the agency to obtain multisite accounts, which enabled geographical expansion to meet the large-scale needs of these businesses, and that of other businesses in the service sector (Figure 2.6).

NOTES

1 Graham Adams, "Burns, William John," in *American National Biography*, ed. John A. Garraty and Mark C. Canes (Oxford University Press, 1999).

2 Gene Caesar, *Incredible Detective: The Biography of William J. Burns* (Englewood Cliffs, NJ: Prentice-Hall, 1968).

3 Caesar, *Incredible Detective*, 26–9.

4 Benjamin Welton, "The Man Arthur Conan Doyle Called 'America's Sherlock Holmes'," *The Atlantic*, November 30, 2013, https://www.theatlantic.com/entertainment/archive/2013/11/the-man-arthur-conan-doyle-called-americas-sherlock-holmes/281618/

5 Caesar, *Incredible Detective*, 33–8.

6 William R. Hunt, *America's Sherlock Holmes: The Legacy of William Burns* (Guilford, CT: Lyons Press, 2019), 22.

7 Hunt, *America's Sherlock Holmes*, 28.

8 Oliver Tatom, "Oregon Land Fraud Trials (1904–1910)," in *Oregon Encyclopedia*, March 17, 2018, https://www.oregonencyclopedia.org/articles/oregon_land_fraud_trials_1904_1910_/#.YiKUrujMJhE

9 Caesar, *Incredible Detective*, 124–59.

10 Caesar, *Incredible Detective*, 161–62.

11 *Proceedings of the Thirty-Sixth Annual Convention of the American Bankers' Association* (Los Angeles, CA, 1910), 106.

12 Scott Harrison, "From the Archives: Aftermath of the 1910 Los Angeles Times Bombing," *Los Angeles Times*, October 2, 2018, https://www.latimes.com/visuals/photography/la-me-fw-archives-aftermath-of-the-1910-los-angeles-times-bombing-20180925-htmlstory.html

13 Kathryn W. Kemp, "'The Dictograph Hears All': An Example of Surveillance Technology in the Progressive Era," *Journal of the Gilded Age and Progressive Era* 6, no. 4 (2007), https://www.jstor.org/stable/25144496

14 Chris Hertig, "Today in Security History: The Death of William J. Burns, American Detective," *Today in Security*, no. April 14, 2021, https://www.asisonline.org/security-management-magazine/latest-news/today-in-security/2021/april/death-of-william-j-burns-american-detective/

15 Caesar, *Incredible Detective*, 198–202.
16 Welton, "The Man Arthur Conan Doyle Called 'America's Sherlock Holmes'."
17 "Wall Street Bombing," 1920, https://www.fbi.gov/history/famous-cases/wall-street-bombing-1920
18 Hertig, "Today in Security History: The Death of William J. Burns, American Detective."
19 "Burns Adds $50,000 to Bomb Rewards…Requires Exclusive Clues," *New York Times*, November 23, 1920, https://www.nytimes.com/1920/11/23/archives/burns-adds-50000-to-bomb-rewards-brings-total-offers-for-wall.html
20 Wall Street Bombing, 1920.
21 William J. Burns, August 22, 1921–June 14, 1924, https://www.fbi.gov/history/directors/william-j-burns
22 "Uncle Sam Teaching Detectives How to Detect," *New York Herald*, November 27, 1921, https://www.loc.gov/resource/sn83045774/1921-11-27/ed-1/?sp=80
23 "The Teapot Dome Trials: 1926–30," https://law.jrank.org/pages/2878/Teapot-Dome-Trials-1926-30.html
24 Hertig, "Today in Security History: The Death of William J. Burns, American Detective."
25 *Sinclair v. United States*, 279 U.S. 749, 1929.
26 "Raymond Burns, Former Chairman of Burns Security Agency, Was 91," *New York Times*, July 8, 1977, https://www.nytimes.com/1977/07/08/archives/raymond-burns-former-chairman-of-burns-security-agency-was-91.html
27 "W. Sherman Burns Is Dead at 86; A Pioneer in Industrial Security," *New York Times*, https://www.nytimes.com/1978/01/07/archives/w--sherman-burns-is-dead-at-86-a-pioneer-in-industrial-security.html
28 "Burns Security Services Elects Grandson of Founder as Chief," *New York Times*, May 4, 1978, https://www.nytimes.com/1978/05/04/archives/people-and-business-burns-security-services-elects-grandson-of.html
29 Borg-Warner, *New York Times*, April 28, 1982, https://www.nytimes.com/1982/04/28/business/borg-warner.html
30 Robert J. Cole, "Merrill Unit to Acquire Borg," *New York Times*, April 13, 1987, https://www.nytimes.com/1987/04/13/business/merrill-unit-to-acquire-borg.html
31 James P. Miller, "Burns Agrees to Be Purchased by Rival Security-Services Firm," *Chicago Tribune*, August 4, 2000, https://www.chicagotribune.com/news/ct-xpm-2000-08-04-0008040352-story.html
32 Caesar, *Incredible Detective*, 19.
33 Val LeTellier, "The Next ESRM Revolution," *Security Management* March/April 2022.

PART II

New Legends Take
On the Old Guard

Starting in 1954 with George R. Wackenhut, founder of The Wackenhut Company, and followed in the next decade by Ira A. Lipman, founder of Guardsmark, and Thomas W. Wathen, who led CPP, three new industry legends used their vision, skills, and hard work to create major competition for the established Pinkerton and Burns agencies.

The early detective agencies were by now primarily providing large-scale security guard services to a growing base of postwar boom industrial, commercial, and residential customers. Thousands of competitors would enter the growing security services industry, but only a few challengers would present a high enough level of competition to shake up the dominance of the Pinkerton and Burns duopoly in the domestic U.S. security guard market.

The legends profiled in Part II had experience in security or law enforcement before founding their respective companies. After military service, and several years as a coach and physical education teacher, George Wackenhut became an FBI agent before founding what would be his namesake company. Thomas Wathen built and took ownership of security company CPP shortly after service as an Air Force investigator and security director, and in 1988 CPP acquired Pinkerton. Ira Lipman began his business career at his father's investigative company and later founded Guardsmark, named in honor of his father.

Each legend attained great success; their leadership styles in many ways shaped their respective companies. They each retired directly or shortly after their companies were acquired, with Lipman carrying on more than a decade beyond Wackenhut and Wathen.

DOI: 10.4324/9781003285564-5

For Chapter 3 the authors interviewed Rick Wackenhut on February 22, 2022, and he graciously shared personal insights and information about his father, the family, and The Wackenhut Corporation. Rick had a long career at the company, starting in 1973. His tenure as a corporate officer included serving as a senior vice president of operations from 1983 to 1986, president and chief operating officer from April 1986 until February 2000, and as president and chief executive officer from February 17, 2000, until the company was acquired by Group 4 Falck in 2002. Rick summed up his father in terms of the values his father held most important in his life. In priority order, George Wackenhut's focus was on "God, Company, Family."

In addition to the research sources cited, information on Ira A. Lipman, his family and career, was developed for Chapter 4 from an interview with his son, Gustave (Gus) Lipman, which was conducted by the authors on January 20, 2022. Information from the Ira A. Lipman website was also very helpful for the authors. Gus Lipman is the eldest of Ira's three sons, who along with his brothers Joshua and Benjamin, worked with Ira at Guardsmark. As with several other companies founded by the legends discussed herein, Guardsmark was a family business.

Our research for Chapter 5 was enhanced by the enthusiastic participation of Tom Wathen's younger sister, Susan (Susie) Wathen, who recounted various tales of Tom and the Wathen family during an interview with the authors on April 15, 2022. Susie was 14 years Tom's junior and the youngest of five siblings.

CHAPTER 3

George R. Wackenhut
"Know-How and Know-Whom"

George Russell Wackenhut in the mid-1950s founded the first security service company that presented a major challenge to the long-standing U.S.-based dominant firms founded by Allan Pinkerton and William J. Burns. George was an outstanding athlete and businessman, and for nearly 50 years would be the majority shareholder of the company. Under his management, and that of his son, Richard R. (Rick) Wackenhut, The Wackenhut Corporation became one of the most powerful security companies in the world during the second half of the twentieth century (Figure 3.1). The company provided large-scale security services to a diverse base of government, industrial, and commercial customers covering government buildings and embassies, manufacturing plants owned by defense contractors, prison systems, nuclear and utility facilities, chemical plants, hospitals, corporate headquarters, and residential communities in the United States, and in many foreign countries.

George Wackenhut was undeterred by the many challenges that wove into his life and career, and was even said to take pleasure at being in the center of controversy. His physical and mental strength, coupled with his strong religious faith fueled his drive to overcome challenges and criticism. The Wackenhut Corporation would become the largest U.S. security company before it was sold in 2002. The name is still used as a security division in Latin America, and remains recognizable in the public domain (Figure 3.2).

EARLY LIFE: DIVING FOR THE BALL

George was born in Philadelphia, Pennsylvania, on September 3, 1919, to William Henry Wackenhut and Frances Hogan. William was described by George as "fastidious, neat to the point of pain" and his mother as "very thrifty and frugal of necessity."[1] George also was known to keep his spaces and belongings well organized. He believed in the importance of maintaining a tidy, proper appearance.

DOI: 10.4324/9781003285564-6   49

FIGURE 3.1   Pictured here is Rick (left) with his father George (right).

George's parents were a tremendous influence and imparted many values to him. Aside from personal appearances and habits, their lessons included the importance of integrity, hard and honest work, and the love of God and family. George was a devout Christian Scientist and would read Bible lessons every day before going to work. His only sibling, a brother named Harry, was also a big influence on George. Harry was

FIGURE 3.2   Rick presenting at the company's inaugural South American Conference in Quito Ecuador in 1998.

(Photo provided and used courtesy of Rick Wackenhut and family.)

11 years older than George, and was like a second father to him. He coddled George when he was young, and guided him early on. George revered and looked up to his older brother, and they remained close throughout their lives. The family struggled during the Great Depression and, like many, experienced the pinch of poverty. During the worst of times the family's dinner consisted solely of potatoes. In some ways, this brought them closer.[2]

The family lived in the suburban Upper Darby area of Philadelphia, and William operated a printing business. In 1935, he lost his business due to the Depression; however, things improved when William soon after became a supervisor in another printing company. During this time Harry dropped out of high school to earn money for the family, and he went to work as errand boy for the Penn Mutual Insurance Company. Harry would go on to a long and successful career at that company.[3] The family's struggles during the Depression taught George to be humble, that it took hard work and sacrifice to survive, and that it took the efforts of the entire family to manage through tough times.

George attended Upper Darby High School, where he was an outstanding student and athlete. A 1937 graduate, he was inducted into that school's Hall of Fame in 2000.[4] Throughout his life and career George was devoted to staying physically fit. His son Rick, in an interview with the authors, recalled how the "neighbors used to chuckle when as a young boy he tagged along with his father who would run around the neighborhood to stay fit." While George was just over six feet tall, he was an imposing figure, his strength of body matched only by his strength of mind. Prior to his career as an investigator and security service founder and executive, he played professional soccer as a goalie, and was a student, teacher, and military instructor in health and physical education.[5]

After graduating from high school, George first went to work in a printing shop, then at a local General Electric (GE) plant. The plant closed amid recession, but GE had required George to attend night school as one of the terms of his employment. As a result, he received credit at The Wharton School of the University of Pennsylvania for completing two business courses. George then worked in the mailroom at C.I. Wood, a commodity firm in Philadelphia. George wanted to get a degree, but could not afford college. However, he was offered an athletic scholarship by Earle "Muddy" Waters, to play soccer for West Chester State Teaching College. Waters remembered the high school athlete who dove relentlessly for the soccer ball while in goal. Waters described George as "always probing, always trying to get better" and described him as "naturally aggressive." At the college, George met Jay Smith, who would later recommend him for service in the FBI.[6]

Military Service, Pearl Harbor, and Marriage

In July 1941, George was drafted into service in the U.S. Army and shipped to Honolulu, Hawaii, as part of the 34th Engineer Regiment. His battalion dug trenches at a coast artillery camp at Kaneohe, on the other side of Oahu from Pearl Harbor. On December 7, 1941, when the Japanese bombed the island, George witnessed the planes circling the island, and smoke coming from the naval base. It was not until later when his battalion was strafed did he realize the planes belonged to the enemy.[7] Rick Wackenhut told the authors that his father recalled seeing the eyes of an enemy pilot as he honed in on the battalion. George would never get over the experience of witnessing the devastation and death of fellow soldiers from the attack on Pearl Harbor (Figure 3.3).

While in service in Hawaii, George was granted permission to take courses of study at the University of Hawaii rather than be on leave, so that he could qualify and apply for Officer Candidate School. He was accepted, and was spared a deployment to New Guinea, when to his

FIGURE 3.3   A fireboat pours water onto the burning battleship USS *West Virginia BB-48* following the attack by Japanese naval aircraft at Pearl Harbor. The USS *Tennessee* is in the background.

(Source: National Park Service Photo.)

astonishment the ship he was on as part of a large flotilla returned to base, as it was needed for another purpose. Shipped instead to the eastern United States, he was assigned as a tactical instructor in ordnance in Aberdeen, Maryland, which was only 60 miles from his home in Upper Darby. While there, he earned correspondence credits needed to obtain a degree in physical education from the University of Hawaii; and while still in the Army, he also played professional soccer part time on weekends for the Philadelphia Nationals.[8]

The dedication to physical fitness and George's resulting strength are reflected in the type of work that the Wackenhut Corp. would focus on and be noted for. The company became a leading security contractor to the defense and nuclear industries, as well as government and prison systems (Figure 3.4). George was an ambitious man. He had become a commissioned officer, and had taken the time and given the effort needed to earn a college degree while in the service. He earned extra money playing soccer part time.

FIGURE 3.4 George Zoley, President of Wackenhut Corrections Corporation; Lawton Chiles, Governor of Florida; and Richard R. Wackenhut, President and Chief Operation Officer, The Wackenhut Corporation; at the Groundbreaking ceremony for the stat medium security prison to be built in Glades County, Florida. Moore Haven, Florida, May 31, 1994.

(Photo provided and used courtesy of Rick Wackenhut and family.)

It was while on Christmas leave in 1943, that he would meet Ruth Johann. Ruth was the stepdaughter of Harry Merz, who had married Ruth's mother, Bessie Blanche Bell. Harry was a family friend and entrepreneur who owned a tour bus company for which George's father had provided printing services. George had met Ruth years earlier through the family friendship, but it was while on leave in Ocean City, Maryland, that he met her again, and asked her out on a date. During one of their dates, Ruth had George take her to a very fancy restaurant. To George's relief, she surprised him when after indicating she would be ordering many of the expensive items on the menu that George could not afford, she told the waiter she was not too hungry and only wanted a shrimp cocktail. Ruth described George as "her knight in shining armor" (Figure 3.5).[9]

The couple's happy marriage brought them two children: Janis who was born in 1945, and Richard who was born on Veteran's Day, November 11, 1947. Ruth was a great supporter of George throughout his career,

FIGURE 3.5 Corporate Officers (Back row left to right) Alan Bernstein, Frederick Thornbury, Cal Harris. (Front row left to right) Rick Wackenhut, Ruth Wackenhut, George Wackenhut. Circa 1987.

(Photo provided and used courtesy of Rick Wackenhut and family.)

and worked for many years alongside her husband within Wackenhut Corp., where she served as the corporate secretary (Figure 3.6). Rick noted that his mother had a very strong personality, and was interested and involved with the company. She insisted that before George hires a company executive officer, they be invited along with their spouse (if married) to the Wackenhut home for dinner so she could size up the prospective hire. Rick recalled Ruth telling George, "I told you so" after George terminated an executive who did not measure up after six months. She had met the candidate at one such family dinner and did not think the executive would work out well for the company.

Rick also recalled that his mother played an integral role in the design of the uniforms for the company. She designed uniforms for several divisions, including for the pre-departure screening services work at airports, and for what was known as the Custom Protection division. The Wackenhut firm was always noted for the distinctive dress of their

FIGURE 3.6   George and Ruth Wackenhut relaxing at their Vero Beach, Florida, home, circa 1998.

security officers, reflecting the meticulous attention to appearance and detail. Both George and Ruth believed uniforms were important to distinguish the company, and allow officers to maintain a dignified, yet commanding, presence. Even into the 1990s when most security officers were attired in simple blue or white shirts and dark pants, Wackenhut guards were custom-fitted and attired in immaculate pressed tan uniforms with a distinctive patch on the shoulder, and trooper style hat.

Teacher and Coach, Always Looking Ahead

George was honorably discharged from the Army on October 22, 1945, and he accepted several teaching jobs to support his family. The first was at Haverford Prep as an instructor in physical education and health, and as varsity soccer coach. He took several summer courses at Teacher's College at Temple University, getting straight A's.

In 1946, he was hired as an instructor at Johns Hopkins University in Baltimore, Maryland. At Johns Hopkins, he initiated a program for students majoring in health and physical education. He also coached wrestling and soccer at the university. Always striving to educate and better himself, in 1949, after three years of night school while working full time, he received a Master of Education from the prestigious Johns Hopkins University.

To supplement his income, George was a reservist in the medical unit for the Army, and in 1950, he would take a physical education post with the Army. The family moved again from Baltimore to Alexandria, Virginia. With the Korean War escalating, George learned that the FBI was hiring candidates without a law or accounting degree. His previous application had been turned down, but with the relaxed regulation, he applied again and this time was accepted for the Bureau. His friend from West Chester State Teaching College, Jay Smith, provided the recommendation required.[10]

An FBI Stint Primes George for a Security Career

George's career at the FBI was brief—from 1951 to 1954—though significant for the training and experience he gained as an investigator, and above all for his reputation and the contacts he would make at the bureau. As head of The Wackenhut Corporation he landed many contracts from retired agents who were security directors at major companies, and his executive staff at the security companies he led had a large contingent of retired FBI, as well as military officers.

After completing FBI training, he was assigned to the Atlanta and later the Indianapolis office, where he was a rising star investigator for the bureau. George earned the respect of his supervisors and fellow agents while at the FBI. His supervisor at the Indianapolis office, Larry Brown, described him as "a tenacious and meticulous agent, one of the best he ever had." Fellow agent Joseph McDonald recalled that George saved his life—when a family member of an AWOL military fugitive they were arresting lunged at him with a knife, George shoved the 200-pound man 15 feet, nearly throwing him out a second-floor window.[11] This was just one of several incidents for which others remembered George, noting his bravery and physical strength. Years of military service, exercise and the study of health and physical education had all resulted in an exceptional ability to handle himself, and in creating an aura of strength that would characterize his life and career.

Working for the FBI required relocating from one home to another, just as in his military days. This, along with the low pay at the bureau, led Ruth Wackenhut to encourage George to leave the FBI, so the family could settle down. George applied for several jobs in the Miami area to no avail. He resigned from the bureau effective May 21, 1954, and looked up a fellow agent named C.W. Bud Thompson who was then with the Dade County (Florida) Sheriff's Department. Thompson told him about an agent named Edward DuBois who had some investigative business in the Miami area. Along with two other retired FBI agents, Kenneth Altschul and William Stanton, Wackenhut and DuBois formed a partnership in July and opened an office in Coral Gables. George was at the time determining the benefits of moving toward providing security guard services, which his son Rick said was a result of wanting recurring work, rather than needing to constantly look for and obtain smaller or temporary investigative assignments. The partnership dissolved less than a year later after a fist fight between George and Edward DuBois.[12]

In 1955, George and the two remaining partners would form Special Agent Investigators, Inc., and Special Agent Guard Services. Their first major security contract was with National Airlines, and the company was soon able to obtain contracts with major companies that had divisions in Florida including International Minerals and Chemicals, Detroit Diesel of General Motors Corporation, Ware Laboratories, Florida Tile Industries, Kraft Foods, Food Machinery and Chemical Corporation, and Grandway Discount Centers. Despite the booming business, Altschul and Stanton accepted jobs elsewhere in private industry, and George bought the partners out.[13]

Late 1958 and early 1959 were critical times for George and his company. The Martin Company (later Lockheed Martin) was looking for a new security vendor. As part of his approach to obtaining the contract, George wanted higher-caliber officers, attired distinctively. George had professional pictures taken of three security officers attired in distinctive powder blue trousers with navy-blue stripes and white shirts with the trousers tucked into black paratrooper boots, and "white helmets, white gloves, white Navy gun belts, and white holsters with a flap that would conceal a revolver with a five-inch barrel." The executive buyers were sold on the idea, and the contract was to start January 1, 1959. On December 31, 1958, Special Agent Security Guards, Inc., was renamed Security Services Corporation, and Special Agent Investigators became a division of Security Services Corporation; and on January 29, 1959, John Ammarell was named executive vice president of the company. Ammarell was a retired FBI agent, who George met when assisting Ammarell at Florida Power and Light (FPL) in finding security coverage for their subcontractor, Air Products Corporation. George was very impressed with Ammarell, and wanted him to run his growing operation.[14]

THE WACKENHUT CORPORATION BECOMES AN INDUSTRY POWER

In September 1959, Security Services Corporation was renamed The Wackenhut Corporation. George would continue to expand the company, developing new divisions and entities. He was building a team, many of whom would stay with the company for many years. John Ammarell worked with George and his companies for the next 28 years in executive leadership positions. Using his contacts with retired military and FBI agents who worked in the security departments for large companies, The Wackenhut Corporation became a powerful security contractor in industry verticals such as defense, utility, and government. The company would ride a continuing wave of outsourcing of services, and for the next 43 years, an expanding need for security services due to industrial expansion and increases in crime. Distinctive uniforms would be a hallmark of The Wackenhut Corporation, projecting strength in the character of the founder. In some quarters the company was ridiculed, with people referring to the officers as "Wackencops" and other derogatory names. Despite this, the formula proved to be highly successful for The Wackenhut Corporation.

Organic Growth and Diversification at the Wackenhut Company

From 1955 until 2002, the company experienced tremendous growth and success, derived from various operating divisions. Developed over time, the business strategy focused on three major businesses worldwide: one providing security services, one providing correctional services and, much later, a business providing staffing services. The company focused on the quality of their services and operations to retain customers and grow organically. The company also expanded service offerings in carefully selected geographic locations worldwide where it could achieve critical mass. George capitalized on his leadership of a talented executive team with a lot of contacts within the security industry. He would later lean on his son, Rick, who would bring in his own management team to perpetuate the company's growth.

Quality service was important to George Wackenhut, and in the 1980s several opportunities emerged for demonstrating high quality. Florida Power and Light, a longtime client where Wackenhut provided nuclear security, asked the company to participate with them so that FPL could attain the prestigious Deming Prize. They did, and once attained, Wackenhut embarked on a process to achieve ISO certification not only at the FPL sites but at additional locations.[15] Rick noted that the company consistently received high marks from its government customers and that the company needed to attain high ratings from auditors as a contractual requirement to retain that business.

The company's expansion included creation of Wackenhut Services, Inc., which was formed in 1960 primarily to provide security services to the federal government. Initial major accounts included the NASA, Kennedy Space Center, and the Nevada Test Site in 1964. In 1983, Wackenhut Services Inc. would be awarded the largest private security services contract for the Department of Energy's Savannah River Plant. These contracts were retained for decades.[16]

For the period ending December 31, 2001, the last full fiscal year prior to the company's acquisition in 2002, The Wackenhut Corporation, together with its affiliates, was the largest U.S.-based global security services provider, with 142 customer support centers in the United States, and additional centers in approximately 40 countries around the world. The Wackenhut Corporation had 68,000 employees and 2001 revenues of $2.8 billion, with the security and correctional services portion of the revenues totaling approximately $1.8 billion. The 2001 Annual Report provides a sketch of the company's scale and influence:

- Wackenhut International, Inc., formed in 1966, along with its affiliates and subsidiaries had provided services, some of which were offered in a greater variety than the company offered in the United States, including central station monitoring, cash-in-transit and others, to approximately 38 countries. International revenues as part of global security services were reported at approximately $172 million (Figure 3.7).
- The Correctional Services division, a 57 percent-owned subsidiary, operated as Wackenhut Corrections Corporation, which was founded in 1984; it had contracts to manage 59 correctional, detention and public sector healthcare facilities for nearly 42,500 beds. The division accounted for $562 million of annual revenues, separate and apart from Global Security Services.
- Staffing Services was formed in 1996, after the acquisition of Oasis Outsourcing, and had become one of the leading outsourcing companies in the Southeast, with a principal concentration in Florida. It contributed a staggering over $1 billion to total annual revenues, exclusive of security and correction services. All told, fiscal year ending revenues for all divisions totaled over $2.8 billion.
- The Custom Protection Officer® program provided highly specialized and trained security professionals to a broad range of customers, including national retailers, financial institutions, and gated communities.
- Wackenhut Services, Inc. was providing security-related services to 12 sensitive government installations, including the Savannah River Site, since 1983; and to 28 commercial nuclear power plants in 14 states, as the market share leader in this niche market.

Despite being a public company, George and Ruth Wackenhut retained control of the company with over 50 percent of its issued and voting stock.[17]

FIGURE 3.7 Listing Common stock on American Stock Exchange, October 9, 1967. (Left to right.) Captain Eddie Rickenbacker, Director of TWC; Morris Goldstein, Vice President of Alfred I. Dupont and Company; George Wackenhut, President; Ruth J. Wackenhut, Secretary; John S. Ammarell, Jr., Executive Vice President; and Victor P. Keay, Assistant Secretary and Assistant to the President.

(Photo provided and used courtesy of Rick Wackenhut and family.)

Controversy and Notoriety

While The Wackenhut Corporation's most widely known controversy today is likely its role in the proliferation of privately operated prisons, other affairs exposing the company's rough seams were documented well before that. In 1967, Governor Claude R. Kirk Jr. of Florida appointed George chief of a private police force to investigate organized crime (Figure 3.8). George was criticized for saying that he and his officers would not limit themselves to suspected criminals but would "investigate everyone and anyone who needs investigating."[18] The company set up a hotline to receive and investigate any tips on crime and within the first six months of operation a progress report provided to state officials

FIGURE 3.8   George worked conducting investigations for the Governor of the State of Florida.

(Photo provided and used courtesy of Rick Wackenhut and family.)

contained information on 1,695 complaints, 33 arrests, and 15 public officials indicted, including three sheriffs removed from office as a result of investigations.[19]

A public outcry ensued on claims of invasion of privacy, and concerns that a private company should not take on a lead role in fighting crime as a government contractor. The role of the company on the project would last for less than a year, during which time George testified at a Senate hearing on the Right of Privacy Act. Despite the sensation in the newspapers and press, George claimed that the program lost money for the company, but the publicity surrounding it spurred new business.[20]

Throughout the 1960s and 1970s The Wackenhut Corporation was alleged to have actively collected information on individuals, to run background checks for their clients and as an outgrowth of George Wackenhut's own purported anti-communist views. The company by 1971 reportedly had files on 2.5 million individuals. In response to the passage of the Fair Credit Reporting Act, it is believed the company reduced the number of files to between 225,000 and 250,000 files, and in 1975 gave many of their files to the Church League of America, a right-wing private organization which was not bound by the disclosure requirements of the law.[21]

Frequent rumors that The Wackenhut Corporation was in the employ of the CIA were never substantiated, though George, reportedly obsessive about high-tech security gadgets in his private life, seemed to relish the suggestion.[22]

George and Ruth Wackenhut built a family home that received some notoriety due to its grandeur. Named Tyecliffe, it took more than five years to build and was completed in the fall of 1974. It was designed by a famous Palm Beach, Florida, architect, John Volk. To decorate it, Ruth used European artisans and craftsmen and materials from all over the world.[23] A brochure on Tyecliffe provided by Rick Wackenhut to the authors, which was from real estate firm Castles by the Sea, described Tyecliffe's approximately 24,000 square feet as

> charming rather than overwhelming ... comfortable rather than formal...a manor house in the finest European tradition. The architecture throughout is meticulously designed to create the enchanting atmosphere of a medieval European manor house in the period extending from the 11th through the 15th centuries. Graced with turrets, winding staircases, alcoves, wood and stone-work, every turn presents an adventure in architectural design. The owner's privacy and safety is ensured through a sophisticated, estate-wide security and fire alarm system, including the entire seawall. The highest point in the manor house affords a dramatic panoramic view of Tyecliffe's gardens, Gables Estates, the shoreline of the city, Key Biscayne, Biscayne Bay, and the sky-scrapers of downtown Miami. No detail was overlooked in the building of this estate.[24]

Rick noted that the locals affectionately referred to Tyecliffe as "the Castle." In 1992, the property sustained extensive damage from Hurricane Andrew before it was sold. It was eventually torn down.

In 1992, a draft report by the House Interior Committee alleged that Alyeska, a consortium of oil companies that operated the trans-Alaska oil pipeline, and its security provider, Wackenhut Corp., may have broken numerous state and federal laws in conducting an elaborate under-cover operation to root out the sources of embarrassing disclosures about the Alaska oil industry. As part of the operation they obtained private phone records and credit reports on industry critics, secretly recorded phone calls and videotaped meetings, stole documents, sought damaging information about Interior Committee Chairman, Congressman George Miller (D-Calif.), and tried to disrupt and obstruct the panel's investigations into the pipeline, the *Exxon Valdez* oil spill, and the covert operation itself. The report recommended that the committee's findings be forwarded to the Department of Justice to consider prosecuting Alyeska and Wackenhut based upon possible violation of federal laws prohibiting obstruction of justice, surreptitious recording, possession of surreptitious recording devices, mail and wire fraud, and access to credit, financial, and other private information.[25]

The Alyeska consortium settled a lawsuit by Charles Hamel, a retired Virginia oil tanker broker, who had helped spur congressional investigations that uncovered safety and maintenance problems on the pipeline. According to statements by former employees, Wackenhut detectives taped Hamel's telephone conversations and got his bank, credit, and other records.[26]

Information given at the inquiry indicated that there was no evidence that Congressman Miller actually came under surveillance, that his phones were tapped, or that he was photographed surreptitiously. George stated that the assignment had been given to a new special investigation division of the company which used covert surveillance techniques that had as its only code of conduct a company policy requiring its agents to obey all laws. He said that company lawyers believed that no laws had been violated.[27] A draft report by the House Interior Committee regarding the incident was published in July 1992, and the Anchorage FBI office investigated allegations of misconduct relating to the incident. Investigations were closed in 1993 and in 1994,[28] and no criminal charges against George or The Wackenhut Corporation were filed.

Controversy around Wackenhut's operation of correctional, detention, and public sector healthcare facilities is not unlike that of other private and public providers of such services. This work is a dangerous undertaking, fraught with issues. Some of the allegations against the Correctional Services division included allegations of mistreatment, harsh conditions, and a lack of treatment programs at the Jena Juvenile Center in Louisiana, which opened in 1998. Two prisons Wackenhut Corrections ran in New Mexico were the scene of stabbings and deaths in 1999. In Texas, a rape scandal involving guards at a jail run by Wackenhut in Austin led to a takeover by state officials.[29] Rick Wackenhut noted that the company always made every effort to correct any missteps.

Controversy and notoriety notwithstanding, George "cultivated an image of probity, toughness and precise military order. His teak-and-granite office was spotless, and he kept a barber's chair in his private bathroom to avoid leaving the office for a haircut."[30]

Group 4 Falck Acquires the Company

George Wackenhut informed shareholders in a filing on May 3, 2002, that the board would consider and vote to approve a merger agreement with Group 4 Falck A/S (Falck) of Denmark, in which the Wackenhut company would continue as an indirect wholly owned subsidiary of Group 4 Falck. Shareholders would receive $33.00 in cash, without interest, for each share of Series A and Series B common stock. With his 51 percent ownership, the outcome was assured.[31]

FIGURE 3.9   (Left to right) Rick Wackenhut, George Wackenhut, Lars Nørby Johansen at Palm Beach, Florida; signing final papers for the sale of The Wackenhut Corporation to Group Four Falk, 2002.

(Photo provided and used courtesy of Rick Wackenhut and family.)

On May 8, George Wackenhut transferred ownership of the company, reported to be the U.S. largest security conglomerate, to Group 4 Falck, which made that firm the second-largest security company in the world (Figure 3.9). George personally received nearly $112 million from the $573 million sale, as well as $18.9 million from options and restricted stock. Wackenhut Corp.'s growth and prosperity arose not only from George's determination and intuition but also from an upswing in crime, overcrowded prisons, and public uneasiness about security and safety. His personal mix of ultraconservatism and kitsch, of showmanship and secrecy, never stood in the way of building a billion-dollar business.[32] Rick said that a favorite phrase of George's, "know-how and know-whom," referred to the services the company and George "knew-how" to provide, for the company partners around the world that "knew-whom" to supply services to.

Though it was a very hard and emotional decision, the family believed the offer was a very good one. Rick noted that the share price paid by Group 4 Falck was about twice what it had been prior to September 11, 2001, and was an opportune time to sell as being in the best interest of the shareholders and the family (Figure 3.10).

FIGURE 3.10   (Left to Right) Ruth Wackenhut, Murray Levine, George Wackenhut, Rick Wackenhut, Marie Zirilli (later to be Rick's wife). Circa 2002 or 2003.

(Photo provided and used courtesy of Rick Wackenhut and family.)

LEGACY

The Wackenhut Corporation's successes and George's legendary career were a result of many factors. George was driven and ambitious, ultimately earning a master's degree by taking night courses, correspondence courses, and earning college credits while working or teaching full time and while in military service. He had the courage and vision to leave a stable government service job, and the energy and skill to found, lead, and build his own company from a small investigative firm into the largest security service in the United States before it was sold.

Through hard and intelligent work, George and Rick recruited a large team of talented executives; and the company secured and retained numerous large contracts with major industrial, government, and commercial customers (Figure 3.11). Many facilities the company protected were vitally important, highly sensitive critical infrastructure facilities, and prime targets for terrorism.

George was a magnetic leader, a listener more than a dictator. "If aggravated you might hear the growl, but he controlled his temper," testified his son Rick, and you also felt his care and love. He was loyal to those around him and commanded and received their respect.

FIGURE 3.11 Through hard and intelligent work, George and Rick recruited a large team of talented executives; and the company secured and retained numerous large contracts with major industrial, government, and commercial customers.

(Photo provided and used courtesy of Rick Wackenhut and family.)

He did things on a grand scale, but was also dignified and humble. For many, he was a tremendous mentor (Figure 3.12). He inspired those around him to be better, encouraging them by his example and by his integrity. He was a religious man who believed that God would provide what was needed. When the Martin account started, things looked grim before a difficult startup, yet George told the staff that "God will provide, it will all work out, and it did." Failure was not an option for him. It was not always easy, and there was a time early on when George passed around a hat at the office so that the company could meet guard payroll.[33]

George Wackenhut's highly successful career was marked by his determination, perseverance, hard work, loyalty, inspired leadership, and organizational skill. Despite controversy, George Wackenhut remains a legend in the security services industry.

FIGURE 3.12 Rick Wackenhut Presenting George Wackenhut with a 40th Anniversary Award for TWC. Circa 1994.

(Photo provided and used courtesy of Rick Wackenhut and family.)

NOTES

1 John Minahan, *The Quiet American: A Biography of George R. Wackenhut* (Westport, Connecticut: International Publishing Group, 1994), 32–3.
2 Richard R. Wackenhut, interview by Michael Hymanson and Keith Oringer, February 22, 2022.
3 Minahan, *The Quiet American: A Biography of George R. Wackenhut*, 27–37.
4 "Alumi Wall of Fame." https://www.upperdarbysd.org/site/Default. aspx?PageID=4665
5 Wackenhut, interview.
6 Minahan, *The Quiet American: A Biography of George R. Wackenhut*, 52–71.
7 Minahan, *The Quiet American: A Biography of George R. Wackenhut*, 101–106.
8 Minahan, *The Quiet American: A Biography of George R. Wackenhut*, 107–32.

9   Minahan, *The Quiet American: A Biography of George R. Wackenhut*, 131–40.

10 Minahan, *The Quiet American: A Biography of George R. Wackenhut*, 155–72.

11 Minahan, *The Quiet American: A Biography of George R. Wackenhut*, 189–92.

12 Minahan, *The Quiet American: A Biography of George R. Wackenhut*, 198–205.

13 Minahan, *The Quiet American: A Biography of George R. Wackenhut*, 248–51.

14 Minahan, *The Quiet American: A Biography of George R. Wackenhut*, 269–73.

15 Todd Brady Schoenrock, "ISO 9000: 2000 Gives Competitive Edge," *Quality Progress*, May, 2002. For more information on the Deming Prize, see https://www.juse.or.jp/deming_en/. For more information on the International Organization for Standardization (ISO), see https://www.iso.org/about-us.html

16 "History," https://www.constellis.com/who-we-are/history/

17 The Wackenhut Corp., *Annual Report 2001*, 2002, https://www.sec.gov/Archives/edgar/data/104030/000095014402002003/g74165e10-k405.txt

18 Jennifer Bayot, "George Wackenhut, 85, Dies; Founded Elite Security Firm," *New York Times*, January 8, 2005, https://www.nytimes.com/2005/01/08/business/george-wackenhut-85-dies-founded-elite-security-firm.html

19 Minahan, *The Quiet American: A Biography of George R. Wackenhut*, 373.

20 Minahan, *The Quiet American: A Biography of George R. Wackenhut*, 368–87.

21 "Guide to the Church League of America Collection of the Research Files of the Wackenhut Corporation, 1931–1973," Tamiment Library and Robert F. Wagner Labor Archives, updated April 20, 2018, http://dlib.nyu.edu/findingaids/html/tamwag/tam_148/dscaspace_ref11.html

22 Matt Schudel, "George Wackenhut Dies," *The Washington Post*, January 7, 2005, https://www.washingtonpost.com/archive/local/2005/01/07/george-wackenhut-dies/49ba2b1f-ee06-4426-9717-7fb3cd75b1a0/

23 "Preservation Demolition of the Tyecliffe Castle, by Allison's Adam and Eve," *Cision PR*, January 25, 2008, https://www.prweb.com/pdfdownload/651811.pdf

24 Castles by the Sea Real Estate, *Tyecliffe Estate Coral Gables [Pamphlet]*

25 Tom Kenworthy, "Alaska Oil Pipeline Company and Security Criticized," *The Washington Post*, July 24, 1992, https://www.washingtonpost.com/archive/politics/1992/07/24/alaska-oil-pipeline-company-and-security-firm-criticized/

26 Michael Parrish, "Oil Pipeline Operators Settle with Critic Who Said They Spied on Him," *The Los Angeles Times*, December 21, 1993, https://www.latimes.com/archives/la-xpm-1993-12-21-fi-4236-story.html

27 Keith Schneider, "Industry Critics Were Target of Pipeline Owner's Inquiry," *New York Times*, November 6, 1991, https://www.nytimes.com/1991/11/06/us/industry-critics-were-target-of-pipeline-owner-s-inquiry.html

28 Documents from 1992 to 1993 obtained by FOIA request: U.S. Department of Justice memos and *Anchorage Daily News* articles regarding The Wackenhut Corporation and Alyeska Pipeline Service Company's alleged involvement in obstruction of justice.

29 George A. Anderson, "Prisons for Profit: Some Ethical and Practical Problems," *America: The Jesuit Review*, November 18, 2000, https://www.americamagazine.org/issue/389/article/prisons-profit

30 Schudel, "George Wackenhut Dies."

31 The Wackenhut Corp., *Proxy Statement and Notice of Special Meeting to Approve and Adopt Merger Agreement*, April 9, 2002, https://www.sec.gov/Archives/edgar/data/104030/000095014402003675/g74655ddefm14a.htm#011

32 Peter Kerr-Jarrett, "A Family Affair," *Broward Palm Beach New Times*, May 23, 2002, https://www.browardpalmbeach.com/news/a-family-affair-6322360?showFullText=true

33 Wackenhut, interview.

CHAPTER 4

Ira A. Lipman
Principles and Profits

Ira Lipman founded Guardsmark in 1963 at the age of 22. His passion for the business is best understood in the context of his early life, as he began in the security services industry as a young boy working for his father, Mark Lipman, who had established a small but thriving investigative service.

Ira would lead Guardsmark to be one of the largest security guard companies in the United States, noted for the quality of service it provided to numerous major institutions and Fortune 500 companies. Its many superlatives led many in the industry to refer to Guardsmark as the Tiffany's of the security industry. As such, Ira exacted exacting standards from himself and his entire staff throughout his career. Underpinning his accomplishments in building a major security company, Ira was a highly principled individual who was devoted to promoting professionalism in the security industry (Figure 4.1). He was a humanitarian, philanthropist, and a loved and respected family man.

EARLY LIFE AND CAREER

Ira A. Lipman was born in Little Rock, Arkansas, on November 15, 1940, to Philadelphia natives Belle and Mark Lipman.[1] We can trace the investigative industry "blood" in the Lipman family to Ira's father, Mark, who as a young man was known as Chick Lipman, and was the youngest of ten children. Mark's two older brothers, Morris, and Lou, were decorated World War I veterans who served under General Pershing in the Forty-Second Infantry Division, nicknamed the Rainbow division. When the older brothers returned home from the war, they set up a savings and loan company in Philadelphia, serving city workers. They had young Mark do "the dirty work," such as skip tracing and background checks.[2]

When the Depression hit, the savings and loan fell on tough times, and by 1934, Mark, who had taken some accounting courses at Temple

DOI: 10.4324/9781003285564-7

FIGURE 4.1   Photograph of Ira, earlier in his Guardsmark tenure.

(Source: Guardsmark photo provided by Gus Lipman.)

University, started taking on cases independently. Mark and his wife, Belle, set out for Houston to do investigative work for some oil industry clients. However, along the way to Houston he had picked up so much business that the couple decided to stay in Little Rock, Arkansas, instead. With clients between Chicago, New Orleans, and Houston, Little Rock was an ideal place to settle. Nearby Hot Springs was also a good source of business, as it was frequented by many people who were on the move, including gangsters, and was a resort area similar in popularity to Las Vegas today.[3]

Mark formed his business, Mark Lipman Services, in 1935, specializing in claims work for lawyers and helping businesses stop theft by their employees. As it grew, the firm began attracting work from Fortune 500 companies.[4] Mark obtained work investigating fraud for large companies such as Pillsbury and Levi's. He would place undercover agents in the plants to uncover fraud and theft. Mark even sat with Sam Walton, founder of Walmart, in the early days to go through register receipts. According to his grandson Gus, Mark was known as the "Dick Tracy of the Southwest." He was a dapper dresser who would smoke up to 12 cigars a day. Only five feet five inches tall, as part of his work "he interrogated suspected criminals, without a firearm and only having a flapjack. He was fearless."[5]

Ira Lipman started work for his father Mark at an early age. By the time he was eight, his father would have him serving as an operative checking for cash register skimming. He would purchase goods and see if the clerks would leave the register open when he made an additional purchase.

The Insider at Central High School in Little Rock

In 1957 Ira was a student at Central High School in Little Rock. The public school became famous during September of that year.

On September 4, 1957, the first day of school at Central High, a white mob gathered in front of the school, and Governor Orval Faubus deployed the Arkansas National Guard to prevent nine black students from entering. In response to Faubus' action, a team of NAACP lawyers, including Thurgood Marshall, won a federal district court injunction to prevent the governor from blocking the students' entry. With the help of police escorts, the students successfully entered the school through a side entrance on September 23, 1957. Fearing escalating mob violence, however, the students were rushed home soon afterward.

Observing the standoff between Faubus and the federal judiciary, Martin Luther King sent a telegram to President Eisenhower urging him to "take a strong forthright stand in the Little Rock situation." Aware that the Little Rock incident was becoming an international embarrassment, Eisenhower reluctantly ordered troops from the Army's 101st Airborne Division to protect the students, who were shielded by federal troops and the Arkansas National Guard for the remainder of the school year (Figure 4.2).[6]

Ira felt empathy for the black students at the school, known in the media as the Little Rock Nine. During the incident, from a pay phone inside the school, he provided real-time tips to NBC reporter John Chancellor about what was happening. Ira kept the secret that he was the source for Chancellor until 1992 when he disclosed it to journalist David Halberstam, who reported it in his book *The Fifties*. In 1995, Ira would establish the John Chancellor Award for Excellence in Journalism at the University of Pennsylvania. Today, it is administered by Columbia University's School of Journalism.[7]

FIGURE 4.2 Photograph of the "Little Rock Nine," as they became known.

(Source: U.S. National Park Service.)

Gus Lipman noted in conversation that the school controversy as well as other moments from his early life in the South left an indelible mark on Ira, who was taught by his parents to respect everyone regardless of race or color. During his travels for business in the South, Ira was particularly upset that African American agents employed by his father were not allowed in the same restaurants and hotels as white people. Ira and his father made it a practice to take their meals with the staff only in places where they could eat together.

Foundational Values

Mark and Belle taught Ira ethical values that would carry him through life, including having a regard for people, a belief in equal justice and opportunity for all people, the value of hard work, and the importance of family. In addition, attention to detail, a value that the Lipmans carried across generations, was a key to their success.

Gus described his grandfather Mark as a leader in the Jewish community, noting how the synagogue congregants and others would go to him for advice. He was "a serious man that people turned to in a crisis and for advice." Gus described his father Ira in similar fashion, as a concerned, thoughtful, and passionate person, a leader who liked people and was always thinking.

Much of Ira's energy might be attributed to his mother, Belle. She was an extrovert, "outgoing, charismatic, and a four-foot-ten dynamo," according to Gus. She was energetic, a world traveler with a zest for life, and an inspiration to her family. Her wide range of passions included opera, literature, and culture. On her 90th birthday in New York, she danced the Charleston. Among her many charitable and service activities she served a term as president of the Little Rock chapter of Hadassah, the Women's Zionist Organization of America. A familiar figure in civic causes, she was honored by the White House, the Office of the Vice President, the State of Tennessee, and the cities of Philadelphia and Memphis.[8] Senator Carl Levin recognized her passing in a memorial remembrance delivered on the Senate floor.[9] Gus noted that when Belle was in her 90s, as the events of September 11, 2000, unfolded, she was on the Amazon River calling regularly to check on the family. Belle lived until the age of 99.

The values imparted to Ira by his parents would in turn be imparted to others, not the least to his sons. He was a firm believer in justice, and he applied solid judgment when he considered what actions to take for the best way forward as an individual and later for his company. Ira demanded honesty, judgment, and courage from himself and all his employees. He would set a high standard and example for those around him.

The patch worn by thousands of Guardsmark security officers contains the words "Truth, Courage, Judgement." As a Jewish family in the South facing anti-Semitism, the Lipmans developed a deep respect for the need to protect the rights of their fellow man. For Courage to be included on the Guardsmark patch signifies the importance Ira placed on this value. To protect requires not only physical but moral courage.

Finding a Career Direction: Custom Security Services

By 1958, the company was working with larger, Fortune 500 companies, and Mark moved his agency to Memphis, Tennessee. When Guardsmark became a public company in 1970, Mark Lipman Services would become their investigative division. Before he passed, Mark would be the division president and a senior vice president of Guardsmark.[10]

After two years at Ohio Wesleyan University, Ira decided he would rather leave school to sell business for his father's firm. Although he left college, Gus noted that his father was always committed to learning. Besides reading a lot, he would later surround himself with subject experts. If he didn't know about something he immersed himself in books. Ira would even have authors come to his office so he could become more knowledgeable on a particular subject.

Ira was so successful at soliciting business that Mark had to ask him to slow down, because they couldn't keep up with the amount of new business. Ira became very interested in politics around this time. He founded and became president of the Memphis Young Republicans; he was also active in and became a leader of the Tennessee Young Republicans. He worked on Richard Nixon's presidential campaign, and later for Nelson Rockefeller's campaign, promoting his "Southern Strategy." However, by 1962 when Rockefeller's campaign suffered a blow due to his divorce, Ira decided it was time to get back to business.[11]

Back full time at Mark's firm, Ira was again selling fraud and theft investigation services to customers when one asked if he could provide a service that was more preventive in nature. In other words, a service that would allow the company to avoid the need for repeated investigation of fraud and losses. Ira had an idea that instead of just providing a protective guard service, he could be proactive by providing a risk assessment, and then design and develop a customized security program to best mitigate problems. Risk assessments and security services based on specific client needs were rather novel at the time and would later become a hallmark service of Guardsmark.

FOUNDING OF GUARDSMARK

In 1963, Ira founded his own company, called Guardsmark (the Mark in honor of his father), in Memphis. The company would focus on providing high-quality service to large accounts in the industrial and corporate security verticals. The postwar economic boom was ongoing, and there were opportunities to provide security services to an expanding industrial and commercial base.

Ira's early success in sales at his father's company carried over to Guardsmark. From the beginning Ira believed that maintaining honesty and truth in his dealings was the correct path to success in life and work. As such, he did everything he could to ensure the truthfulness of his representations, the quality of service to be provided, and that his employees would be honest and truthful in their work on behalf of the company and its customers.

Ira met Abe Plough, of Schering-Plough, early on while in Memphis, and the chemical giant would become one of the first major customers for Guardsmark. Abe Plough was a mentor to Ira and imparted some of his wisdom from his chemical business to Ira. Plough told him not to fear raising his billing rates; "Earn your rates every day and don't sacrifice service." Otherwise, he would never sustain quality at Guardsmark. Ira took that advice. Guardsmark was known as a company that would not sacrifice quality in pursuit of revenues by competing at low prices or by paying low wages.

Other early key accounts included St. Jude's Children's Research Hospital, and a new RCA television plant that was built in Memphis. After completing an exhaustive proposal for RCA, Guardsmark was awarded the contract which Gus said was "a transformational deal for the company."

In a 2006 presentation to the International Security Forum in Beijing, China, Ira noted that Guardsmark was founded on the twin pillars of quality and enduring excellence. By investing in his employees, Ira believed that he could ensure better service than his competitors. Through quality control of all phases of the company, he could also ensure client retention.[12] Managers at Guardsmark were held to exceedingly exacting standards, and bonuses would be affected if the exacting standards were not met. The company was reluctant to hire anyone from within the high-turnover security industry. "I don't want their bad habits," said Ira Lipman, the firm's president, and owner. "My impression was that Guardsmark's screening and supervisory standards were better than the competition's," said Robert McCrie, publisher of the security business's leading newsletter.[13]

Setting High Professional Standards

Early on Ira surrounded himself with retired military people. His son Gus remarked that having military experience was "pretty much a requirement to work for Guardsmark then." He noted that exacting military standards of discipline at Guardsmark stemmed from the hiring of prominent military veterans. D.D. Nelson, who served in the Air Force under General Curtis LeMay, would head operations in the East, and R.A. Henry, a decorated Marine who was at Guadalcanal during World War II, would head up operations in the West. At Guardsmark, The Nelson-Henry Award was named for the late D.D. Nelson and the late R.A. Henry, two of the company's prominent early leaders.[14]

Ira saw early on that with the rapid boom in security services, many small companies with little or no professional standards were flooding the industry and providing service at low rates. He implemented exacting and thorough screening tools used by police forces, such as the Minnesota Multiphasic Personality Inventory (MMPI), to ensure that his employees did not have underlying emotional problems that might interfere with executing their duties. He insisted on only having people who he could be assured would protect his clients, their employees, and visitors.[15] The rigorous selection process at Guardsmark would include:

- Checking work and school history back to age 18
- Ten-year residential history
- Polygraph where permitted by law
- Ten-panel drug test and random drug testing
- A zero-tolerance program for illegal drug use
- Psychological testing to determine if candidates could handle stress
- An independent review of employee files

Ira invested in Guardsmark employees by providing them with the highest wages, medical benefits, retirement plans, a college tuition reimbursement program, and incentives for officers and managers to obtain security certification such as the ASIS Certified Protection Professional certification (CPP)®. Officers and managers would not just go through training programs, but initial and ongoing "learning and development programs."[16]

Ira insisted that at Guardsmark employees be treated with respect and dignity. Due to his early experience with religious and racial discrimination, and his sense of ethics and justice, Guardsmark would have a diversity program and equal opportunity in employment and for promotion.

Ira's influence on high professional standards went well beyond his own company. He was a driving force behind the creation of NASCO (the National Association of Security Companies) and led the call starting in the 1980s for private security companies to have access to FBI criminal history records. He embarked on a decades-long lobbying effort to urge policymakers to enact legislation to authorize such access. The effort successfully culminated in the 2004 passage of the Guardsmark-inspired Private Security Officer Employment Authorization Act, which granted all employers of security officers the authorization to request FBI screening on their officers.

The programs and exacting standards of excellence implemented at Guardsmark and through his leadership of NASCO would result in great success. In several speeches, Ira said that Guardsmark's success proved that "principles and profits were not mutually exclusive but go hand in hand."[17]

Key Events Shape Guardsmark

Besides landing key early accounts, Gus told us of other watershed moments for Ira and Guardsmark. In 1968, Gus noted that Guardsmark security officers were part of the protective detail in Memphis at a hospital where the body of Martin Luther King lay after he was assassinated. He noted that Ira was totally committed to ensuring that there would be no harm done despite the charged atmosphere.

After the assassination, news spread quickly and riots broke out in more than 100 cities across the United States. In the week following the shooting in Memphis, hundreds of buildings were burned, thousands of arrests were made, and more than 40 people lost their lives.[18]

In 1970, Ira married his secretary, Barbara Kelly, and the couple would have three sons who followed Ira later on into the business. His sons—Gus, Joshua, and Benjamin—would all work for the company in distinct roles. At the time Ira and Barbara were in New York, and commuting from their home in Chappaqua was proving difficult. By 1972 they would move to Memphis, where they resided until 2002.[19]

In 1970, Arkansas billionaire Jack Stephens and his firm Stephens, Inc., took Guardsmark public at a multiple of 40 times earnings. It was the first IPO for Stephens, and in the same year they would take Walmart public as well. Nine years later, with the stock undervalued, Ira took the company private. He was "tired of Wall Street pressuring him to make more acquisitions."[20]

The company would grow at a 10 percent compounded rate until selling in 2015 without acquisitions and remain highly focused on being the premier supplier of security service to aerospace and defense, hospitals, oil and chemical facilities, Fortune 500 companies and their headquarters, as well as Class A Office Buildings. Retail and government work, where price was often a paramount concern to the buyer, were not verticals that Guardsmark specialized in or entered. Gus stated that Ira viewed his main competition as in-house corporate security, and by proving Guardsmark could do the job at their standards or better, business would continue to grow. Ira did not waver from the beginning in leading a company founded and focused on providing quality security services, and the success of Guardsmark is a testament to his hard work and focus.

In 1979, Gus said the Iran hostage situation, along with plane hijackings, became a major concern for Ira (Figure 4.3). Ira made it known that these situations would affect the United States with increasingly dire consequences. He had a keen understanding of the dynamics of evolving security risks. What was happening overseas would find its way to the States. He let his staff know to assist clients through risk assessments and mitigation.

FIGURE 4.3 Iranian students overrun the U.S. Embassy in Tehran (November 4, 1979) (Public Domain).

In congressional testimony and opinion articles, he was among the first security experts to urge that metal detectors be installed at every airport to screen passengers; that carry-on luggage be scrutinized fully; and that frequent fliers be given special identification cards to speed them through security checkpoints so guards could focus on more potentially problematic travelers. Many of those recommendations, by Ira Lipman and others, were adopted by the federal Transportation Security Administration, including for thorough baggage checks and for government-issued passes given to qualifying travelers to expedite entry—today known as Global Entry cards.[21]

Ira was outspoken regarding restricting security officers carrying weapons. In 1988, only one-half of 1 percent of the 7,000 guards employed by Guardsmark nationwide would carry a firearm. Lipman also barred his personnel from packing canisters of Mace or any other device capable of inflicting bodily harm. The company guards would carry weapons only when they were safeguarding high security risks such as substantial amounts of cash, negotiable instruments, or nuclear power facilities. Ira stated, "I've always felt that it is unnecessary for security officers to carry a weapon in 99 percent of cases." Likewise, he said in an interview at his corporate headquarters, "If you're going to carry a gun, who are you going to shoot? The only person who should be permitted to take a human life is a police officer, and then only in self-defense or to save another life." Guardsmark at the time was the sixth largest U.S. security company, a $125-million-a-year company with 79 offices covering 400 cities.[22]

Gus remarked that the 1993 World Trade Center bombing and 1995 Oklahoma City bombing were also significant events, as these international and home-grown terrorist acts illustrated the risks of mass casualty events. These events, as with the Iran crisis, would prove to show increased demand for more sophisticated security solutions. Ira noted that Guardsmark would employ more former FBI agents than any other company, and the company largely comprised employees with military and/or law enforcement experience.[23] Surrounding the company with extraordinary security experts was a sound business practice for Guardsmark, as it would be for several of its major competitors. The experts were drawn to Guardsmark in the knowledge that the firm paid handsomely for quality work.

In 1994, Gus graduated from the Wharton School of Business with a B.S. in economics. He began his full-time security career at Guardsmark soon after, working out of the San Francisco office starting as an account manager. He quickly received several promotions and was a West Coast regional manager within two years. Ira would increasingly rely on Gus and his sons as the company grew over the next few decades.

The Family Faces Adversity

In 1994, Mark Lipman passed away. It was the beginning of a tough stretch for the family. He had been a profound influence for his family, not to mention the many businesses that had benefited from Mark Lipman Services, which, as noted earlier, was the investigative division of Guardsmark from 1970 until 2015. In 1973, Mark teamed up with Robert Daley, a former deputy police commissioner of New York City, to write a book titled *Stealing: How America's Employees Are Stealing Their Companies Blind*. He also lectured widely about crime. In recognition of his efforts to further criminology, the library at the Center for Studies in Criminology and Criminal Law at the University of Pennsylvania's Wharton School was named after him in 1985.[24]

In 1996, Barbara Lipman suffered a massive stroke. Six weeks later, Ira would need triple bypass surgery. Flowers were sent by many, including competitors hopeful to acquire Guardsmark. The family would not be ready to sell and instead was interested in growing the business.

Fortunately, Ira had built up a strong personnel structure within Guardsmark, he had his sons and longtime professionals with him at the company, and the company had made several key management hires. Vice President of Major Accounts, James "Jim" Antonelli had been with the company since 1971. Weldon Kennedy, retired deputy director of the FBI, would be hired in 1997 and would stay with Guardsmark for the next 16 years. Thanks to their leadership the company survived through a difficult period, and Gus noted that during that time Ira recognized his mortality. It was a humbling experience.

GUARDSMARK MOVES ON

As Ira learned from his father, Mark, the three sons learned from Ira. The security business was in their blood. Gus rose through the ranks and became the Chief Operating Officer in 2005, operating out of the New York office. His brother Josh later became Vice Chairman, involved primarily in finance and legal issues out of the Memphis office. Benjamin would become Senior Executive V.P. of Sales. Guardsmark maintained its customer relationships due to the continued quality of the service they provided. The reputation of the company was always maintained, because Ira and his team adhered to the principles of service he demanded from day one.

By 2015, the industry was changing, and private equity was enabling companies to grow more quickly through acquisition than organic growth due to the low cost of capital. The competition was increasing as more large companies had entered the U.S. market, and Ira and his sons did not want to bring on a partner or acquire other companies. Doing so would be antithetical to the way things had been done in the company for its entire history. Many companies pursued Guardsmark, but Universal Protection, which had been expanding exponentially, made a generous offer which the family felt was in their best interest to take. In 2015, Universal acquired Guardsmark. Ira served as Vice Chairman of Universal Protection until Universal merged with Allied-Barton in 2016. Ira passed away three years later in 2019, and Barbara passed in 2020.

A LEGACY OF PHILANTHROPY, HUMANITARIAN, AND INDUSTRY AWARDS

In addition to his prowess as a businessman, Ira left a legacy of philanthropy, humanitarianism, and contributions to the security services industry. His legacy will be felt by many for generations to come. Following is a partial list of the numerous endowments, philanthropies, and organizations Ira supported; and a sample of awards he received, and articles and books he published on the security industry.

Endowments

Guardsmark Professorship at The Wharton Business School
Ira A. Lipman Center for Journalism and Civil and Human Rights at Columbia University
Ira A. Lipman Chair in Emerging Technologies and National Security at the Council on Foreign Relations
Ira A. Lipman Professorship at the Wharton School at the University of Pennsylvania
Ira A. Lipman Professorship in Journalism at Columbia University
The John Chancellor Award for Excellence in Journalism
The Lipman Family Professorship of Criminology, Law, and Public Policy at Northeastern University

Humanitarianism

Chairman of National Non-Profit Organizations, The National Conference of Christians and Jews, and the National Council on Crime and Delinquency
First Chairman of the Ethics Committee of the United Way of America
Member of the Council on Foreign Relations
Board member of numerous organizations, including The Simon Wiesenthal Center and The New York Historical Society

Awards and Honors

1983 Distinguished Service Award from the NAACP
1985 Humanitarian of the Year Award, National Conference of Christians, and Jews
2004 The Dean's Medal of The Wharton School of the University of Pennsylvania, where he served as member of the Board of Overseers from 1991 to 2016

Authored Books and Articles

Author of *How to Protect Yourself from Crime* in 1975; its fourth edition in 2012 was titled *How to Be Safe*

Wrote and published numerous articles for *The New York Times* and *The Washington Post*, and published the monthly *Lipman Report*, a management newsletter

REFLECTIONS ON A LEGENDARY CAREER

Ira Lipman made major contributions to the security industry and to humanity at large. He was at the forefront in enhancing the reputation of the industry by lobbying to increase the ability of security companies to screen, train, and pay security officers higher wages. He set out to provide a better-quality company and stuck to his principles.

From the start Ira focused his energy on providing high-quality service, attracting, retaining, supervising, and training the best people to work with him to provide the best service for his customers. With a concern for his employees, he provided them with better pay and benefits, and in return he demanded excellent performance. This strategy enabled Guardsmark to prosper, and the company sustained an elevated level of quality required by discerning top-shelf private companies, enabling consistent yet measured, profitable growth.

Ira refused to forsake his beliefs in order to grow his business through predatory pricing, or to go into verticals he deemed would be of less value to the Guardsmark brand. He would not operate as a commodity business, paying low wages and charging low prices to get customers. In this manner the reputation of his company solidified his prospects with discerning buyers of high-end security services. He lived up to his promises, and Guardsmark was extraordinarily successful.

Ira co-founded a professional organization for security services leaders. Through this vehicle and other initiatives, he regularly engaged in lobbying efforts that elevated security issues in the national consciousness.

Ira Lipman and Guardsmark were recognized as leaders in their commitment to "values-driven management." Ira and Guardsmark were lauded for being ahead of the time in adopting a code of ethics for Guardsmark in 1980. The code was included in the book *Eighty Exemplary Ethics Statements* and praised for its then-unique inclusion of "employee wellness."[25]

Ira believed that having security officers underpaid and undertrained would imperil society. In lectures and in print, he predicted that demand for security service would continue to grow, led by an increase in commerce, crime, and a move to outsourcing, and that with technology evolving, low wage security officers would not be able to handle more sophisticated requirements to provide service. With increased demands on providing security to meet today's challenges, it still remains to be seen if the standards and wages for the security industry will rise.

Ira's success at Guardsmark was proof as he said that "principle and profit are not mutually exclusive."[26] He made sure to deliver what he promised. He achieved remarkable success, and at its peak in 2015, when he sold Guardsmark, it topped $500 million in revenues, had 18,000 employees, and more than 125 offices serving 400 cities in the United States, Canada, Puerto Rico, and the United Kingdom. Major corporations that used Guardsmark for all or most of their security ranged from Lockheed Martin to General Dynamics; from Charles Schwab to BASF, Microsoft, MillerCoors, Harley Davidson, Ford Motor Company and Discover Financial; from *The New York Times* to *The Washington Post*; from Federal Express to Time Warner (Figure 4.4). For 50 years, Guardsmark handled the security for St. Jude's Research Hospital, the country's only comprehensive cancer center for children. Guardsmark easily could have been bigger, but Ira chose to grow organically starting in 1977 without an acquisition.

As a boss he was a very demanding and exacting taskmaster, but fair, and by all accounts he never made a decision without evaluating

FIGURE 4.4   Photograph of Ira, later in his Guardsmark tenure, in a board room.

(Source: Guardsmark photo provided by Gus Lipman.)

whatever ethics might be involved. Weldon Kennedy, the aforementioned former FBI deputy director, who joined Guardsmark as its vice-chairman from 1997 to 2014, recalled that Ira

> was hard to work for but I don't think any person would tell you he was unfair or made erroneous decisions. But it was almost impossible for people to completely fulfill the standards that he set for the company. He set them high because he wanted to be the best in the business, which in my opinion he was, without anybody anywhere near close to him.[27]

NOTES

1   Sam Roberts, "Ira Lipman, Security Man Who Spoke Out for Air Safety, Dies at 78," *New York Times*, September 27, 2019, https://www.nytimes.com/2019/09/27/business/ira-lipman-dead.html

2   Gustave (Gus) Lipman, interview by Michael Hymanson, January 20, 2022. A skip tracer chases down someone who is hard to find—that is, someone who has "skipped town."

3   Lipman, interview.

4   "Mark Lipman, 88, Investigator Who Founded a Private Agency," *New York Times*, May 25, 1995, https://www.nytimes.com/1994/05/25/obituaries/mark-lipman-88-investigator-who-founded-a-private-agency.html

5   Lipman, interview. A flapjack is a small, leather beavertail-shaped self-defense weapon with a weighted end, easily concealed. It is also known as a slapjack, slap, or sap.

6   "Little Rock School Desegregation," in *Martin Luther King, Jr. Encyclopedia* (Stanford University Martin Luther King, Jr. Research and Education Institute). https://kinginstitute.stanford.edu/encyclopedia/little-rock-school-desegregation

7   Roberts, "Ira Lipman, Security Man Who Spoke Out for Air Safety, Dies at 78."

8   "Belle Ackerman Lipman," *Commercial Appeal*, August 19, 2009, https://www.legacy.com/us/obituaries/commercialappeal/name/belle-lipman-obituary?id=14828060

9   "Remembering Belle Ackerman Lipman," *Congressional Record* 155, issue 131: (September 16, 2009), https://www.govinfo.gov/content/pkg/CREC-2009-09-16/pdf/CREC-2009-09-16-pt1-PgS9428-3.pdf

10   "Mark Lipman, 88, Investigator Who Founded a Private Agency."

11   Lipman, interview.

12 Ira Lipman, "The Model Private Security Industry" (paper presented at the Beijing International Security Forum, September 20, 2006).

13 "A Man the Guard Firms Love to Hate," *Time*, March 9, 1992, http://content.time.com/time/subscriber/article/0,33009,975007,00.html

14 "Guardsmark Honors Top Performers of Fiscal Year 2014," *PR Newswire*, August 28, 2014, https://www.prnewswire.com/news-releases/guardsmark-honors-top-performers-of-fiscal-year-2014-273084081.html

15 "A Man the Guard Firms Love to Hate."

16 Lipman, "The Model Private Security Industry."

17 Lipman, "The Model Private Security Industry."

18 Alan Taylor, "The Riots That Follwed the Assassination of Martin Luther King," *The Atlantic*, April 3, 2018, https://www.theatlantic.com/photo/2018/04/the-riots-that-followed-the-assassination-of-martin-luther-king-jr/557159/

19 "Biography of Ira A. Lipman," https://iraalipman.com/biography_of_ira_a_lipman/

20 Richard Behar, "Ode to Whistleblowers: Ira Lipman (1940–2019), From Civil Rights to the Security Industry," *Forbes*, November 21, 2019, https://www.forbes.com/sites/richardbehar/2019/11/21/ode-to-whistleblowers-ira-lipman-1940-2019-from-civil-rights-to-the-security-industry/

21 Roberts, "Ira Lipman, Security Man Who Spoke Out for Air Safety, Dies at 78."

22 Robert Wiedrich, "Disarming Security Guards," *Chicago Tribune*, May 31, 1988, https://www.chicagotribune.com/news/ct-xpm-1988-05-31-8801030646-story.html

23 Lipman, "The Model Private Security Industry."

24 "Mark Lipman, 88, Investigator Who Founded a Private Agency."

25 "Rest in Peace, Ira Lipman (1940-2019), Guardsmark Founder/CEO and NASCO Co-Founder" (September 17, 2019). https://www.nasco.org/rest-in-peace-ira-lipman-1940-2019/

26 Lipman, "The Model Private Security Industry."

27 Behar, "Ode to Whistleblowers: Ira Lipman (1940–2019), From Civil Rights to the Security Industry."

CHAPTER 5

Thomas W. Wathen
No Fear of Flying

Thomas W. (Tom) Wathen began his security career while in the Air Force, but achieved his legendary status by transforming a small, California-based security company into a leading national firm, culminating in the acquisition of Pinkerton's.

Tom's early life helped set the stage for his later success. He inherited his father's affable nature and zest for sales, and his life and career were marked by his application of the values he was taught. Among these were: your word is your bond; be fair, generous, and hard-working; protect those around you. His passion for the security industry may have only been exceeded by his passion for flying (Figure 5.1).

EARLY LIFE

Tom was born in Vincennes, Indiana, on October 5, 1929, the firstborn child of William H. "Jack" Wathen and Dorothy M. Stumpp. According to Tom's sister Susie, he got his nickname from his aunt, as he reminded her of a departed beau. Jack lost his father at age 13 and left school to work for the Schultheis & Sons Furniture store, unpacking crates (Figure 5.2 here). He was a hard worker, and during the Depression while others were losing their jobs, he worked on commission and became a successful salesperson at Schultheis. His hard work, friendly personality, and reputation for honesty served him well, and he would become floor manager and then office manager, before retiring at age seventy, five years beyond the required retirement age for store employees.

While sharing about Jack, Susie recalled a family trip with her parents, sister Barbara, and Tom to Washington D.C. when she was young. Jack longed to step inside the Pentagon, and though members of the public were not allowed entry, Tom and Jack took a chance and approached the guard, who was nearly seven feet tall. "Could we step inside for just a moment?" they asked. As Susie tells it, "The guard noticed my father's

DOI: 10.4324/9781003285564-8

FIGURE 5.1   A photo of Tom at Flabob Airport.

(Used with permission and courtesy Flabob Airport/Tom Wathen Center.)

Knights of Columbus ring and the men began chatting and before you know it, we were given a brief tour at the Pentagon."

Jack was self-taught and an avid reader. Susie described him as fair, honest, protective, and kind, the same qualities she used to describe Tom. As a parent Jack was strict, but he never hit any of the children. Susie stated that Tom also learned values from his mother, whom she described as gentle, sweet, and protective. She helped out with the family's finances during the Depression working as a bookkeeper for her father's butcher shop, but later was a homemaker taking care of the five Wathen children.

Dinner was an almost sacred time, when the family would gather to converse, and outside interruptions such as phone calls were not allowed. In the Wathen home, structure and clear expectations were their own form of discipline, often making punishment unnecessary. Susie recalled Tom speaking about the time he had failed to clean up the family garage as promised after school, instead of staying out with his friends. When Jack got home and saw that the garage had not been cleaned, he said, "I am disappointed in you Tom, since your word was not honored." Tom said that from that day, he resolved to be more self-disciplined, and to make sure his word was his bond. He was ashamed that he had let his father down.

FIGURE 5.2   A photo of Tom with his sister Susie.

(Used with permission from Susan "Susie" Wathen.)

Physically, Tom was tall like his father and brother Bob (Bosco), about six feet three inches, and was described by Susie as handsome and well-liked. Like Susie and their father, he had a gift of gab, and mention is made in articles and by industry persons describing him as decidedly affable.

Vincennes is a small rural town by the Wabash River whose locals have long been mostly employed by the regional Samaritan Hospital, and Vincennes University. Across the river on the Illinois side was the small O'Neal Airport, and when Tom was a young teenager, he would ride his bike there. He became fascinated with flying and would sweep out the hangar in return for rides on the small planes. Susie confirmed the story that her mother forbade Tom to continue going there once she found out what he was doing, as "mom was terrified of anything happening to her son."

A Passion for Aerospace and Security

After graduating from Lincoln High School in Vincennes, Tom attended Vincennes University, before enrolling at Purdue University to study aeronautical engineering. As Tom proved not to be the best mathematician, the dean of students suggested he pursue another line of study unless he could improve his math skills. Tom transferred to Indiana University to study police science.

Tom graduated from Indiana University in 1951 with a degree in Police Administration. He joined the Air Force, where he was stationed at Wright-Patterson Air Force Base, and, later, the Pentagon. Tom would receive an award as a Distinguished Alumnus of the University in 1990.[1]

From 1951 to 1958, Tom worked as an industrial security officer with the Air Force, and then as a special agent for the Department of Defense.[2] His duties there, which included background checking for vulnerabilities at various military facilities and work as a security director,[3] helped prepare him for success in his career as a security services business owner.

Gone West

Seeing an opportunity to marry his love for aviation with his skills in security management, Tom left government service and moved to California, where he became a security director for production of the X-15 rocket plane and the B-70 bomber at North American Aviation.[4] Susie noted that Tom's move to California was a big deal for Tom and the whole family. He "loved California, and he would gleefully point out the lemon tree outside of his office headquarters years later." He became a licensed pilot and bought an airplane to pursue his passion for flying. Susie said it was likely bought on credit, since he "did not earn too much when he first went to California."

Over the next few years Tom took security management positions in other West Coast businesses, including the RCA Corporation, where he worked as security director for military electronics. He became corporate security director for the Mattel Corporation in 1963.[5]

After a year at Mattel, Tom had a falling out with his boss, and accepted a job at California Plant Protection (CPP), on the condition that he retained some equity. The company reportedly had fewer than 20 employees and under $163,000 in annual revenues. Tom bought 49 percent of the company for what some might have considered a bargain at $60,000. Within nine months he owned the company fully. He had bought the corporation with all its liabilities, including a $17,000 unpaid tax bill from the IRS. His so-called bargain was a huge headache. He had no experience owning a business. However, as a security director he had experience as a customer of private security guard businesses, and he based his operation on providing the type of service he wanted to receive as a customer.[6] Despite the initial financial struggle, the company grew, anchored in customer service and personnel training.

GROWING CPP

Tom started growing CPP by concentrating on providing customers with the type of uniformed security guard service that he had wanted as a customer. He was in the right place, during a period when the need for guard services was starting to expand along with the economy. Susie said he approached building the company with great enthusiasm and confidence and was always looking toward the future. A spirited leader, he focused CPP's services on protecting factories and offices. For a while Tom tried to diversify the company's offerings into alarms, uniforms, and executive protection services, but this was short-lived. The company was most successful when it stuck to what it did best—providing uniformed, unarmed security guard services. Tom did, however, recognize that he might need to diversify if technology advances made traditional guard service outmoded.[7]

Understanding Risk Profiles—His Own and His Customers'

When Tom was building out his business, he recognized that having a better trained security officer was one way to differentiate his service from others. He required guards to call once a week to hear a recording where he spoke about different aspects of security; those who logged their calls were eligible for a randomly awarded prize. He produced his own training films to be used for basic guard training as well as on job sites. Eventually he had a certification program within the organization for which passing was required for promotion. The upgraded training and improvements in officer screening were not overly expensive, and the company was able to compete on price in the highly competitive West Coast market. He also lobbied in California for a training requirement and background check on guards who carried firearms. Only a small percentage of his security own officers were armed, which kept his insurance risk profile low.[8]

Tom's background in government security helped him to identify areas to help out his customers with their costs. He told of landing his first big account by doing a security survey for a multisite prospect where he identified that the prospect could save money and secure the properties "by installing alarms and access controls, using radios, putting a fence up, and making one guard do for two buildings."[9]

The company focused on uniformed security guard service, and CPP also advertised heavily to bolster the image of his security service. His ads displayed active and healthy security guards to counteract the public perception of less active guards. To inspire loyalty, he awarded merit badges and pay raises for officers who passed certain tests to sharpen their skills and knowledge. His management style was active; for example, he carried out routine security checks on job sites himself. Likewise, he personally screened the guards hired for the firm's security work at the 1984 Los Angeles Olympics (Figure 5.3).

By 1986, the small firm had become the fourth largest security company in the United States, behind Borg-Warner Protective (the owner of Burns and Wells Fargo), Pinkerton's, and Wackenhut. Tom partly credited a company profit-sharing program designed as an incentive plan for managers for the company's rapid expansion.[10]

FIGURE 5.3   Olympic Torch Tower of the Los Angeles Coliseum on the day of the opening ceremonies of the 1984 Summer Olympics. CPP provided security services during the Olympics.

(Source: U.S. Department of Defense Air Force Photograph.)

Organic Growth

CPP grew steadily during the late 1960s and early 1970s, and by 1980 the company had 30 offices in seven states. The company's growth in uniformed guard services took off during the "golden era" in the 1980s. Tom had realized that to expand more rapidly he might need to absorb short-term losses with a new office opening, and between 1980 and 1984, CPP opened 104 offices in another 31 states, which "moved the company into the industry's big leagues."[11]

Between 1977 and 1986, the company averaged 35 percent annual growth, and by 1986, CPP had about 23,000 employees at 130 offices in 38 states. The Van Nuys, California, headquarters staff had grown to 70.[12]

STORM CLOUDS

On December 7, 1987, Tom was in Vincennes as his mother Dorothy passed. The time was, according to Susie, an "emotional whirlwind" for Tom because it occurred while CPP was acquiring Pinkerton's. Susie recalled that as the close-knit family was gathered in Vincennes, he received a phone call and told the family, "I've just bought Pinkerton."

On January 26, 1988, CPP completed its acquisition of Pinkerton's, the nation's oldest security firm. CPP bought the 137-year-old company from American Brands, which doubled the number of CPP employees to 50,000, and increased its expected annual revenue from $250 million to about $650 million. The move, according to security expert Robert McCrie, allowed the firm to "vie with Borg-Warner's security guard unit as the biggest player in the $6-billion security guard market."[13]

The newly merged company would initially operate under the name CPP/Pinkerton.

A Challenging Acquisition

Susie said that Tom was always fascinated with Pinkerton, having read much about founder Allan Pinkerton, and she recalled a visit with Tom to Allan Pinkerton's grave in Chicago. Despite Tom's enthusiasm and confidence that the big deal would work out, some in the industry believed the acquisition would prove difficult for CPP.

With a reported loan to repay of about $95 million and razor-thin margins, success was not assured for Tom. However, Lloyd Greif, the investment banker who arranged financing for the deal, noted that the synergies would work and that Pinkerton's had the "strongest name in the business." Only 55 percent of the debt was due to be repaid within seven years. Tom began cutting costs right away by shutting down Pinkerton's Manhattan corporate headquarters and about 125 duplicate offices and laying off 400 staff. About $12 million in yearly costs was eliminated. He still had to be frugal though. His competitor Richard Wackenhut (see Chapter 3) commented at the time, "Tom has his hands extremely full...he's been a success story. But it's a little too early to tell yet how he's going to do with the purchase of Pinkerton's." Similarly, Robert McCrie said Wathen was "one of only a few people in the whole industry who have the ability to turn around Pinkerton's, which is clearly required" [...] but because of Wathen's debts, "how well he's doing is still a big question mark."[14]

Tom would succeed through hard work, and operational and financial restructuring, but it was not easy. Susie remembers Tom always working to manage the company finances. In December 1988, the company needed to borrow $20 million to keep up with loan payments. Then in early 1990, there was a partial stock offering, the first for Pinkerton's. Most of the proceeds would be used to reduce debt. The company posted net income of $6.32 million in 1989, compared to a net loss of $592,000 on sales of about $650 million in 1988, which marked a turnaround. In comparison, in 1987, Pinkerton's lost $11.2 million, "mostly because it tried to increase its revenues by bidding low on security contracts." The company cash flow allowed it to pay interest on its debt, but even after the stock offering, it had little financial or operational flexibility.[15]

Susie recalled the excitement being on the floor of the American Stock Exchange with Tom when the company went public, and Tom remained enthusiastic and looking to grow the company. The infusion of cash through the public offering and an additional loan was a shot in the arm for Tom. He refinanced Pinkerton's debt, obtaining "extremely favorable rates" and a four-year moratorium on repayment of principal, and began talking about more acquisitions and revitalizing the investigative side of Pinkerton's. Tom stated, "I love to grow, [...] Growth has always turned me on, and now we'll be able to go out and beat up on people again."[16]

Help from a Friend

In 1990, Tom turned to a longtime friend, Albert J. "Al" Berger (Chapter 9), who had been a California Plant Protection board member, for help with the merger and to prepare for the initial public offering. Berger became the chief operating officer of Pinkerton in 1990, and Tom noted, "I needed help consolidating the administrative and financial operations. [...]I don't claim any expertise in that area." With Berger's help, Pinkerton followed up its initial offering with a secondary stock offering in April 1991 and further reorganized senior debt. With operational changes Berger initiated, Tom said that the company had the means to "make Pinkerton something more than a vanilla commodity by offering services that enhance the value of our work." Among other things, the company had a computerized scheduling and billing system and implemented radio-based systems for gathering security data from far-flung sites. With operations in order, Tom took over the chief operating duties and Berger went back to being a consultant and outside board member.[17]

The GM Deal and a Change in Operational Leadership

In 1992, with the help of the proceeds from the secondary offering, Pinkerton bought General Motors' internal uniformed security business for an undisclosed price and agreed to provide security to GM locations around the United States for six years. It was purportedly the largest transfer of an in-house security force to a private security company. The company had also acquired several smaller security companies. In April 1994, Pinkerton Security & Investigation Services named Denis R. Brown as the company's president and chief executive officer, and Tom would continue to serve as the Chairman of the Board. Brown stated that "As technology becomes a more vital part of the security industry, companies such as Pinkerton must look to the future and anticipate the changing demands of the marketplace."[18]

It was a conflicted time for Tom. His first wife Gabby, who had been ill for many years, passed in July, and while Tom was by far the largest Pinkerton shareholder, it was time for him to step back from day-to-day operations. He had managed the firm for the past 30 years.

Tom would have preferred that someone from the industry take over day-to-day management of the company, but the board was looking for a fresh perspective. Still, Tom stayed on as Chairman until the firm was sold.[19]

WINDS OF CHANGE

Responding to changes in technology, the company started to become less focused on uniformed guard services and more focused on security systems integration services, monitoring, consulting, investigations and pre-employment services. In fiscal years 1996, 1997, and 1998, security officer services accounted for approximately 92 percent, 89 percent, and 87 percent, respectively, of the company's revenues.

In 1998, the company won a long-term contract expansion to provide security services to General Motors Corporation and Delphi Automotive

Systems in North America. With a projected value to exceed $1.1 billion over the next eight years, the agreement represented the world's largest commercial contract for the outsourcing of security services. This contract, in addition to various acquisitions, led to additional growth, such that the company by 1999 had approximately 48,000 employees, and revenues for the fiscal year ending in 1998 of just over $1 billion. However, revenue growth was stagnating, and financial results were disappointing. The company reported that

> operating profit was $7.4 million, or 0.7% of service revenues in 1998, as compared with an operating profit of $26.4 million, or 2.6% of service revenues in 1997. Operating profit decreased due to a decrease in the gross profit margin, higher operating expenses and the write-down of long-lived assets and other special charges.[20]

Despite less than stellar financial results, the inherent value of the company was apparent. Seizing on an opportunity to sell, Tom and the Pinkerton shareholders were rewarded handsomely when the company accepted an offer of purchase by Securitas AB of Sweden.

Securitas Acquires Pinkerton

On February 22, 1999, Pinkerton's Inc. announced an agreement to sell the company to Securitas AB of Sweden for $384 million. The price at $29 per share was 72 percent above Pinkerton's previous closing price of $16.88, underscoring the value of a famous name in the security business. Tom held a 30.6 percent stake in the company and had already agreed to sell his shares to Securitas. "An even stronger indication of investor enthusiasm was apparent in Sweden," reported *The New York Times*, "where Securitas's shares jumped 15 percent, or 18.5 kronor ($2.31), to 139.5 kronor, in trading on the Stockholm Exchange."[21] The windfall for Tom Wathen was quite substantial considering his initial $60,000 investment plus the IRS tax liability of $17,000 when he bought CPP. He had built an empire and managed to prevail after taking a chance on acquiring Pinkerton.

LEGACY

The authors interviewed Donald (Don) W. Walker, a highly respected security industry executive, on July 5, 2022, for his recollection of Tom Wathen as a leader and person. Subsequent to our interview on October

13, 2022, Donald passed away. In a tribute to him it was noted that Walker was a leader and, like Wathen, also a legend within the security profession.

> In addition to serving as President of ASIS, he was one of the co-founders of the ASIS CSO Roundtable and also served as President of the CSO Center. Walker's commitment to building community and knowledge within the security profession was steadfast as he was active in ASIS International, for four decades.[22]

Walker stated that he first came to know Tom Wathen in the mid-1970s, after he had retired from the FBI. It was not until 1991, however, when Walker sold his company, Business Risk International (BRI), to Pinkerton that he came to work under Tom as an executive vice president. Walker would later work with Thomas Berglund (profiled in Chapter 11) and become chairman of Securitas Security USA. Walker stated that

> Tom was more of a risk taker than I thought. He was an entrepreneur, with an engaging and charismatic personality. He was a man who meant what he said, and who you could take at his word.... Tom was very focused out of necessity on cost control, and though he had to lay off staff as a result of the [Pinkerton] acquisition, Tom felt a loyalty to retain those Pinkerton employees who had extensive longevity at the company. He loved the security industry and held a deep commitment to the security officers.

Befitting Tom's love of the industry and the Pinkerton heritage, Don Walker noted that he and Tom arranged for the donation of Pinkerton memorabilia to the Library of Congress, with some also housed at the Ann Arbor, Michigan, offices of the Pinkerton consulting division of Securitas.

The authors interviewed Al Berger on June 12, 2023. Berger said he first met Tom at a Young President's Association meeting in Arizona. They became friends and in 1975, when Tom was having some difficulties with a partner he asked Berger to serve as a director on the Board of CPP. Berger would serve on the Board from 1975 until 1994. According to Berger:

> Tom was a cordial, outgoing, good guy. People were attracted to him. The Pinkerton acquisition was hard on Tom since the Board required him to relinquish operational control after many years of running the company, but on balance in retrospect it was positive.

Tom's career was marked by great success, yet Susie Wathen noted, "He had control over his business career, but not so over his personal life." His first and second wives both passed away from illness, and he would marry twice more before he passed in 2016. Despite personal setbacks, his success allowed him to enjoy the finer things. He purchased large homes in Bel-Air and Montecito, California, and traveled extensively. In addition to flying planes, he would own several yachts, including one which he named *Seacurity*.

After the sale of Pinkerton's in 1999, Tom bought Flabob Airport in Riverside, California, to be used as a campus for his Thomas W. Wathen Foundation, later renamed the Tom Wathen Center. The facility is used to inspire lifelong learning about flight and is the home of Chapter One of the Experimental Aircraft Association (EAA), the first of some 900 chapters. Tom's obituary reports that

> Under Tom's guidance, Flabob became the home of an aviation-themed public charter secondary school, of a branch of Spartan College of Aeronautics and Technology, and of the headquarters of the world's oldest pilot fraternity. It has offered field trips, Air Academies, and aircraft restoration projects to thousands of young people from toddlers to high school students. Its at-risk intervention projects have diverted young gang members to useful lives in aviation. Dozens of young people have earned pilot and mechanic certificates, and have had their lives positively changed.[23]

FIGURE 5.4   A photograph of Tom in his retirement.

(Used with permission and courtesy Flabob Airport/Tom Wathen Center.)

Susie noted that Tom was a devout Catholic and looked up to by everyone in the family. Their parents were extremely proud of the man he had become. When Tom's mother passed, he helped his niece buy the family home in Vincennes; he helped Susie buy an apartment in Chicago and helped his sister Margaret financially with her family farm.

Tom's legendary career was marked by his enthusiastic leadership and the personal qualities he used in the development of a major security services company. In a similar vein as Ira Lipman (see Chapter 4), Tom was proud to have played a part in disarming largely unregulated armed private security officers. He had an outsized influence and effect on many people, in and outside of his family. He was deeply respected by his family, his competitors, and his staff (Figure 5.4).

NOTES

1　"College of Arts and Sciences Distinguished Alumni Award: Thomas W. Wathen," 1990, https://honorsandawards.iu.edu/awards/honoree/5010.html

2　Pinkerton's Inc., *Annual Report 1998*, 1999, https://www.sec.gov/Archives/edgar/data/78666/0000898430-99-001129.txt

3　James F. Peltz, "He's Buying Security's Holy Grail: CPP's Owner Feels Special Responsibility to Enhance Reputation of Pinkerton's," *Los Angeles Times*, December 22, 1987, https://www.latimes.com/archives/la-xpm-1987-12-22-fi-30463-story.html?_amp=true

4　Barnaby J. Feder, "Chairman of Pinkerton's Adds to His Responsibilities," *New York Times*, April 14, 1992, https://www.nytimes.com/1992/04/14/business/business-people-chairman-of-pinkerton-s-adds-to-his-responsibilities.html

5　Feder, "Chairman of Pinkerton's Adds to His Responsibilities."

6　Michael Barrier, "Tom Wathen's Security Blanket," *IndexArticles*, 1990/2004, https://indexarticles.com/business/nations-business/tom-wathens-security-blanket/

7　Alan Goldstein, "Plant Protection Service Blossoms: 4th Largest Security Firm in U.S. Seeks to Shake Industry's Shabby Image," *Los Angeles Times*, June 17, 1986, https://www.latimes.com/archives/la-xpm-1986-06-17-fi-11813-story.html

8　Barrier, "Tom Wathen's Security Blanket."

9　Barrier, "Tom Wathen's Security Blanket."

10　Goldstein, "Plant Protection Service Blossoms."

11　Peltz, "He's Buying Security's Holy Grail."

12　Goldstein, "Plant Protection Service Blossoms."

13　"CPP Security Completes Acquisition of Pinkerton's," *Los Angeles Times*, January 26, 1988, https://www.latimes.com/archives/la-xpm-1988-01-26-fi-38676-story.html

14   Barry Stavro, "Buyer Seeks to Pay Off Detective Agency's Debt," *Los Angeles Times*, December 11, 1988, https://www.latimes.com/archives/la-xpm-1988-12-11-fi-313-story.html

15   John Medearis, "Pinkerton's Going Public to Ease Debt," *Los Angeles Times*, February 20, 1990, https://www.latimes.com/archives/la-xpm-1990-02-20-fi-969-story.html

16   Barrier, "Tom Wathen's Security Blanket."

17   Feder, "Chairman of Pinkerton's Adds to His Responsibilities."

18   "Brown Named President, CEO," *UPI Archives*, April 21, 1994, https://www.upi.com/Archives/1994/04/21/Brown-named-Pinkerton-president-CEO/6584766900800/

19   Donald W. Walker, interview by Michael Hymanson, July 5, 2022.

20   Pinkerton's Inc., *Annual Report 1998*.

21   Barnaby J. Feder, "Securitas of Sweden to Acquire Pinkerton's in $384 Million Deal," *New York Times*, February 23, 1999, https://www.nytimes.com/1999/02/23/business/securitas-of-sweden-to-acquire-pinkerton-s-in-384-million-deal.html

22   "In Memoriam: Don W. Walker, CPP," October 18, 2022, ASIS International, https://www.asisonline.org/publications--resources/news/blog/in-memoriam-don-w-walker-cpp/

23   "Thomas William 'Tom' Wathen, 1929–2016," *Santa Barbara News Press*, June 27, 2016, https://www.legacy.com/us/obituaries/newspress/name/thomas-wathen-obituary?id=7383634

PART III

A New Wave of Competitors in a Golden Era

In Part III, we examine legends who built two major U.S.-based security companies starting in the early 1990s: U.S. Security Associates and SpectaGuard, which operated first as Allied Security, and then from 2004 as AlliedBarton. While William C. (Bill) Whitmore, Jr. spent his entire security career at SpectaGuard and subsequent entities formed by merger and acquisition, Charles R. (Chuck) Schneider and Kenneth W. (Ken) Oringer were senior executives at Baker Industries for 15 years before they co-founded U.S. Security Associates in 1993. Meanwhile, Albert J. (Al) Berger was a longtime chemical industry owner and executive before turning his attention to the security service industry at CPP/Pinkerton and then SpectaGuard and Allied Security.

Schneider and Oringer's legendary industry careers began in 1978, when Chuck as chief executive officer and Ken as chief financial officer led the Baker Industries division of Borg-Warner Corporation to become the largest security company in the United States. Baker started in 1965 as a small (less than $6 million) supplier and manufacturer of smoke detectors. In 1967, Solomon Baker, the founder of Baker Industries, obtained the rights to use the venerable Wells Fargo and Pony Express names. The company began to expand, operating as Wells Fargo Guard, Armored Services, and Alarm; Pony Express Courier; and Pyrotronics for the smoke detector segment.[1] But it was under Chuck's leadership, and with Ken directing numerous acquisitions—including the 1982 acquisition of Burns International—that Baker was transformed into the largest

DOI: 10.4324/9781003285564-9

U.S.-based security service company. Chuck and Ken left Baker in 1993, and co-founded U.S. Security. The partners then built the company into one of the largest U.S.-based security companies. By 2010, the company had revenues of over $1 billion and was the fourth largest security provider in the United States. Seven years later revenue would exceed $1.5 billion, and the company employed over 55,000 security associates.

Meanwhile, after a police career spanning eight years starting in 1973, William C. (Bill) Whitmore, Jr. began rising through the ranks of SpectaGuard, a regional security service company. Starting with his promotion to chief operating officer in 1990, and then as chief executive officer and chairman in 2003, Whitmore built the company, then operating as Allied Security and later AlliedBarton, into a $2.1 billion security company with over 60,000 employees by 2015. He retired in 2018, two years after AlliedBarton merged with Universal Services to form Allied Universal, as chairman of the board of that company.

Al Berger was a longtime CPP board member, but through his association with Tom Wathen, he would become a board member, consultant, and then president of Pinkerton. Following his tenure at Pinkerton, Al became a partner at Gryphon Partners, and became a part-owner of SpectaGuard, and ultimately the company chief executive officer from 1998 to 2003, and a chairman from 1998 to 2006. His impact on these companies during the time was extraordinary, turning around Pinkerton and being instrumental in bringing the company public, and with SpectaGuard growing the firm with Whitmore from $84 million to over $1 billion in revenues during his time with those companies.

U.S. Security Associates and Allied Security competed in the U.S. market with Burns, Pinkerton's, Wackenhut, and Guardsmark, but the golden age in which these national companies flourished would be a prelude to significant changes beginning at the turn of the twenty-first century. Large-scale mergers and acquisitions, new legends, and companies fueled by the active participation of global investment firms would have a significant impact in changing the competitive landscape of the security services industry.

Information for Chapter 6 was enhanced by an interview the authors conducted with Chuck Schneider on November 16, 2021. He also provided a taped segment recounting an experience in the U.S. Navy. Both authors of this volume worked under Chuck while at U.S. Security Associates and can attest to his strong and effective leadership. He achieved great success for himself and earned the respect of his associates every step of the way.

Information for Chapter 7 was enhanced by interviews with Ken Oringer on April 16, 2021, and November 29, 2021. Author Keith Oringer is Ken's son; and along with author Michael Hymanson, each frequently conversed with Ken regarding his career. The authors, as mentioned earlier, were employed at U.S. Security Associates, Keith as the third employee of the company, and Michael after his own firm was acquired by U.S. Security Associates. Ken peacefully passed away on September 28, 2022, and many tributes to his memory were sent to Keith and the Oringer family.

While we were unable to interview Bill Whitmore (Chapter 8), Al Berger provided us with information on his time working with Bill, as well as extensive information on his rise as an executive and owner, first in the chemical industry, and then in the security services industry.

Information for Chapter 9, Albert J. Berger, was enabled through our interviews with Al on June 12 and August 14, 2023. In addition to information on Bill Whitmore, he provided information on Tom Wathen (Chapter 5), from his days at both CPP and Pinkerton, as well as his fascinating story about his family, chemical and security industry experience.

NOTE

1 Baker Industries, *Annual Report 1985*, 1986.

CHAPTER 6

Charles R. Schneider
Engineering Success

Charles R. Schneider, known for most of his life as "Chuck," began his security industry career in 1978 as an executive with Baker Industries, which was acquired by Borg-Warner and operated largely under the Wells Fargo brand, and from 1982 also under Burns International. Chuck was at Borg-Warner until 1993, as chief executive officer of Borg-Warner's Protective Service division.

In 1993, Chuck and Ken Oringer (profiled in Chapter 7 of this volume) co-founded U.S. Security Associates, Inc., where Chuck served until 2014 as chairman and chief executive officer and until 2018 as chairman of the board of directors. The co-founders built U.S. Security Associates from an initial investment into a billion-dollar company and the fourth largest security company in the United States.

Chuck parlayed his education, drive, leadership, and management skills, which were based on principles of fairness and objectivity, to obtain spectacular business results (Figure 6.1). His educational background in engineering supported his methodical organizational approach to management, while his early career experiences in business enhanced his desire and ability to lead people.

EARLY LIFE AND EDUCATION

Chuck was born on June 13, 1940, the youngest of three children. He and his siblings were first-generation Americans. His parents, Fred, and Hildegard were of German descent, having emigrated from Switzerland to the United States in 1925.

The family lived in Wesleyville, a small borough of Erie County in northwestern Pennsylvania. Chuck's father was an electrical engineer, his mother a homemaker. Chuck noted in the interview that their focus on the importance of education, and their ongoing support and guidance,

DOI: 10.4324/9781003285564-10

FIGURE 6.1   Charles "Chuck" Schneider speaking at an International Security Ligue Meeting.

contributed to his academic and business success. At Wesleyville High School, Chuck excelled in academics and athletics, where he played on the football and basketball teams.

In 1958, Chuck attended Penn State University on an ROTC Naval scholarship. In 1962, he received a B.S. degree in mechanical engineering and then entered the U.S. Navy for a four-year active-duty stint. With his father's background in engineering, it is no surprise that Chuck would be gifted with analytical skills. He developed those skills through his engineering education and naval experience and applied them throughout his career—first at a manufacturing company and as a division manager for a musical equipment manufacturer; later, and perhaps surprisingly, as a chief executive officer for large-scale security companies. As with other legends who pursued education as a foundation for success, Chuck worked hard to be well educated, both through formal schooling and through practical experience. In every job he held, he strove to acquire as many skills and as much knowledge as possible.

Service in the U.S. Navy

Chuck's naval service was significant to his career as well as his personal life. In 1964 while in the Navy, he met Enid Hennessey, the daughter of Captain James L. Hennessey. The couple was married in 1965 at a full naval ceremony at the Brooklyn Navy Yard shortly before Chuck shipped out to sea (Figure 6.2). Thankfully, this separation was short. During their many years together, the couple had two daughters, a son, and ten grandchildren. Until her passing in 2017, Enid was an active supporter of Chuck's career, and Chuck credits her for much of his success.

FIGURE 6.2   A photo of Chuck Schneider and his wife Enid Hennessy on their wedding night in 1965.

In the Navy, Chuck was primarily assigned as a chief engineer, managing destroyers along the East Coast. Here, Chuck honed his management skills, learned to correct mistakes and how to effectively lead and direct fellow service members.

In the video that Chuck provided us on November 18, 2021, he recalled that in the Navy he worked under a demanding, but effective, officer, John D. Exum. Chuck said that Captain Exum taught him many valuable lessons in leadership.

Chuck described his first encounter with Captain Exum. Reporting for his first assignment on the destroyer USS *Noa*, docked at Mayport, Florida, Chuck met Captain Exum in the ship's wardroom after he had finished his initial paperwork on board. Most of the crew was onshore at the time as it was at the start of a weekend, but not Exum. Captain Exum greeted Ensign Schneider and requested that Chuck "let him know the status of the forward fire and flushing pump." Chuck advised Exum he would check on the pump in the morning—it was not considered an essential part; thus, Chuck thought his answer would be acceptable. Captain Exum looked squarely at the newly commissioned ensign and repeated that he wanted Chuck to find out the status of the pump. Chuck said he realized "Exum meant business," so he went to the forward engine where he found that the pump in question was not in its place, and was likely out for repair at the tender, a support ship docked alongside the *Noa*. Chuck told Exum what he found, and Exum then stated, "I'm not interested in where it is, sailor, I want the status of the part."

Chuck hurriedly went to the tender and found and memorized information from a repair memo on what was being done to the pump. He returned to the wardroom and advised Captain Exum on the information the captain had wanted in the first place. The incident took about an hour in all but proved an invaluable lesson in leadership for Chuck—one of many such lessons Captain Exum taught him. First, Captain Exum had taken the time to train the newly assigned officer when Exum could have been off the ship instead, enjoying time off. Second, he taught Chuck the meaning and importance of completed staff work. Exum wanted a complete answer, and in this case, Chuck needed to do whatever it took to get an answer. Exum had established a "required standard of performance."

The USS *Noa* was the top-performing destroyer in the Atlantic. It was also the ship that plucked astronaut John Glenn out of the Atlantic when his spaceship returned from its three-orbit mission around the earth. If its staff did not perform to lofty standards, they were assigned elsewhere. While some sailors did not take well to Exum's style, Chuck did.

Chuck learned from the captain that establishing and then demanding performance standards from his staff led to better results. Subordinates who could not provide an elevated level of performance after being given guidance and a chance to produce would not have a long career working for him. Chuck applied the leadership and management lessons he learned from Exum. As a manager, Chuck believed it was important to make requests clear and require that a full and complete answer be provided. It would be necessary to communicate clearly and have subordinates provide useful information in a concise and accurate manner. In that way, decision-making would be facilitated based on facts.

In addition to the many technical lessons learned as a naval officer, Chuck recalled that during his military service, he developed an acute interest in managing people. This spurred his decision upon honorable discharge to enter Harvard Business School in 1966. He graduated from Harvard in 1968 with an MBA degree.

Chuck later recalled that some credit for his management success was due to Harvard professor John Hammond, who he described "as a great influence and thinker." Chuck did a business case study while at Harvard for Hammond, which enhanced his decision-making ability, and he sought Hammond's advice on several problems during his career. He learned it is wise to seek out the advice of respected mentors.

Building Skills with People and Processes

After graduation, Chuck accepted a job as director of marketing with Carlisle, Pennsylvania-based P.R. Hoffman Company, a division of the Norlin Company. The company provided quartz crystals for use in new industrial applications, including in the watch industry.

Chuck was a problem-solver, and his marketing and management abilities were recognized by the parent company after he solved a manufacturing issue which improved output at the Hoffman division. In 1969 when Norlin purchased Chicago Musical Instruments, of which Gibson Guitars (Gibson) was a subsidiary, Chuck was promoted to Gibson as director of marketing after the passing of a manager there. Chuck was subsequently promoted to general manager and then president at Gibson. In our November 16, 2021, interview, Chuck said, "I enjoyed working with people," and by combining his technical and analytical background with a penchant for managing people and processes, he was learning how to become an effective business leader.

LAUNCHING A SECURITY CAREER AT BAKER INDUSTRIES

In 1978, Chuck was recruited and then hired as Group Vice President for Baker Industries, and his career in the security guard services industry began. Chuck and his family relocated from Pennsylvania to the Parsippany, New Jersey, area, where Baker had its corporate headquarters. During our interview, Chuck noted that at first that he was reluctant to enter the service industry, having spent his career to date in the manufacturing sector. However, the prospect of managing a large and growing business was exciting.

Baker Industries was a diversified security services firm operating primarily under the Wells Fargo brand name, with guard, armored car, alarm, and smoke equipment divisions. Chuck was assigned to lead the guard, armored car, and alarm services division, and to report directly to Malcolm Baker.

At Baker, Chuck met Ken Oringer, who had been hired just before him at Baker Industries as their chief financial officer. Theirs was a fateful meeting, as together, 15 years later they would co-found U.S. Security Associates.

Baker was one of the largest security companies in the United States. They were in active competition with Pinkerton, Burns, Wackenhut, Guardsmark, and many smaller regional and local security service providers. The security industry was expanding rapidly during the decade. On January 12, 1978, Selwyn Raab of *The New York Times* wrote:

> Pinkerton, the nation's largest and oldest private security company, with 33,000 guards, reported that business had increased by more than 60 percent since 1970... In 1976, Pinkerton's nationwide income* (*sic*) was more than $200 million... Spurred by the rising crime rate in the country during the last decade, the guard business has catapulted from a small cottage industry—with less than $1 billion in gross income—into a recession-resistant $12-billion-a-year giant. An estimated total of a million people is employed as full-and part-time guards, double the number of police officers in the country.[1]
>
> [Note: * Should be "revenue."]

Baker meanwhile reported 1977 sales of $185 million and net income of $6 million after an extraordinary loss of $1 million.[2]

Borg-Warner Acquires Baker Industries

In late 1977, Borg-Warner Corporation made an offer to pay $118 million in cash for Baker Industries, the protective services company.[3] The deal closed in January 1978.[4] Borg-Warner was pursuing a diversification strategy apart from its primary auto component manufacturing base and was looking to enter a growing, recession-resistant industry. Later that year a *New York Times* reporter commented that "When the Borg-Warner Corporation, the $2 billion producer of auto parts, announced that it was acquiring Baker Industries back in 1977, there were those in Wall Street who seriously questioned the wisdom of the deal."[5] Baker's manufacturing division was struggling due to price deterioration in the smoke detector segment and unusually large inventories. An official at Borg-Warner stated that "they bought the company for its guard, armored car and courier services and these divisions are ahead of expectations."[6]

Chuck recalled that Baker had pursued a policy of acquiring diverse security companies and then leveraging the new business under the Wells Fargo name. He believed that there was a clear need to focus on operations to improve service and profits, and not rely on the power of the Wells Fargo brand name alone. To more effectively manage the profit centers within the company, Chuck used his technical engineering thought process and operating vision to initiate new systems to improve operations, emphasize service, and better understand who was making money for the company.

Chuck also recognized early on that there were few or no barriers to entry in the security guard industry, but there was a lot of competition. By developing better systems, the company could compete more effectively because it would be offering a better service and gaining market share through organic growth, capitalizing on competitor weakness. The strategy worked as the division prospered and Borg-Warner soon recognized the potential for future profits and growth in the security guard industry.

Borg-Warner Acquires Burns International Security

Thus, in 1982, Borg-Warner acquired Burns International Security, which became a subsidiary of their Baker Industries division. Burns was acquired for $82.5 million and had 36,000 employees and revenues of $240 million.[7] The division was now the largest security guard company in the United States.

To date, Chuck's role at Baker had been highly successful. He proved that even in less than stellar economic times, the industry could thrive. By 1982, it was reported that

> Baker Industries, the parent of Wells Fargo acquired five years ago, put Borg-Warner into the protective services business, which just happened to be on the verge of explosive growth, in part, ironically, because a faltering economy makes people more aware of security. As the economy goes down, the crime rate goes up—and so do the profits of protective services firms. Last year, Baker and the rest of the company's protective services group—which includes Wells Fargo alarm, guard and armored car services, Pony Express courier services, an industrial fire protection unit, and now Burns Security, enjoyed a 24 percent increase in revenues and a 51 percent rise in earnings.[8]

Chuck noted that he was assigned to turn Burns around and incorporate the business into the Borg-Warner Protective Services unit. Burns was losing customers at a fast pace and had been offsetting the loss of business with price increases. Burns also was facing extreme competition, and their strategy of raising prices to offset the loss of business was failing. Customer retention was suffering, and large and small customers were balking at price hikes. Chuck noted that one critical profit center was the nuclear division, for which there was less competition; retaining that business while turning around the rest of the business needed to be a focus. The company, however, was in competition with the growing Wackenhut Corporation.

Burns headquarters relocated from Briarcliff Manor to Borg-Warner's Parsippany, New Jersey, office. The move was completed in 1985.[9] During this time Chuck began examining each customer's contribution to profits, to identify and correct specific issues. He stabilized the nuclear division, and with help from others brought in from Baker, succeeded in turning around the struggling Burns.

Mentors Help Chuck Succeed as a Leader

In addition to the aforementioned Captain Exum and Harvard professor John Hammond, Chuck gave credit for his management success to long-time Borg-Warner chairman and chief executive officer, James Bere, and James "Jim" Gavin, a senior vice president of finance who also held various other senior roles at Borg-Warner. He said they were excellent communicators who assisted and supported him while managing the business at Borg-Warner. Jim Gavin and James Bere were leading executives in their day; among other honors and achievements, both were included in a delegation of prominent Illinois businesspeople who met with President Gerald Ford during an evening reception on July 21, 1975.[10]

Their influence was apparent in the way Chuck led at Borg-Warner and later at U.S. Security Associates. Chuck clearly communicated to his staff and required a level of competency in the prosecution of their work. At the same time, he recognized that promotion from within bolstered morale and fostered company spirit. His interest in people helped him motivate staff at Borg-Warner and U.S. Security to achieve results.

Chuck was instrumental in the Borg-Warner security division becoming the world's largest protective services company in the United States, and in 1986, his excellent performance was rewarded with a promotion. He was named president and chief executive officer of the Borg-Warner Corporation's Protective Services Group, replacing colleague and sometime mentor James J. Gavin Jr., the group's chairman and vice chairman of Borg-Warner. Gavin had filled in for Malcolm F. Baker, who had resigned in June as the interim president. The Borg-Warner Protective

Services Group was at the time the world's largest protective services company, with 55,000 employees and 500 branch offices in the United States, and included the Wells Fargo guard, alarm, and armored car companies; Pyrotronics, an alarm division; Burns International Security Services; and the Pony Express Courier Corporation.[11]

Soon after the promotion, in 1987, "Merrill Lynch Capital Partners signed an agreement to buy the Borg-Warner Corporation of Chicago for $48.50 a share, or $4.23 billion, and convert the huge industrial organization into a private company."[12] Chuck indicated that the leveraged buyout by Merrill strengthened his position at the company. He was retained and continued running the division after the leveraged buyout. Revenue and profits at the security division continued to grow, and he managed and directed the division to enable it to take advantage of opportunity within the security services industry.

Departure from Borg-Warner

However, by 1992, Borg-Warner, with eight major divisions, was looking to streamline and sell off divisions. It was reported that

> functional responsibility for Baker Industries' corporate and administrative activities would be transferred from Parsippany, N.J., to Chicago. Baker Industries' revenue through 1991 exceeded $1.5 billion, but Donald C. Trauscht, president of Chicago-based Borg-Warner, said transferring responsibilities to Chicago would streamline the organization with improved operating efficiency, quicker decision-making, and more effective communication with business units.[13]

Chuck was invited to stay with the company and relocate to Chicago; however, he believed the relocation of the office violated his management agreement. In August 1992 Borg-Warner closed the security firm's head office in Parsippany, New Jersey, and moved the office to Borg-Warner's headquarters in Chicago, along with four other members of Baker's headquarters staff. Chuck subsequently filed suit, and after a 15-month legal battle, he was granted his wish to leave the company, saying, "we will remain friends."[14] He reaffirmed in his 2021 interview that "we parted on good terms."

Chuck's departure from Borg-Warner was an opportune moment. He and former colleague Ken Oringer had discussed going into business. The two men realized that their futures would be more secure by controlling their own company, and no longer working as executives for other owners.

CHUCK CO-FOUNDS U.S. SECURITY ASSOCIATES

In late 1993, Chuck and Ken founded U.S. Security Associates in Morristown, New Jersey, along with Ken's son, Keith Oringer, a co-author of this book. With "only a desk and a chair" at their office, but a world of experience and some of their own seed money, Ken and Chuck sought funding to acquire a security guard company as a platform for larger things. They pitched their idea to Chicago-based private equity firm Golder, Thoma, Cressey, Rauner (GTCR), and convinced GTCR to provide them with funding (Figure 6.3). Chuck noted that at the time it was one of the first guard industry investments made by a private equity company. It would be a harbinger of things to come: in later years, private equity investment firms began making many medium- and large-scale investments in the security services industry.

Once GTCR approved money to fund an acquisition, the search for a platform company ensued, but the partners needed to act fast as GTCR had given them a tight deadline to find a target. In a major break for

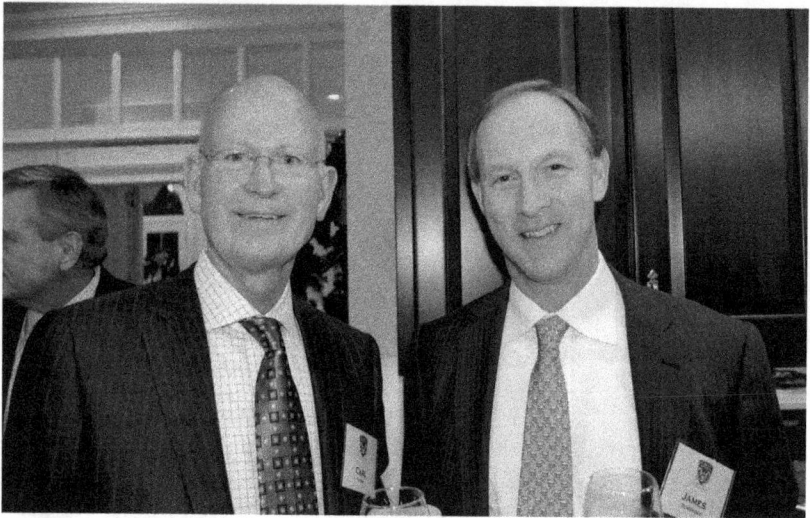

FIGURE 6.3 A photo of Carl Thoma (left) and James TenBroek (right), from U.S. Security Associates 20th Anniversary Celebration held on December 18, 2013, at Chuck's house. Carl Thoma was Co-Founder and Managing Director of Golder Thoma Cressey & Rauner (GTCR). He is currently Founder and Managing Partner of Thoma Bravo. Jim TenBroek is the Former Managing Director at Windpoint Partners and currently Co-Founder and Managing Partner of GCP (Growth Catalyst Partners).

(Photo provided by Chuck Schneider.)

Chuck and his partner Ken, Tim Reynolds, a banker they knew from prior business, advised the partners that Figgie International was looking to sell their guard service company, Advance Security Engineering (Advance). Although Figgie had received a letter of intent from their former employer, Borg-Warner, it was not yet signed and in November 1993, Harry Figgie agreed to meet with Chuck and Ken.

Chuck noted that Harry Figgie liked the partners as they reminded him of how he too had started. Figgie agreed to sell Advance to the partners for $27 million along with a 5 percent equity stake to be retained by Figgie International. Chuck and Ken got an additional bridge loan from GTCR for the acquisition and a letter of intent was signed several days after the meeting with Harry Figgie. The partners were on their way to building U.S. Security Associates into a billion-dollar business. On February 26, 1994, Figgie International sold its Advance Security Unit to closely held U.S. Security Associates of Morristown, New Jersey.[15]

With the purchase of Advance, operations initially continued under the Advance name. Advance had a network of 30 branches and revenues of $70 million, which enabled the company to grow across various geographical markets. In 1995, Advance was rebranded as U.S. Security Associates. What followed was an outstanding record of growth and success due to the management skills of Chuck, and the financial savvy of his partner, Ken.

Implementing Systems and Controls for Operating Efficiency

Chuck used his industry operating experience at Baker to initiate system controls at U.S. Security. Chuck said that he instituted systems to better control a largely decentralized operation more efficiently. Reporting structures were streamlined and designed to get the most pertinent information to the right people in the organization. Chuck said the systems and controls put in place included consolidated standard invoicing; one-call customer service lines; design and implementation of ease-of-use technology to provide branches with computer generated analysis of their profits and operations; a structure of decentralized branch unit presidents reporting to the corporate office; and provision for assignment of dedicated account managers. Chuck engineered the company as he liked, and his strong and effective leadership produced desired results. The company kept growing and was consistently profitable.

Seeing the possibilities for the company, in 1999, Wind Point Partners bought out GTCR. The investment by Wind Point turned out to be beneficial for Wind Point and partners Chuck and Ken, and Wind Point stayed with the company until 2011. When Wind Point sold their position Chuck was quoted to have thoroughly enjoyed working with Wind Point over the past twelve years as U.S. Security grew to be the fourth largest provider of security services in the United States. U.S. Security is a much better company as a result of its partnership with Wind Point.[16]

Right Partners, Right People

Chuck told us that having the right business partners and having the "right people in place" was essential to the company's success. Along the way he assembled an exceptionally talented management and sales team. One notable hire was Alton Harvey, initially a regional sales manager who convinced Chuck in 2002 to allow him to develop and head up a National Accounts program, which served only multisite national companies. Chuck said, "I was concerned that national accounts were extremely low margin, and I needed Alton to assure me that we could both grow the company and remain profitable. Alton said he could get the job done." The National Accounts program was formed, and Chuck stated that it proved an enormous success. Chuck said that by 2018, it accounted for approximately $650 million year of the approximately $1.5 billion in annual companywide revenue.

Alton Harvey, who eventually became senior vice president of sales at U.S. Security, in a personal interview for this chapter, provided helpful insights regarding the national accounts. Alton said:

> Many of the accounts I visited were looking for us to provide the same level of service to other areas where they had facilities around the country. When Chuck was concerned about profit levels, Chuck agreed to let the customers know that we would need to maintain our profit levels, and that we had to base our pricing on wages in any given area. We started out getting large accounts with Georgia Pacific, International Paper, and then a bunch of transportation companies. That led us to other verticals as the client company security managers spoke about our service to each other. A big break came when we expanded our Walmart work from a few stores to an entire region and then some more. Once we gained more traction, we had a bit more leeway for the really large accounts, and it took a team to build up national accounts.

Alton described Chuck as an "outstanding leader, who was a great listener. You would propose something, and he would examine and take apart your idea with an analytical and professional approach before making a decision. He was always fair."

Innovative Programs; Certifications and Awards

As U.S. Security celebrated its 20-year mark with an event on December 18, 2013, company leadership highlighted key drivers of its astounding growth over the two decades. Among the success factors, a company pamphlet listed the following timeline of administrative and technological programs initiated and developed at U.S. Security.[17]

1995 Post-Positive: 24-hour post monitoring for quality control to identify attendance and punctuality problems at cold start locations

1998 Past-Positive: automatic confirmation that the branch team has completed every step of an employee background investigation through verification of documentation by corporate HQ

2000 Responsive Management: proprietary communication technology with built-in accountability to communicate with clients on an agreed-upon schedule, to document concerns and issues, and follow through to resolution

2003 USA Link: providing security information for customers through a portal

2004 Enterprise Security Manager: a dashboard for multisite clients to view all phases of client specific service

2004 Tour-Positive: real-time monitoring of security officers in motion, enabling clients to track the location of any officer through the officer's Android device

2005 USA Training Academy: professional trainers use two-way video and voice collaboration over the internet to train officers on a wide range of internally developed training programs

2007 USA Visitor Management System: digitized documentation and registration of site visitors and vehicles

2007 Gate Master: digitized recording of truck movements and deliveries at warehouse and distribution facilities

2008 The Daily Trainer: program for security officers to call a toll-free number daily to answer a site-specific security related question

2009 Weather Watch: an optional program to alert customers of dangerous weather events in their area

2010 Instant Alert Equipment Monitoring: digitized system to immediately notify customers when their equipment is not within defined tolerance levels

2011 Red Box Alert: Fire Extinguisher monitoring utilizing the tour positive device

2012 Security Information Systems: a secure web portal for clients to have a real time dashboard for the entire security operation

2013 Electronic Site Inspection System: real time digitized documentation of site inspections

In addition to these programs, in 2004, the company became the first security company to obtain ISO 9001:2000 status at headquarters and at each branch office. The ISO standards required the company to have sophisticated and proven operating systems, audited and certified by the International Organization for Standardization (ISO), an international standard-setting body composed of representatives from various national standards organizations. In 2006 and again in 2012 U.S. Security Associates was recognized as one of the world's best training and development companies by the American Society for Training and Development (ASTD). Starting in 2007, the company was named a Top 100 Training Company by *Training* magazine.

In June 2008, the company earned certification under the Department of Homeland Security's SAFETY Act. In 2012 U.S. Security was selected as a 2012 World Class Customer Service honoree by Smart Business Network. The company was also ranked as a G.I. Jobs Top 100 Military Friendly Employers in 2013. Systems were not just tools to tout in a brochure, but a means to execute performance to meet the needs of customers who were becoming more demanding of quality security services, especially after a decade of heightened security risks.

Employee Morale and Company Growth

During a time when the industry was plagued by high customer turnover, U.S. Security prided itself on an over 90 percent customer retention rate. Managers were rewarded with quarterly and annual bonuses based on customer retention, branch growth, and profitability. Beginning in 2006, the company began an annual "Winners Circle" to foster morale and reward top-performing managers and outstanding security officers. The event would be held over several days each year at luxury hotels with celebratory dinners, awards, and various activities both planned and optional. For example, when author Michael Hymanson took part in 2014, the Winners Circle was in Atlanta and included a visit to the High Museum where there was a large exhibition celebrating the Wild West. More than a mere networking event, the Winners Circle was a chance to cement friendships with colleagues, many of which continue today. It is illustrative of how so many of the leadership legends profiled in this book took a personal interest in their colleagues, and treated them with respect, dignity, and fairness. Winners Circles continued until Allied Universal acquired the firm in 2018.

The record of growth described in a U.S. Security pamphlet documenting its two decades of success includes the following company annual revenue milestones:

1995 $100 million
1997 $200 million

2001 $300 million
2004 $400 million
2005 $600 million
2009 $700 million
2010 $800 million
2012 $1.3 billion

U.S. Security Associates Acquired

On July 29, 2011, Wind Point Partners sold its share in U.S. Security Associates to affiliates of Goldman Sachs Capital Partners. U.S. Security was at the time providing security services for over 3,000 clients, with 146 branches across the United States and Puerto Rico. Chuck continued to lead U.S. Security Associates for several more years as chief executive officer, and remained as chairman, invested in the company.[18] It was reported that U.S. Security Associates had been sold for $640 million.[19] In less than 17 years, U.S. Security had grown from a startup to a billion-dollar security service powerhouse (Figure 6.4).

FIGURE 6.4 A graph from 2002, when Windpoint was the private equity, until 2011, when the company was sold to Goldman Sachs Capital Partners. The stock went from 2 cents to $36.36 when Goldman Sachs Partners purchased the company.

Chuck was still chairman and a major shareholder of U.S. Security Associates when it was acquired on October 16, 2018, by Allied Universal, for a reported sum of approximately $1 billion. U.S. Security at the time employed more than 50,000 security professionals, and generated 2017 pro forma revenues of approximately $1.5 billion, and adjusted EBITDA of approximately $95 million.[20]

REFLECTIONS ON A LEGENDARY CAREER

Chuck stated that throughout his security industry career it was "a good business to be in." It had stability in bad times and was always growing. We asked Chuck if September 11, 2001, had a significant impact on the company, and Chuck noted its effect for U.S. Security was "mostly felt in the New York area." During the 2008–2009 financial crisis the company still prospered. Its business was diversified among many industry verticals, which shielded it from downturns in any one particular vertical. Service to the broad range of industry verticals included office buildings, corporate headquarters, transportation, warehouse, logistics, residential, healthcare, education, and retail. Accounts were both national and local across a broad swath of the United States.

Chuck noted that the development of technology in his opinion most impacted the industry rather than any particular historical event. The use of technology to obtain data from diverse parts of the company, such as different branches throughout the country, and the ability to process information, made a substantial difference in the successful operation of the business. As stated, Chuck was a master at engineering systems to promote efficiency and better service with excellent financial results. Mirroring comments from other legends, Chuck told the authors that he believes the industry's most urgent needs are to improve the quality of services and the professionalism of the officers. He feels that the security officer on the line can be trained better and paid better, and that the industry needs to do a better job in getting customers to recognize the advantages of this.

Chuck noted that the keys to building a good security company were hiring the right people, using technology effectively, defining a strategy and "sticking to your lanes and keeping things simple." For example, rather than expanding to Europe, he believed U.S. Security and its customers were better served by focusing on the U.S. market, which was big enough. Chuck said he believed that by focusing on what you do well, and doing it better than your competitors, you could keep the customers satisfied.

Chuck provided guidance and encouragement to those who had the benefit of working with him. As a leader, he encouraged those around him to be better managers, because it would help them achieve superior

FIGURE 6.5 A 2017 photo of Chuck Schneider retiring as a board member from the International Security Ligue at the Antibes, France meeting.

results and become better people in the process (Figure 6.5). When author Hymanson attended a managers' orientation at the Roswell headquarters, Chuck gave the initial presentation to the group where he explained that the key to effective management was to treat the security officer with respect, as they were the backbone of the business. Later that day, as he did with countless other groups at headquarters for training, he had dinner with them in a collegial setting. Significantly, the CEO took the time to get to know the line staff.

Chuck was focused on results with the goal of creating a meritocracy. He used the highest level of objectivity in evaluations and promotions of employees, whom he always called "associates." The result was a culture of high-performance standards, fairness, respect, and recognition for associates at all levels of the organizations he led.

Chuck was particularly adept at applying lessons learned to manage better and to lead staff and entire divisions and companies. He used his analytical mind to design solutions and to simplify those things that were complex.

FIGURE 6.6 Chuck Schneider at his alma mater Penn State in 2019.

Furthering his mark on the application of engineering principles for the design, planning, and control of operations in the management of service businesses, Chuck was the driving force behind Penn State University's service enterprise engineering (SEE) program (Figure 6.6). The program started in the late 1990s, and Schneider has served as the chair for the SEE board since its inception. The university established a service engineering minor degree within the engineering school in 2018.[21]

NOTES

1 Selwyn Raab, "Private Guards: Now a Growing, Troubled Industry," *New York Times*, January 12, 1978, https://www.nytimes.com/1978/01/12/archives/new-jersey-pages-private-guards-a-growing-troubled-industry-private.html

2 "Companies Report Earnings," *New York Times*, March 4, 1978.

3 Robert Cole, "Borg-Warner Seeks Baker Industries," *New York Times*, November 8, 1977, https://www.nytimes.com.1977/11/08/archives/borgwarner-seeks-baker-industries-diversified-industrial-company.html

4 Daniel F. Cuff and Dee Wedemeyer, "Protection Never Dull to Head of Borg Unit," *New York Times*, September 29, 1986, https://www.nytimes.com/1986/09/29/business/business-people-protection-never-dull-to-head-of-borg-unit.html

5 Robert Metz, "Borg-Warner's Smoke Detector," *New York Times*, December 29, 1978, https://www.nytimes.com/1978/12/29/archives/market-place-borgwarners-smoke-detector.html

6 Metz, "Borg-Warner's Smoke Detector."

7 "Borg-Warner," *New York Times*, April 28, 1982, https://www.nytimes.com/1982/04/28/business/borg-warner.html

8 Mark Potts, "Borg-Warner Succeeds by Breaking the Cycle," *Washington Post*, April 1, 1982.

9 Bob Fetonti, "William J. Burns, America's Sherlock Holmes, Vol 3.3," *Briarcliff Manor-Scarborough Historical Society*, no. October 31, 2020, https://www.briarcliffhistory.org/the-briarcliff-notebook/william-j-burns-americas-sherlock-holmes

10 The Daily Diary of President Gerald R. Ford, July 1, 1975 (President's Daily Diary Collection, Box 76), https://www.fordlibrarymuseum.gov/library/document/0036/pdd750721.pdf

11 Cuff and Wedemeyer, "Protection Never Dull to Head of Borg Unit."

12 Robert Cole, "Merrill Unit to Acquire Borg," *New York Times*, April 13, 1987, https://www.nytimes.com/1987/04/13/business/merrill-unit-to-acquire-borg.html

13 William Gruber, "Borg-Warner Revamps Control of Subsidiary," *Chicago Tribune*, May 5, 1992.

14 William Gruber, "Borg-Warner Executive Gets Wish to Leave," *Chicago Tribune*, November 19, 1993.

15 "Company News: Figgie International Sells its Advance Security Unit," *New York Times*, February 26, 1994.

16 "Wind Point Partners Sells U.S. Security Associates," news release, July 29, 2011, https://www.wppartners.com/overview/ussa-sale

17 U.S. Security, *Two Decades of Success*, 2013.

18 "Wind Point Partners Sells U.S. Security Associates."

19 "Goldman Sachs Merchant Banking Acquires U.S. Security Associates," news release, August 3, 2011, https://mergr.com/goldman-sachs-merchant-banking-acquires-u.s.-security-associates

20 GlobeNewswire, "WENDEL: Allied Universal Completes Acquisition of U.S. Security Associates for Approximately $1 Billion," news release, October 26, 2018, https://www.globenewswire.com/news-release/2018/10/26/1627970/0/en/WENDEL-Allied-Universal-completes-acquisition-of-U-S-Security-Associates-for-approximately-1-billion.html

21 Andrew Krebs and Miranda Buckheit, "Who's the Man Behind the Chair? An Interview with Chuck Schneider of the Service Enterprise Engineering Board," *Penn State College of Engineering Industrial and Manufacturing Engineering (IME) Newsletter*, 2019, https://www.ime.psu.edu/assets/magazine/2019.pdf

CHAPTER 7

Kenneth W. Oringer
The Artful Closer

Kenneth W. Oringer (Ken) was a prominent chief financial officer for several of the largest security guard companies in the United States. Ken was born in Brooklyn, New York, in 1931. Ken's security industry career began in 1978 at Baker Industries, which was acquired by Borg-Warner Corporation, and largely operated under the Wells Fargo brand. It was where Ken achieved his early life goal of becoming a chief financial officer; and where he directed numerous acquisitions and several divestitures in the security industry. But it was at U.S. Security Associates where his hard work, dedication to his education and profession, and ability as a negotiator and financial executive allowed him to achieve extraordinary success not only as an executive, but as an owner. In 1993, Ken co-founded U.S. Security Associates with Charles R. (Chuck) Schneider, whom he met while at Borg-Warner (see Chapter 6). Within 20 years he negotiated and structured more than 50 acquisitions and enabled U.S. Security Associates to become the nation's fourth largest security services company with revenues of more than $1.3 billion.[1]

EARLY LIFE AND CAREER

Ken was born in Brooklyn, New York, in 1931 during the Great Depression, and his family had little money. The family resided in Sheepshead Bay, Brooklyn where his father worked as a chiropractor, eventually building a practice that allowed the family to buy a home in 1942. Both Ken and his sister enjoyed a loving and supportive family life in Brooklyn. They were treated fairly and with respect, and the lessons his family imparted served him well throughout his career. Ken's parents stressed the need for their children to get a solid education and apply themselves at school so they might succeed in their chosen careers.

Ken attended James Madison High School, noted for famous graduates including Ruth Bader Ginsburg, Bernie Sanders, Charles Schumer,

DOI: 10.4324/9781003285564-11

FIGURE 7.1   Kenneth W. Oringer graduation picture NYU 1951.

(Photo provided by author Keith Oringer.)

and Joe and Frank Torre of baseball fame. He studied hard and aspired to advance his knowledge to pursue a good life. His first thoughts were to become a stockbroker (now termed financial adviser), and during high school, he authored a paper on the New York Stock Exchange.

His family helped support his education, and he earned a BS in accounting at the prestigious Stern School of Business at New York University (NYU) in 1951. Ken recognized early on that education would form a foundation for his future success. Once he was in college, his goal was to become a professional in accounting and finance, and he aspired to be a chief financial officer. This sharp vision drove his commitment to complete an advanced education and enabled his success as it sharpened his mind and business ability (Figure 7.1).

Law Degree, Military Service, and Marriage

Ken was committed to pursuing excellence in his field through higher education and obtaining practical experience. He developed a keen interest in the law. During the Korean War, his deferred draft status allowed him to earn a J.D. degree at Fordham Law, and in 1954, he was admitted to the New York State Bar.

In 1954, Ken began service in the U.S. Army, where he honorably served the country until 1956. In the Army, Ken stated that he obtained "valuable experience auditing government contractors as a contract termination specialist." His work auditing Army contracts with large companies, including Chrysler and American Car and Foundry, saved the government tens of millions of dollars. Ken recognized that attention to financial details could pay big dividends for those he worked for.

In 1956, after honorably completing his service with the U.S. Army, Ken married Cecile Small, and the couple moved to Long Beach, Long Island. Cecile supported his career, and the couple raised a family, having a daughter and son.

Breaking into Accounting, Tax, and Finance

One day after his military discharge Ken began his career in 1956, at a salary of $100 per week, as a semi-senior accountant at the Big 8 accounting firm, Arthur Young (later Ernst & Young). There he started honing the skills needed to achieve a chief financial officer position at Arthur Young, where he remained until 1963. At Arthur Young, Ken worked with major Fortune 500 companies, including Standard Oil Company of New York (Mobil Oil), Indian Head Textile Mills, Inc. and others, saving these companies millions of dollars in taxes. His first assignment was for the Mobil account, where he helped consolidate more than 200 companies. His excellent work led him to be assigned to complex tasks at the company, which included a thorough analysis of Mobil's crude oil extraction, oil shipments, and refining processes.

Not satisfied with a bachelors and a law degree, in 1959, Ken earned his Certified Public Accountant (CPA) license from New York State and was transferred to the tax department at Arthur Young. Now an attorney and CPA, while at Arthur Young, Ken went back to school at night, using his military benefits to pay for his LLM, a master of law in Taxation degree, from New York University, which he finished in 1962.

Developing Financial Acumen

Ken's fine work at Arthur Young on behalf of their client, Indian Head, had particular significance for his career. While working on the account, Ken met James J. Gavin, the Chief financial officer of Indian Head. Gavin liked and respected Ken and recruited him to Head of Taxes at Indian Head. Ken would also later work in finance with Gavin at Borg-Warner, where Gavin would be a top executive.

Ken learned many lessons from Gavin, both in finance and in how to conduct himself. In addition to being an accomplished executive, Jim Gavin was also a compassionate man. His wife, Zita, stated that

> before retiring as vice chairman of Borg-Warner Corp. in 1985, he [James Gavin] juggled family life and philanthropic ventures but put God first.... He was very strong in his faith, and he never let the world take over material things. They weren't important to him. His main objective was to share his wealth with the poor.[2]

Ken and Gavin shared a consideration for people less fortunate than themselves. Ken was always impressed with Gavin's skills as a chief financial officer and as a person of faith and integrity. Ken told us that he referred to Jim Gavin as his rabbi. Following Gavin's example allowed Ken to prosper as a financial executive, and as a creditable person.

The position at Indian Head was a large step up in Ken's career. Indian Head was a spinoff of Textron Inc. and was rapidly growing as a conglomerate. Ken found opportunities there to hone his skills and use his education to develop practical financial and tax law expertise. Ken was not only a man behind the numbers, but he wore many hats at the firm. Ken told us that his work with Indian Head included travel to Europe and South America, where he oversaw the reorganization of many companies.

On one of his first assignments in 1964, Ken was tasked with reviewing the tax position and the financial condition of the accounts of South America–based Joseph Bancroft Company. The company was encountering multiple issues. Bancroft owned a patent for Banlon, which crimped synthetic fibers, but the company was having problems collecting royalties from licensees. Ken discovered that some governments in South America didn't allow the repatriation of money which the corporation earned there. That meant that Indian Head and other companies were not allowed to take money out of the South American countries. Ken also discovered and corrected numerous problems with the way Indian Head's South American general manager was performing his job. The problems occupied much of Ken's time for several years, but he reorganized 11 Bancroft licensees in South American countries to take care of the royalty collections and was able to repatriate 20 million BRZ (Brazilian cruzeiros) for Indian Head, valued at the time at $6 million.

As a result of his success with Bancroft and other projects, his hard work at Indian Head was recognized, and he received several promotions. Indian Head and Ken were doing very well. It was reported that Indian Head, Inc. realized an increase of 11 percent in earnings on a sales gain of 18 percent in the annual period ended November 29, 1969, setting records for the fourth consecutive year.[3]

Ken used the opportunity at Indian Head to show his understanding of complex tax laws. He made sure purchase prices paid to acquire companies were allocated to assets rather than to goodwill. He saved Indian Head hundreds of thousands of dollars in taxes. Ken caught the attention of the company's new president, Marshall Smith, when he turned around the operations of a subsidiary in which Indian Head provided financing to dealers distributing school buses and ambulances. Various distributors were not paying interest and principal on loans to Indian Head, so Ken had the vehicles repossessed and then sold to recoup what was due to the company. Proceeding in this fashion enabled Indian Head to sell the division to Borg-Warner Acceptance Company for $20 million, and in 1974, Ken was named treasurer of Indian Head.

SEARCHING, THEN FINDING A SECURITY CAREER AT BAKER INDUSTRIES

In 1975, ownership changes were underway at Indian Head as the billionaire Baron Hans-Heinrich Thyssen-Bornemisza acquired the company's stock. The baron was a Dutch-born Swiss citizen with a Hungarian title and heir to a German fortune. In both business and art, Baron Thyssen built upon his enormous inheritance. He diversified his father's war-shattered company, the Thyssen-Bornemisza Group, into glass, plastics, automobile parts, trading, and container leasing. From its profits, the baron would expand his father's collection into a private art holding rivaled only by the collection of the queen of England.[4]

The baron at the time wanted to increase his U.S. holdings substantially, starting with the purchase of Indian Head. Afterward, Ken was offered the newly created position of International Treasurer for the baron, which would require him to be based in Monaco. Despite being wined and dined across Europe and New York, Ken and his wife Cecile decided they would rather remain in New York than have their children remain in their local schools. Ken said that they chose "family before glitz" (Figure 7.2). While Ken was driven to success, he valued his children and family much more.

Ken recognized that his future was not to be with Baron Thyssen, and he was recruited and subsequently hired as vice president of finance at the private Gottesman family company.

Gottesman, a billionaire, traded stocks and, according to Ken, at the time controlled 5 percent of the world's paper manufacturing. Ken evidenced much internal politics at Gottesman, and his nearly two-year stint there was the shortest of his career with any one company. In 1978 Ken left the Gottesman company, and a headhunter named Marty Bauman introduced Ken to the Baker Industries Company, which was looking for a chief financial officer.

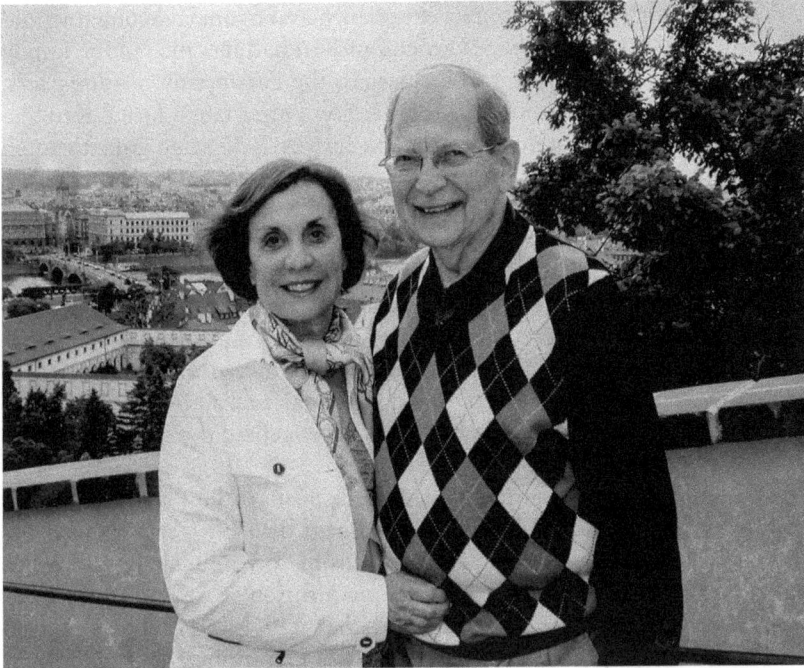

FIGURE 7.2   Ken in his later years with his beloved wife Cecile Oringer.
(Photo provided by author Keith Oringer.)

Ken met with the company founder, Solomon Baker, to interview for the job. At the time Baker was in the process of being acquired by Borg-Warner. Jim Gavin, with whom Ken had worked at Indian Head, was now at Borg-Warner and he supported him for the job. Ken accepted the offer from Baker, which was based in Parsippany, New Jersey. When Ken was appointed Chief Financial Officer and Vice President of Finance in 1978, he achieved the career goal he had set out for from the beginning. Little did he know at the time that it would be the start of his legendary career in the security industry.

Baker was a leading security company and owned Wells Fargo Guard Services, Wells Fargo Armored Car, Wells Fargo Alarm, Pony Express Courier, and Pyrotronics Inc., their large fire and safety device manufacturing division. Security was a growing industry, and once acquired by Borg-Warner, Baker Industries would become their Borg-Warner Protective Services division. Ken's work at Borg-Warner would hone skills specific to the security industry.

Ken attributes his professional relationship with Gavin as one of the keys to his success. Just as they did while at Indian Head, he and Gavin would again manage extensive merger and acquisition activity and have a solid working relationship. His experience and financial acumen would be needed to succeed at Borg-Warner. But Ken had just moved the family to Short Hills, New Jersey, to be closer to the Parsippany headquarters, and he was concerned about his tenure. Soon after being hired, Ken discovered that in addition to other top executives, Baker had gone through six chief financial officers during the previous seven years. Nonetheless, as he had done before, he quickly proved his worth to the company, and he stayed at Borg-Warner for 15 years.

Gavin had great trust in Ken, and he was allotted $20 million per year for acquisitions. He made good on the company's expansion plans by wisely acquiring accretive security businesses and disposing of non-performing units. In all the deals that he negotiated and structured at Borg-Warner, he masterfully applied his legal and tax background to ensure that they were properly handled and benefited the company to the fullest extent possible.

One of his first assignments was to dispose of the Pyrotronics division, which manufactured smoke and alarm devices. Ken arranged for the sale to include all assets at a good profit for the new Borg-Warner ownership. He followed that with the acquisition of key alarm services companies including the 3M company's alarm division; and he arranged for the construction of a central monitoring station and armored car depot in Clifton, New Jersey. According to Ken, from 1978 until 1982, the armored car division grew from $50 million to over $200 million and the alarm division from $60 million to over $200 million. Unlike those before him, Ken's position at Baker was neither tenuous nor short-lived.

Teaming Up with Systems Engineering Expert Chuck Schneider

In 1978, while at Borg-Warner, Ken met Charles (Chuck) Schneider, and they would later team up to found U.S. Security Associates, Inc. Their experience at Borg-Warner allowed Ken and Chuck to recognize the advantage they could give to customers by building a large national company to improve service for existing customers and attract new ones. They recognized they could not only reduce costs through a centralized but locally run efficient business but also improve and standardize training programs for their guard force. They identified the best geographical locations for Borg-Warner's expansion, and with Gavin's support and funding, Ken and Chuck were able to significantly expand the company's security division. A highlight of that expansion was the 1982 acquisition by Borg-Warner of Burns International Security. By 1993, the $185 million security division became the national security service industry leader with over $1.76 billion in revenue.[5]

While at Borg-Warner, Ken learned another important lesson. The company had operations in Spain through the Wells Fargo armored car division. There, they were competing with Prosegur, which was that country's leading security guard and armored car company. Ken was instrumental from 1987 to 1989 in arranging a merger of the company's Spanish armored car business with Prosegur, so that the division could best compete. They became equal partners with Prosegur in the armored car business in Spain. The Spanish division became highly profitable as the respective firms consolidated the number of armored car stops and achieved other operating and management synergies. His experience with this deal and his prior work overseas enabled Ken to recognize the complexities of foreign law, and the hurdles domestic companies had in operating internationally. It influenced his and Chuck Schneider's later decision to focus U.S. Security Associates' business on providing security guard services primarily in the United States.

A Season of Change

In 1987, Merrill Lynch Capital Partners took Borg-Warner private in a leveraged buyout.[6] According to an article in *The New York Times*, "The surprise takeover—known as a leveraged buyout because it would involve a substantial amount of borrowed money—would be among the largest transactions of its kind. A Borg-Warner spokeswoman, Patricia Yoxall, acknowledged that management did not participate in the financing but said management will remain intact.[7]

During the time Merrill Lynch Capital Partners was negotiating to buy Borg-Warner, senior executives at Baker Industries enlisted Donaldson, Lufkin, and Jenrette to act as an exclusive financial advisor to explore the valuation, negotiation, and formation of a new company for a potential purchase of Baker's security business. An agreement signed on May 29, 1987, called for Chuck Schneider to become President and Chief Executive Officer of Acquisition Corp., Ken Oringer to become Chief Financial Officer and Paul L. Rathblott to become Chief Administrative Officer if the new company succeeded in buying Baker. The Merrill groups' offer prevailed, but, despite the setback in becoming owners, the senior executives were retained by new ownership. For now, Ken's future as chief financial officer of the Baker protective division would continue, but by no means was it the last deal that Ken and Chuck would undertake in the pursuit of becoming owners (Figure 7.3).

Ken recalled a significant deal in 1991 when Borg-Warner acquired Globe Security. Globe was making approximately $100 million in revenue but was in bankruptcy. Ken dealt with the bankruptcy trustee, who was employed by Willkie and Farr, a prominent law firm. Ken negotiated

FIGURE 7.3   A photograph of the Baker Partners and their spouses from January 29, 1991.

an agreement with the trustee; however, according to Ken, the bankruptcy process required that other companies could bid on Globe, based on the agreement he had negotiated. Ken noted that as he had performed due diligence on Globe and negotiated the initial deal, he had knowledge that Borg-Warner could increase their bid without jeopardizing the ultimate profitability of the deal. Competing against several other major firms, Borg-Warner prevailed at the ensuing auction. Ken once again used his financial expertise and ability to negotiate to benefit his company.

By 1993, 15 years after his start with Baker Industries, successor firm Borg-Warner decided to take the Protective Services Division public as Borg-Warner Security and spin off the automotive divisions to shareholders. With management changes underway, Ken and Chuck needed to move on. The result was the founding of U.S. Security Associates, Inc.

PLANTING SEEDS FOR U.S. SECURITY ASSOCIATES

In 1993, Ken and Chuck began looking for opportunities to form their own security company after negotiations with foreign-based Securitas, Securicor, and Group 4 to establish U.S. divisions under their control did not materialize. They then put in $2.5 million of their own money to establish a new security company, and they received $12.5 million in equity funding from a Chicago private equity firm, Golder, Thoma, Cressey, Rauner (GTCR). GTCR gave the partners six months to "make things happen."

In Ken's next and biggest break, the partners found out from a banker that Figgie International was selling their security company division, Advance Security. Advance had revenues of $70 million and had a national branch network, which the partners felt would be an ideal springboard to build a large national security company. There were 30 branch offices in many states and a central headquarters in the growing Atlanta area.

While Figgie had executed a letter of intent with Borg-Warner to buy Advance, Henry Figgie, the CEO of Figgie International, liked Ken and Chuck and decided to sell to the partners. The purchase price for Advance was $27 million, and to enable a deal, the partners took on additional bank debt and gave 5 percent of the equity to Figgie. Ken used his analytical expertise to determine that this deal would be ideal for the partners (Figure 7.4). The deal was closed in February 1994,[8] and in 1995, Advance was rebranded as U.S. Security Associates. The new company was on its way to becoming an industry giant (Figure 7.5).

In April 1994 Thomas W. Wathen stepped down as president and CEO, and Denis R. Brown took over as the new president and CEO at Pinkerton.[9] U.S. Security Associates executives believed the timing was right to make an offer to acquire the firm, since Tom owned 33.3 percent of the shares, and in May 1994 with just $70 million in sales it launched a friendly takeover of publicly traded Pinkerton. The stock was trading at $14 a share, and U.S. Security Associates offered $24.00—a 71 percent premium. Ken Oringer, his son Keith, Chuck Schneider, Jim Tenbroek of GTCR, and Carl Thoma of GTCR worked on the takeover attempt. The Pinkerton board ultimately rejected the offer, however, and Keith notes that "we thought about a hostile takeover but decided against it based on our discussions internally, and with an outside consultant."

Five years later, Securitas offered $29 a share and was successful in buying Pinkerton.[10]

Acquisitions and internal growth required additional funding. In 1997 after a market sell-off, Bank of America as their primary lender put pressure on the partners as they were not meeting loan covenants. This hurdle needed to be overcome. Ken stepped up efforts to collect outstanding receivables and the company put on additional new profitable business. With additional cost controls Ken put in place, the company avoided losing funding and their equity in the company. It was a turning point for Ken and the company.

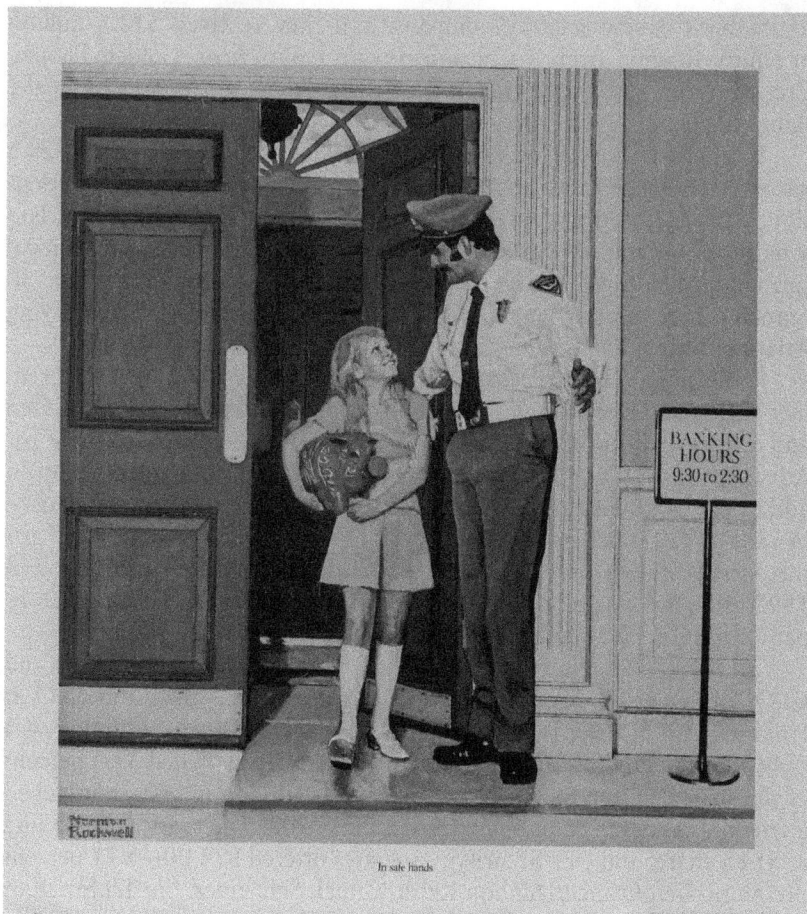

FIGURE 7.4 "In Safe Hands" by famed artist Norman Rockwell was commissioned by Harry E. Figgie Jr., Chairman of Figgie International, which was the parent company of Advance Security at the time. The painting prominently displays the Advance Security shoulder insignia of the security officer. The painting was presented to Ken on the occasion of the First Anniversary of the founding of U.S. Security Associates, Inc., November 15, 1994.

(Photo provided by author Keith Oringer.)

Expansive Acquisitions and Successive Investors

In 1999, Wind Point Partners bought out GTCR. Wind Point was supportive of U.S. Security's growth plans and allowed further acquisitions. Between 1994 and 2014, Ken would oversee more than 50 acquisitions,

FIGURE 7.5 Ken and Chuck in photo with Advance Security senior management after closing acquisition, February 26, 1994. Pictured left to right Chuck Schneider, President and CEO, U.S. Security Associates; Rick Massimei, President, Advance Security; Larry Nelson, V.P. Controller; Ken Oringer, Executive Vice President and Chief Financial Officer U.S. Security Associates; Jim Flowers, Vice President, A & R and Administrator.

(Photo provided by author Keith Oringer.)

and along with organic growth, the company had many years of strong and sustained growth.

Ken noted that Wind Point's faith in the company paid off for them, as their initial investment of $40 million led to a profit for them of more than $300 million when Goldman Sachs Private Equity purchased their interest in U.S. Security in 2011.

After the initial acquisition of Advance Security, as chief financial officer and executive vice president, Ken was responsible at U.S. Security for negotiating the following acquisitions, along with many others not listed below:

1994 Bedway Security
1995 D.B. Kelly Associates
1995 Employers Security Company
1996 Nation Wide Security
1997 Owl Security & Investigation
1998 Murray Guard

1999 Superior Building Services
2000 Atlantic Security Guards
2003 Arko Executive Services
2004 Bell Security
2004 Atlas Security & Patrol
2005 Progressive Security Concepts
2005 Cognisa Security
2006 John C. Mandel Security Bureau
2008 Nation Wide Services
2009 Vanguard Security
2010 Day & Zimmerman
2011 Corporate Security Solutions
2011 Bowles Security Services
2012 Andrews International
2012 Morris Protective Services
2013 Control Capitol Security
2013 Diamond Detective
2013 Cauley Security

Ken described the 1998 Murray Guard acquisition as being of particular note. Roger Murray Jr., the company owner, was an attorney and a tough negotiator. Ken leveraged his reputation as a fair and honest businessman to structure a deal that preserved operations management and allowed Murray to continue to operate in their home state of Tennessee. It was a big win for U.S. Security.

Again, in 2004, Ken used his reputation and the good offices of his friend, Robert D. McCrie, professor at John Jay College of Criminal Justice, to earn the trust of the family that owned Bell Security, which facilitated the acquisition. The company founder, Marcel Sapse, had died, and his widow desired to sell to a trusted buyer. The acquisition allowed U.S. Security to significantly expand its presence in the vital New York metro area market.

In 2005, Ken engineered the acquisition of Cognisa, which added significant revenue to the company. Ken met with Cognisa's chief financial officer over dinner and negotiated what turned out to be a very smooth transaction. Cognisa was the U.S. arm of Securicor. The Cognisa acquisition catapulted U.S. Security into the upper echelons of security companies in the United States (Figure 7.6). For a comparison of revenues and market share among leading security companies as of early 2003, see Table 7.1.

FIGURE 7.6 2003 marked the 10th anniverary of U.S. Security Associates. A photo from the company's celebration of such held on November 14, 2003. Pictured left to right Chuck Schneider, President and CEO; Jim TenBroek, Managing Director, Windpoint Partners—Currently Founder and Managing Partner, Growth Catalyst Partners; and Kenneth W. Oringer, Executive VP & Chief Financial Officer.

(Photo provided by author Keith Oringer.)

TABLE 7.1   U.S. Private Guard Contractor Key Operating Statistics 2003

Company (Parent)	Revenues ($ million)	Market Share (%)	Employees (1,000)	Owner Country
Securitas U.S.A. (Securitas)	2608	23.7	100	Sweden
Wackenhut (Group 4 Securicor)*	1489	13.5	38	U.K.
Allied/Barton	900	8.2	36	U.S.
Akal Security*	500	4.5	8	U.S.
Guardsmark	465	4.2	18	U.S.
TransNational Security Grp.	386	4.0	15	U.S.
U.S. Security Associates	375	3.5	17	U.S.

(*Continued*)

TABLE 7.1   (Continued)

Company (Parent)	Revenues ($ million)	Market Share (%)	Employees (1,000)	Owner Country
Initial (Rentokil-Initial)*	293	3.4	14	U.K.
ABM Security Services	250	2.7	12	U.S.
Cognisa (Group 4 Securicor)	146	1.3	6	U.K.
Other Guard Contractors	3610	32.8	258	U.S.
U.S. Total	**11,022**	**100.0**	**522**	—

Sources: Regulatory filings, annual reports, Web pages, press reports. The companies' financial reporting period may vary due to differing accounting practices. A detailed list of source material can be found in the appendix of the Congressional Research Service report.

* Statistics include North American guard operations outside the United States. Paul W. Parfomak, *Guarding America: Security Guards and U.S. Critical Infrastructure Protection*, 2004, https://digital.library.unt.edu/ark:/67531/metadc809152/

Goldman Sachs Private Equity Takes a Majority Stake in U.S. Security

As chief financial officer, and because of his legal acumen, Ken was a key player in the deal with Goldman Sachs. In addition, Ken had developed a good banking relationship with the Royal Bank of Scotland. He was by now an extremely respected financial executive and was an owner and major shareholder who was highly capable of negotiating and dealing with major financial institutions. His lead role in acquisitions and the company's organic growth from the national accounts division and at the branch level fueled significant company growth. By 2011 the 1994 startup had grown to a more than $900 million security company giant. U.S. Security Associates had become the fourth largest security guard company in the United States.

Acquisition by Allied Universal

By 2014, the company grew revenues to over $1.3 billion. Throughout his tenure, Ken had a critical role in directing the company's finances, ensuring its financial stability, and overseeing the many acquisitions that catapulted the company into the highest ranks of the security guard services industry. Four years later, U.S. Security Associates would be acquired by Allied Universal for $1 billion.

While preparing this chapter the authors spoke with two colleagues of Ken about their impressions of him. Denman Brown, Director of Credit and Collections, reported directly to Ken from 1997 to 2014, and described being interviewed for the job.

> I was called back for a second interview which lasted about an hour and one half, same time as the first. That first interview was the most challenging one I ever encountered. At the second interview, Ken asked me why he should hire me. I told him, "Because I'm going to tell you the truth, no matter." I left the interview thinking there was no way I would be hired, but received a call that I was hired soon before I reached home...Ken knew the financial aspects of the security business inside and out. He knew what he was looking for, and required excellence, and you did it over until he was satisfied. He was always supportive and had your back, but he also knew how to strike a balance when my position conflicted with other departments.

Mark Reed, who reported directly to Ken Oringer from 2000 to 2012, first as a division controller, and from 2002 as corporate controller, said:

> Ken was a world class CFO, and a cut above all CFO's I ever met. He was knowledgeable about all things related to finance and taxation at a large company. He was demanding and operated at a high level and expected things to be done right and on time. Yet he was tolerant, understood people and was the ultimate mentor. He had a "New York" style, which some people at the Atlanta area headquarters had to adapt to, but he was always open, fair, and straight with you.

REFLECTIONS ON A LEGENDARY CAREER

Ken stated that looking back at U.S. Security "we made the right calls throughout." Besides the acquisitions, he attributes the success of the company to their ability to provide excellent customer service and solid employee recruitment, screening, and training. He noted that the company had developed superior operating systems, had expertise in managing cash in the business, and treated employees well.

Ken was instrumental in building security guard giants at Borg-Warner and U.S. Security Associates. He was a master in negotiating acquisitions. He was purposeful in advancing his career through dedication to education and his profession through hard work, and by applying a keen understanding of tax, accounting, treasury, and law in his position as a chief financial officer and as a founder and owner of a major security services company. Ken was 62 years old when he co-founded U.S. Security Associates. While he achieved success in his security industry career at Baker and Borg-Warner, his extraordinary success at U.S. Security was achieved at a stage in life when others might have retired. His story illustrates that success can be achieved not only early on but also much later in life. Author Michael Hymanson can attest to Ken's honesty and integrity. When Michael's company, Pan-American Investigation Service, Inc., was acquired in 2006 by U.S. Security Associates, Ken was tough, but in all dealings before, during, and after the close Ken displayed integrity and honesty. While Ken had a serious approach to his work, he always retained a sense of humor and humility. Michael also had the pleasure of working at U.S. Security Associates for more than ten years with Ken, his son Keith, and Chuck Schneider. His respect and admiration for his colleagues is immeasurable.

Security industry executive John Harford, Vice President of Corporate Development at Allied Universal, spoke to the authors on November 22, 2022, and paid tribute to Ken's memory. John worked with Ken and Chuck Schneider (Chapter 6) while at Baker Protective Services from 1982 to 1990, and then while at U.S. Security Associates, from 1995 to 2018, where he was last employed as vice president of mergers and acquisitions, subsequent to the 2018 acquisition of U.S. Security by Allied Universal. John recalled that while he was working for Security Bureau, Inc. between 1990 and 1995, Harry McFarland, a former colleague who was a general counsel at Wells Fargo and then Baker Protective Services, told him that Ken had developed what remains a commonly used acquisition deal structure as described below.

> Ken was like a father to me. His mentorship aided greatly in my professional development, and I am forever grateful for his guidance and wisdom. He very simply was one of the most accomplished men I knew, who despite his lofty achievement always remained humble, keeping faith and family first. It was a genuine privilege to work under his tutelage. Very few people understand his significance in shaping our industry. Ken developed an acquisition deal structure which is still commonly used in many security company acquisition transactions. This included the practice of using multiples of monthly revenue rather than earnings as a means of presenting and reaching agreement on an offer price to

a seller, establishment of revenue guarantee periods, and provision for a purchase price holdback with final payment to the seller based on a reconciliation of revenues as of an agreed upon date. I will miss him much but celebrate his life as one well lived.

For his extraordinary business success, and as a person of great integrity who cared deeply for people, he is duly recognized as a legend of the security services industry.

NOTES

1 U.S. Security, *Two Decades of Success*, 2013.
2 Lisa Black, "James J. Gavin Jr.: 1922–2007," *Chicago Tribune*, March 6, 2007.
3 Clare M. Reckert, "Indian Head Cites an 11% Profit Rise," *New York Times*, December 24, 1969, https://www.nytimes.com/1969/12/24/archives/indian-head-cites-an-11-profit-rise-sales-show-18-advance-in-the.html
4 Jonathan Kandell, "Baron Thyssen-Bornemisza, Industrialist Who Built Fabled Art Collection, Dies at 81," *New York Times*, April 28, 2002, https://www.nytimes.com/2002/04/28/nyregion/baron-thyssen-bornemisza-industrialist-who-built-fabled-art-collection-dies-81.html
5 "Borg-Warner Security Corp., a Chicago-based Supplier," *Chicago Tribune*, February 3, 1994.
6 Matt O'Connor, "Buyout," *Chicago Tribune*, April 14, 1987.
7 Robert Cole, "Merrill Unit to Acquire Borg," *New York Times*, April 13, 1987, https://www.nytimes.com/1987/04/13/business/merrill-unit-to-acquire-borg.html
8 "Company News: Figgie International Sells its Advance Security Unit," *New York Times*, February 26, 1994.
9 "Brown Named President, CEO," *UPI Archives* (April 21, 1994). https://www.upi.com/Archives/1994/04/21/Brown-named-Pinkerton-president-CEO/6584766900800/
10 Barnaby J. Feder, "Securitas of Sweden to Acquire Pinkerton's in $384 Million Deal," *New York Times*, February 23, 1999, https://www.nytimes.com/1999/02/23/business/securitas-of-sweden-to-acquire-pinkerton-s-in-384-million-deal.html

CHAPTER 8

William C. Whitmore Jr.
A Steady Hand

In 1981, after serving eight years as a police officer, William C. (Bill) Whitmore Jr. landed his first security industry job at SpectaGuard, a regional security firm based in King of Prussia, Pennsylvania. He began as an assistant security director at the Spectrum arena, where the Philadelphia 76ers basketball team and the Philadelphia Flyers hockey team played their home games. He moved up quickly, becoming security director, then director of operations and vice president of operations, before becoming chief operating officer in 1990.[1] In 2003, he was named president and chief executive officer; he became chairman in 2006. During his tenure as a senior executive from 1990 to 2016 significant changes occurred at the company. With ongoing organic growth and strategic acquisitions, the company—operating as Allied Security and then AlliedBarton Security—became a leading U.S.-based security giant.[2]

Under Bill's leadership, Pennsylvania-based AlliedBarton grew to operate in more than 120 offices across the United States, serving more than 3,300 customers, including 200 members of the Fortune 500. The company serviced clients "across diverse end-markets, including, for example, commercial real estate, higher education, healthcare, financial services, government services, aerospace and defense, petrochemicals and retail."[3] By 2016, AlliedBarton had more than 60,000 employees and revenues of more than $2.2 billion. When AlliedBarton merged with Universal Services to form Allied Universal, Bill became chairman of Allied Universal, the largest U.S.-based security company, with over 140,000 employees and more than $4.5 billion in revenues.[4]

EARLY LIFE AND CAREER

Bill was born in Pennsylvania, on March 7, 1952, the son of William C. (Bill Sr.) and Marie Whitmore. Bill Sr. was a lifelong resident of King of Prussia, Pennsylvania, until his passing at the age of 93, in 2019. He graduated

DOI: 10.4324/9781003285564-12

from Upper Merion High School in 1944, where he was class president, and after high school, he enlisted in the United States Navy where he became a decorated combat veteran of the Pacific Theater. In 1953 he graduated from Drexel University with a BS in Electrical Engineering and was employed by Alan Wood Steel and later Westinghouse Corporation, until he retired in 1981. Bill's father also served as scout master for a local Boy Scout troop.[5]

King of Prussia, Pennsylvania, where father and son grew up, was at the time of Bill's youth largely a farm community. Bill said that his own

> membership in the Boy Scouts had a big influence on him as it offered a well-conceived program for character development. You could attain small wins at a young age, and as you became older, you received more responsibility and larger tasks—and greater rewards as you achieved milestones.

After high school Bill worked as a laborer, became a volunteer firefighter, and became interested in law enforcement. He would serve as a police officer from 1973 to 1981; while employed he studied business part time at Montgomery County Community College and later at the Philadelphia College of Textiles and Science (renamed Philadelphia University), where he earned a degree in police science in 1982. While a policeman, Bill also dabbled in real estate rentals and had a small delivery service, but "decided to drop those so I could focus on one thing and do it well," and in 1981, he went to work for SpectaGuard security company as an assistant security director at the Spectrum arena in Philadelphia. Within a few months he was promoted to security director (Figure 8.1).[6]

FIGURE 8.1 The Spectrum (center) was the oldest of the four venues which made up the South Philadelphia Sports Complex in this 2004 view from the Wells Fargo Center (1996). The Sectrum was in operation from 1967 to 2009. Citizens Bank Park (right) is the complex's newest (2004) facility, while Lincoln Field (2003) is just out of view to the far right.

KEY ROLE AS SPECTAGUARD EXPANDS

Bill was promoted to chief operating officer at SpectaGuard in 1990 and for the next eight years the company concentrated on providing security guard services to corporate customers in the Philadelphia and Boston metro areas. In 1998, Albert J. "Al" Berger joined with Gryphon Partners to acquire SpectaGuard. SpectaGuard set out to consolidate the highly fragmented and largely undermanaged U.S. contract security officer industry. Berger was named CEO and Chairman. The first major acquisition took place in 1998, when SpectaGuard acquired Effective Security, Inc., a provider of contract security officer services to the New York metro area market. The acquisition of Effective Security resulted in sales increasing from $84 million in 1998 to $178 million (Figure 8.2).[7]

FIGURE 8.2   Bill and Jeanie Whitmore (seated) pictured here with Al and Carol Berger.

(Photo provided courtesy Al Berger.)

Berger told the authors during a June 12, 2023, interview that he was introduced to owners of SpectaGuard through a lawyer acquaintance. Berger said:

> I saw SpectaGuard as a well-managed company with low account turnover and a dominant position in the Philadelphia market area. They were doing the right things, and as a partner with Gryphon, saw an opportunity to grow the company.

Effective Security had grown in the New York metro area into the leading area security services company after starting in the mid-1970s as a division of Yonkers-based cleaning company, Colin Service Systems, before relocating to its new headquarters in White Plains, New York. The president of Effective, Robert M. Diamond, was a well-known security industry figure in New York, and had been a chapter chairman at the New York chapter of ASIS International, as well as president of the Associated Licensed Detectives of New York.

Colin Service Systems was, likewise, itself a success story. In 1913, Samuel Colin began working as a part-time window cleaner. In 1935, he was joined by his son George, and with six employees, George convinced his father to expand into cleaning and janitorial services.[8] Run by successive generations, not only did the Colin family build and sell Effective, but in 2004, the company generated over $70 million in sales providing janitorial services throughout the Northeast. Colin Service Systems was sold to ABM Industries, itself a provider of janitorial as well as security services.[9]

Effective customers included many Class A office buildings, as well as banking, education, and area corporate accounts. The acquisition of an established New York City–based company would be repeated by legend Steve Jones (Chapter 14) when Universal (later Allied Universal) acquired T&M Protection Resources in 2013. As home to many Class A office properties and financial company headquarters, the New York City market was important for many of the national security companies.[10]

Contributing to SpectaGuard's success, organic growth had averaged about 16 percent per year for the three years prior to the acquisition. Bill said that the fast level of organic growth was in part attributed to hard work in achieving a customer loss rate of under 5 percent in an industry experiencing client losses of 20 percent; a reduction in guard turnover by having a good relationship with employees by paying guards a decent wage with benefits; and by changing the company's customer mix. Despite his start in the business doing security work at the Spectrum arena, the company had shifted its focus to commercial security.

> We came to realize the business we wanted to get into was commercial security and not the event market … for big events you

may need eighty people, but then there's the question of what to do with them because there won't be an event that big again for months.

The company also leveraged an electronic protection division which it started in 1987. The division included a new building with a control center providing monitoring services, along with sales of access systems, phone, and video systems. The company began marketing integrated asset protection and provided in-depth evaluation of a company's or institution's security needs to determine the best use and placement of electronic and traditional guard service.[11]

BECOMING A NATIONAL COMPANY LEADER

On March 2, 2000, SpectaGuard acquired Allied Security (Allied) of Pittsburgh, forming what it called the largest privately held security services company in the country. Allied-SpectaGuard became the fourth largest U.S. security company, with 16,000 employees and 47 offices. The combined company revenues for the prior year totaled more than $378

FIGURE 8.3   Bill with Ron Rabena at Allied SpectraGuard.

(Photo provided courtesy Ron Rabena.)

million.[12] The company leveraged Allied Security's national reputation and footprint to advance from a regional to a national security company and soon take the name Allied Security (Figure 8.3).[13]

Bill Leads Allied Security under New Ownership

Bill was promoted to president and chief executive officer in 2003, and became chairman in 2006, replacing Berger. He was implementing a successful strategy as Allied pursued

> a strategy of focusing on lucrative vertical markets in well-established metro markets. The company was providing premium contract security officer services to quality-conscious customers in seven vertical markets throughout the United States: high-rise office buildings, corporate complexes, shopping malls, financial institutions, universities, hospitals, and industrial sites.

Allied placed several levels of customer relationship managers in direct and ongoing contact with customers to "promptly and effectively anticipate and respond to the needs of customers and security officers." Sales and marketing efforts were designed to focus on quality-conscious customers located primarily in urban centers and other concentrated business districts in major metropolitan areas and select suburban areas with a high density of businesses. Allied management saw that many businesses in these markets desired and utilized high-quality security officer services and chose service quality over service price and capitalized on this opportunity.[14]

The period of Bill's senior leadership would be marked by several changes in ownership and highly selective acquisitions that bolstered the company's size and reputation as a national security leader. The success of the company did not go unnoticed by major financial firms.

In March 2003, four months after Allied Security filed a registration with the Securities and Exchange Commission for an initial public stock offering, the offering was scrapped when it was announced that Allied Security would be acquired by MacAndrews & Forbes Holdings Inc., an investment vehicle of the financier Ronald O. Perelman.[15] The aggregate purchase price was $263.6 million—more than $155 million higher than what Gryphon had paid to acquire Allied less than four years earlier.

With additional funding Allied Security would make new acquisitions, including the purchase for approximately $45.8 million on December 19, 2003, of PSB (Professional Security Bureau), a provider of high-quality contract security services to corporate customers primarily in the northeast United States. Then on March 19, 2004, Allied acquired

SSI, a provider of high-quality contract security services to universities and corporate customers primarily in Boston, for $11.3 million. But the biggest deal would be the acquisition of Barton Protective Services for $180 million in cash on August 2, 2004. As of July 31, 2004, Allied and Barton together employed approximately 36,000 security officers. On a combined basis, the companies provided contract security officer services to over 2,100 clients, including more than 100 of the Fortune 500 companies, in 39 states and the District of Columbia. Pro forma revenues for 2003 were listed at over $667 million.[16]

Continued growth would follow, and operating as AlliedBarton Security Services, on July 20, 2006, the company acquired Initial Security LLC for approximately $73.9 million. Revenues from 2004 to 2006 were reported as having grown from $873 million to $1.26 billion.[17]

Al Berger told the authors:

> Bill performed a key role in transitioning acquisitions, and I helped mentor Bill. He was a hard worker. Bill had become an excellent manager. He was able to provide detailed rationale and a clear vision when leading the managers. I had my eye on Bill as a guy who could run the company, and I was confident that Bill was the right man to take over the CEO position as I wanted to retire. At the same time, McAndrews and Forbes had the financial strength and an aim to grow the company, and they were a good fit for the growing company. They made a lot of money from their investment.

AlliedBarton Attracts High-Profile Investors

In August 2008, an all-cash acquisition of Allied Security was made by The Blackstone Group from MacAndrews & Forbes Holdings Inc. for a total consideration of about $700 million. By 2008, AlliedBarton employed approximately 51,000 security officers, had 118 offices nationwide, and served a client base that includes about 200 Fortune 500 companies in 45 states and the District of Columbia. For the 12 months ended June 30, 2008, the company had pro forma revenues of about $1.6 billion.[18]

Bill said that despite the recession caused by the financial crisis the company bucked the downward trend and grew revenues from 2006 of $1.2 billion, to 2010 revenue of $1.7 billion.

> The good news for our industry is that during an economic downturn, there is a focus on crime … there is a concern with protection, a concern with preventing workplace violence. Those things still exist, and a company like ours is here to fill that need.

Helping to attain growth, the company foresaw certain industry trends, including the consolidation of contracts to single large providers and acted. The pipeline of business for large clients looking to consolidate services with one supplier was the strongest source of growth for the company. Bill put together a national accounts team that worked with customers embarking on similar initiatives. That program did not exist in 2007, but by 2011 it grew to roughly $400 million. Bill said

> we sat down and wrote a plan. The plan needed to fall in line with the vision and cultural values you promote as a company, and you need a team that is willing to embrace those values and work toward the goals outlined in your strategic plan.

The goal of the organization was to protect the people, property, and the assets of clients, and Bill was the leader in setting the goal, communicating the goal to associates, and seeing through its achievement. Staff performance was closely monitored, and managers held accountable for performance. Outlining the rationale for this, Bill said:

> Goals get translated into an annual performance plan, goals get translated into compensation metrics as basic as performance planning documentation for individuals, which is then cascaded into the company. Then we sit down and measure people on how they did against those goals and how well we did as an organization. That's the accountability part, that we hold people accountable for doing it. It's a mentality that is shaped by management from an employee's first day on the job. From the beginning of the first day, employees are schooled in the company's goals, strategy, and values. They are given a copy of the company's cultural primer, *Dare to be Great*. Employees are expected to know its contents. Anyone can learn the software and technology of the job, but you want people to lead.

With *Dare to Be Great* as the template and Whitmore providing leadership, the culture of accountability took root throughout the expansive AlliedBarton footprint. Bill motivated employees, explaining the mindset this way:

> One thing I always tried to be clear about is that *Dare to be Great* is exactly what it says, I'm daring you to do something great. You walk in every day and say to your employees, "I want us to be better and better." It's been said over and over again, it's teamwork. If your company is made up of leaders who can work together for a common cause, and who are there for each other

in good times and bad, I think those are the companies that survive. I think if we meet all of our plans, then it is a win-win-win for customers, employees and shareholders. That is what I define as a success.[19]

Bill also focused on an issue close to his heart: hiring military veterans. In 2013, the company hired more than 5,000 veterans through its *Hire Our Heroes* program. Jerold Ramos, director of strategic recruiting and military liaison at AlliedBarton, said in an article for the website *Chief Learning Officer*® that

> Mr. Whitmore challenged us to create a military recruiting strategy. In the past employers shied away from veterans because they were afraid that they would be deployed. But he wanted to bring American heroes to the table. We can train them to do private security, but what they bring to the table is a sense of loyalty, justice, leadership, and trustworthiness. That's what makes a great security officer.

Ramos served in the Navy during the Vietnam War, and when he returned in the early 1970s, he was a high school dropout with few job prospects and a young family to support. His first job was as a grocery store security guard. Ramos said that when he came home from the war, he had no direction and got into the security industry just to earn a paycheck. Eventually, Ramos earned his GED certificate and went to college. He joined AlliedBarton in 2002 as a recruiter, and, like his boss Bill Whitmore, he moved up the ranks quickly. He cited Whitmore as one of his greatest sources of inspiration. Ramos said that Bill had the ability to motivate others through just a few words. "He doesn't just give you marching orders. He tells you the reason behind it and gives you support." This, Ramos said, was the difference between being a leader rather than a boss. Ramos said that he saw himself as a product of Whitmore's "higher calling."[20]

Under Bill's leadership, the company's sustained growth continued to interest financial firms. In June 2015, the French investment firm Wendel "agreed to acquire AlliedBarton Security Services, one of the largest providers of security guards in the United States, from the Blackstone Group for about $1.67 billion, including debt." Wendel said it would make an equity investment of about $670 million for a 96 percent stake in the security firm, with the remaining stake owned by AlliedBarton's management. AlliedBarton posted revenue of $2.18 billion for the 12 months ended March 31, 2015, and employed more than 60,000 people.[21]

FIGURE 8.4   Photograph of Bill in 2016, from the Press Release of the AlliedBarton Security Services and Universal Services of America merger.

AlliedBarton and Universal Services Merge

On August 1, 2016, Wendel announced that AlliedBarton Security Services had completed a merger with Universal Services of America, creating the leading security company in North America. The combined company would operate as Allied Universal, having 140,000 highly trained employees at the time of the merger. The combined firms were expected to "have total annual revenues of approximately $4.5 billion and adjusted pro forma synergized EBITDA of approximately $440 million." Steve Jones (Chapter 14), the chief executive officer of Universal Services of America, became the chief executive officer of Allied Universal and Bill Whitmore was elected as the company's chairman of the board (Figure 8.4).[22] Two years later, Bill retired.

LEGACY

Bill Whitmore was a highly successful security industry leader who along with Al Berger transformed SpectaGuard security company from a mid-sized regional security provider into a multibillion-dollar leading North American security company. The company under his leadership grew steadily through organic growth and a series of well-chosen strategic acquisitions, fueled by the support of private equity investors and ongoing company profits. Its roster of Fortune 500 customers made it one of the most recognized security companies in the world, and a leader in the U.S. market. The company maintained a large presence in virtually every major market in the United States and had a large network of branch offices throughout the country.

On November 9, 2022, the authors had the pleasure of speaking with David Buckman about his impressions of Bill's leadership and management style. David worked with Bill for over 11 years, from April 2005 through August 2016, as executive vice president and general counsel of AlliedBarton. After the merger of Universal Services and AlliedBarton, David continued with Allied Universal, where Bill remained until 2018 as board chair. In July 2021, subsequent to the acquisition of G4S by Allied Universal, David became global general counsel for Allied Universal.

David first met Bill when he interviewed for the general counsel position at AlliedBarton. David said he felt a "strong rapport" with Bill right away. After another round of interviews with other AlliedBarton executives and ownership representatives, David was hired. David described Bill this way:

> [O]utgoing, a great conversationalist, easy to be around, and having a steady temperament. He was not a typical "schmoozer," but had a way of relating to all types of people. He has a great sense of humor and enjoyed telling stories. Bill would let you know if he was disturbed about something in a business context, but he was always in control of his emotions. With Bill, what you see is what you get. He had a high degree of self-awareness and determination to improve himself. He was keenly aware that he had advanced from a police officer to a leading role in private security as a chief executive officer of an industry-leading company.
>
> A life-long learner, Bill worked hard on what would make him and others around him successful. He was an avid reader with a strong intellectual curiosity; a sophisticated businessman, who knew all the details of the business and was fluent in the business metrics, with a sophisticated understanding of finance and capital markets. Bill's mental math skills are as fast as anyone I've met.

David said Bill's leadership style "evolved as the business grew."

> You got the sense that he always had bigger plans and was always looking to do more and do it better. He didn't shoot from the hip, but followed a consensus approach, gathering his senior

team to talk things through. Once he made a decision, he had processes in place to execute strategy and measure results but without overly formalized systems. As the company grew, Bill struck a balance between being in the field and directing from the corporate office. While in the field he would meet with branch personnel, security officers, and frequently with customers, never losing the pulse of the operations and the company's employees.

In addition to directing Allied Universal, Bill was busy with additional industry and civic activities. From June 2004 to January 2009, Bill served on the Private Sector Senior Advisory Committee of the Homeland Security Council, appointed by President George W. Bush. Bill is a board member emeritus of the Philadelphia Police Foundation, and former chair of the Philadelphia University Board of Trustees.[23]

In 2011, Bill authored a book titled *Potential: Workplace Violence Prevention and Your Organizational Success*. Based on a national survey commissioned by AlliedBarton, Bill determined that efforts to prevent workplace violence need to begin with an organization's c-suite taking steps to change corporate culture. Rather than being complacent, companies should nurture employee engagement, encourage individual growth, and build a practice of ethical decision making. People need to know how to reach the designated person or team in charge of resolving workplace conflicts and other issues, and how that information is treated. Leaders also need to create a culture of zero tolerance for bullying and other forms of intimidation in the workplace. Bill said, "another important step in preventing workplace violence is providing continual training on the subject, not just to managers and supervisors, but to all employees."[24]

In 2012, Bill Whitmore received the Edgar B. Watson Award from the National Association of Security Companies (NASCO). The award recognized his contributions to the private security industry and was presented during the annual ASIS convention at the Marriott Philadelphia City Center Hotel on Tuesday, September 11, 2012.[25]

Bill was also a founder, supporter, and chairman of the Ed Snider Youth Hockey and Education Organization, which was named after the late Ed Snider, former chairman Comcast-Spectacor and the founder of the Philadelphia Fliers.[26] The organization has a mission of using the sport of ice hockey "to build lives and unite communities, helping educate young people to succeed in the game of life." A professional hockey player and board member for Snider Hockey, Wayne Simmonds, said Snider Youth Hockey "makes impossible dreams possible for thousands of deserving boys and girls."[27]

Through hard work, brilliant strategy, and operational execution with a steady hand, Bill transformed SpectaGuard into a major national security services company that numbered many Fortune 500 companies, major institutions, and Class A office properties among its long-standing customers. Bill's success at growing Allied attracted the attention and interest of increasingly strong investment firms that helped fund company expansion. Eventually, global investment companies Wendel and Warburg Pincus engineered the deal that cleared the way for AlliedBarton to merge with Universal Services, creating the largest U.S.-based security services company. During his security career, Bill set an example in leadership and management excellence, guiding the growth, and fostering the prestige of a highly respected security services company.

NOTES

1 Rita Pyrillis, "AlliedBarton's Bill Whitmore: A Higher Calling for Security," March 24, 2014, https://www.chieflearningofficer. com/2014/03/24/alliedbartons-bill-whitmore-a-higher-calling-for-security/

2 Bill Whitmore, "Milestones and Rewards," *New York Times*, December 15, 2012, https://www.nytimes.com/2012/12/16/jobs/alliedbartons-ceo-on-milestones-and-rewards.html

3 "Blackstone to Sell AlliedBarton to Wendel," news release, June 30, 2015, https://www.blackstone.com/news/press/blackstone-to-sell-alliedbarton-to-wendel/

4 Joseph N. DiStephano, "AlliedBarton Security merging to form industry giant," *The Philadelphia Inquirer*, May 4, 2016, https://www.inquirer.com/philly/business/20160504_AlliedBarton_Security_merging_to_form_industry_giant.html&outputType=app-web-view

5 "William Whitmore Sr., 1926–2019," *The Times Herald* (Norristown, PA), June 28, 2019, https://www.legacy.com/us/obituaries/timesherald/name/william-whitmore-obituary?id=12452232

6 Whitmore, "Milestones and Rewards."

7 Allied Security Holdings LLC, *Annual Report 2007*, 2008, https://www.sec.gov/Archives/edgar/data/1301566/0000950136080 01365/file1.htm

8 Penny Singer, "Generations: Keeping It in the Family," *New York Times*, June 8, 1986, https://www.nytimes.com/1986/06/08/nyregion/generations-keeping-it-in-the-family.html

9 ABM Industries, *Annual Report 2005*, 2006, 55, https://stocklight.com/stocks/us/services/nyse-abm/abm-industries/annual-reports/nyse-abm-2006-10K-06719417.pdf

10 Universal Protection Service, "Universal Protection Service Acquires the Security Officer Services Division of T&M Protection Resources, LLC," news release, January 2, 2013, https://www.prnewswire.com/news-releases/universal-protection-service-acquires-the-security-officer-services-division-of-tm-protection-resources-llc-185431472.html

11 Elizabeth Bennett, "Growth's secure for SpectaGuard," *Philadelphia Business Journal*, May 29, 2000, https://www.bizjournals.com/philadelphia/stories/2000/05/29/smallb1.html

12 "Company News: SpectaGuard Says it has Acquired Allied Security," *New York Times*, March 3, 2000, https://www.nytimes.com/2000/03/03/business/company-news-spectaguard-says-it-has-acquired-allied-security.html

13 Whitmore, "Milestones and Rewards."

14 Allied Security Holdings LLC, *Registration Statement*, September 20, 2004, https://www.sec.gov/Archives/edgar/data/1301573/0000950 13604003024/file001.htm

15 "Company News: Allied Security to be Bought by Investment Firm," *New York Times* January 18, 2003, https://www.nytimes.com/2003/01/18/business/company-news-allied-security-to-be-bought-by-investment-firm.html

16 Allied Security Holdings LLC, *Registration Statement*.

17 Allied Security Holdings LLC, *Annual Report 2006*, 2007, https://www.sec.gov/Archives/edgar/data/1301566/0000950136070 02252/file1.htm

18 "Moody's Assigns Ratings to AB Merger Sub (Allied Security)," news release, August 5, 2008, https://www.moodys.com/research/Moodys-assigns-ratings-to-AB-Merger-Sub-Allied-Security--PR_160507

19 "How Bill Whitmore Secured the Future of AlliedBarton Security Services by Emphasizing Culture and Strategy," November 1, 2011, https://sbnonline.com/article/how-bill-whitmore-secured-the-future-of-alliedbarton-security-services-by-emphasizing-culture-and-strategy/

20 Pyrillis, "AlliedBarton's Bill Whitmore: A Higher Calling for Security."

21 Chad Bray, "Wendel Agrees to Acquire AlliedBarton Security for $1.67 Billion," *New York Times*, June 30, 2015, https://www.nytimes.com/2015/07/01/business/dealbook/wendel-agrees-to-acquire-alliedbarton-security-for-1-67-billion.html

22 Wendel SE, "AlliedBarton and Universal Services of America Finalize Merger, Creating the Leading Security Services Company in North America," news release, August 1, 2016, https://www.prnewswire.com/news-releases/alliedbarton-and-universal-services-of-america-finalize-merger-creating-the-leading-security-services-company-in-north-america-300306813.html

23 "Meet Our Team," accessed November 24, 2022, http://jandrinvestment.com/the-team/

24 Joel Griffin, "Leadership's Role in Preventing Workplace Violence," February 29, 2012, https://www.securityinfowatch.com/security-executives/protective-operations-guard-services/article/10635378/

alliedbarton-president-and-ceo-bill-whitmore-shares-his-insights-on-workplace-violence-prevention-in-webinar

25 "AlliedBarton's Bill Whitmore to be Honored by NASCO at ASIS 2012," September 7, 2012, https://www.securityinfowatch.com/security-executives/protective-operations-guard-services/news/10775718/alliedbarton-president-and-ceo-bill-whitmore-to-receive-nascos-edgar-b-watson-award

26 "Meet Our Founder," accessed October 29, 2022, https://snider hockey.org/about/

27 Ed Snider Youth Hockey & Education, *Snider Hockey 2017 Impact Report*, 2018, http://sniderhockey.org/assets/documents/partials/core_buttongroup/T1YQg.pdf

CHAPTER 9

Albert J. Berger
The Right Formulas

Were it not for a chance encounter with Thomas Wathen (Chapter 5) at a business association meeting that led to Albert J. "Al" Berger's appointment by the Wathen-led CPP Security as a director in 1975, his legendary security career may not have occurred. From the late 1950s and until 1987, Al was a successful chemical and industrial company executive and owner. While Al served part-time as a board member from 1975 at CPP and Pinkerton, he started working full-time in the security industry as president at Pinkerton from 1990 to 1994. He would then become a partner at Gryphon Partners, buying SpectaGuard and Allied Security (Allied), where he served as chief executive officer from 1998 to 2003, and as chairman until 2006 for their holding companies.[1]

At CPP, Al was instrumental in overseeing the acquisition of Pinkerton, and the turnaround of a struggling company. At SpectaGuard and Allied, he served as a mentor to Bill Whitmore (Chapter 8) and as chief executive officer guided the company to become a leading U.S. national security company. The result was the rapid transformation of SpectaGuard during his tenure there from a regional company with $84 million in revenues into a national security leader, operating subsequently as Allied Security and then AlliedBarton with revenues exceeding $1.26 billion at year end 2006.[2]

EARLY LIFE AND EDUCATION

Al was born on August 30, 1936, to Molly Isaacson and Samuel J. Berger. His mother was born in Montreal, where her Romanian-born Jewish parents had emigrated to before settling first in Philadelphia, and then New York City around 1926. Al's father was born in Bavaria, Germany, as Baptiste Berger-Schmitt, before taking his naturalized name, as Samuel J. Berger. His father was an orphan, and Catholic, and emigrated to Boston around 1928, where he worked for an uncle as a baker.

DOI: 10.4324/9781003285564-13

During his interview with the authors on August 14, 2023, Al described in detail his early life in New York, and the influence his parents had on his life and career. His mother worked in the family store that his father established in the Stuyvesant section of Manhattan, on First Avenue between 13th and 14th Streets in New York City. The store was a combination bakery, dairy, and canned goods retailer.

Al's mother had studied opera, and Al noted that she sang in the Metropolitan Opera chorus. She had an interest in culture and learning, interests which she imbued in Al. Al's father was described as very diligent, and he taught Al by his example and through his words that one must make sure that things be done well and right. The family, like most during the Depression, lived modestly, struggled, and was faced with rationing during World War II. Al noted that ingredients for the bakery were scarce and valuable, and that any waste was costly, which meant things had to be done correctly the first time around.

From an early age, Al was an avid reader and a diligent worker. He described a series of jobs he held from early childhood through to his full-time career company. When he was six or seven years old, he sold shopping bags in front of the family store. Al said that the money saved enabled the family to buy a TV set in 1947. He worked at the family store from an early age alongside his parents up and through high school. He said that he learned to measure ingredients (especially helpful in his later chemical career), to wait on customers which taught him about the value of customer service and people, and to stock shelves where he learned the value of inventory control and cost control.

It was not until after he was eight years old that Al attended public school. The family had moved to the Williamsburg section of Brooklyn, which was where his maternal grandparents lived. It was then that he learned more about his Jewish roots and had a Bar mitzvah.

When Al was young, he had a fondness for chemistry, and his father bought him a chemistry set and built a worktable for his projects. Al was also interested in sports, and he said that he joined the Police Athletic League club where he learned to box and play baseball. He also enjoyed playing football. As a teenager, he spent summers working as a waiter in the Catskills and had a job cleaning cabins for the Grace Line. During the holiday season, he would deliver the yellow pages. All said all the work he did taught him the value of learning about who he worked for, and with. He developed people skills that were valuable in his career.

Al was a good student, and despite his desire to attend Boys High School in Brooklyn, his parents insisted that he accept a place at the prestigious Stuyvesant High School in Manhattan.

Al described this move as a "life changer." He obtained an excellent education and was able to continue to help the family as their store was close by the school. If classes were in the morning he worked at the store in the afternoon, and if classes were in the afternoon, he worked at the store in the morning. At Stuyvesant, Al excelled at football and was offered a scholarship at several schools, including New York University (NYU). NYU, however, stopped its football program, and Al decided to attend City College of New York (CCNY).

A Mentor and Higher Education

During the summer before attending City College, Al got a job hauling calves, beef, and veal, which were chilled on dry ice, into delivery trucks for the Berliner & Marx company on 14th Street and Tenth Avenue in New York City. Within two weeks he was promoted to supervisor. Mr. Berliner was described by Al as a mentor to him, and wanted him to stay with the company, but Al embarked on an education to study Engineering. The promotion at Berliner & Marx "gave me confidence which was helpful in my career."

Yet another job that Al worked at was during his second semester at CCNY, for the Curtiss-Wright Corporation. There, Al used electro-mechanical calculators to determine dimensions in the design of exhaust manifolds. A bulletin board at the company led to his applying for, and subsequently accepting, a job with the Atomic Energy Commission, where he worked on measuring radioactivity, and testing specimens from actual nuclear bombing. He received top-secret clearance, and a supervisor at the company introduced him to another mentor, Tony Segura, with the Foster D. Snell division of Booze Allen Hamilton. Al learned more about researching papers to produce chemical abstracts, and his career in the chemical industry was starting to unfold.

MILITARY SERVICE AND A CHEMICAL INDUSTRY CAREER

The Korean War brought the draft, and Al enlisted in the Marines. It enabled him to continue working in the chemical industry. Al proudly served the Marines from 1957 to 1959 on active duty, and until 1962 in the reserves. In 1959, he started his first full-time job, with Witco Company, where he engaged in the product development of additives and coatings to produce concrete with improved physical properties. Al was transferred to California in 1961, and shortly after, the Dow Chemical Company bought the division. Al continued to work full-time in the chemical industry, foregoing further higher education, which was interrupted by his military service and successful career.

Al noted that in 1964, after he had moved to California, his father Samuel passed away Al relocated his mother, and younger siblings, sister,

Elaine, who was born in 1943, and brother Neil, born in 1951, to be close to him and so he could help provide for them.

In 1964, Al founded his own company, Coating Composites, which made additives to strengthen concrete and manufactured protective coatings. Al sold the company in 1992, to the Sauereisen Company of Pittsburgh, Pennsylvania.

CAREER IN THE SECURITY SERVICES INDUSTRY

A Chance Meeting

As noted in Tom Wathen, Chapter 5, Al said he first met Tom at a Young President's Association conference in Arizona. They became friends, and sometime in 1975, Tom was having some difficulties with a partner, and he asked Al to serve as a director on the Board of CPP. So began an entry into the security service industry, which would lead years later to a legendary career first at CPP-Pinkerton, and then for SpectaGuard and Allied Security.

While serving on the board at CPP, Al continued to work in the chemical industry as founder and owner of Coating Composites, and at HCC Industries from 1985 to 1987, where he served as president and reorganized operations to set the stage for the company to go private.

A Consequential Role at CPP and Pinkerton

In 1988 and 1989, while on the board of CPP, Al served as a consultant to CPP in the acquisition of Pinkerton. Al said he was initially opposed to the acquisition, "because the company did not have enough management talent" at the time. By this time, Al said he was "tiring of the cumbersome regulatory processes in the chemical industry."

From 1990 to early 1994, Al would serve as president and a Vice Chairman at Pinkerton. The board insisted on his running the company when Pinkerton was acquired by CPP. He said

> the prospect of managing a large integration presented a challenge, and an opportunity to guide managers at the company and see them prosper. I took pride in harnessing their energy, and in seeing a turnaround at Pinkerton, which was losing money.

Al said he was focused during the integration of Pinkerton on managing costs, and, according to Tom Wathen, Al helped "in consolidating the administrative and financial operations." With Al's help, Pinkerton's followed up an initial offering with a secondary stock offering in April 1991 and further reorganized senior debt. The operational changes Al initiated "made Pinkerton something more than a vanilla commodity by offering services that enhance the value of our work."[3] According to Al, "it was hard work at Pinkerton, but within eighteen months we were able to take the company public. I liked cleaning things up, and Tom was able to monetize his Pinkerton ownership."

At Gryphon Partners, CEO for SpectaGuard, and Allied Security

Al said that after his tenure at Pinkerton ended in 1994, he was introduced to Gryphon Partners by a recruiter of chief executive officers, named Bill Meyers. Gryphon along with Texas Pacific Group were looking for investments, and they made Al an offer to become a partner at Gryphon. "I did some research and found that SpectaGuard, a Philadelphia area security company with offices in Boston as well, was a well-run company that had the potential to grow much faster." Despite an inclination to retire, Al agreed to participate in the acquisition of SpectaGuard and was named the company chief executive officer and chairman in 1998.

Growth commenced, first with the Effective Security purchase, also in 1998, and then with the acquisition of Allied Security in 2000. That acquisition was significant, and Al said that "it gave us a national footprint, and Allied had great people." Al described his working relationship and mentoring of Bill Whitmore (Chapter 8) in our June 12, 2023, interview; and his support for Bill to become his successor when Al retired as chief executive officer. Both Bill and Al worked together on the Allied integration with SpectaGuard, and the combination of acquisitions and organic growth was spectacular. From the time of the Effective acquisition to year end 2002, the company revenues went from $168.8 million to over $510 million.[4] SpectaGuard took on the name Allied Security and was a force in the U.S. security services market (Figure 9.1).

Al was a very savvy and accomplished executive, versed and experienced in managing people, business, and the financial aspects of large companies; having been successful in his chemical industry career, at Pinkerton and now at Allied Security. He ascribed his success to being proficient at

> listening to people. I got along with people in the field and worked with them as a peer and not as a boss. I was also able to drill down to find solutions and had the ability to analyze the big picture. The work took patience and courage.

FIGURE 9.1   (Left to Right) Bill Whitmore, Mort Feinberg, and Al Berger, photo taken circa 2009 or 2010. Mortimer J. Feinberg was a Dean at the Baruch School of Business, City University of New York, and a leading industrial psychologist and consultant to business leaders globally, including to both Pinkertons and then Allied. He contributed articles to the *Wall Street Journal*, authoring and co-authoring six books before he passed away in 2015.

Al possessed an innate intelligence, keen business sense, and described himself as a "conservative risk taker." He knew the travails of a tough life, and the value of hard work from his early days, which carried him through his entire career.

MacAndrews and Forbes Buys Allied, Acquires Barton

In February 2003, SpectaGuard was acquired by MacAndrews & Forbes Holdings Inc. (MAFCO) for approximately $263.6 million. The company growth strategy included "the acquisition and integration of complementary businesses in order to increase our density within certain geographic areas, capture market share in the markets in which we operate and improve profitability or expand our service offerings to our customers."

FIGURE 9.2   Al speaking at a company function in 2003.

The company acquired Professional Security Bureau, Ltd. in December 2003 for approximately $45.8 million and, in March 2004, acquired certain assets and liabilities of Security Systems, Inc., for approximately $10.6 million. In August 2004, the company acquired Barton Protective Services for $181.3 million (Figure 9.2).[5]

Al said that Ron Perelman of MAFCO, asked him to remain as chairman. Al had already put aside his retirement for the past five years while he was chief executive at the company. Al said that Perelman was very supportive, and there was no second guessing on what we were doing at Allied. Al also wanted to help Bill Whitmore move seamlessly into the role of chief executive, and so Al stayed on as chairman until 2006, and then as a board of managers member up to 2008.

Mission Focused Management

Al noted that:

> I participated in the preparation of three Harvard Business School case studies in the late eighties, early nineties, one about my initiatives at HCC and two pertaining to the acquisition of Pinkerton's by CPP. The HCC paper laid out the management compensation plan for the three presidents running operations in three different States, each making different product lines for their own customer base. The chief executive officer at HCC who hired me, had introduced my manager's compensation plan at an executive conference at Harvard, and unbeknownst to me my interview and plan would form the basis of a case study. Each plan proposed a budget based on a management forecast (which was agreed to be an improvement over the previous year) payroll; and bonuses would be directly related to the increase, though failure could be grounds for separation.
>
> Harvard professors and some students felt that the consequences for executives not meeting goals laid out for them in the HCC plan were too severe. Nevertheless, the case paper was studied by Harvard students over at least a five-year period, and my own son, Adam, experienced it in a class at Harvard. I had never mentioned it to him previously.
>
> The two CPP-Pinkerton case studies centered on the process of CPP buying Pinkerton, and the process in deciding to take Pinkerton public, were eventually used as part of "final" finance exams for several years at Harvard.
>
> I mention this because it reveals a trait that has driven me at every position I have held, which is the necessity and importance of mission focus. It was something I lost in my own business, Coating Compositions, after I turned operations over to a chief operating officer, but I subsequently regained mission focus as an executive at HCC Industries.
>
> My mission focus in the security business had been to make acquisitions to provide major growth, get liquidity for the company and chairman, and triple revenue in five years for the private equity owners. Of course, the fundamentals of operating a security business must take into account quality of service, such as quality assurance underlies the material manufacturing business. That said, forecasting, budgeting and constant reminders to managers and employees of a company's mission and goals, is what a chief executive officer must be doing.

Ron Rabena was senior vice president of operations at the time of the Gryphon acquisition of SpectaGuard and remains today with Allied Universal as chief client officer. Regarding Al Berger, Ron told the authors:

> I was introduced to Al when SpectaGuard was sold to Gryphon group. He became our CEO after acquisition. Al was one of the brightest executives I have met. He was intelligent, innovative and had high IQ as well as high emotional intelligence.
>
> He had a wealth of knowledge in the security industry and painted an Incredible vision for us to grow profitable while improving our brand. His approach was calm, deliberate and measured.
>
> He took over the leadership of a young company and mentored us on how to operate at the next level. He rarely raised his voice but always made his point and was usually spot on. He encouraged risk taking and let us learn from our mistakes.
>
> He made us laugh as he always used real life examples. He was not afraid to be direct but would never take shots at your weaknesses only your strengths. He was instrumental in my personal growth and a great mentor to me during his days as our CEO.
>
> I remember when we were attacked on 911, his calm, direct and insightful leadership was so impressive. He handled us and the entire circumstances with incredible leadership.
>
> I still stay in contact with him over the years and always learn from every conversation.
>
> I respect him, trust him and learn from him every time we speak.
>
> A true role model...He also was a great mentor to Bill Whitmore over his tenure. He was instrumental in Bill's growth.

LEGACY AND CHARITABLE WORK

Al Berger's career as a senior executive in the security services industry was marked by monumental events at two of the leading companies of his time. He led a turnaround and the integration of Pinkerton with CPP, while president of the company from 1990 to 1994. He was then instrumental in taking Pinkerton public within 18 months of the acquisition. But the best was yet to come.

In 1998, he became an owner with Gryphon Partners of SpectaGuard, and while chief executive officer of successor company, Allied Holdings LLC., he oversaw a huge increase in revenues during which the company

FIGURE 9.3 (Left to right) Mark Derosier, Carol Berger, Virginia "Ginny" Derosier, and Al Berger.

became a leading U.S.-based, national security services company. As chief executive officer from 1998 to 2003, chairman through February 2006, and then as a board of managers member until 2008; revenues from the acquisition of Effective Security resulted in sales increasing from $84 million in 1998 to $178 million and to over $1.26 billion by year-end 2006. As of December 31, 2006, Allied provided security services to over 3,300 clients in 44 states and the District of Columbia, including approximately 200 Fortune 500 companies. As of February 2007, the company employed approximately 51,400 individuals in 112 offices nationwide [6]

Al was a successful businessman and leader in both the security services industry and the chemical industry. His business success has permitted him, alongside his second wife, Carol Auerbach, to support a variety of charitable activities through his own donor-advised fund, and the Isaac and Carol Auerbach Family Foundation (Figure 9.3).

Al is a member of the National Advisory Committee for Foundations, Inc. He has served as a member of the Patron Leadership Council for the Manhattan Theatre Club and on the board of directors. He also served as a member on the board of the Bellevue Arts Museum.[7] Al noted that he and Carol have endowed a chair in cybersecurity at Drexel University and a fellowship for the Campaign for Grade-Level Reading.

Al is proud of his children, Adam, and Erica, from his first marriage to the late Phylis Berger. He said he leads a very happy life now and is glad to be relieved of the sleepless nights that accompanied being a business owner.

Al sees the greatest challenge for security companies today is "to provide good health care coverage, and childcare for company employees. It is also incumbent on security companies to properly screen and monitor their employees." To be successful, the security company owner must "have money, good officers, and managers that know the business. This is best when managers are promoted from within the organization. It is important that you set an example for your employees and customer." And make sure you do things right. Throughout his career, Al was mission focused, and the results can be summarized as mission accomplished. He had the right formulas for success in both the chemistry and security services industry.

NOTES

1 Allied Security Holdings LLC, *Annual Report 2006*, 2007.
2 Allied Security Holdings LLC, *Annual Report 2006*, 2007.
3 Feder, "Chairman of Pinkerton's Adds to His Responsibilities."
4 Allied Security Holdings LLC, *Annual Report 2006*, 2007.
5 Allied Security Holdings LLC, *Annual Report 2006*, 2007.
6 Allied Security Holdings LLC, *Annual Report 2007*, 2008.
7 Drexel University College of Computing and Informatics, n.d., Dean's Executive Advisory Council.

PART IV

Scandinavians Build Global Companies

The three Scandinavian legends profiled in the next chapters—Jørgen Philip-Sørensen (Chapter 10), Lars Nørby Johansen (Chapter 11), and Thomas F. Berglund (Chapter 12)—had significant roles in creating and/ or leading the world's largest security companies during their respective tenures. The authors were aided in their work for this chapter by interviews with the legends, Thomas Berglund on March 11, 2022, and Lars Nørby Johansen on January 5, 2023. We were also aided by an interview with Waldemar Schmidt on November 7, 2022, along with written information he provided to us. We are grateful to him for his role in facilitating the interview with Lars. Waldemar is a highly respected Danish-born business executive, academician, and author. His business career included tenure at global cleaning giant, ISS A/S, culminating as chief executive officer from 1995 to 2000. He was a close friend of the late Jørgen Philip-Sørensen, and served with both Sørensen and Johansen on corporate and/ or organization boards, including Group 4 Falck and Group 4 Securicor. Chris Holliday also assisted the authors on Chapter 10 by providing us with various photos and newsletters, and granting us an interview on September 16, 2022.

Swedish-born Jørgen Philip-Sørensen came from an illustrious family of security leaders, and developed Group 4 into a global security giant. Danish-born Lars Nørby Johansen was a business executive who transformed Danish-based Falck from a fire safety, rescue, and assistance (ambulance) company into a European security leader. It became a global security company when he merged Falck with Sørensen's Group 4 to form Group 4 Falck. Swedish-born Thomas F. Berglund was a business executive who significantly expanded the global presence and size of Securitas through acquisitions of U.S.-based Pinkerton's and Burns. At the time of their retirements from the security service industry—Lars in 2005, Sørensen in 2006, and Berglund in 2007—the three Scandinavian legends had built the world's largest global security companies.

The global security companies they developed all had their origins early in the twentieth century as night watch (guard) companies with ties to the Philip-Sørensen family, unlike the largest U.S. security companies— Pinkerton's, founded in 1850, and Burns, founded in 1909—which began as detective agencies. The following information on the origins of these global companies was provided courtesy of Waldemar Schmidt as part of a presentation he prepared and gave at a family seminar for the children, grandchildren, and family advisors of Jørgen Philip Sørensen after his passing in 2010. Additional information from the presentation is also cited in Chapter 10.

In 1901, Marius Hogrefe established a small Danish security guard company, Kjøbenhavn-Frederiksberg Nattevagt (Kjobenhavn-Frederksberg Nightwatch). In 1905, Jørgen Philip-Sørensen's grandfather, Carl Julius Philip-Sørensen, became employed at the company and rose to managing director. The company was renamed in 1908 as Dansk Nattevagt (Danish Nightwatch), and in 1918 became United Guarding. It later became known as ISS Securitas, and was eventually acquired by Falck.

In 1934, Carl Julius established what would become Securitas AB in Helsingborg, Sweden by acquiring Helsingborg Nattevagt (Helsingborg Nightwatch). His son, Erik Philip-Sørensen, was managing director. In 1947, Erik Philip-Sørensen became the sole owner of Securitas AB and expanded it internationally. In 1981 he split the company into London-based Group 4 Securitas, and Stockholm-based Securitas AB.[1] Jørgen would develop Group 4, and years later Thomas Berglund would measurably expand Securitas, with both companies becoming global giants.

In 1906, Sophus Falck founded Denmark's Falck, which largely remained a family-run fire safety, rescue, and assistance company until Johansen became chief executive officer in 1988. In 1993 Falck acquired ISS Securitas as a platform security service company for Falck to start the process of becoming a global security company.

The success achieved by the legends profiled in Part IV was the result of hard work, business skill, and inspired leadership based on carefully developed strategies that were successfully implemented. These legends largely deployed a "Scandinavian business model" that has a focus on decentralized operations and a respect for employees that includes promoting individual initiative, providing opportunities for advancement through a commitment to training, and fairness in labor relations.

Employees are expected to be attentive to the needs of the company and the customers so that all stakeholders benefit. Lars told us that

> [D]irecting a company with tens or hundreds of thousands of employees requires something that binds. There must be a culture and vision that entails the importance of people and shared values. It must also of necessity be operated as a decentralized system, because a hierarchal system of control can't fully work in such large enterprises.

While the three legends profiled in this segment shared in the tenets of the model, each developed the vision and culture of their respective companies through their unique personal leadership and management styles.

NOTE

1 "Memorial Information: Nils Jørgen Philip-Sørensen," accessed September 23, 2022, http://www.jpsmemorial.co.uk/journal/2010/2/3/tribute-by-waldemar-schmidt-english-danish.html

CHAPTER 10

Jørgen Philip-Sørensen
Traversing the Globe

Nils Jørgen Philip-Sørensen, also known as Philip to his friends and as JPS in professional life, was active in the security services industry for over five decades starting from the late 1950s. Along with the contributions of his father and grandfather, JPS represents the third generation of Philip-Sørensens who made their name nearly synonymous with the global security industry (Figure 10.1). The Philip-Sørensen family is in large part responsible for creating the Europe-based global security powerhouses, Securitas, and Group 4 Securicor, later known as G4S.

In addition to being organizational leaders, JPS and his father, Erik Philip-Sørensen, played major roles in the development of professionalism in international security, notably through their substantial participation and contributions at the International Security Ligue. Erik Philip-Sørensen was a founder of the Ligue in 1933, served as its secretary general and later chairman from 1934 to 1963; JPS served as its chairman from 1980 to 1986.[1]

Erik is a legend in his own right, yet we chose to spotlight JPS, as his five-decade career in the security services industry—which included 35 years as chief executive officer of the Group 4 companies—culminated at the time of his retirement 2006 in the creation of the world's largest security company (Figure 10.2). With the acquisition of Securicor in 2004, Group 4 Securicor (G4S) would report in 2005 revenues of approximately £4.2 billion (over $7 billion at that year's exchange rate), while operating in over 100 countries, with more than 410,000 employees.[2]

Philip (JPS) was a global entrepreneur with diverse interests. The creation of the world's largest security company was his masterpiece. It was something that would have made his father and grandfather proud. They were the security service entrepreneurs of their time and founded ISS Securitas and "Swedish Securitas," respectively. While Group 4's major competitors acquired security companies at high prices in Europe and America, Philip established Group 4 subsidiaries in many fast-growing new world countries with his cunning strategy. Philip achieved his life's

FIGURE 10.1   Father and son: Erik and Jørgen Philip-Sørensen at a security conference.

FIGURE 10.2 A young Erik Philip-Sørensen pictured here, father to Jørgen Philip-Sørensen.

ambition through the mergers with Falck and Securicor: to become chairman and largest shareholder of the world's largest security company.[3]

FAMILY ROOTS IN THE SECURITY
AND CLEANING INDUSTRY

Carl Julius Philip-Sørensen was born in Sweden in 1883 and led a colorful life before he was employed by a Danish security company in 1905, which was later renamed the United Guarding Company. JPS said that his grandfather "came from the theater business. He was a very creative man who kept a pen and paper near his bedside table."[4]

In 1934, while employed at United Guarding, later named ISS Securitas, Carl proposed to the company chairman, C.L. David, that instead of having the guard leave the premises unmanned from four or five in the morning, that they fill the gap until customers opened their business with a team of cleaners. In this way, Det Danske Rengørings Selskab (DDRS, Danish Cleaning Company) was established, and the contract cleaning industry in Denmark was born. The cleaning business was not organized the same way as the security business, and the cleaner's job was considered the lowest in society. Carl was concerned for their welfare and wanted to professionalize the cleaning industry, and, to his credit, agreements were made with unions for the workers' benefit.[5]

Soon Carl became a director and a pioneer in the security industry. He started a guard school and introduced a watch clock so that customers could get documentation of what the guards really did. When his only child, Erik Philip-Sørensen, was a year old, Carl suddenly left him and his mother.[6]

Erik strove to impress his father; JPS in turn wanted to impress his own father who was strict with JPS.[7] Erik worked for four years as a manufacturing apprentice in Jutland before he obtained a job as a security guard in the security company his father managed in Odense. After two years, in 1931, he became employed by the security company in its Copenhagen location. Erik was active in the guard company's commercial activities, but his entrepreneurial spirit moved him to follow his own path, and in 1934 he left Denmark for Sweden, where he got a job in AB Hälsingborg's night watch guard company, which was founded by his father. Three years later, the 28-year-old Erik managed to buy exactly 50 percent of the company for SEK 30,000 by investing SEK 5,000 that he borrowed from a relative. The purchase price would be equivalent to about $120,000 today. Shortly afterward, Erik bought additional shares from another businessman and became a majority shareholder in the company.[8] At the time of his divestiture to his sons, the company was the largest European security company with a value of over $100 million.[9]

Erik Philip-Sørensen's Acquisitions Set the Stage for Sons Jørgen and Sven

Over the following years, Erik acquired control of several other companies in the Swedish security industry. Business prospered and prominent investors, including Lars Magnus Ericsson (founder of the telecom company Ericsson), invested in the company's various technology projects.

At an early stage, Erik took an interest in ethical and moral issues facing guards and watchmen. As the business expanded and employees with diverse backgrounds were hired, he established a motto—"honesty, vigilance and helpfulness"—to be at the core of all company operations. The simple, three-word motto is to this day represented by the three red dots of the Securitas AB logo. Shortly after acquiring the company Swedish Nattvakt, an international expansion of the business began with establishments in the UK and Japan, and in 1972, all companies owned by Erik Philip-Sørensen were united under the Securitas brand.[10]

Jørgen's Early Life

JPS was born in Malmo, Sweden, on September 23, 1938, where Erik was running Securitas at the time, but JPS was brought up in Denmark where his grandfather Carl was operating the Danish Securitas. JPS was not the greatest of students. He left school in agreement with the headmaster so as "not to waste each other's time" any further.[11] JPS stated himself that he was not very bright at school, but was very happy:

> I learned a lot, maybe less about important school subjects but more about sport, companionship, music and leadership. But above all, I learned about people! And that, in particular, has been of enormous help in my career as a businessman. And I have no hesitation in saying that this is largely due to what the teachers gave me during my school days.

He was promoted each year, but each summer, "the Headmaster told me that I was moved up on trial! My Parents got rather accustomed to the news and were not very pleased!"[12]

A source who requested to remain anonymous told the authors that father and son did not appear to have a close relationship, but it was respectful, and that JPS was competitive with Erik, the latter having retained an interest in competitor Securitas while JPS was running Group 4. Perhaps the early years of physical distance were a factor in the overall father–son relationship; regardless, there is no doubt that Erik's success provided JPS with a similar desire to prosper. The younger brother Sven would be involved for some time in the family business but would exit it at a far earlier time than JPS.

The mark of Erik Philip-Sørensen on the security industry is perhaps best reflected by the words of JPS:

> Anyone who has had the opportunity of meeting my father will know that his enthusiasm and dedication are contagious. His dedication to the profession has been his biggest influence on me. So too have his sense of humor, his decision making and his respect for the common man. And at the age of 83 he still has the stamina to talk all through the night about the security business.[13]

LEARNING THE SECURITY BUSINESS THE HARD WAY

Without continuing to higher education, JPS entered the security business as a security guard. In 1958, he moved to Birmingham, UK, where his father sent him to work for Plant Protection, a company Erik had started seven years earlier above a grocery store. JPS would work very hard, struggling at times with his English, especially in situations where he needed to assert himself.[14] The lack of a formal degree did not deter his quest for knowledge, as Chris Holliday described JPS as an avid reader, with many interests.

Within two years Erik sent JPS to Belgium with £5,000 (approximately $10,000 today) to start a new business[15]—one might guess it was a kind of challenge or test of the younger man's business sense and willingness to take risks. Getting new business was not often easy. A prospective customer once threw JPS down the stairs, blaming JPS for a business loss in the Belgian Congo because of his Swedish ancestry.[16]

At one of his first contracts in Belgium, the customer observed JPS shoveling coal into the furnace on the premises. Perhaps not realizing that the security company he'd just hired was brand-new and understaffed, he remarked, "When I first saw you, you were wearing a uniform selling security. The next time, when we signed the contract, you were in a business suit. Now, you're in a boiler suit. What company is this?" JPS responded, "I am the company." But soon he would recruit and grow the Belgian security company into a sizeable one.[17]

While JPS started out doing most everything at the company he later was able to be more strategic; he expanded operations directly and through partnerships in many countries globally. He made bold choices in business and pursued opportunities around the world in areas others considered risky at the time.

In 1964 JPS returned to the UK and the family business, to become operations director for what became known as Group 4 Total Security when Erik consolidated the UK group of companies. JPS was appointed managing director in 1965, and by 1968, he became chief executive of the company and remained in that position for the next 35 years. In 1974, JPS and Sven acquired majority ownership of their father's company.[18] Erik did not just give the company to Sven and JPS. They had to bid against a multinational Swedish company for control of the company. The business was at the time Europe's largest security firm.[19]

A FAMILY RIFT

Five years later JPS and Sven divided the company, and by 1981 the company employed almost 24,000 people, had offices in 15 countries and annual revenues of 1.9 billion SEK (in 1981 the equivalent of approximately $400 million) making it one of the world's largest security firms.[20]

The international operations developed as Group 4 Securitas, operating primarily in the UK, while Swedish operations continued as Securitas. The holding company Skrinet would acquire Securitas from Sven in 1983, and two years later, Skrinet sold Securitas to Investment AB Latour.[21] Sven had a 75 percent stake in Securitas, and Jørgen had 100 percent of the stock of Group 4 and a 25 percent stake in Securitas. After Sven sold Securitas, JPS soon thereafter sold his 25 percent stake. JPS would go on to build Group 4 into a global powerhouse, but the sale of Securitas by Sven created a family rift, and the brothers did not speak from then on. JPS was quoted as saying,

> When my brother Sven sold his stake, it was kind of like selling the family silver ... I've tried to send him birthday cards for years but never get a response. Even at our father's funeral [Erik Philip-Sørensen died in August 2000 at the age of 92] he didn't want to talk to me.[22]

BUILDING GROUP 4 GLOBALLY

Group 4 began building services in Europe, and by the end of the 1980s it was operating in 24 countries. A further expansion was underway in Eastern Europe, along with the establishment of a division to provide service to the previously private corrections (prison) sector. In January 1991, JPS introduced the first issue of *Group 4 Magazine*, noting that

[It] is being published quarterly and circulated to the management of Group 4 Securitas (International) in the 24 countries where we have operating, associated or affiliated companies. With the continued growth of the business, the time has come to supplement the news you already receive nationally with a publication that focuses on the international influence of Group 4.

The first magazine notes the opening in Hungary of a security division and the dramatic changes and opportunities for commercial expansion arising from the fall of the Iron Curtain (Figure 10.3). Group 4 is noted as becoming the first Western security company to operate in Hungary. The division opened with 350 employees serving government and commercial establishments (Figure 10.4). In addition to Hungary, the magazine notes the opening of a branch in Czechoslovakia, and other Eastern European nations at the request of "newly-elected governments who need practical assistance in their efforts to modernize and demilitarize their industrial security service."

In addition, the magazine announced that Group 4 would be forming a new division to service custodial or prison correction-related services

FIGURE 10.3 Then Chairman Jørgen (far right) and Hungarian colleagues are shown one of the military establishments, previously occupied by Soviet troops, to be protected by Group 4.

FIGURE 10.4 Jørgen (right) and Gabor Majtenyi, Director of the Ministry of Finance, congratulate each other on the signing of the Hungarian Joint Venture.

as a joint venture with American company Carter Goble Associates, to be called Group 4 International Correction Services BV. The group was said to be seeking contracts in the United States, Australia, and Europe, initially, and eventually in other parts of the world:

> Group 4's first interest in custodial work was announced three years ago when our UK operating company, Group 4 Total Security, joined forces with Tarmac Construction to form a consortium capable of designing and building prisons, following government indications that it was prepared to put such work out to private enterprise. Until then, the British government Property Services Agency (PSA) had been totally responsible for all prison construction.

Additional services in the sector were to include prisoner transport.[23]

The Group 4 magazine's third issue, published later in 1991, notes that the company was operating in 31 countries, "with openings in India and additionally in South America through joint ventures in Argentina, Chile, Brazil and Uruguay, where industrial development is occurring at a very fast rate." The company noted the visit to the Worcestershire, England, headquarters of several prominent Indian executives, welcomed by David Hudson, managing director of Group 4 Securitas Hindustan.

Another article announced, "in our search for suitable marketing opportunities we learned of the British Steel Challenge roundthe-world yacht race and decided very quickly that sponsorship of this marvelous event would be ideal for Group 4."[24]

The operation in India was highly successful from the start. Sixteen embassies, including the American embassy, which alone required a guarding force of 500, were being protected in India by Group 4 Securitas Hindustan. The guard force of the division reached a total of 1,400 within several years. David Hudson, managing director, said,

> We inherited 550 guards—over 600 if you include the part-timers—and we immediately began a program of training to ensure they were equipped to serve as first line of defense for the US embassy, its warehouses, offices and diplomatic residences, of which there are over 130, all scattered around New Delhi and its surrounding areas.[25]
>
> (Figure 10.5)

The growth of Group 4 would continue through expansion in many countries, and then with major mergers and acquisitions. During the 1990s—considered the golden age of security service—JPS continued to

FIGURE 10.5 Pictured here, after the Group 4 signing, are (left to right), Regional Security Office Frank E. Juni, Managing Director David Hudson, the then U.S. Ambassador to India, and Administrative Counselors Nick Ackerman and Cristobal Orozco.

expand Group 4 across the globe. Following is a summary of its global expansion.

1991 Group 4 acquires businesses in Belgium and Turkey
1993 Group 4 acquires businesses in Austria and Canada
1994 Group 4 establishes operations in the United Arab Emirates and the Ukraine, and all activities in Spain are sold to Securitas AB
1996 Group 4 starts activities in Bangladesh; Group 4 begins a joint venture with British Gas to provide meter-reading services in the UK and establishes AccuRead
1998 Group 4 starts activities in Bangladesh[26]

A Key Sponsorship

JPS was an avid supporter of yacht racing and, as noted earlier, began a sailing sponsorship through Sir Chay Blyth's British Steel Challenge in 1992. A writer for *Yachting World* documented that "Group 4 was teamed with an up-and-coming former fireman, Mike Golding." After that first race,

> Group 4 continued their sponsorship for another four years. Golding went on to win the 1996 race convincingly and the association ignited in Philip-Sørensen an enduring passion for sailing and the teamwork required by it. [...] [Later,] Group 4 bought the Challenge yacht Golding had raced and funded him for a successful attempt to break Chay Blyth's 'wrong way' solo circumnavigation. [...] Jørgen Philip-Sørensen also solely owned Mike Golding Yacht Racing and oversaw the running of the sailing business. He had many other business interests, including owning Danish Yachts in Skagen.[27]

Integrating Security and Technology

By 1992, Group 4 was heading a £400 million empire. When not traveling to more than 31 countries in which the company had subsidiaries, JPS could be found at the Group 4 Learning Center in the Cotswolds. "It has the air of a retreat, but at some point in their career, guard or manager, each member of Group 4's staff, and indeed many of their customers, will spend time here, probably at the training center."[28]

JPS was also an early proponent of integrating security with technology. He reported that "Group 4 is no longer simply a guarding company. It has developed its expertise in complementary elements of this service, combining manpower with high technology in a number of ways." He believed early on that a guarding business owned in isolation will never succeed.[29] With the introduction of System 4 International BV, the company began to enable integrated services for their customers. The systems included design and installation of surveillance equipment, electronic time recording systems, and magnetic card access devices, as well as an expansion of alarm systems and alarm response.[30]

Over the next 12 years the business systems went through several phases of increasing sophistication. The initial phase consisted of stand-alone alarm systems. This led to the development of larger systems with control center connectivity, then to networked and integrated devices with single control interface, and then to fully integrated electronic security systems and devices providing a package of building management solutions.[31] By 2004, the Security Systems component of Group 4 Securicor security business was 13 percent or approximately $572 million of the group's total turnover reported as DKK 27,612 million ($4.4 Billion). Manned security was 78 percent of turnover and cash services 8 percent.[32]

FACING OBSTACLES

Correction system security work would prove to be controversial for G4S. From the start, problems were reported with these services in various locations, resulting in reputational issues for the company.

In 1993, Group 4 was seriously embarrassed when, in a two-month period, eight prisoners escaped from a prison transport service run by the company. One prisoner leapt from the dock of a Derbyshire court, where he was facing burglary charges. Two others slipped out of vans, and another on burglary charges was mistakenly released by guards who did not know how the bail system worked. In Australia, Group 4 Securitas operated the Mount Gambier jail and Port Phillip Prison. There were a number of suicides shortly after Group 4 took over. A jury involved in an inquest for a prisoner being remanded in transit ruled that if the prisoner had been given medical treatment, he would have almost certainly survived. After the verdict, the family started civil proceedings against Group 4, and the suit was settled out of court. A judge in another incident issued a punitive ruling to Group 4 after delays in getting prisoners to court caused the halt of a major criminal trial. Issues like these prompted many years of public debate over privatizing the corrections system.[33]

Additional issues in England occurred when in March 2000, six Romanian immigrants escaped from a Group 4-run holding center in Cambridgeshire, with 12 additional asylum seekers escaping again in 2003 by scaling a perimeter fence. Three prisoners also escaped from a courthouse in October 2001 after attacking Group 4 security officers and locking them in a cell. In December 2001, a vehicle transferring prisoners from Cambridge to a Bedford prison crashed, resulting in the escape of a 20-year-old who later gave himself up. Despite the negative press, a Group 4 spokesperson claimed that they had reduced by 82 percent the number of escapes compared with when the police and government prison officials undertook the service and that the company conducted more than six million movements successfully and without incident.[34]

MAJOR MERGERS AND ACQUISITIONS

In May 2000, Falck acquired Group 4 Securitas (International) for 8.75 billion Danish crowns ($1.07 billion), creating the world's second-largest provider of security services. Falck offered 7.74 million of its own shares to buy privately held Group 4 Securitas from Jørgen Philip-Sørensen, who afterward would own 37.5 percent of Falck.[35] The acquisition resulted in JPS becoming chairman of Group 4 Falck.

Two years later, in March 2002, Group 4 Falck acquired U.S.-based Wackenhut Corp.[36] With the acquisition, Group 4 Falck attained a strong position in the U.S. market but picked up additional prison security business, which it would soon divest.

After the subsequent acquisition of Securicor in July 2004, Group 4 Securicor (G4S) became the world's largest security company. JPS would remain as chairman of G4S until his retirement in 2006, although his original retirement date had been set for September 2005. Soon after Group 4 acquired Securicor, it was agreed by the board of directors of G4S that Lars Nørby Johansen would step down as chief executive and leave the board after the annual general meeting on June 30, 2005, and that JPS would remain as chairman until June 30, 2006.[37] The relationship between JPS and Lars Nørby-Johannsen (see Chapter 11) has been the subject of much speculation, and what was once a close business relationship between the legends ended with the replacement of Johansen at G4S.

LEGACY

JPS was described by colleagues as a remarkable businessman and an inspirational leader. He was a proponent of greater regulation in the security industry. In 1971, he "initiated the campaign for licensing of the UK private security industry. His ambition was realized with the Royal Assent of the Private Security Bill in 2001." He was also

a great supporter of many charities including Save The Children, The Foundation for Liver Research, the European Centre for

Allergy Research and was a founder member of the Nelson Mandela Children's Fund; and in 2000, he was awarded a CBE (Commander of the Order of the British Empire) for services to the private security industry and in 2008 he received the Knight of the Danish Flag from Queen Margrethe II of Denmark.[38]

Despite the reputational risks that JPS faced as he ventured into far-flung countries and through the operations in private prisons that came with bad press, his personality belied any inside turmoil that may have resulted from these activities.

A source who requested anonymity told the authors that JPS was attentive to all aspects of the business. He was numbers-focused and required managers to utilize a dashboard which helped them tailor their reporting to include the details he wanted to know in a concise manner. He had an intense business focus and would carry cash-in-transit boxes containing detailed information on the business for each country he was visiting and which he used to conduct meetings in each of the visited locations (Figure 10.6). But he measured the stature of the company by the number of employees and was cognizant that the effects of his decisions weighed heavily on the employees. Once guidelines were established, he would allow managers to run their enterprises within their respective jurisdiction of the G4 empire. He was an enabler who empowered employees. He was a natural communicator, able and eager and enjoying opportunities to speak with employees and people at all levels.

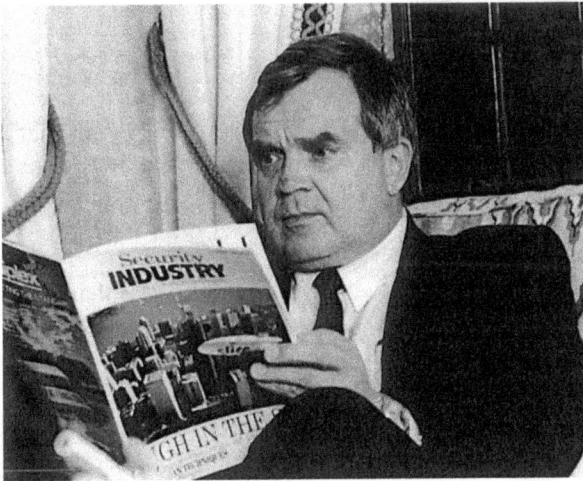

FIGURE 10.6   Jørgen taking a moment to read a security publication and keep abreast of the latest developments in the industry.

FIGURE 10.7 Jørgen (right) presenting the certificates at the first joint training course for IMS and Group 4 supervisors in Belgium.

JPS established the management development program at Farncombe and in Belgium. Managers were taught how to implement and manage service level agreements (Figure 10.7). One such manager who achieved remarkable success was David Hudson, who, as mentioned earlier, directed operations in India. Hudson grew that operation into one that employed more than 130,000 security officers.

Memorial Service Family Address by Mark Philip-Sørensen

There is no greater description of the legacy of JPS than that which was given by his son Mark at JPS's memorial service. It is clear that Mark and his siblings had a great respect, admiration, and love for his father. In Mark's words:

> My father was a great lover of jazz and before I share my words with you, I would like to read some lyrics of song sung by Louis Armstrong which we all listened to together with him on his last day.
>
> (Mark then read aloud the lyrics to "Dream a Little Dream of Me.")

Clear blue skies, birds tweeting, Louis Armstrong playing and a Swiss train tooting. These are the last memories we have, of being with our father.

In those last few hours everything was peaceful and perfect. He couldn't have planned a better day to leave us. In fact ... it was a fantastic day.

Nils Jørgen Philip Sørensen was a remarkable man. He was a husband, a father, and a grandfather. He was an entrepreneur, a leader, and a friend. Nothing can replace him.

Well ... maybe ... apart from the carrying of a leather bag, the sound of a glass of whisky with ice chinking, the smell of a Cohiba cigar, and the love of a toy plane!

Born in 1938 to Eric and Britta as the eldest son, he was a naughty boy at the beginning but soon grew to become a natural leader. Chanting those famous Securitas words vigilance, integrity, and helpfulness. And from this little boy with blue eyes and blond hair and some may say a sneaky, inquisitive but gentle smile.

He has achieved, he has seen, and he has done things, that many of us can only dream of.

Throughout his work with G4S, Ecover, and many other companies under his guidance, he has met all types of people from all over the world. "You may have only spent a few minutes with my father but as with everyone he would leave a permanent impression of inspiration for them to build business or career on. This is a gift which is truly unique."

On November 3, 2006, JPS was awarded an honorary MA degree from the University of Worcester in recognition of his contribution to the West Midlands economy. This was one award he was very proud of.

The number of people here today and the letters we have received is a clear demonstration that JPS did succeed at school and he did understand **PEOPLE.**

On visiting him in Switzerland before Christmas I had the opportunity to discuss a few things with him. These were:

1. that he needed to set his sights low each day and
2. that there was no room for heroes.

On this memorable occasion he agreed that it would be a good idea to take on board these two points. Although I feel that this helped him, looking back now I feel that even THIS must have been a great challenge for him. Why, because he always set his sights high and he was and **still IS** a hero to all of us today.

During those last few weeks in the Clinique Genolier my sisters, Susse and I noticed that he had been using his signature smile to its maximum effect. [...] Even though he was there for a relatively short period of time I know that they had great loyalty towards him and held him very close to their hearts. This is a testament to his endearing personality.

He was a confident man and very rarely lost for words. Always able to do an impromptu speech which would be memorable, and touching, or say a few wise words during a meeting, dinner or party. [...] We will never forget that he had a great love of England and a fondness for everything British. No more so than the love of his Farncombe home and Estate where as a large family we had many memorable Easter BBQs and Christmas Carols.

There was a time, when they used to say, that behind every great man, there had to be a great woman, but in our father's case I believe there were three. Three women who he respected and loved greatly.

There was his mother, Britta, who **GAVE** him his sense of fun, love of family gatherings and, I think, taught him to embrace everything expensive and glamorous.

Then there was our mother, Ingrid, who in those early Group 4 days, stood by and supported him while she was bringing up my sisters and myself.

And finally there is Susse who supported him on his long travels abroad, and who brought him closer to us **AGAIN** and **CARED** for him over the last 12 years. [...]

Was it Philip or Jørgen, Mr. Sørensen or JPS even I am not sure, but one thing I am sure of is that when he answered the phone, he would say those words...

"Sørensen here!"[39]

NOTES

1 "About Us: History," accessed March 14, 2022, https://www.security-ligue.org/about-us/history

2 G4S, *Annual Report 2005*, 2006, 4, 6, 44.

3 Waldemar Schmidt, "Memorial Information: Nils Jørgen Philip-Sørensen," http://www.jpsmemorial.co.uk/journal/2010/2/3/tribute-by-waldemar-schmidt-english-danish. html

4 "Still Sore." Forbes, April 1, 2022. https://www.forbes.com/global/2002/0401/024sidebar.html

5 Waldemar Schmidt, 2010, *The Philip-Sørensen Family's unnoticed influence on the global security services industry* [PowerPoint presentation].

6 "About Erik Philip-Sørensen." accessed September 24, 2022, https://www.epss.se/om-erik-philip-Sørensen/

7 "Still Sore."

8 "About Erik Philip-Sørensen."

9 "Still Sore."

10 "Erik Philip-Sørensen (1909-2001)." accessed September 24, 2022, https://www.loomis.com/en/about-loomis/history/founder-erik-philip-Sørensen

11 "Jørgen Philip-Sørensen." Obituary, *The Times*, February 19, 2010. http://www.jpsmemorial.co.uk/the-times-obituary/

12 "Commencement Speech at Dean Close School, 26 May 2007." http://www.jpsmemorial.co.uk/dean-close-commemoration-2007/

13 *Group 4 International Magazine*, January 1992.

14 "Jørgen Philip-Sørensen." Obituary.

15 "Jørgen Philip-Sørensen." Obituary.

16 Roy Stemman, "Celebrating an Impressive Career." *G4S International*, June 2006. http://www.jpsmemorial.co.uk/jps-g4s-retirement-article/

17 Roy Stemman, "Celebrating an Impressive Career."

18 Roy Stemman, "Celebrating an Impressive Career."

19 Paul Conroy, "The New Guard." *The Age*, March 27, 1998. https://www.theage.com.au/

20 "Erik Philip-Sørensen (1909–2001)."

21 "Our History." https://www.securitas.com/en/about-us/our-history/the-1980s-and-1990s/

22 "Still Sore."

23 *Group 4 International Magazine*, January 1991.

24 *Group 4 International Magazine*, August 1991.

25 *Group 4 International Magazine*, January 1992.

26 "G4S History." accessed April 15, 2022, https://www.g4s.com/who-we-are/our-history

27 Elaine Bunting, "Farewell to a Great Sailing Fan." Yachting World. (January 19, 2010). https://www.yachtingworld.com/blogs/elaine-bunting/farewell-to-a-great-sailing-fan-9361

28 *Group 4 International Magazine*, January 1992.

29 *Group 4 International Magazine*, January 1992.

30 *Group 4 International Magazine*, May 1992, 17–18.

31 G4S, *Annual Report 2004*, 2005, 18. https://www.g4s.com/-/media/g4s/global/files/annual-reports/ara_2004.ashx

32 G4S, *Listing Particulars on the Proposed Merger of the Security Business of Group 4 Falck a/S with Securicor PLC*, June 2004, https://www.g4s.com/-/media/g4s/corporate/files/financial-presentations/fa-040604-listing_particulars_final_document.ashx

33 Paul Conroy, "The New Guard."

34 Rebecca Allison, "G4: A History of Blunders." *The Guardian*, August 15, 2003. https://www.theguardian.com/uk/2003/aug/15/immigration.immigrationandpublicservices

35 "Falck Buys $1.1B Group 4." *CNN Money*, May 2, 2000, https://money.cnn.com/2000/05/02/europe/falck/

36 The Wackenhut Corp. *Proxy Statement and Notice of Special Meeting to Approve and Adopt Merger Agreement*, April 9, 2002. https://www.sec.gov/Archives/edgar/data/104030/000095014402003675/g74655ddefm14a.htm#011

37 G4S, *Annual Report 2004*, 2005.
38 "Tributes Paid to Pioneer of the Security Industry." *Evesham Journal*, January 28, 2010. https://www.eveshamjournal.co.uk/news/4877338.tributes-paid-to-pioneer-of-the-security-industry/
39 "Family Address Given on 26 February, 2010 in Worcester, UK." http://www.jpsmemorial.co.uk/address-mark-philip-Sørensen/

CHAPTER 11

Lars Nørby Johansen
Gaining Trust through Solutions

Lars Nørby Johansen (Lars) is a legend in the security services industry for his dynamic leadership: first at the security service division of Danish fire safety, rescue, and assistance company Falck (Falcon) A/S, and then at successor security companies. Lars was chief executive officer of Falck Redningskorps (Rescue Corps) A/S and Falck Holding A/S beginning in 1988, served as president and chief executive officer of Group 4 Falck A/S from June 2000 to May 2004, and was president and chief executive officer of Group 4 Securicor from May 2004 to June 30, 2005.[1]

During his career as a security executive, Lars transformed Falck into a global security service power. Lars oversaw Falck's masterful strategy and execution. He directed Falck's acquisition of ISS Securitas as a platform security company; listed Falck on the Copenhagen Exchange to raise capital; and, after expanding in Europe, merged Falck with Group 4, acquired U.S.-based Securitas, and then acquired London-based Securicor.

By 2005, Group 4 Securicor was competing with Securitas as the world's largest security company, operating in over 100 countries, with over 360,000 employees, with global revenues of approximately $5.5 billion.[2]

When Group 4 Falck and Securicor merged in 2004, the Falck rescue company was demerged from the security group.[3] Lars resigned from Group 4 Securicor effective June 30, 2005 but remained chairman of Falck until 2014. Two years after he resigned from Group 4 Securicor, the company was renamed G4S, and remained variably the world's largest or second largest global security services company until it was acquired in 2021 by Allied Universal.

EARLY LIFE

Lars Nørby Johansen was born on August 16, 1949, in Nyborg, Denmark, to Vita Nørby and Jørgen Johansen. Jørgen owned a grocery store that during Lars' childhood was the third largest in the city. During

DOI: 10.4324/9781003285564-16

his childhood, his mother stayed at home, helped in the store, and cared for Lars and his older sister. Lars described his father as cautious and financially restrained. In contrast, he spoke of his mother as being inquisitive and energetic, pursuing a variety of interests such as languages and culture. Lars took after his mother. The family was not wealthy but Lars enjoyed a "light and playful childhood." Reading formed an important component of Lars' life, and when he was 14, he was recommended by his school to be a book setter at the local library, as he was the best student. Reading opened his mind to a world he had previously not known as a carefree youth mostly interested in playing outdoors with his friends.[4]

As a youth, Lars always "loved red fire engines, became a teacher, and then made his dream come true by heading Falck, a company that ran a fire service." He was a brilliant student who excelled in Latin and ancient Greek history. He had an early interest in sociopolitical affairs and took part in demonstrations against apartheid and the Vietnam War.[5]

From 1974 to 1983, Lars worked as an associate professor in social sciences at the University of Odense (now University of Southern Denmark) and at Harvard as a guest lecturer. He earned a Master of Science in Economics and Management from Aarhus University in 1983, but left teaching and research to pursue a career in business.[6] He became disillusioned with what he came to believe was the elitist nature of the university life, and after years as a lecturer and assistant professor, he left his family in Odense to go to Copenhagen to change careers. He would find the change engaging and a means for self-discovery.

LEAVING ACADEMIA FOR THE PRIVATE SECTOR

Not long after arriving in Copenhagen in 1983, Lars became a management consultant for the Danish education academy Denmark's Forvaltningshøjskole (School of Management); later he worked as deputy chief executive at Assurandør-Societetet (now the Danish Insurance Academy), from 1985 to 1986.[7]

While his job at the management school was a teaching role, it was no longer lecturing. He was engaging with business people on practical situations. His first "real boss job" began at the insurance academy, where he was responsible for leading employees in getting member insurance companies to realize more value from their membership. The new job taught him how to be responsible for employees; it also showed him that authority lay not in being a dictator but rather in getting people to do what you want them to do because they believe that what you say is right. "Giving orders," he said, "is okay if you're putting out a fire, but in day-to-day contexts sticking out commands won't do, and nothing good will come of it." Lars stated that business life taught him lessons in leadership; namely, to explore how you act in relation to others as a leader and how you are viewed by others. It taught him how people deal with situations, and how to push yourself and others to get things done.[8]

Next, Lars began working as an executive heading up claims management at Baltica, Denmark's largest insurance company. Peter Christofferson, the chief executive officer at Baltica, introduced Lars to the Falck Company which was looking for an executive manager. Christoffersen saw great potential in Lars due to his charisma and ability to impose structure and make things happen. Within two years Lars was the top managing director at Falck. At the time, Falck was in financial distress; its family ownership sold the firm to Baltica in 1988.[9]

Lars said that he

joined an insurance company, worked there for two years and then was given the chance of heading the insurance company or taking charge of a company that owned and ran privatized fire brigade services in Scandinavia. I always had a childhood dream of being a firefighter and owning a fire engine. So there was never a contest—I went to join that company (Falck).[10]

Lars' fast ascent at Falck was a prelude to big changes at the company, and there would be great rewards—but these came with a personal price.

GROWING FALCK'S SECURITY COMPANY

In 1991, Baltica sold 55 percent of its shares in Falck.[11] Baltica's plan to use Falck's customer base to sell insurance backfired, when potential insurance subscribers left Falck after being solicited by Baltica. In addition, the ambulance business was losing share to rival companies and profits were weak. To counter competition from rivals Baltica sold a majority interest in Falck, keeping a 45 percent stake for themselves. Lars had to restructure Falck by closing call centers and laying off people. He raised prices to allow the company to make a profit, and learned then that profit was necessary to ensure a company's continued viability and existence. Initially viewed with great hesitancy by Falck staff, Lars became more of a hero for helping to save Falck.[12]

Under Baltica, Falck had acquired several alarm companies as part of a strategy to offer safety and insurance in Denmark and other Nordic countries. In 1993 Falck was just the third largest security company in Denmark, behind the leader ISS Securitas and Securitas AB of Sweden (Figure 11.1).

When ISS decided to sell their security division to repurpose their company, Falck outbid Securitas for the business. The acquisition of

FIGURE 11.1   A photo of Lars Nørby Johansen from the early 1990s while employed by Falck.

(Photo provided and used courtesy of Lars Nørby Johansen.)

ISS Securitas was the platform Falck used as a springboard to expand Falck's small security component into a security leader. It was part of a well-planned move that Lars and his senior management team had carefully formulated, to expand first in Europe and then globally.[13] Waldemar Schmidt, the former CEO of ISS, told the authors in a personal interview that revenues at ISS Security were about $50 million at the time. Lars told the authors that Falck saw an opportunity for growth in the security business. Their work in the fire safety industry, along with having a small presence in the security industry, gave them confidence that they could compete with Securitas. He said the ISS Securitas acquisition saved them much time as Falck right away had a strong European presence. There were ties between Falck and ISS Securitas as Danish companies, and the shared cultural values assisted with the integration.

GOING PUBLIC AND ACCELERATING ACQUISITIONS

In 1995, Falck was listed to trade as a public company on the Copenhagen Stock Exchange. Going public enabled Falck to obtain capital needed to fuel additional acquisitions and expand. Falck soon acquired security businesses in Germany, Poland, Estonia, and Lithuania.[14]

By 1999, Falck was a major European security provider operating in the contract security guard, alarm, and cash-in-transit businesses. Global security leader Securitas reported that Falck was one of its largest competitors in Europe. In addition to Falck's leading position in Denmark, it was now a major competitor for Securitas in guard, alarm, and cash-in-transit services in Sweden, Finland, Norway, and Poland.[15]

In 1999, Falck acquired NVD, the largest security company in the Netherlands.[16] By 2000, Falck was operating in nine countries and was Europe's second largest security company with approximately 31,000 employees, and revenues of 7.2 billion DKK (Danish Crowns) or approximately $880 million.[17]

TWO LEGENDS MERGE THEIR FIRMS

In May 2000, Falck acquired rival Group 4 Securitas for 8.75 billion DKK ($1.07 billion), creating the world's second-largest provider of security services. As a result, Group 4's owner, Jørgen Philip-Sørensen (Chapter 9) would own 37.5 percent of Falck. The combined company, Group 4 Falck, would trade as a public company listed on the Copenhagen Exchange. Group 4 Falck soon had 115,000 employees in 50 countries, with a strong position in Europe and a global reach that included the Middle East and India. Group 4 Falck revenues would eventually exceed 15 million DKK or approximately $1.8 billion. With the merger, Group 4 Falck obtained critical mass and high density in its operations, creating a unique platform, and strengthening the full-scale security service concept offered by both companies.[18]

Lars told the authors that the merger was very well received by investors. Falck's leadership had discussions for several years with Jørgen Philip-Sørensen. Both strong businessmen, Lars and Jørgen Philip-Sørensen joined forces, with Lars appointed chief executive officer and Sørensen elected chairman of the board. Lars said that Sørensen was warmly welcomed back to Denmark when the company headquartered in Copenhagen. Regarding the merger of Group 4 with Falck, Waldemar Schmidt told the authors that Lars wanted to build a large company, and for Sørensen, it was a way to monetize the private Group 4. Lars told the authors that the Group 4 Falck merger went very smoothly and that in addition to enlarging Falck, it had benefited Sørensen to have Group 4 Falck now listed as a public company.

While the older Falck rescue and assistance businesses struggled to keep up, Lars had built up Falck's widespread security business. It had only taken Lars seven years from the time of the ISS acquisition to transform the Falck company into a global security services leader.[19]

Lars said that while the plan had been to grow the fire safety business along with the security business, it became apparent that the security business was able to grow faster and that there were no measurable gains by tying the services of the companies together. Additional acquisitions in the security service segment soon followed, including a major acquisition that allowed Falck to enter the U.S. market.

GROUP 4 FALCK ACQUIRES WACKENHUT CORPORATION

In March 2002, Group 4 Falck agreed to buy The Wackenhut Corporation for $573 million so Falck could expand in the United States. Wackenhut had more than 40,000 employees and demand for security guards was rising after the September 11, 2001, attacks. With a market of $14 billion for security in the United States, Falck and its bigger rival Securitas (which had bought U.S.-based Pinkerton's and Burns over the preceding three years) expected the U.S. market to grow faster than other markets (Figure 11.2).[20]

FIGURE 11.2 (Left to right) Lars Johansen, Gary A. Sanders—the President of the Securities Service Division and Senior VP of North American Operations—and then U.S. Secretary of State Colin Powell join in celebrating the acquisition of Wackenhut in Washington D.C. in 2002.

(Photo provided and used courtesy of Lars Johansen.)

Lars said that he had visited the Miami area several times and developed a warm and friendly relationship with the Wackenhut family. He told George and Ruth Wackenhut that "the Vikings had returned to the U.S." Lars said the reaction of investors to this acquisition was not as positive as with the Group 4 merger, and there was some criticism due to the cultural differences. Yet while the cultures of the companies were quite different, the Europeans viewed Wackenhut as a prize due to its industry leadership position in the United States. Because of the distinct company cultures, Lars said that the integration process entailed having Wackenhut continue to be operated in the United States much as it had before. However, Wackenhut's corrections business would be spun off (Figure 11.3).

Following The Wackenhut Corporation purchase, Falck sold a 57 percent stake that it owned in Wackenhut Corrections Corporation (WCC) to executives of WCC for $132 million. WCC would continue as a separately listed public company.[21] The sale removed any conflicts of interest arising from Group 4 Falck's separate prison management business

FIGURE 11.3   On board the tall ship *Danmark*. Picture (left to right) are Gary A. Sanders, COO Alan Berstein, Lars Nørby Johansen, the ship's captain, and Jørgen Philip-Sørensen.

(Photo provided and used courtesy of Lars Johansen.)

overseas. In May 2004 Group 4 Falck would also sell its own detention and prisons business, Global Solutions Limited (GSL)—for £208 million—to London-based venture capitalists Engelfield Capital and Electra Partners Europe. Selling GSL was a condition set by the European Union commissioner for competition to get approval for the £1.7 billion merger of Group 4 and Falck.[22]

GROUP 4 FALCK ACQUIRES SECURICOR, FALCK IS DEMERGED

In 2004, Lars concluded merger talks with British rival Securicor Security Services and announced that Group 4 Falck and Securicor would join forces in the last quarter of 2004. The combined group was proposed to create a global security operation with

> turnover approaching £3.8 billion and an estimated market value of more than £1.6 billion. Johansen had been conducting talks with his counterpart at Securicor—Nick Buckles—for the past 12 weeks, with an official announcement confirming the merger presented to the London Stock Exchange on February 24th.[23]

Requiring anti-trust approval, in May of 2004 the Commission on European Committees issued a statement of non-opposition to the merger of Group 4 Falck with Securicor, subject to some agreed upon divestitures. The report noted that the Group 4 Falck was the second largest global security services provider with operations in more than 85 countries around the world. Group 4 Falck was now organized in three primary business divisions: security services (guarding and alarm services); rescue and safety services; and global solutions, including justice services (such as prisoner transportation and immigration services). Securicor was described as an English company listed on the London Stock Exchange operating in three principal areas: guarding and alarm services, cash services, and justice services. In 2003 the pro forma worldwide turnover of Group 4 Falck was approximately 3.7 million euros (merger assets only) and Securicor 1.97 million euros. Prior to the merger, Group 4 Falck was to be demerged into two new separate companies: Falck A/S and Group 4 A/S. The global solutions and the fire safety and rescue services were transferred to Falck A/S; and the guarding, alarm, and cash services business transferred to Group 4. Group 4 would continue to trade publicly on the Copenhagen Stock Exchange. Lars would lead the integration process, and Nick Buckles, chief executive officer of Securicor, was to be responsible for head office integration. Buckles would succeed Lars as chief executive "at the appropriate time."[24] That time would come soon.

The shares of Group 4 Securicor were scheduled to close in July 2004, with trading to be on both the Copenhagen and London Stock Exchanges. The Skagen 2004 Trust (Jørgen Philip-Sørensen's family trust) would own 13.60 percent of the company, making the Trust the largest shareholder of the company. The head office would be near Gatwick Airport in England, and the headquarters office of Group 4 Securicor in Copenhagen would be closed once the integration was complete.[25]

Lars said that the merger of Group 4 Securitas with Securicor was part of a vision to be a world leader in global security, and that there was a strong strategic rationale behind it. Securicor had focused on security over the last few years, having previously operated in other areas, including communications; Group 4 Falck had also increasingly been focused on security services. The merger was expected to enable synergies through the consolidation of businesses in key European and North American markets, including the UK, France, and the Netherlands, and, to a certain extent, Canada, Hong Kong, and South Africa. In other markets the merger was to enable an increase and strengthening of its position by obtaining critical mass and density. Lars noted that

> Most importantly, the merger strengthened our position in developing markets, which is very important for us because the growth in those markets is very strong: it's far above average; and so is the margin. In fact, Securicor and Group 4 Falck were two of the biggest companies in those markets and by merging the two groups we are much stronger [...] and in terms of our electronic security offering, it's very important for us, partly for the business in its own right, as well as in combination with our guarding operation, to be able to offer combined packages to our customers.[26]

Lars told us that with the merger they had succeeded in attaining a size comparable to Securitas.

Vision and plans aside, the merger complicated Lars' continued hold on the company. Securicor

> had something of a rocky ride on the financial markets during the last three years, its prospects taking a significant hit when its American aviation security subsidiary Argenbright Security was sued (the company having been responsible for security screening on two of the fateful flights that hit the World Trade Centre during the terror attacks perpetrated on September 11). Nick Buckles had reassured London leaders that Securicor had more than £1 billion of insurance coverage in place, but Securicor also was reported to have been experiencing difficulties with its German operations.[27]

LARS EXITS GROUP 4 SECURICOR

Despite having big plans for the newly formed company and having negotiated the acquisition of Securicor, what ensued was the early departure by
Lars from the company, effective June 30, 2005. Jørgen Philip-Sørensen, in
the chairman's column of Group 4 Securicor's 2004 Annual Report, wrote:

> [T]he board has determined that with the businesses perform-
> ing well, integration on track and the new management team
> working together successfully, Nick Buckles will assume the chief
> executive role this summer. It has [...] been agreed that Lars
> Nørby Johansen will step down as chief executive and leave the
> board after the annual general meeting on June 30. Lars was one
> of the main architects of Group 4 Securicor. I have, as chairman,
> found him a most inspiring and visionary chief executive and it
> has been a privilege to work with him. His creativity is outstand-
> ing and is envied by many. He leaves the company in a healthy
> and prosperous position and we wish him continued success in
> whatever he decides to do in the future.

Lars in his column wrote:

> "When I look back, I am proud of what we have achieved in a
> very short space of time through the commitment and hard work
> of everyone in the organization Group 4 Securicor had by now
> [...] I've enjoyed my time in the security industry and specifically
> as CEO of Group 4 Falck and then Group 4 Securicor. I know
> that the business is in safe hands and wish my colleagues all the
> very best for the future." The company reported having 360,000
> employees operating in over 100 countries.[28]

His forward-looking vision for Group 4 Securicor was never fully realized. Lars wanted to "lead a company that would act in a responsible
manner, and behave as a market leader should behave." He credited high
rates of customer retention at Group 4 Falck to the company paying well,
and respecting trade unions, with which they had a regular dialogue. He
believed as a large employer, the company could offer a wide range of
careers which would be beneficial in the longer term. He said:

> Our clients have increasingly become more global in their out-
> look. We must feed the needs of those customers. You cannot do
> so by selling "standard" products. No two countries are identi-
> cal, and no two industries are the same, which is why we must

be flexible enough to provide tailor-made security solutions combining different components [...] The development of integrating
systems and software that will enable our customers to combine
manned security with electronic alternatives is the future.[29]

That strategy called for a 6 percent organic growth per year, additional
growth through acquisitions, and a strengthening of the company position
in each of its markets: manned security, security systems, cash services, and
justice services. The goal was to become the "first choice provider for key
users of integrated security services," to deliver cost synergy targets while
maintaining a focus on day-to-day business performance, and the use of best
business practices. Expansion was to focus on higher-growth countries.[30]

The strategy and growth that was projected was never realized
after Lars' and then Sørensen's departure from the company. Waldemar
Schmidt, who in addition to being former CEO of ISS is also an expert
in corporate governance, told the authors that the decision to acquire
Securicor in the drive for growth was complicated in that Securicor had
a large, cash-intensive cash-in-transit component and lingering issues
that included its acquisition of Argenbright's airport security business.
Schmidt agreed with the authors that the eventual sale of G4S to Allied
Universal was a result of a stagnant stock price, the failure to execute
the strategy, and bad press arising from various incidents over the years.
These included G4S' inability to staff required manpower needs at the
2012 London Olympics, and continuing difficulties with its private
detention services.

There has been much speculation regarding Lars' early departure and
what became of the business relationship between Lars and Sørensen.
After his resignation from G4S, Lars moved back to Copenhagen. He
and Sørensen would subsequently only exchange a few words. Lars said,
"I think he congratulated me when I got married. But otherwise nothing."[31] In our interview Lars spoke well of Sørensen as a leader who
ventured into areas others did not. He said the merger of Group 4 with
Falck was smooth, and that Sørensen had benefited greatly by the listing
of Group 4 Falck as a public company.

For Lars, the exit proved to be something of a relief for him, as
well as an education in and of itself. Lars told us that a benefit of going
through the expansion of Falck's security business throughout the world
was that, once demerged from Group 4, its leaders had learned many
lessons to enable Falck to grow internationally. He was justifiably proud
of his record of growing Falck's security business, and told the authors
that his 16 years as chief executive officer of Falck was a great journey
which resulted in the creation of a lot of value; but the "high moment in
my career was the demerger of Falck."

Lars served as chairman of Falck until 2014. Upon his retirement, he said, "I have been on a fantastic journey with Falck, during which the organization has evolved from a Danish rescue and assistance service provider with 6,000 employees into a global player with operations on six continents."[32]

LEGACY

Within seven years from the time of the ISS Securitas acquisition, Lars had created the world's second largest global security services company. He transformed Falck from a small fire safety and rescue company into a large organization offering security guarding and integrated services, and he did so in a dynamic way. Group 4 Securicor became about as large as Securitas under his leadership, and challenged the global leader in markets around the world.

Nels Pedersen, Director of Group Communications at Group 4 Falck, said that Lars ran a continuously developing, good healthy business on a sound commercial basis while simultaneously retaining the legacy of Falck's founder, Sophus Falck, in aiding people in need and limiting accidents. Lars had "shown a remarkable ability to predict and evaluate general trends in society, in both domestic and international matters" and cultivated a strong network in politics, culture, and the finance industry.[33] Lars was also noted to have been a strong proponent and practitioner of developing and sustaining a positive relationship with unions by working through various committees and councils.[34]

Waldemar Schmidt told the authors that Lars was a brilliant businessman and had a very corporate approach to business. While Jørgen Philip-Sørensen would go from country to country meeting with operations staff and holding meetings with partner companies, "Lars was more inclined to go from country to country meeting with financial people. He is quite brilliant and was a great businessman."

Lars has remained continually active as a board member and advisor to numerous companies and organizations. A partial listing of Lars' nonexecutive chairmanships through the years includes the following:

Chairman of the board of William Demant Holding A/S
Chairman of the board of the Danish Growth Council
Chairman of the board of Copenhagen Airports A/S
Chairman of the board of Codan A/S and its subsidiary (Codan Forsikring A/S)
Chairman of the board of Montana Møbler A/S
Chairman of the board of the Rockwool Foundation
Chairman of the board of the Foundation for Entrepreneurship— Young Enterprise

Chairman of the board of the University of Southern Denmark
Deputy Chairman of the board of Arp-Hansen Hotel Group A/S[35]

Of note, the Foundation for Entrepreneurship was established in 2010 by an inter-ministerial partnership between four ministries, on the basis of the Danish government's overall strategy at that time for education in entrepreneurship. The Danish government "set up the Partnership for innovation and entrepreneurship in education to strengthen and coordinate efforts to integrate innovation and entrepreneurship in education."[36]

Lars' interest in promoting research on corporate and social governance is evident by his involvement with Copenhagen Business School's Center for Corporate Governance (CCG), where he served as chairman of the advisory committee. The CCG is a "virtual center, which brings researchers together from several departments and institutions inside as well as outside of Copenhagen Business School." The overall focus of the center is to deliver timely and relevant research to society, including the business community. It is one of the largest centers of its kind in Europe and aspires to have a world-class research environment.[37]

Earlier in his career, he chaired the Nørby Committee, which was named after him and which, in 2001, proposed the first Danish national corporate governance code. In subsequent years, this was followed "by similar initiatives in all four Nordic countries and, by December 2005, comprehensive corporate governance codes based on the comply-or-explain principle were part of the mandatory listing requirements on all primary exchanges."[38] From the early part of the twenty-first century, corporate governance codes have been the main form of self-regulation in the Nordic countries' private sector.

According to Lars, the art of leading is to draw resources out of people so you gain all the knowledge that is within the organization. He acknowledged that organizations need a hierarchy to support authority and provide support; however, he said, "also I gave it body and substance by handling things my way […] the hierarchy works best where you fill it with a personality and an authority that comes when people view what you are doing is right."[39]

Lars told the authors that he believes

the security industry will continue to grow and thrive as we are living in a turbulent and insecure world. While there are enormous developments on the technology side of the business, people basically just want peace of mind and security is a basic need. I was always struck by the low margins in the security business and I hope that the industry could better reach customers to understand that security is not a basic commodity but a valued service.

FIGURE 11.4 Present-day photo of Lars Nørby Johansen.

(Photo provided and used courtesy of Lars Johansen.)

While Lars' work allowed him to discover things about himself and confirmed his extraordinary ability as a business leader, he also suffered several personal setbacks along the way, including divorce and losing the friendship of some former associates. His greatest happiness, it seems, came during the time when Falck operated as a venerable fire safety, rescue, and assistance firm. His delight in his work at the Falck safety business was evident as his face lit up in our interview whenever it was mentioned, yet he rightfully retains a great deal of pride in having built a global security company, creating value for numerous stakeholders. His ability to gain others' trust and his influence on the business of management and corporate governance will be felt and recognized for generations (Figure 11.4).

NOTES

1 G4S, *Annual Report 2004*, 2005, https://www.g4s.com/-/media/g4s/global/files/annual-reports/ara_2004.ashx

2 G4S, *Annual Report 2004*.

3 Commission of the European Communities, *Merger Procedure Article 6(1)(b) Decision: Group 4 Falk / Securicor*, May 28, 2004, https://ec.europa.eu/competition/mergers/cases/decisions/m3396_en.pdf

4 Kathrine Lilleør, *Life and Management: Lars Nørby Johansen* (Bianco Luno, 2011), 1–18.

5 "How a Childhood Ambition Changed Lars's Life," *This is Money* (February 28, 2004), https://www.thisismoney.co.uk/money/news/article-1513533/How-a-childhood-ambition-changed-Lars-life.html

6 Oticon Foundation, "Changes to the Board of William Demant Holding A/S," news release, February 23, 2017, https://attachment.news.eu.nasdaq.com/a4844bb15dc5931e9a442fed7f9d1b8e8

7   Oticon Foundation, "Changes to the Board of William Demant Holding A/S."
8   Lilleør, *Life and Management: Lars Nørby Johansen*, 20–36.
9   Nils Mulvad, "Unclear Exit from G4S by Two Danish Business People," *Private Security Network*, no. January 10, 2020. https://privatesecurity.network/stories/unclear-exit-from-g4s-by-two-danish-business-people/
10 "How a Childhood Ambition Changed Lars's Life."
11 "G4S History," accessed April 15, 2022, https://www.g4s.com/who-we-are/our-history
12 Lilleør, *Life and Management: Lars Nørby Johansen*.
13 Gordon Adler, Waldemar Schmidt, and Els van Weering, *Winning at Service: Lessons From Service Leaders* (Chichester, UK: John Wiley & Sons Ltd., 2003), 19.
14 "G4S History."
15 Securitas AB, *Annual Report 1999*, Securitas AB (Stockholm, 2000), 19–33.
16 Commission of the European Communities, *Merger Procedure Article 6(1)(b) Decision: Group 4 Falk / Securicor*, 23.
17 Waldemar Schmidt, *Winning at Service: Lessons from Service Leaders*, 23.
18 "Falck Buys $1.1B Group 4," *CNN Money*, May 2, 2000, https://money.cnn.com/2000/05/02/europe/falck/
19 Mulvad, "Unclear Exit from G4S by Two Danish Business People."
20 Bloomberg News, "Expanding in US, Falck Buys Wackenhut Security," *New York Times*, March 9, 2002, https://www.nytimes.com/2002/03/09/business/company-news-expanding-in-us-falck-buys-wackenhut-security.html
21 Wackenhut Corrections Corporation, *Securities Prospectus*, August 6, 2003, 40, https://www.sec.gov/Archives/edgar/data/923796/000095014403009400/g83842sv4.htm
22 Bill MacKeith, "Private Companies That Run Detention Centers in the UK," *Melting Pot Europa*, February 23, 2005, https://www.meltingpot.org/2005/02/private-companies-that-run-detention-centres-in-the-uk/
23 IFSEC Global, "Group 4 Falck Confirms Merger Deal With Securicor Security," March 8, 2004, https://www.ifsecglobal.com/mergers-and-acquisitions/group-4-falck-confirms-merger-deal-with-securicor-security/
24 Commission of the European Communities, *Merger Procedure Article 6(1)(b) Decision: Group 4 Falk/Securicor*.
25 G4S, *Listing Particulars on the Proposed Merger of the Security Business of Group 4 Falck A/S with Securicor Plc*, June 2004, https://www.g4s.com/-/media/g4s/corporate/files/financial-presentations/fa-040604-listing_particulars_final_document.ashx

26 "Lars Johansen—Group 4 Securicor PLC (Interview)," *The Wall Street Transcript*, January 10, 2005, https://www.twst.com/interview/lars-johansen-group-4-securicor-plc

27 IFSEC Global, "Group 4 Falck Confirms Merger Deal With Securicor Security."

28 G4S, *Annual Report 2004*.

29 Brian Sims, "Two's Company," *Building*, March 4, 2005, https://www.building.co.uk/twos-company/3047516.article

30 G4S, *Listing Particulars on the Proposed Merger of the Security Business of Group 4 Falck A/S with Securicor Plc*.

31 Mulvad, "Unclear Exit from G4S by Two Danish business people."

32 "Lars Nørby Johansen to Retire as Falck Chairman and Be Replaced by Thorleif Krarup," *Falck Global*, March 20, 2014, https://www.mynewsdesk.com/falckglobal/news/lars-noerby-johansen-to-retire-as-falck-chairman-and-be-replaced-by-thorleif-krarup-294657

33 Waldemar Schmidt, *Winning at Service: Lessons From Service Leaders*, 93–4.

34 Waldemar Schmidt, *Winning at Service: Lessons From Service Leaders*, 134.

35 "Lars Nørby Johansen to retire as Falck Chairman and be replaced by Thorleif Krarup."

36 "Foundation for Entrepreneurship: History," https://ffefonden.dk/om-fonden/. (Foundation for Entrepreneurship 2022).

37 Copenhagen Business School Center for Corporate Governance, *Annual Report 2017*, 2018.

38 Per Lekvall et al., *The Nordic Model of Corporate Governance* (2014), 39, https://papers.ssrn.com/sol3/papers.cfm?abstract_id=2534331

39 Lilleør, *Life and Management: Lars Nørby Johansen*, 40, 69, 117.

CHAPTER 12

Thomas F. Berglund
Success by Lifting Others

From 1993 until 2007, Thomas Fredrik Berglund was chief executive officer of Sweden-based Securitas AB (Securitas). During this time, the company grew organically and through acquisitions, rapidly expanding first in Europe and then in the United States. Upon acquiring Pinkerton and Burns in 1999 and 2000 respectively, Securitas became the leading security services company in North America and the world. Accounting for currency changes, Securitas sales in 1994, Berglund's first full year as chief executive officer, climbed from 6834 MSEK (Million Swedish Krona),[1] or approximately $900 million, to 60,235 MSEK,[2] or approximately $8.6 billion in his last full year as chief executive officer in 2006.

The company achieved this record of growth in large part by adhering to a model which company management developed under Berglund's leadership and then implemented throughout the organization in a systematic fashion. Key components in the model included the following:

- Employee development and empowerment
- Ensuring all employees internalized the company's values such that they could implement them no matter what role they filled
- Focusing on specialization of services to be provided
- Segmenting customers to better identify and serve their particular needs.

On March 11, 2022, the authors had the pleasure of interviewing Thomas Berglund, an affable man, with a sense of humor and humility. From the start, it was apparent that his wide-ranging curiosity about matters both practical and philosophical, and application of ethical principles in his life and career, mattered more to him than any personal success. Thomas defined success not by his own achievements but by his enabling of others to succeed. He attributed the success of the company not to his own abilities, but to the collective efforts of the executive team, as well as

DOI: 10.4324/9781003285564-17

> We strive to
> keep it simple.
>
> Thomas Berglund

FIGURE 12.1   "We strive to keep it simple." A photo of Thomas Berglund from Securitas's May 2000 Management Bulletin.

(Provided and used courtesy Thomas Berglund and Securitas.)

the front-line security officers and managers at Securitas. He modestly acknowledged that while "the art in business was keeping it simple," there was a lot of hard work behind the company's success (Figure 12.1).

EARLY LIFE AND EDUCATION

Thomas Berglund was born on June 18, 1952, in Stockholm, Sweden, the youngest of four children. His father, Tage, was a line manager in the automotive industry, and his mother Eva, was a homemaker. Thomas said that he grew up in a Christian family, an open-minded family with strong fundamental values. His parents taught him that "life's meaning lay beyond what was good for oneself; it was for what one might do for others." They taught him that when you decide what to do with your life, it should be more about how to contribute to others than yourself. And they taught him the value of being honest, working hard, and making every day count.

Thomas said that "the Ten Commandments are not a bad place to start." In our conversation he expressed concern that young people today are not learning how to relate with one another and are not given the tools to think about the meaning of life, something that is very important to him. He noted that someone once said, "Don't count your days, but make your days count." That quote is attributed to Muhammad Ali.[3]

Thomas noted that he grew up in a dynamic era of the 1950s to the 1970s, during which time the effects of World War II still lingered, and in a period when a lot of people were trying to build a better life for themselves and for society, having felt the effects of that war as well as the Vietnam War. He described the era as one of tremendous growth, opportunity, and change that may only be eclipsed by today's technological revolution.

During his formative years, the family moved in and around the suburbs of Stockholm where he received his early education. He described himself as not a good athlete, but early on he had an interest in politics. As a teenager, he was an idealist and wanted "to change the world." He recalled that in high school, he had "tough discussions about politics, literature and other things" with one of his teachers; he contacted the teacher fifty years later and had a meaningful three-hour discussion with the teacher about life. It was "like we had met a few weeks later rather than fifty years later." Thomas said that that teacher, as well as others, taught him more than just subject matter—they gave him a broad perspective on life. Thomas said that "people today are more and more educated but know less and less about life."

After graduating from high school, Thomas worked in politics for the center-right Liberal Party in Sweden. From the time he was "about twenty-three to twenty-six," he earned a bachelor's degree at the prestigious Stockholm School of Economics. He noted that his education there "gave him a theoretical understanding as to how things worked in business," but he found out that "managers really needed to learn by experience how to think and handle various situations." He observed, "having an education is important for giving you certain tools, but having a broad perspective helps you to be a better manager."

FROM GOVERNMENT SERVICE TO PRIVATE INDUSTRY

Thomas became employed full-time after college by the government when the Liberal Party came to power. He reflected with a chuckle that "when you are young, you know nothing, and they want to employ you in the government." An idealist, he became a bit discouraged with government when he realized it was not so easy to change the world.

Thomas said he worked for the government until he was aged 32. He did "big and small things and became a speech writer for the prime minister, who then became the minister of foreign affairs" (Figure 12.2). His experience in government taught him that while it can do good things for people, a bureaucracy was not always an efficient or the best way to accomplish things. It taught him about how politics worked, and also

FIGURE 12.2 Ola Ullsten, pictured here during his time as Prime Minister of Sweden from October 1978 through October of 1979. Berglund was a speech writer for Ullsten at the time.

how it sometimes didn't work. When the government changed hands to the control of the center left Social Democrat Party, despite an offer to stay Thomas decided to work for a private consultancy, the Swedish Management Group, which was owned by the Swedish Employer's Confederation (SAF).

The SAF advanced free enterprise causes based on their determination that the government could fund services, but that the administration of some services could be served better by private industry. Thomas noted that a popular line of thinking in government was that it could "pay less and get higher quality," but that model did not work well. Informed by his work with the SAF and his experience in government, he observed that this was particularly the case for children's schooling. Looking to start a privately operated preschool, he traveled to the United States to learn more about privatization of services. In October 1983, he took part in the introduction of private prekindergarten schooling through a company named Pysslingen; the name derived from a children's short story collection by Swedish author Astrid Lindgren called Nils Karlsson-Pyssling (translated in English as "Simon Small").

The Swedish suburb of Sollentuna contracted with Pysslingen to operate two childcare centers, to "break the municipal monopoly" on the provision of social services.[4] Thomas said it was jokingly termed by some in Sweden as "Kentucky Fried Children."

Some in Sweden thought private education was for the rich. But Thomas said he enabled privately run education funded by the government to be made equally available and affordable for the poor and the rich.

Despite a ban on grants for independent day care centers, Pysslingen became the first company in Sweden to run independent preschools.

By 1992, independent school reform spurred the creation of many more private schools. In 2011 Pysslingen was one of many schools acquired by AcadeMedia,[5] which is today a publicly traded company with approximately $1.3 billion in revenues, northern Europe's largest education company, and where Thomas is a board member.[6] As Thomas noted, the model of private industry managing publicly funded services has become increasingly used throughout Europe, and he is involved now in running publicly funded healthcare companies that are privately managed.

When Thomas and his colleague were researching how to implement the Pysslingen concept, they met with executives of several service companies to learn management techniques for getting more out of available resources. He learned then that in order to sell your services, "getting better quality by paying less was more than addressing control of the cost side; you must deliver a quality service that will provide value to the buyer."

BERGLUND'S SECURITY INDUSTRY
CAREER AT SECURITAS AB

In 1984, Thomas received an offer to work for Securitas, which had new ownership. The company had deteriorated and, under the current CEO, was pursuing a strategy of providing a broad array of services in Sweden. Thomas said that he and a few others almost quit the company because of their disagreement with leadership about the direction of the company. Rather than the broad-based services approach, they saw that industrial plants and companies needed to have more specific and specialized services provided.

Fortunately, by 1985 the new ownership from Investment AB Latour, and its chairman, Gustaf Douglas, began looking to refocus the business on security rather than be a provider of a broader range of services. It began to shed non-security-related businesses, and to acquire security companies, first in Europe, and then in the United States.[7] A new chief executive officer, Melker Schörling, was appointed in 1987. Thomas said that Schörling was a good teacher and influencer, and that he knew how to manage people—all skills that are vital in the service business.

In 1988, Securitas acquired a major Swedish lock company, ASSA, and from 1989 to 1991, under Schörling's leadership, acquired companies in Norway, Denmark, and Portugal, as well as Hungary. In 1991, the company was listed on the Stockholm Exchange. Additional acquisitions in the next few years expanded operations to France, Switzerland, Austria, Germany, and Spain.[8] Thomas described the security business at the time as being formed around a simple concept of "guards, locks and alarms." These three segments of the security services industry would be expanded going forward.

Thomas's first assignment at Securitas was in the finance department, but Håkan Winberg—who would become the chief financial officer of the company through 2007, as well as Thomas's best friend—remarked to him, "Why don't you go into management since you don't understand finance very much?" It proved to be timely advice, for it was from there on that his career at Securitas really shone. His first assignment in operations was to supervise technical installations in the Stockholm area. He then managed the security guard business for the company. By 1993, after a series of promotions, he was appointed chief executive officer.

Leading Securitas in the Tradition of Integrity, Vigilance, and Helpfulness

Every member of Securitas wears an insignia which contains three red dots, signifying the company's values of Integrity, Vigilance, and Helpfulness. Under the emblem, Securitas "unites individuals in our efforts to do a good job and to develop ourselves and the Company" (Figure 12.3).[9] It was the way Thomas described his career in leadership and management at Securitas. He learned that the building block of good management of a service business was to first understand how to serve the customer. That took learning and an understanding who they were and what they needed. He learned that there were many different types of customers, each of whom would need a certain combination of guard, lock, alarm, or cash handling services.

It is important to Thomas that managers demonstrate active interest in the services and programs their company provides. He learned that good managers cannot be stuck on their own ideas about how things work. He found that it was the security officer, the technician, and the cash handler who could give him the most useful details on how things

FIGURE 12.3   The three red dots of Securitas's logo represent the company's values of integrity, vigilance, and helpfulness.

were going in the business, what worked, and what was involved at the level where services were provided. This type of boots-on-the-ground information provides managers with a world of insight into the customer and their needs, and how the company can improve its relationships with different clients.

He said that once you have knowledge of the customer and how things are provided, a strategy has to be put in place for the best way to organize and deliver service to best meet the needs of the customer. He noted it is in the implementation of the strategy where the hard work really takes place. For one thing, there was no way that the company could manage everything from a central location. What then really becomes important is to have an "understanding of what makes people tick." He said a traditional view of organizing was that you have a boss, then more bosses, then supervisors, and then guards. He felt you need to turn that upside down and enlighten and empower the front-line people. "The boss is still the boss, and has the responsibility, but you can also delegate the authority to the front line." Management can give guidance, but still leave it up to the field staff to execute the work well. Thomas led by the model on which Securitas built its foundation.

The Securitas model is described in the Annual Report of the company in 2000. They noted that as an important player in the market, Securitas assumed responsibility for setting high standards, performing professionally, to achieve higher customer satisfaction and enhance growth and profitability.

Models and structures are tools, but it is people who make the difference. It is important that employees are developed, and the organization transfers its values so that everyone in the organization understands what the company does and that each individual is committed to every detail. Common values are formulated around the company's basic duty to protect homes, workplaces, and the community, and the values are driven by the company ethic of Integrity, Vigilance and Helpfulness, as mentioned earlier. The development of the company, growing organically as well as through acquisition, happens within an organizational structure in which the right people are recruited and hired. Operations are focused on obtaining detailed knowledge about the company services so that quality service and profits are enhanced, and the organization builds self-confidence. Complementary services to existing, as well as new customer groups, results in increased specialization; and organic growth is driven through the resulting service and customer segmentation.[10]

The management process at Securitas is visualized and taught through a representational model: the Securitas toolbox. In this, each manager receives an actual wooden box. Each tool within the box is a reference on how to manage and symbolize components of the Securitas model. The "value chain" defines the link between the customer's needs and how the business is organized to meet those needs. "Six fingers" form a framework for financial follow-up, so that each manager's performance is clearly measured. A flat organizational structure allows for quick decision-making, with the right person being in the right place to serve the needs of the customer.[11] At the height of Thomas' tenure at Securitas, with administration offices in London, Stockholm, and Dublin, there were only 35 central administrators. One step down to the country division there were 1,000 administrators. Instead of the field waiting for orders to come from the top and then filling out paperwork, the model adopted was to have the field react to the market and not to a bloated head office.[12]

Thomas pointed proudly to a management training program he initiated early on and ran for 18 years. Four to five times a year he met with managers in different countries, where Thomas and his executive team learned directly from the front-line managers, and they in turn learned key lessons, such as how to solicit feedback on customer satisfaction through key performance indicators, and how to propose potential solutions to address their "pain" points.

Rather than restrict himself to talking with the fifteen or so top-level headquarters employees, Thomas spent a lot of time traveling to meet with customers and the company's employees. He preferred to get out and see the company's operations in person. It sent a message that the leader cared enough to want to know the details.[13]

Securitas Becomes the Leading Security Services Company Worldwide

From 1994 to 1997, under Thomas' leadership, Securitas became the leading security company in Europe, operating in 14 countries, with over 40,000 employees and sales of approximately $1.5 billion. During his first three full years as CEO, sales and the number of employees nearly doubled. In the previous ten years, average annual revenue and income growth averaged over 27 percent per year. In addition to the guard services division, impressive growth was attained in the Securitas Direct home alarm segment and business alarm segments, with over 75,000 and 125,000 customers, respectively.[14]

Thomas said it took ten years to build out the European market. Securitas then turned its attention to the North American security services market. It was at the International Security Ligue, an organization of leaders from the major security companies in the world where he served as chairman from 1996 to 2007, that he heard that Pinkerton might be available to be acquired. After many discussions with Pinkerton's CEO, Denis Brown, a deal was struck. Later, Securitas learned from management at Pinkerton that Burns Security might also be looking to be acquired. In 1999, the company acquired Pinkerton, and one year later it acquired Burns International.

Thomas stated that the size of the market was no restriction, and the amount the company could grow was more a question of "our own energies." Along with the acquisitions of Pinkerton and Burns came the acquisition of two U.S. regional companies: First Security and American Protective Services. With those transactions, Securitas became the largest security provider in North America with a 20 percent market share. Acquisitions in Latin America would add an additional 20,000 employees in that region.[15] In 2001, the first full year that Pinkerton and Burns were part of Securitas, sales from the prior year rose by 48 percent to $4.8 billion, including a 7 percent organic growth, with income rising by 39 percent to $1.36 billion.[16]

Thomas said that at the time the U.S. acquisitions were being discussed, executives in Europe thought that there must be a big need for security in the United States since it must be quite violent there. They thought there would be a lot of costly armed guard services with lots of risk, and that with such a big need, their services must be very advanced. He said all three assumptions proved wrong. What they found was a largely "static guard," and the only really interesting thing about the market was the number of large customers. They believed that there was a potential to refine the business in the United States, as they had done elsewhere by tailoring services to different segments of the market and introducing a better quality of service.

Thomas found it odd that a large U.S. company would have a call center, with operators all based in Minnesota, for example, calling prospective customers across the country using a scripted message. When he saw that process, he knew that there was an opportunity to use the Securitas model to expand business. Rather than rely on remote call centers, the local managers Securitas retained or hired would need to use their local marketplace knowledge to identify and develop business. A local sales manager could be used to open the door to a new prospect, but it was the local operations manager that would ultimately become the point of contact and establish trust with local customers.

Of this approach Thomas went on to explain:

> We brought to the U.S. and elsewhere, a model in which our management needed to feel that they were part of something bigger than themselves. There was no compromise on this concept, and we only brought in people who bought into this—to get the acceptance required that we listen to people and talk to them so that they too could learn, and we could lead them. Our decentralized concept empowered local managers, but that also

required us to have tight financial controls to measure and assess performance.

He noted that one hurdle when they entered the United States was dealing with labor unions. Although Securitas had a very good relationship with unions in Europe, some of the union leaders in the United States brought in consultants to have bad press published about the company. They even brought in some union leaders from Europe to the United States, to paint the company in a bad light. On September 11, 2001, Thomas was on his way to Chicago for a meeting with the top leadership of the Service Employees International Union (SEIU). The terrorist-hijacked airplanes had caused their devastation on the U.S. Eastern seaboard, halting all travel throughout the country. Thomas' trip was sidetracked. A conference call ensued, in which he told the SEIU "we can choose to fight or make a deal." He noted that he subsequently met with the SEIU president, Andy Stern, several times, and established trust. They found common ground and things went smoothly. Thomas noted, "unions are not sent by the devil but are here to help the common person." He felt that it all comes back to putting trust in people to open up common ground.

In 2001, Securitas was reorganized into a divisional structure with five specialized divisions for greater business focus. These would be North American and Europe Guarding, Large Alarm Systems, Home Alarms (Securitas Direct), and Cash Handling. With the acquisition of Loomis, Fargo & Company, the company became a major player in the U.S. cash handling business. From 2001 to 2004, additional acquisitions were made across Europe, including Bell Group plc in the UK, and Eurotelis in France, to become the market leader for banks and other high security clients. In 2005, the U.S. guarding operations underwent extensive structural work, resulting in a clearer organization, a single brand, and more efficient methodologies.[17]

We asked Thomas about the decision to change the Pinkerton and Burns operating names in the United States to Securitas. As has been outlined earlier in this book, both names were long associated with security services in the United States, and the brands well established. Thomas said that while they had internally discussed this, the decision was actually prompted by the U.S.-based managers who requested the change. As with the companies that they had acquired in Europe,

> nothing about using the Securitas name was forced. We came with an old-fashioned way of operating. We had to be humble, and we taught the managers what we knew. They saw the success of other companies we acquired that were operating under the Securitas name and wanted to change.

Thomas did acknowledge the power of the Pinkerton brand for detective services, and Securitas to this day retains the brand name for its consulting and investigative division.

For 2006, the last full year that Thomas was CEO, total sales at Securitas were 60,235 MSEK or $8.6 billion, with the guarding division accounting for 49,085 MSEK, or approximately $7 billion. The guard division had approximately 195,000 employees in more than 30 countries; the Loomis division had 20,000 employees and sales of 11,474 MSEK, or about $1.5 billion. The Securitas Systems and Securitas Direct units were spun off to shareholders and listed on the Stockholm Exchange. The remaining organizational structure would include Security Services North America, Security Services Europe, and Loomis Cash Handling. The strategy for development remained consistent: "professionalism, specialization and segmentation to reflect the constantly growing and differentiated needs of customers, creating new markets and specialized activities with their own business models." Thomas reported that "Security is one of mankind's most basic needs. It embraces our physical security and our ability to direct and control conditions in our daily lives. Security is an indispensable part of human welfare. It is the foundation of our values." Reflecting on his decision to turn over control of the company to new leadership, Thomas noted that

> it seems only natural to recommit ourselves to Securitas' overriding values of Integrity, Vigilance and Helpfulness at a time when the Group once again enters a new phase in its development, and when I myself have decided to move on after twenty-two years with the company, including fourteen years as President and CEO.[18]

The cash-in-transit business proved to be the least successful of the Securitas divisions. Thomas told us that the business had changed from the transportation of money to more of a cash handling service with increased liability. "We were no longer just transporting money but becoming a middleman and booking money. That took on a different culture from the guard and alarm business."

When the company announced that the cash-in-transit division would be listed rather than sold, the share price fell by some 11 percent. Financial results were impacted by listing costs and a large provision for an insurance claim arising from the sale of the German cash-handling business. However, the company retained its guidance saying it saw full-year pretax profit rising at the same rate as last year.[19] In 2008, Loomis was spun off and listed as a separate company on the Stockholm Exchange.[20]

Since Thomas left the company, Securitas has remained one of the largest global security services companies in the world. Sales in 2021 totaled MSEK 107,700, or approximately $11 billion. At the end of 2021, the company announced an agreement to acquire Stanley Security, a leading security integrator, which they expect "will lead to improvements in operating margins and a combination of global presence, connected technology and intelligent use of data." With a high-profile integrator, the company could better offer a complete turnkey security operation, melding guarding with a multitude of physical security options. The operating groups are now organized into three business segments—Security Services North America, Security Services Europe, and Security Services Ibero-America—covering services in 46 countries.[21] The Security Direct home alarm business proved to be a lucrative one. Thomas said that it has been sold twice to private equity and now has a value three times that of the guarding business.

REFLECTIONS ON A LEGENDARY CAREER

Thomas stated that when Securitas first entered the U.S. market, market segmentation, specialization, and the understanding of the customer's security needs were more sophisticated in Europe than in the United States. He believes that this has now changed, and that segmentation in the United States has become more sophisticated than elsewhere.

He regards September 11, 2001, as a pivotal moment for the security services industry. It forced a renewed focus on security to stop small incidents in order to prevent large-scale incidents. Security, he said, has moved from a focus on the protection of assets, to embrace the concept of risk management in which vulnerability is assessed and security and systems are designed to mitigate risk. Technology has also become much more sophisticated in its application in the security industry (Figure 12.4).

Thomas said he started early on working with competitors to raise standards across the entire industry, because:

> If you go it alone, they think you are either stupid or aloof. We were trying to build a common thread. A common theme in the industry was pay less so you can make more money. But we felt that if you pay too little you would not get good people to work for you. We deserved to be trusted, and paying low wages was not the way to earn customer or employee trust.

As an example, he pointed to what happened with airport security. "The customers paid a cheap price; wages were low, and the TSA took over providing service. You cannot grow that way."

FIGURE 12.4   Smoke rises from the site of the World Trade Center in New York City, September 11, 2001. Thomas cites 9/11 as, without question, a momentous and pivotal period for the global security services industry.

(Photo by Paul Morse. Source: U.S. National Archives.)

Thomas said that certainly mistakes were made along the way, but it is easy to be wise afterwards. His record at Securitas is remarkable. He did not found the company but led it during the period of its most significant growth. He led by being true to his own, as well as the company's, values. Thomas said the motivation for his success came "from seeing his own people succeed; to give meaning to every employee in the organization. It is in building something together that we lift each other, giving employees something more than a pay raise," which he described as a short-term lift only. Good pay was an essential element, to be sure, but only one element in the formula for success.

Lars Nørby Johansen (profiled in Chapter 11) told the authors that Thomas was "someone we all looked up to," and he "paved the way for us because of the way he managed and in how he started the consolidation in the industry."

Tony Sabatino, currently the chief executive officer of Paragon Systems, a division of Securitas, was in 2000 a vice president of operations in the Southwest Business Unit of Burns International when Securitas acquired Burns. Today he is the chief executive officer of Paragon Systems, a division of Securitas. Tony provided the authors with his impressions and recollection of Thomas Berglund as a leader; and the impact Thomas had on his own career.

Thomas Berglund was one of the most influential people to me in my early career. I was very fortunate to be one of ten Burns International employees to attend the Global Manager's Meeting in Barcelona in September 2000 shortly after Burns was acquired. At the Barcelona meeting, which was led by Thomas, I experienced a leader who displayed an infectious pride of the security industry, had an empathetic understanding of the routines, duties, and challenges of a security services manager and meaningfully conveyed that he wanted each of us to do well, and had figured out how to universally translate a common group of tools to a diverse group of employees from throughout Europe and North American. I left Barcelona inspired and knew I wanted to work with Securitas. (Figure 12.5)

One year later I was selected to participate in Securitas Executive Training (SET), a yearlong program comprising of six weeklong sessions. Thomas personally taught the sessions and challenged us to operate within the Securitas Toolbox but broadened our thinking, widened our approach, and deepened our commitment through our work with fellow employees, clients, and industry stakeholders. He and I engaged one another several times during those sessions, sometimes I prevailed and sometimes I learned another perspective, but I personally felt driven by his desire to make us better managers. Our SET team was together on 9-11-01 in Madrid, Spain. I was with Thomas when he fielded calls from the media, and I witnessed how he represented our company and our industry. We did not cancel our meeting but rather Thomas guided us to recognize the magnitude of the global situation but also the importance of our session and our role in society to keep our clients safe. He led us through an important executive training session over the next days within an atmosphere he created where it was ok to learn and debate but also ok to recognize the magnitude of what was happening on the global stage. We were all impacted by the events of 9-11 but we were also very glad to be there.

Thomas summed things up when he told us, "Your organization starts with the customer, and then having the best people to manage and provide the service; and in this way you make wonderful music." It is collective success that matters most to Thomas, and in the final analysis that *is* what matters the most (Figure 12.6).

SECURITAS Securitas International Meeting 2000 **SECURITAS**

At Securitas, dreams come true!

BARCELONA – "Dreams come true!" With these words, Securitas CEO Thomas Berglund concluded the International Meeting in Stockholm in 1998. Two years later, in October 2000, Thomas Berglund repeated these same words in Barcelona, and to underscore their relevance he cited some figures: "When I said sales would reach SEK 30 billion by 2003, you all thought I was crazy. But look at this – you've already done it!"

With SEK 50 billion in sales and 210,000 employees in more than 30 countries, Securitas has very quickly become the world's largest security company.

The story began in Sweden in 1934. As the company made its first acquisitions in the late 1980s in Portugal, Norway and Denmark, the plot began to thicken. The Securitas story is as eventful as it is fascinating.

Not easy

Dreams come true – they really do. And at Securitas, they've come true more than once. However, as Thomas Berglund pointed out, after several years of major acquisitions, it is now time to concentrate on what these acquisitions are meant to bring: profit.

"It won't be easy. I know that right now many countries are struggling with their acquisitions," he said, addressing an audience of almost a thousand at Teatre Nacional de Catalunya and asking them:

"Is it easy in Germany?"

"No!" said the Germans.

"What about in France?"

Same answer.

And so it continued.

"Even in Texas it's a challenge," Thomas pointed out. "We're all asking ourselves why we do this – and then we do it again. I suppose we must enjoy it. But I'd like to quote Jan-Ove Nilsson, Country President, Sweden: "It's hell being a manager. And if you're good at it, they give you even bigger hell!""

Help in the form of a toolbox

Fortunately, there is help available in a little wooden box. At the sixth International

"If we can just get everybody to use all these tools, there's no stopping us!" CEO Thomas Berglund got help from the Caretaker when picking up the parts from the Toolbox.

Meeting, Securitas employees from all around the world had the opportunity to become acquainted with the Toolbox. Some of the delegates were already familiar with it, but for others, the Toolbox was a new and important source of inspiration for their work. This box, with its eight tools,

"Each one of you here in the audience makes a difference"

became the focal point of those intensive days in Barcelona.

"We are gathered here in Barcelona so that you can see that we have been successful before, and so we can share our experiences with each other," Thomas said. "Each one of you here in the audience ma-

kes a difference. There are no consultants here, no professors. Just us – Securitas people."

Let the meeting begin!

SECURITAS
Securitas International Meeting

"Wait…haven't we met before?" The meeting in Barcelona was a good opportunity for nearly 1,000 employees to meet and exchange knowledge.

"There are no consultants here, no professors. Just us – Securitas people," Thomas Berglund said when he opened the 6th Securitas International Meeting from the stage of Teatre Nacional in Barcelona.

FIGURE 12.5 "There are no consultants here, no professors. Just us— Securitas people." Thomas Berglund's comments in kicking off the 6th Securitas International meeting from the stage of the Teatre Nacional in Barcelona. Pictured is an excerpt from a company newsletter about the meeting from 2000.

(Provided and used courtesy Thomas Berglund and Securitas.)

FIGURE 12.6   Collective success. A company photo of Securitas employees at the Barcelona company meeting.

(Provided courtesy Tony Sabatino.)

NOTES

1   Securitas AB, *Annual Report 1997*, 1998, 8.
2   Securitas AB, *Annual Report 2006*, 2007, 4.
3   "Muhammad Ali Quotes," https://www.goodreads.com/quotes/200873-don-t-count-the-days-make-the-days-count
4   Rianne Mahon, "Rescaling Social Reproduction: Child Care in Toronto/Canada and Stockholm/Sweden," *International Journal of Urban and Regional Research* 29, no. 2 (2005): 351, https://doi.org/10.1111/j.1468-2427.2005.00588.x
5   "Our History," accessed March 12, 2022, https://academedia.se/om-academedia/historia/
6   "Financial Information," accessed March 12, 2022, https://academedia.se/investerare/finansiell-information/
7   Gordon Adler, Waldemar Schmidt, and Els van Weering, *Winning at Service: Lessons From Service Leaders* (Chichester, UK: John Wiley & Sons Ltd., 2003), 13–14.
8   "Important Events in Our History," https://www.securitas.com/en/about-us/our-history/timeline/
9   Securitas AB, *Annual Report 1997*, 3.

10 Securitas AB, *Annual Report 1999*, 2000, 6.
11 Securitas AB, *Annual Report 1999*, 7.
12 Waldemar Schmidt, *Winning at Service: Lessons From Service Leaders*, 146–47.
13 Waldemar Schmidt, *Winning at Service: Lessons From Service Leaders*, 91.
14 Securitas AB, *Annual Report 1997*, 3–5.
15 Michael C. Williams Rita Abrahamsen, *Security Beyond the State: Private Security in International Politics* (New York: Cambridge University Press 2011), 45–46.
16 Securitas AB, *Annual Report 2001*, 2002, 4.
17 "Important Events In Our History."
18 Securitas AB, *Annual Report 2006*, 3–9.
19 Maria Akerheim, "Securitas CEO Plans to Resign; Unit Taken Off Block As Net Falls," *The Wall Street Journal*, August 11, 2006, https://www.wsj.com/articles/SB115526199836632975
20 "Important Events In Our History."
21 Securitas AB, *Annual Report 2021*, 2022, https://www.securitas.com/en/news/regulatory-press-releases/securitas-ab-full-year-report-januarydecember-2021/

PART V

Today's Global
Security Leaders

The three legends profiled in Part V—Helena Revoredo Gut (Helena), Stephan Crétier (Stephan) and Steve Jones (Steve)—come from vastly different backgrounds; all are principals and have been directly instrumental in building three of the top four largest global security service companies of today. Active in the security industry since 1997, Argentina-born Helena Revoredo controls the voting shares of Madrid-based Prosegur through the family holding company, Gubel SA. Prosegur has large contract security and cash-in-transit businesses. Canadian Stephan Crétier founded GardaWorld (Garda) in 1995, and it too has substantial contract security and cash-in-transit businesses. California-born Steve Jones has since 1996 built what is now Allied Universal, with headquarters in the United States and the United Kingdom, into the world's largest security services company. Securitas, last referenced in Chapter 12, rounds out the top four. After many years as the world's largest security company, Securitas currently ranks second in size to Steve Jones' Allied Universal. In addition to large contract guarding segments, each of today's four largest companies has been expanding its respective security technology capabilities to augment its overall security programs.

Magnus Ahlqvist joined Securitas in August 2015 as Divisional President Securitas Services Europe, and since March 1, 2018, has been the CEO of Securitas. He is the Chair of the International Security Ligue.[1] While not featured as a legend, his leadership in the industry to date has been impressive.

The highly educated Helena has been ably assisted by her son Christian Gut, who has served as chief executive of Prosegur since 2008.

After the tragic loss due to a car accident of her husband, Prosegur founder Herberto Gut, Helena boldly took over at Prosegur in what largely remains a male-dominated business. Today, Prosegur revenues exceed 4 billion euros. As an accomplished businesswoman and philanthropist, Helena is a model for women who will lead companies. In 2009 she said that "Companies and institutions now value human capital first and foremost, and women have a great deal to contribute in this regard."[2]

Stephan also completed a formal education, but attributes his business success to life experiences. Stephan transitioned from an early career as a baseball umpire to the security industry, and borrowed money to start Garda. He describes himself as an owner-operator, and today the company has revenues of approximately C$4 billion (Canadian dollars). His story illustrates a fighting spirit, an engaging man driven to achieve success, someone who is not afraid to make things happen when others would walk on by.

Steve has built Universal Protection Service, now Allied Universal, into the world's largest security company through sheer determination, grit, leadership, and business skill. When his hopes for a career as a professional football player ended due to injury, Steve directed his unbounded energy to the business world. Seeing an opportunity in the security services industry, he began a journey that included acquiring more than 100 companies. The result of his hard work has been that Allied Universal today has revenues of over $20 billion and is one of the world's largest employers.

For Part V, the authors obtained written information directly from Helena Revoredo Gut. We also interviewed her son, Christian Gut, on March 13, 2023. Stephan Crétier was interviewed by us on January 16, 2023. Our final interview for the book was conducted with Steve Jones on November 6, 2023.

NOTES

1   Source: securitas.com Group Management, Magnus Ahlqvist, President and CEO of Securitas AB, https://www.securitas.com/en/about-us/group-management/magnus-ahlqvist/

2   "People: The Key to Business. An Interview with Helena Revoredo," *IESE Alumni Magazine*, September 2009, https://media.iese.edu/research/pdfs/E114.pdf

CHAPTER 13

Helena Revoredo Gut
Resilience and Vision

Helena Revoredo Gut (Helena) was born in Rosario, Argentina, as was the man who became her husband, Herberto Gut (Herberto). They both graduated from the Catholic University in Buenos Aires, where the couple lived before moving with their children to Madrid, Spain, in 1976. It was there that Herberto founded Prosegur Compañía de Seguridad, S.A. (Prosegur), now one of the world's largest security service companies. In 1997, after Herberto tragically died as a result of a car accident, Helena became a Prosegur director, and then its president in 2004 (Figure 13.1).

A public company, Prosegur is also a family company. Share control has been maintained through the family holding company, Gubel S.A. (Gubel). While Helena gave the majority shareholding in Gubel to her children, Helena has retained 100 percent of the voting rights.[1] Helena has provided strategic oversight of Prosegur since 1997. Her eldest son, Christian, earned a degree in Economics and Business Administration from Centro Universitario de Estudios Financeros, Madrid, and has been a director since 1997, and CEO since 2008 (Figure 13.2). He told the authors that "after about eighteen months learning various business lines at Prosegur, I earned an MBA from INSEAD, France, and worked from 1998 to 2001 in mergers and acquisitions at the Rothschild bank." He would rejoin Prosegur in 2003, where from 2004 to 2007 he served as Managing Director, Prosegur Spain. "I hired a new CEO, and was the deputy, until I became CEO of Prosegur Group in 2008." In 2017, Christian was named chairman of Prosegur Cash (Figures 13.3 and b).

Helena's daughter, Chantal, has served on the board since 1997, and as director of Prosegur Cash since 2016.[2] In 2020, Helena gave additional responsibility in Gubel to her younger daughter, Bárbara, who had worked as vice-secretary and secretary, and to her younger son, German, to carry out the duties that Bárbara was previously responsible for.[3]

Christian told the authors that his father was a hands-on operator, who took the company "from 0 to 350." He allowed that he is like his father in being a hands-on manager, but his mother is more of a strategic thinker. He said that his parents were hard-working, had a great deal of

DOI: 10.4324/9781003285564-19

FIGURE 13.1   Helena Revoredo Gut.

(Photograph used with permission and provided by Helena Revoredo Gut.)

FIGURE 13.2   Helena Revoredo Gut and her son Christian Gut at the Madrid Stock Exchange, March 17, 2017.

(Photograph used with permission and provided by Christian Gut.)

FIGURE 13.3 (a) and (b) Additional photos of Christian Gut from Prosegur Cash's IPO at the Madrid Stock Exchange, March 17, 2017.

(Photographs used with permission and provided by Christian Gut.)

FIGURE 13.4   A photograph of the distinctive yellow Prosegur armored money transport van from Lisbon, Portugal.

(Credit: Shutterstock.com)

perseverance, and imparted in their children humility, which he believes has served the company and family well. He views providing security as a humble task.

As of December 31, 2021, Prosegur comprised 234 companies, including 44 joint ventures. In 2021, revenues were approximately €3.5 billion, with security services accounting for 49.6 percent, and cash-in-transit services 43.4 percent.[4] Fiscal year 2022 was marked by a recovery from the pandemic, with overall revenues increasing by 19.1 percent, to €4.17 billion, led by the contract security division with €2 billion and cash services at €1.87 billion. Profits recovered as well, with net income increasing by over 92 percent to €84.1 million. As of December 31, 2022, the company employed approximately 150,000 employees operating in 31 countries across Europe, Asia, Australia, Africa, Latin America, and the United States (Figure 13.4).[5]

EARLY LIFE AND EDUCATION

Helena was familiar with the business world from childhood; her father, D. Juan Federico Revoredo Johnson, was a renowned businessman and an owner of the Pittmetal Company. Prior to her work at Prosegur, Helena worked in banking and the metallurgical industry.[6] Family life and education played a significant role in Helena's development as a leader and person. Helena proclaimed to the authors that she was her parents' only child. "My education was very important to them, and they always told me I could do anything I wanted in life."

> As long as I worked very hard for it, I could achieve anything. I always saw myself as becoming an entrepreneur. I do not know whether it is big or small, or in what area of activity. I cannot point out a single teacher but the frame of mind my university transmitted to its students led me towards that path.

Early jobs in the banking and steel industry "reinforced my idea of developing my own business."

PROSEGUR IS FOUNDED AND FAMILY SETTLES IN SPAIN

After Herberto and his family moved to Buenos Aires, he completed his studies and graduated with a degree in Business Administration from the Catholic University in Buenos Aires. It was partly by chance that he came to start Prosegur. Herberto wrote a study on methods of determining optimal routes for efficiently and safely transporting money, and in 1975 he became a consultant to the Juncadella Company, the leading cash-in-transit company in Argentina. Juncadella sent Herberto to Spain to explore the prospect of starting a security company there. Seeing that there was opportunity to develop business in Spain, Herberto, Helena, and their children moved to Spain in 1976. Herberto was given a 16 percent share of the startup which was funded by Juncadella and several banks. Six years later, Herberto bought out the other shareholders. His main competition in the market was from Esabe, the largest company operating in the space, and from Wells Fargo. Those companies would be acquired by Prosegur.

In the 1980s Prosegur began to concentrate on the less capital-intensive security guard services vertical, and as part of this strategy signed an agreement with ADT and secured important contracts to guard nuclear facilities, General Motors, and other large companies. The company grew rapidly and began to acquire companies in Spain, Europe, and Latin America. In 1987, Prosegur went public. At that time, it was the largest security company in Spain, and the only one with a global footprint.[7]

In 1995 Prosegur expanded to Latin America. Herberto had returned to Argentina and bought 50 percent of the local Juncadella group. He would not be able to enjoy the fruits of this development, however, because tragedy struck two years later. On May 31, 1997, Herberto died in a traffic accident while back in Madrid. Three people who accompanied him were seriously injured. At the time of Herberto's passing, Prosegur had operations in four European countries in addition to Spain and in four South American countries. The company had 25,000 employees and revenues of 67,000 million pesetas (approximately $470 million).[8]

HELENA STEPS UP TO RUN PROSEGUR

Helena told the authors that after her husband's passing,

> I had my hesitations about my capability for running a large organization but on the other hand I was sure I wanted to keep Prosegur, as I regarded it as my husband's and my own life project. I was never uncomfortable interacting with male counterparts, whether at school, work or at other activities. I was fortunate to have great support from my children, who shared my convictions. I also had the support of my fellow workers. I sensed that is how they wanted the company to continue, and I profited from that common vision.

Helena continued these reflections, noting,

> There are things that are inside of you. I have always been close to private business because of my father, and then I accompanied my husband, who was a born entrepreneur. I have a fondness for undertaking new projects and taking risks. Business life satisfies me a lot.[9]

Helena described how her resilience was forged from her family life, and from a resolve to carry on what her husband had started. In those early days, Helena said,

> I sensed a feeling of orphanage in the company, so I knew a change in the management style was necessary. New people were needed, and the selection of such people was my first worry. My strategy at the beginning was to have a humble approach to this new situation, listening to people and reassuring everyone in the company of our long-term commitment to Prosegur. Later, Prosegur's opening to international markets was my next challenge.

PROSEGUR'S GLOBAL EXPANSION AND RESILIENCE

In 2001, Prosegur acquired the Argentina-based cash-in-transit and security services business group, Juncadella, folding it into Prosegur Internacional. The acquisition enabled Prosegur "to expand into South America, specifically Argentina, Brazil, Chile, Uruguay, Paraguay, and Peru. In the same year, the Group expanded into France."[10]

From 2002 to 2011, Prosegur completed mergers and acquisitions which "strengthened the Group's position in countries in which it already had a presence, and additionally enabled it to establish itself in countries such as Colombia, Mexico, Ecuador, countries in Central America and Germany."[11] Christian told the authors that the company has focused on being the leading company wherever they have business operations.

In 2008, Christian was appointed managing director. He is currently chief executive officer and executive chairman. Christian has an undergraduate degree in economics and business studies, and a Master of Business Administration, from INSEAD Business School. He is also a member of the board of trustees of the Prosegur Foundation. Christian is joined on the board of Prosegur by Helena and his sister, Chantal Gut Revoredo. Chantal has an economics degree and Master of Business Administration from IESE Business School. Like Christian, she has been a director of Prosegur since 1997 and is a member of the board of trustees of the Prosegur Foundation.[12]

Various restructuring moves since 2011 have enabled Prosegur to further expand. It now has a presence in Asia (initially Singapore and India, then China in 2012, the Philippines in 2018, and Indonesia in 2019) and, since 2013, Australia. Prosegur entered South Africa in 2016, after which it acquired additional companies in Portugal and Spain. During this time company leadership implemented a business model called "One Group, Three Businesses." The business of the group is now structured along three business lines: Security Services (which included Cybersecurity Services beginning in 2014), Cash Services, and Alarms Services. In 2017, Cybersecurity Services became a sub-group of the company, and the company entered the U.S. market starting in 2019. After the acquisition of the Brazilian company Cipher, S.A. in 2019, the Cybersecurity Services business line was rebranded as Cipher. Another subgroup focusing on added-value outsourcing to financial institutions and insurance companies, and associated technologies, was created and named Prosegur AVOS.[13]

Prosegur thus today "carries out its activities through five business sub-groups or areas: Prosegur Security, Prosegur Cash, Prosegur Alarms, Prosegur Cybersecurity (or Cipher) and Prosegur AVOS." The business is operated on a decentralized model, with each subgroup operating independently. Global support is provided by specific company departments in finance, human resources and external affairs, risk management, legal, and mergers and acquisitions.[14]

Expansion into the U.S. Market

The expansion to the U.S. market began in earnest after Command Security agreed on September 18, 2018, to be acquired by Prosegur. The transaction closed on February 21, 2019.[15] Command had revenues of approximately $126 million and net profits of about $553,000.[16] Command was the largest of four acquisitions that Prosegur would make for the U.S. market. In addition to Command, the company acquired Best Security Industries and Viewpoint, plus Cipher had some U.S. business. The companies acquired were noted as being highly recognized in, and having deep knowledge of, the technology, remote monitoring, cybersecurity, and security services markets; and that by adding their capabilities, Prosegur was looking "to create a nationwide pure player in Enterprise Risk Security, focused on providing clients with the most integrated and advanced security solutions."[17]

Christian told the authors that prior to acquiring Command as a platform for entry in the U.S. market, the company had concentrated on building its business in Latin America. He noted that there had been earlier conversations with Chuck Schneider of U.S. Security, but the excessive cost of entry into the U.S. market, in which companies were being purchased for high multiples, did not warrant an investment until the Command opportunity arose. He said that Prosegur's experience in the public markets facilitated the purchase of publicly traded Command. With no large companies left to acquire, he sees expansion mostly through organic growth in the United States, and he hopes for Prosegur to be a billion-dollar company in the U.S. market within five years.

Navigating Loss, Recession, and the Pandemic

Besides leading the company after the tragic loss of Herberto, Helena and Christian faced additional challenges due to the global financial crisis of 2007–2009 and the COVID-19 pandemic starting in 2020. Helena described the global financial crisis as the first global crisis that she experienced. She said that while crises of this type cause many companies to go out of business, recessions also "provide great opportunities for those that can detect them."

How can business leaders identify these opportunities? I think it calls for special abilities, rather than specific skills. Being able to assess negative situations with a certain degree of optimism is important, as is being alert at all times and not lowering your guard. Opportunities emerge only in specific cases.[18]

Reflecting on the crisis, the Prosegur 2009 annual report noted that while economic changes impact the security sector, the industry has its own drivers that have a far greater impact on the future evolution of the market. These include:

> [T]he level of outsourcing of security services, the increased level of banking, the greater number of big/multinational companies, an increase in the number of bank branches and ATMs, and in general increased standard of living and wealth in all social classes, are important indicators with great relevance to the future progress of the sector. The positive evolution of some of these sector drivers, accompanied by the company's continual innovation, its search for excellence and the implementation of the cross-selling commercial policies, makes it possible for us to face the current situation from a privileged position.[19]

Christian told the authors that COVID was especially hard on the company. With a substantial portion of their business in Latin America, he said Prosegur was severely impacted due to vacancies, volume declines, and currency impacts. He said that the crisis "taught us that we needed to restructure cost and business structures."

In addition to business closures and successive temporary stoppages in activity, the company experienced reduced access to credit, and enormous economic uncertainty. In the first half of 2020 alone, sales fell 13.6 percent, EBITA fell 33.3 percent, and net profit fell 60 percent. But, due to measures implemented, Prosegur "achieved a significant improvement in the generation of operating cash, favored by the efficiency in receipts and the containment of expenses. In record time, the company deployed a series of measures to ensure the well- being and protection of employees." This included promotion of telework where possible and "the deployment of the communication and security infrastructure necessary for employees to carry out their work with the best possible guarantees." The company instituted necessary health and safety measures to protect employees where remote work was not possible. Of special note was the deployment of a digital passport that allowed employees to manage access to facilities from their mobile phones and establishing mechanisms and protocols for monitoring positive cases. These measures, along with others such as the use of technology for temperature measurement, verification of the use of masks or control of social distancing, were introduced on the premises of the company's clients to guarantee the safety of their own employees and workspaces.

In 2022, Christian reported on a new strategic plan for the company, under the name Perform & Transform. Its goal would be "to consolidate our world leadership in the security market and to accelerate the profitable growth of our operations." The Perform part of the strategy is to increase efficiencies and continue ongoing process improvements; Transform is the development of solutions and services as the key to the future of the company. "It includes the deployment of a technology and digitalization to support the company operating model to implement innovation and transform markets across more than two thirds of company sales by the end of the plan." In the same report Helena noted that beyond the financial results, Prosegur would continue to work on

> transformation initiatives and strive to become a company driven by technology, according to our intention to remain a pioneering and ground-breaking company open to continuous innovation. We believe that protection in today's world means providing maximum possible peace of mind in the physical and digital environments of our clients, the members of our teams, and the general public. This also implies an active and concrete commitment to the societies in which we operate, and to the preservation and future of the planet as a whole.[20]

The plans and actions were successful. The annual report for 2022 indicated revenues had increased by approximately 20 percent, net profits increased by over 58 percent, and new programs grew rapidly across the company's operating divisions.[21]

A Successful Family Enterprise

When her husband tragically passed in 1997, Helena showed determination by taking control of Prosegur, and has since strategically guided the company. In an industry traditionally dominated by men, Helena proved that the path to success in this or any industry is open to women around the globe who are willing to take risks, be confident, and utilize a variety of skills necessary to succeed in business. Helena told the authors, "My husband struggled from the beginning to create a strong company culture and he greatly succeeded in doing so. I did my best to keep and enhance that culture through the years and the natural transformations." While Prosegur was already well established when Helena took over, her strategic guidance and Christian's hands-on-management have resulted in record levels of revenues and profits. This was accomplished through measured geographic expansion, selective acquisitions and partnerships, organic growth, and moving into new vertical initiatives. Along with

Garda, Prosegur is among the few companies that have been successful in both the cash-in-transit business and security guard service business.

Helena gave credit to her children for the success of Prosegur in her written notes to the authors, and said that "to begin with, Christian is highly motivated. [His] becoming the managing director was a turning point in the company." She continued,

> He is a very accomplished and educated person, has a very quick understanding of situations and is a sound decision maker. He has further developed our international footprint, turned Prosegur into a highly innovative company and throughout the years has developed a strong leadership. Chantal's involvement in the Board of Directors is also very enriching as she has a very deep under-standing of the company, having worked herself for several years in different areas of Prosegur. In family-owned companies or in entrepreneurial families, business is of the utmost importance, but family comes first. There is never good understanding in busi-ness if there is no harmony among family members. Love and mutual respect are the key. And of course, family members should not come to the business and less into the family business unless they are very motivated and trained to resume its responsibility.

Christian told the authors that the segmentation of the business into five separate operating units, sharing branding and some central functions, along with a commitment to be the leader in the local markets where they compete, has been a key to Prosegur thriving in all five areas. New disruptive players in the industry are changing the rules of the game, and Prosegur intends to be at the forefront of the changes in physical and dig-ital security solutions. He believes that tomorrow's successful companies must invest in digital transformation. The old legacies must be upgraded, and systems will need to be widened, with a focus on superior IT systems. He said that the company is investing in Israel and other places around the globe; "it is all about bringing people together."

CIVIC, CHARITABLE, AND PROFESSIONAL ENDEAVORS

Helena has long been involved in civic, charitable, cultural, educational, and professional business activities within and outside Prosegur. She is highly educated, holding a PADE from the IESE Business School. She was the first woman to sit on the board of Endesa, Spain's largest electric util-ity company (Figure 13.5).[22]

The Prosegur Foundation has supported educational and cul-tural projects since 1983. Helena, Christian, and Chantal are all board

FIGURE 13.5   A photograph of Endesa's Besós combined cycle thermo-electric plant—located in Barcelona, Spain—with two thermal units fueled with natural gas.

(Credit: Shutterstock.com)

members and active in the foundation. The foundation is fully funded by the company and has the support of its entire organizational structure to address its mission. The mission of the foundation is to support the education of children and young people, convinced that education is the best tool for their development. It promotes the social and labor inclusion of the most vulnerable groups, trying to generate changes in attitude toward more supportive values. The foundation develops corporate volunteering actions, "to add the solidarity of our professionals to the Company's social work"; and it orients activity to the United Nations 2030 Agenda to contribute to the achievement of the Sustainable Development Goals. The foundation has supported over 13,000 scholarships since 2008, and currently supports thousands of youths in schools and in environmental education training.[23]

Helena's interest in management education led her to chair Euroforum, an institution that promotes executive development. She is a member of IESE's International Advisory Board (IAB), which advises the school on current trends in economics and management and is committed to social causes. In the mid-1990s she drove the creation of the foundation's presence in 12 countries across Europe and Latin America where the company also operates. The foundation supports projects such as the reconstruction of schools in Argentina and the integration into the workplace of people with limited physical or mental abilities. In the cultural arena, the foundation provides scholarships for students at the Reina Sofia School of Music.[24]

In 2009, Helena was asked, "How do you imagine the corporate world in 2020?" to which she replied,

> I do not know what it will be like, but I can tell you how I would like it to be. I'd like to see companies where talent is truly valued and enhanced, because I think that is where the added value is. A company where a flexible work environment is accepted and understood as a benefit for both employers and employees, where mobility is readily available, and the job market is accessible to many people. I would also like to see organizations with a growing interest in corporate social responsibility [...] Progress depends more on a transformation of how society thinks than on institutionalized actions, and education plays an important role because schools really transform social attitudes. Much of the success in gender equality has been achieved through academic institutions, especially universities, where women have demonstrated that they measure up on academic terms.[25]

In written comments to the authors, Helena said that today,

> I believe women are very close to reaching an equal footing with men in the business world. This is especially true in the most sophisticated and competitive areas of activity because of women's outstanding performance in universities and higher degree studies. Maybe in activities that require lower skills, the gap is more significant.

Helena has been a forward-looking leader whose story provides inspiration and an example for men and women in how to lead a global enterprise with integrity, intelligence, and a consideration for the needs of customers, employees, and society. She has a love of family, and has provided guidance to her children, to the Prosegur staff and to numerous beneficiaries of the Prosegur Foundation. Her strong will, perseverance, intelligence, and talent as a manager are a beacon for anyone looking to succeed in the security services industry.

NOTES

1   "An Armored Queen Who Ranks Among the Most Powerful Women in Spain," *Punto Biz*, July 21, 2022, https://puntobiz.com. ar/actualidad/una-reina-blindada-que-rankea-entre-las-mujeres-mas-poderosas-de-espana-202272113440

2   "Director Profiles," 2022, https://www.prosegur.com/accionistas-inversores/gobierno-corporativo/consejos-adm-com-delegadas/perfiles-consejeros

3   Consuelo Font, "Helena Revoredo: The Millionaire Leader of Prosegur Prepares for Retirement," *El Mundo*, February 22, 2020, https://www.elmundo.es/loc/famosos/2020/02/22/5e3c2e6721efa05 97c8b468b.html

4   Prosegur Compañía de Seguridad S.A., *Note Issue Prospectus*, March 30, 2022, 43, 49, https://ise-prodnr-eu-west-1-data-integration. s3-eu-west-1.amazonaws.com/202204/ee4c2f83-4fbf-4e74-b48d-48108f76063a.PDF

5   Prosegur Compañía de Seguridad S.A. and Subsidiaries, *Consolidated Annual Accounts and Directors' Report for the year ended 31 December 2022*, 2023, 173–79, https://www.prosegur.com/dam/jcr:aca7fe46-4919-47aa-95e8-e1dbd6f51c32/Conso%202022.pdf

6   "An Armored Queen Who Ranks Among the Most Powerful Women in Spain."

7   "Herberto Gut Beltramo," in *Real Academia de la Historia, Diccionario Biográfico electrónico* (2018), https://dbe.rah.es/biografias/25990/herberto-gut-beltramo

8   "Herberto Gut, President and Founder of Prosegur, Dies in an Accident," *El País*, June 2, 1997, https://elpais.com/diario/1997/06/02/economia/865202407_850215.html

9   "An armored queen who ranks among the most powerful women in Spain."

10   Prosegur Compañía de Seguridad S.A., *Note Issue Prospectus*, 44.

11   Prosegur Compañía de Seguridad S.A., *Note Issue Prospectus*, 44.

12   Director Profiles.

13   Prosegur Compañía de Seguridad S.A., *Note Issue Prospectus*, 44.

14   Prosegur Compañía de Seguridad S.A., *Note Issue Prospectus*, 44.

15   Command Security Corporation, *Securities Deregistration Statement*, February 22, 2019, https://www.sec.gov/Archives/edgar/data/864509/000149315219002443/forms-8pos.htm

16   Command Security Corporation, *Securities Deregistration Statement*, 3.

17   "Prosegur and Best Security Industries Announcement," 2019, https://www.prosegur-eas.com/Prosegur-and-BSI-Announcement

18   "People: The Key to Business. An Interview with Helena Revoredo,"
      IESE Alumni Magazine, September 2009, https://media.iese.edu/
      research/pdfs/E114.pdf

19   Prosegur Compañía de Seguridad S.A., *Annual Report 2009*, 2010,
      105.

20   Prosegur Compañía de Seguridad S.A. and Subsidiaries, *Consolidated
      Annual Accounts and Directors' Report for the year ended 31
      December 2021*, 2022, 15–19, 163–66, 80.

21   Prosegur Compañía de Seguridad S.A. and Subsidiaries, *Consolidated
      Annual Accounts and Directors' Report for the year ended 31
      December 2022*, 2023, 173–79, 95.

22   "Profile: Helena Revoredo," *Forbes*. https://www.forbes.com/profile/
      helena-revoredo/?sh=551a1acd15e5

23   "Discover our Social Commitment," accessed March 6, 2023,
      https://www.fundacionprosegur.com/en/

24   "People: The Key to Business. An Interview with Helena Revoredo."

25   "People: The Key to Business. An Interview with Helena Revoredo"

CHAPTER 14

Stephan Crétier
The Disruptor

Canadian-born Stephan Crétier (Stephan) once described himself as "more a business person who has experience in security than a security person who became a business person."[1] But Stephan developed an acumen for security as well as a fondness for the industry. His story illustrates that if not for fate and circumstances, his talents and drive would have fostered his success in virtually any industry. His entrepreneurial spirit is evident in the story of his building, owning, and managing GardaWorld Security Corporation (Garda), a global security leader. He is a proud Canadian who relishes what his team at Garda is creating, and the unconventional paths he takes which others might forego.

Stephan's path to building Garda started after an initial career as a baseball umpire and part-time work in the off season as a store detective. With little income from those endeavors he looked for another career, and he was recruited for a job at a security company. While managing that security company, Stephan was rebuffed by the owner when he requested equity; in 1995 along with his longtime partner and now wife Stéphany Maillery, he took out a second mortgage for C$25,000 (Canadian dollars) to start his own security business. From there Stephan built, and today leads, Garda, now a C$4 billion global security service provider, with 120,000 professionals operating in 45 countries around the world.[2]

Not one to sit back and rest on his laurels, Stephan shaped his success by constantly applying a keen understanding of where he had been and where he wanted to go. Stephan is a tough and disciplined competitor, who in his inimitable way once said, "You're either on the menu or you're looking in the menu."[3] He has been looking at the menu ever since he started Garda.

EARLY LIFE IN CANADA

Stephan was born in Montreal on August 8, 1963. His parents came to Canada in the 1950s, his father from Italy and mother from Switzerland.

 DOI: 10.4324/9781003285564-20

Stephan's father worked for many years as a maître d' in restaurants before becoming a union leader. His father's work with the union helped Stephan to recognize how unions can contribute to the welfare of their members. It also gave him an appreciation of the value of good industrial and labor relations. His mother was a hardworking aesthetician for 31 years. His parents struggled, and they separated for a time; seeing their struggle instilled in Stephan a desire to succeed. By age ten he was both competitive and combative and argued with the umpires when playing baseball. When one of the coaches he competed with told Stephan he was going to go to umpire school to learn the rules and beat him, Stephan said he would go too.

In high school he was bullied by his teachers even more than fellow students because he spoke French in a largely English-speaking school. He said, "it was either you survive or you get bullied. I think I learned quite fast: choose your fights." By the time he was 16, Stephan was umpiring for provincial championships; at 18, national-level games, and when he reached 20, World Cup games. "You needed to be thirty-five to umpire a major competition, an international competition. I got the exemption. I was chosen as the umpire and chief for the final—youngest to do that in the history of the sport."[4]

Lessons Learned from Baseball and College

Seeking more big-time baseball experience, Stephan attended umpire school in Maine and started umpiring Triple-A baseball in the United States for the next four years. Stephan said he learned valuable lessons from baseball, because as an umpire he was running the show and also dealing with the stress of spectators and players not agreeing with the calls. He learned to communicate with ballplayers from diverse backgrounds from all over the world (Figure 14.1). The link between sports and business was not lost on Stephan.

> I run my business like a baseball game ... the baseball coach and the CEO are talent managers ... and every morning I get up, and I wonder if I have the best lineup. Everyone knows in your organization it's exactly that. [...] Like positions in a baseball game you want to compartmentalize the company and the talent and always thinking the right person at the right place.[5]

Stephan told the authors that the greatest challenge in the business is finding the right people and talent.

Like other business legends, Stephan worked while studying and he earned a degree in Industrial Relations at the University of Montreal and then an MBA at California Pacific University. Stephan said that while

FIGURE 14.1   Stephan sporting a baseball cap, harkening back to his earlier days as a triple-A umpire. During that time, for four years he had the opportunity to travel the United States and hone his interpersonal skills interacting with the various personalities in coaches and ballplayers.

his education gave him a good understanding of business, doing it in the United States gave him

> maybe a more American style of doing business which is more predatory than the usual culture in Canada. In Canada, you grow a business and you just sell it. I'm more in the philosophy of building empires than trying to just build a company and flip it.[6]

Stephan told the authors that he is extremely proud of being an owner-operator and has been proud to continue to own a large portion of his business.

Transition to the Security Industry

At 25 and earning only about $800 a month, Stephan saw that freedom from financial burdens would not come from umpiring. To survive, in the off season when not umpiring he was working in the parks department for the Canadian city of Laval and part-time as a store detective. A recruiter he enlisted for help changing careers noted the store detective job on his resume, and Stephan soon accepted a job offer for director of operations at a security company. After six months he was the chief executive officer at the security firm. He reorganized the business and in the process developed an affinity for the security industry. After five successful years there, he asked the security company owner to sell him 10 percent of the business but was rebuffed.[7] In five years, he had grown that business from C$4.8 million to C$32 million.[8]

BUILDING GARDAWORLD

Stephan resolved to own his own company. In 1995 at age 32 he sowed the seeds of GardaWorld with an initial investment of C$25,000 from a second home mortgage. The company initially operated as Trans-Quebec Security Inc. First-year revenues for the company were C$600,000. In 1998 the company began an expansion in Canada, was renamed Trans-Canada Security Corporation, and listed shares on the Alberta Stock Exchange under TSV Ventures at C$0.10/share. That same year the company completed its first acquisition—Admari Group in Quebec City. That was followed in 1999 with the purchase of Garda Security Group, one of the leading security providers in Eastern Canada; the company changed its name to GardaWorld Security Corporation.[9]

The early years for Stephan and Garda were marked by several brushes with near-collapse. Stephan told the authors that there were at least four times when he nearly did not meet payroll, as he was always "stretching the machine." Stephan said that "I was never shy in calling my customers to tell them that we provided the service you required, but we need to be paid so we can continue providing that service." He told the authors that these trials taught him to "to be a disciplined buyer."

By 2002, operating profit at Garda grew to C$73M. Within the next two years, Garda added a consulting and investigative division, cash-in-transit, and aviation security services. The company also began trading on the larger Toronto Stock Exchange under the symbol GW. The acquisition in 2003 of Secur, the cash-in-transit division of Quebec credit union Desjardins, was Garda's ninth acquisition. Aviation security services were started in 2004, beginning a

> partnership with the Canadian Air Transport Security Authority (CATSA), after winning the contract to perform pre-boarding security screening at Toronto Pearson International Airport. The company stepped up to the challenge and created a world class screening operation now present in twenty-eight airports across Canada.[10]

Stephan told the authors that he saw the decision in the early 2000s to move more aggressively into the cash-in-transit business as a great opportunity.

> My background in labor relations allowed me to understand the challenges that the credit union was having with the unions and I was able to benefit from this. Today, our cash-in-transit business is a global leader and represents about twenty percent of our business.
>
> (Figure 14.2)

Stephan said that he saw how "Securitas and Melker Schörling operated that business alongside their guarding business, and "I was able to take that model and adapt it to how I operated Garda."

In 2005, Garda made a big move into the United States and bolstered its guard, cash-in-transit, and global consulting and investigation services

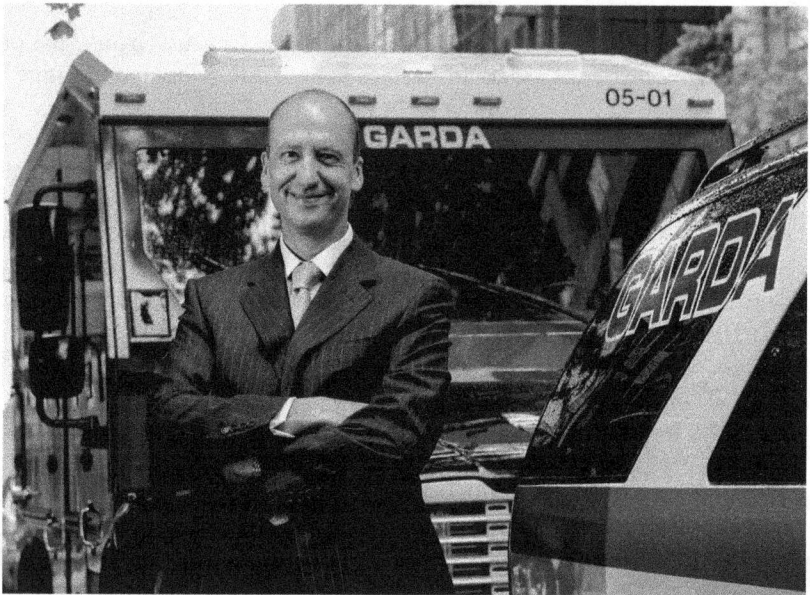

FIGURE 14.2 (Montreal, June 14, 2005) Newly in the cash logistics business, Stephan—at the Annual Meeting of GardaWorld Shareholders—announces that the net profit for the first quarter that ended on April 30 had almost tripled, and the company intended to double its size within five years (Montreal, June 14, 2005.

(Photo Source: GARDA.)

with the $67 million acquisition of Vance International. With 3,700 employees, Vance provided services through offices in Virginia, New York, Florida, London, and Mexico City.[11] Then in 2006, Garda continued expanding the cash-in-transit business in the Midwestern United States with the acquisition of seven local companies and began a global expansion throughout the Middle East by merging its high-threat operations of Vance International (which alerts business and individual clients to threats worldwide) and consulting firm Kroll Security International (KSI). Stephan said at the time that the

> Global security consulting services are essential to business success in high-risk markets today and Garda is meeting that need by continually strengthening its presence around the world. The integration of KSI with Vance International, our leading security consulting, investigations, and physical security division, is a logical and significant expansion of Garda's global presence and scope.[12]

Managing through the Financial Crisis of 2008

Like many other companies, Garda faced challenges during the financial crisis in 2008. After a decade of successfully buying small companies to become Canada's largest security and cash-handling business, Stephan used debt to acquire "eighteen companies over a 16-month period." Garda paid $391 million for ATI Systems International in 2007, creating a global cash-in-transit firm and the second largest behind Brinks in the United States; but Garda sued ATI for inflating the value of the company and misrepresenting its finances. Then on September 15, 2008, Lehman Brothers filed for bankruptcy, and Garda's stock price plummeted to $.60 per share down from $10 after reporting disappointing earnings and violations of loan covenants. Investors fled, including Montreal fund manager, Sebastian van Berkom, who sold his entire stake in Garda. Berkom said, "he (Stephan) kept reassuring us everything was fine when the acquisition wasn't working out," but Stephan was undeterred, and said "forget the investors, forget the banks-they were playing darts with my picture." Stephan sold off two businesses at a loss for $92 million; but Garda's remaining operations continued to perform well. Garda restructured its debt and the stock price and the company recovered.[13] To raise money, Garda sold Vance to Andrews International in 2009. Stephan told the authors that competition was heightened in the United States, but "we were well-paid, and then the low stock price enabled me to take the company private." Stephan had turned a perilous situation to his advantage by taking prudent steps and investing in Garda when others were fleeing.

Garda Goes Private, Global Growth Continues

In 2012 Garda was taken private by a group led by Stephan, with financial backing from Apax Partners, a leading private equity investment group. The authors asked Ashish Karandakir, a partner at Apax, why they invested in Garda. Ashish said that prior to meeting with Stephan, Apax "had spent time evaluating investing in Loomis and Brinks along with Garda." He continued,

> While I had strong conviction in our thesis around the security industry, we had no jockey to ride the horse. Our perception of the industry was it lacked ambition. Stephan made up for the lack of ambition from his competitors and more. Stephan was not concerned about the next year or two but wanted to build a business for the next twenty years. Stephan wanted to build the largest, best run security business in the world – he already believed he had built the best run business – for him, the question was around scale. This stood out for me [...] coming out of the meeting, I had conviction Stephan would be a great steward of the business and a money maker not just for Apax Fund investors but for those that would follow.

Apax originally met with Garda to provide financing to enable them to make a transformational acquisition, but those plans did not materialize due in part to the low share price of Garda. Stephan realized his ambitions necessitated private capital, and Apax and Stephan started discussing a potential private buyout of Garda.

Ashish said, "The pursuit of Garda over its competitors was a 'no brainer' for us to execute our thesis." He elaborated,

> First, Garda had the most ambitious, skilled, and seasoned management team in the industry. Security services are a management execution intensive industry where you make dollars from picking pennies. Management was a buyer, not a seller. Stephan and his team were interested in rolling 100% of their proceeds. I have been doing this a long time and I have never seen a management team with more conviction in their business plan. I famously asked Stephan if he wanted to take some proceeds off the table and Stephan said "everybody rolls 100% or gets rolled over."
>
> Second, Garda shares were trading at a discount [...] Finally, Garda had not just a cash- in-transit business but a high-quality security guarding business which was in the early innings of emerging as a consolidator – even if we got our thesis around cash wrong, we had a solid hedge in the guarding business.

This is how we found our way to investing behind Stephan and Garda over a longer period of time and not as it was originally intended."

For Stephan, taking Garda private while the share price was depressed was a financial bonanza. He told the authors that he was able to retain about 26 percent of the equity in Garda at the time of the Apax transaction, and he would increase his share of the company over time.

In 2013, Garda rebranded its cash-in-transit and aviation services and consolidated its position in Canada with acquisitions of Intercon Security and Total Security Management. Cash-in-transit, operating as GardaWorld Cash Services, "signed a 12-year, $1.4 billion strategic agreement with Bank of America to manage the banks' cash processing and check imaging services in 32 locations across the USA, adding more than 1000 Bank of America employees."

A year later GardaWorld Cash Services completed the acquisition of G4S Cash Solutions in Canada. The acquisition added 2,400 employees to its cash-in-transit operations.

Additional expansion in Africa and the Middle East would occur in 2015 and 2016; in 2016, GardaWorld Aviation Services "signed a five-year contract with the Canadian Air Transport Security Authority (CATSA) for pre-board screening operations in the Central and the Prairies regions of Canada" (Figures 14.3a and b).[14] The authors asked Stephan how he was able to operate globally, with all the varying regulations and differences in markets. He said

we adapt to local markets and hire local people to run our business. We were the first global company to operate in Kurdistan, and we brought in intelligent local operators. In areas where the regulatory or operating climate is difficult, it creates a barrier to entry and actually helps us.

Garda Expands in U.S. Presence and Forms New Divisions

In 2017, Stephan and Rhone Capital, a global leader in alternative investments, completed the purchase of all Garda shares held by Apax Partners and secured C$2.2 billion in refinancing. (Stephan told the authors this deal enabled him to have a 40 percent ownership stake.) In 2018, Garda expanded into the United States, first with the purchase of United American Security LLC (UAS), which had 24 branches and 3,600 employees in 16 states; and then in 2019, with the acquisition of Whelan Security, which was operating with 34 branches in 31 states with 10,000 employees.

(a)

(b)

FIGURE 14.3   (a) Stephan visiting Malawi's operations, May 18, 2021, and (b) Celebrating GardaWorld's rebrand in Rwanda, May 21.

(Photo ©Cyril Ndegeya; provided by Stephan Crétier and used with permission.)

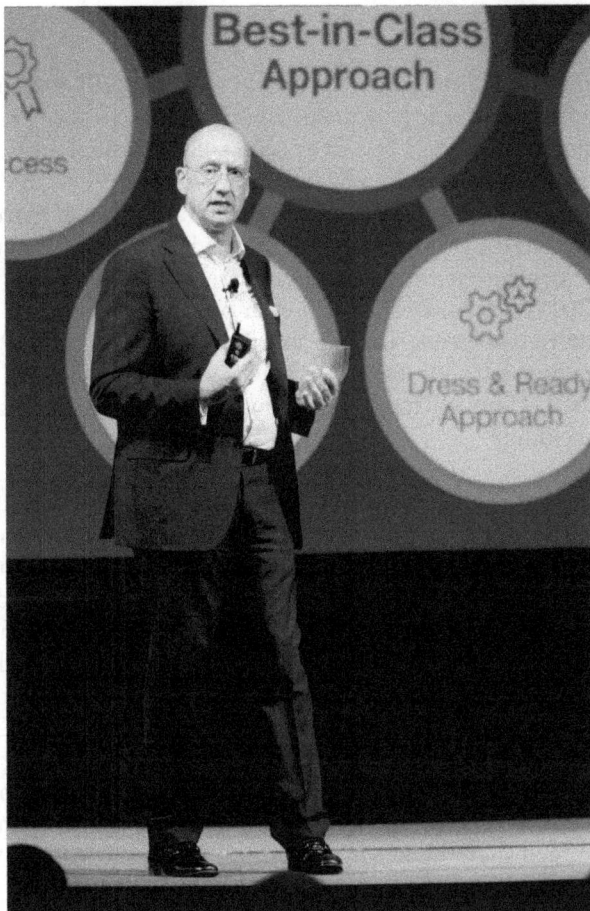

FIGURE 14.4 GardaWorld's Las Vegas Leadership Summit in 2020; Stephan speaking to 700 leaders across all operations.

Garda's consulting and technology divisions would also expand between 2018 and 2020. It acquired global risk and crisis management consultancy NYA, which had one of the largest and most experienced crisis intervention teams in the world; and then World Aware, a U.S. risk management firm. Security technology services were bolstered when Garda acquired U.S.-based ECAMSecure and U.K.-based Drum Cussac. In 2020, Garda combined Drum Cussac, NYA and FAM International Security to "take risk management to the next level as new brand Crisis24" (Figure 14.4).[15]

The Battle for G4S

Having built Garda into one of the world's leading global security companies, Stephan was ready to make what would have been the biggest deal in company history. The target was G4S, and Stephan was primed for something bigger than he had ever done before.

In October 2019, a C$5.2 billion recapitalization of Garda by BC Partners, the largest private buyout in Canadian history, resulted in BC owning 51 percent of the shares, with Stephan holding 49 percent.[16] Earlier in 2019, Garda considered a cash offer for some or all of G4S, a company more than twice Garda's size. Garda then opted not to pursue a deal, but soon after the BC deal, the COVID pandemic had made the valuation of G4S much more appealing. G4S was also going through problems including

> charges that some executives had defrauded the Ministry of Justice, the loss of a contract to run a Birmingham prison, and Norway's wealth fund shunning investments in the firm. It sold off most of its cash-handling business in February 2020, to U.S. peer Brinks, and in July announced plans to lay off some employees at its retained UK cash operations, which have attached pension obligations. Seeing the disruption at G4S, Stephan said that G4S needed an owner, not a manager. In September 2020, Garda made an offer to purchase G4S for $3.8 billion. The offer was quickly rejected by the G4S board as too opportunistic, coming at a time of severe turbulence in global financial markets, and the board urged shareholders not to take any action.[17]

A bidding war would ensue when Allied Universal made offers for G4S. Garda ultimately did not match a higher Allied offer, and the bidding process concluded with G4S accepting Allied Universal's offer. Stephan told the authors that "we will never know if this deal would have been good for Garda. We are a disciplined buyer and were not going to pay more than what we thought the company was worth."

Garda Emerges Strong from the Pandemic

Though Garda did not acquire G4S, with BC's backing, Garda was in a strong position to pursue other opportunities. In 2020, Moody's Investor Services reported that Garda was benefiting from strong market positions in security guard and cash-in-transit segments, "which provides them with competitive advantages in winning contracts; stable businesses with high contract renewal rates and recurring revenue; and good customer and geographic diversity." Garda was noted to have good liquidity, with "moderate exposure to social risks" primarily due to security services to high-profile clients such as Western governments and embassies in higher-risk areas in the Middle East and Africa.[18]

In 2022, Garda used a term loan of $700 million to fund the $675 million acquisition of Dallas-based Tidel Engineering (Tidel), a leading cash automation solutions provider in North America. Moody's viewed the acquisition of Tidel positively

> because it will enable Garda to offer end-to-end proprietary service and product offerings capable of outsourcing its clients' entire cash ecosystem. Tidel's well-known brand, leading market position in the US and a large underpenetrated cash management market at retailers, will provide strong growth opportunities both in the US and offshore.[19]

Rating agency Fitch reaffirmed the company credit rating after the debt issue and noted that Garda performed well during the pandemic. Garda signed new business due to "increased demand in some areas (security services at pharmacies, healthcare providers, governments, financial institutions and grocery retailers) offsetting declines in other areas (event management)." Garda increased margins through pricing power in some of their operating segments and initiated cost controls to reduce operating costs.[20]

On August 24, 2022, Garda announced that it had "deployed over $1.3 billion to solidify its industry leadership position, while also revolutionizing service delivery models. The acquisition of ARCA marks GardaWorld's 10th transaction in 2022." ARCA was described as a global leader in cash technology solutions and a global market leading manufacturer of teller cash recyclers for financial institutions. ARCA was joined with Garda's global cash ecosystem integrator and financial technology company, Sesami. To help finance the deal and support its global strategic vision, Garda concluded an agreement with the Government of Québec through Investissement Québec, for a $300 million investment "by way of a private placement in GardaWorld preferred shares."[21] Stephan told the authors that any idea that the cash system will go away is a myth. We are instituting intelligent devices in the business, and where we do not handle cash, we are handling other transactions. We have spent a billion dollars and we are the leading global player in this segment of the business. We have world-class positions in all three segments of our business: guarding, cash-in-transit, and consulting.

In December 2022, Garda's Crisis24 division completed a deal with Palantir. Stephan told the authors that the market put a $1.4 billion value on that business. According to Stephan, the "strategic partnership is a paradigm shift in the delivery of security risk intelligence." He went on:

> It will allow Crisis24 to conquer new frontiers as the most powerful and advanced source of risk intelligence and analytics in the world. We are privileged to partner with Palantir, a world-renowned software and AI powerhouse, as a strategic growth ally to maximize Crisis24's full-service integrated risk solutions. More importantly, we are bringing together two entrepreneurial companies who are leading in their fields to uniquely leverage the power of man and machine.[22]

GARDA'S RISE AS A GLOBAL SECURITY COMPANY

The growth of Garda was steady, if not spectacular, with a strategy of expanding in Canada first before expanding globally and into different verticals. Stephan took the company public early on and used the resulting capital to fund expansion. He overcame financial adversity during the 2008 financial crisis, recapitalized, and obtained additional financial backing to make acquisitions, fund organic growth, and take the company private. Business lines were expanded from security guard services to include the large cash-in-transit component, aviation security, investigation, and consulting services, and, of late, new technologies in physical security and cash services.

Stephan and his team also invested considerable company time and effort in building the reputation and quality of service provided to customers. Garda announced in 2016 that it was the first company in the world to hold ISO 18788:2015. ISO Certifications covered every service that the company provided throughout the world to include the following:

- Management system for private security operations (ISO 18788)
- Management System for Quality of Private Security Company Operations (PSC.1-2012)
- Quality Assurance Management (ISO 9001)
- Environmental Management (ISO 14001)
- Societal Security—Business Continuity Management (ISO 22301)
- Occupational Health and Safety Management (BS OHSAS 18001)[23]

A Focused and Inspired Leader

Ashish Karandakir of Apax told the authors that "Stephan is a trifecta—
he is a player, coach, and team owner. If I were to draw a likeness, [I'd
say he compares] to the Cowboys owner Jerry Jones. That is quite rare."

> He can run the business down to the smallest branch, set the
> strategy for the business, hold leaders accountable and finally he
> allocates capital to the highest returning projects. The combina-
> tion of these three skill sets makes him a durable entrepreneur, as
> most have one or two but not all of these skills.
>
> [...] From a private equity investor perspective, Stephan is the
> most aligned entrepreneur/CEO one can hope to partner with.
> He does what he says, says what he can do and not what he
> needs to say. He sets a high bar for himself and others and he
> follows through [...]
>
> Stephan lives and breathes this business. He is always on.
> During our five- year partnership there was not a time that
> Stephan missed a step on what was going on in the business –
> and it is a business where things go wrong every day! In a low
> margin business, the leader needs to have a handle on costs:
> Stephan knows where every nickel is spent and does not engage
> in irrational extravagance. While the Apax Funds were investors
> nobody at Garda had assistants, including Stephan who booked
> his own travel and managed his own diary! This was mandated
> by Stephan not by Apax. Despite being very self-assured, Stephan
> is open to feedback and change in opinion as the facts change.

Jean-Michel Filiatrault, Senior Vice President, Corporate Development at
Garda, provided the authors with this description of Stephan as a leader:

> Stephan is a results-oriented leader that has repetitively demon-
> strated to his teams over the years how the impossible can actu-
> ally be accomplished when one is focused on the end-game and
> the game plan execution. He will say words like "game plan",
> "lineup", and the importance of "keeping your eye on the ball".
> This sports talk is deeply rooted into Stephan's past and his no-
> nonsense, tried-and-true management style. Attitude, nerve and
> staying focused have always been second nature to him.
>
> Stephan spends the majority of his time managing talent, cre-
> ating leaders of their own around him, and an environment
> where high-performance individuals are truly aligned and com-
> mitted to creating extraordinary results for themselves and one
> another.

Describing his own philosophy, Stephan said, "the role of a leader is true alignment [...] and I think that's something I do extremely well [...] Garda has consistently provided a quality service that delivers value to customers" [...] I go everywhere as a proud Canadian [...] and wherever I go people love the Canadian. We still have a very strong brand." While he believes that technology is important, it will not simply replace people.

> You look at the growth of the security industry, the people side of the business. Since cameras have been there, it's unbelievable. The growth is there. The aspect of combining with technology is important. That's the future. We have a big business in the US of remote monitoring, which is attached to artificial intelligence, so you're able to have one person looking at 7000 cameras and then just the analytical, he's able to focus on what's happening in there. So definitely there's a change in there, but it remains a people business.[24]

Stephan told the authors that

> if you can get capital, there are so many incredible businesses that you can start and build. The world will always need security, and there are so many angles to the standard business. For example there is the hospitality aspect. You just need to be good.

He said he is not "a detailed manager, but I manage details. I get branch office rankings from all over the world, every day. I have been creating value." When asked about the effect on the industry of large global investment companies, Stephan noted that there are positives and negatives.

> It brings credibility and capital to the industry. The industry still needs consolidation. But they are not always long-term holders; they look at it as a spreadsheet business. We are the best because we are owner-operators, very profitable and not a top-down business. We are not a Chinese buffet, but we are very good in what we focus on.

Service and Awards

The Stéphan Crétier Foundation was founded in 2006 by Stephan and his wife, Stéphany. The foundation's mission is to give back to the community by supporting various Canadian not-for-profit organizations. Among the foundation programs is the Bolo (be on the lookout) Program, "an innovative and results-driven project focusing on public safety awareness as well as the public's assistance in locating Canada's most wanted fugitives." The foundation also supports the Vimy Foundation, which preserves and promotes Canada's World War I legacy as symbolized with the victory in the battle at Vimy Ridge in April 1917. In 2018, Stephan and Stéphany provided a major donation to the Montreal Museum of Fine Arts (Figure 14.5).

In 2011 Stephan was named among the most influential Canadian CEOs of the decade, and in December of 2012, he received the Queen Elizabeth II Diamond Jubilee Medal (Figure 14.6). His influence in the security industry includes becoming the first Canadian appointed to the Board of Directors of the International Security League (Ligue Internationale des Sociétés de Surveillance). Stephan also plays an active role as a board member of several organizations, including the Montreal Economic Institute, a leading free market think tank; the Hirshhorn Museum, a Smithsonian institution based in Washington, DC; and TransCanada.[25]

The proud Canadian has come a long way from fighting with coaches and teachers, and calling balls and strikes. The company that Stephan started with a $25,000 second mortgage has grown impressively,

FIGURE 14.5   A photograph of the exterior of the Montreal Museum of Fine Arts.

(Credit: Shutterstock.com)

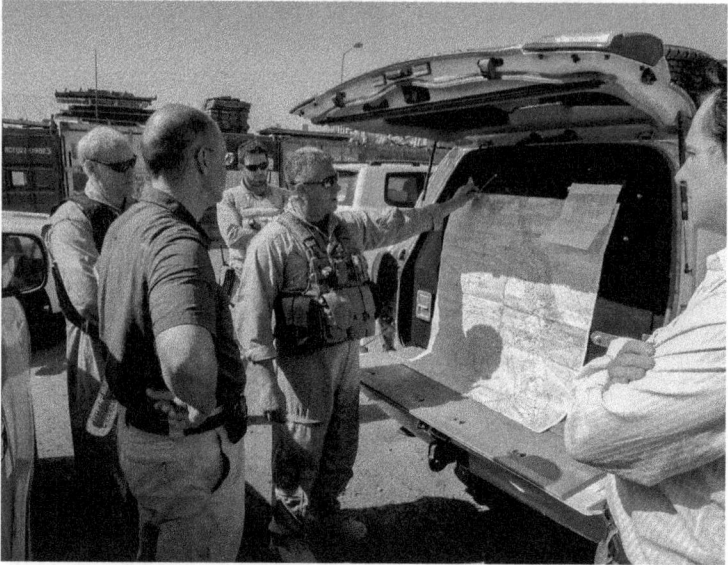

FIGURE 14.6   Stephan Crétier visiting GardaWorld's Security operations in Basra, Iraq, the same year he was named the most influential Canadian CEO of the decade.

(Photo from October, 2011.)

as Stephan took calculated risks and "stretched the machine" to make things happen. The result of his hard-driving yet endearing, inspired style was building Garda into a C$4 billion security services company that continues to grow. Stephan is still going strong, and his legacy is still being written. Stephan told the authors that his bankers and investors refer to him as "the disruptor" and throughout his career he has managed to turn convention on its head, doing what others would not do and creating immense value in the process.

NOTES

1   Gordon Pitts, "Stephan Cretier: The New Wonder Boy," *The Globe and Mail*, July 1, 2007, https://www.theglobeandmail.com/report-on-business/stephen-cretier-the-new-wonder-boy/article1077809/

2   "Stephan Crétier: Founder, Chairman, President and Chief Executive Officer," accessed November 14, 2022, https://www.garda.com/about-us/stephan-cretier

3 Goldy Hyder, *Business Council of Canada podcast*, podcast audio, Stephan Crétier, Founder, Chairman and CEO of GardaWorld, https://thebusinesscouncil.ca/publication/stephan-cretier/

4 Hyder, *Business Council of Canada Podcast.*

5 Hyder, *Business Council of Canada Podcast.*

6 Pitts, "Stephan Cretier: The New Wonder Boy."

7 Hyder, *Business Council of Canada Podcast.*

8 Pitts, "Stephan Cretier: The New Wonder Boy."

9 "GardaWorld, A Success Story," accessed November 14, 2022, https://www.garda.com/about-us/gardaworld-a-success-story

10 GardaWorld, A Success Story.

11 "Garda World Security Buys Vance International," *Security Infowatch.com*, November 28, 2005, https://www.securityinfowatch.com/security-executives/protective-operations-guard-services/press-release/10592411/securityinfowatchcom-garda-world-security-buys-vance-international

12 "Garda Takes Over Kroll Security International," December 7, 2006, https://www.upi.com/Defense-News/2006/12/07/Garda-takes-over-Kroll-Security-Intl/24111165513089/

13 Sean Silcoff, "Rebounding Garda Back in Acquisition Mode," *The Globe and Mail*, August 28, 2012, https://www.theglobeandmail.com/report-on-business/rebounding-garda-back-in-acquisition-mode/article4506404/

14 GardaWorld, A Success Story.

15 GardaWorld, A Success Story.

16 Garda World Security Corporation, "Completion of GardaWorld Recapitalization for C$5.2 Billion," news release, October 30, 2019, https://www.garda.com/press-release/completion-of-gardaworld-recapitalization-for-c52-billion-0

17 Yadarisa Shabong, "UK's G4S Rejects 2.95 Billion Pound Offer from Canadian Security Firm GardaWorld," September 14, 2020, https://www.reuters.com/article/uk-gardaworld-m-a-g4s-idUKKBN2651P4

18 Louis Ko and Donald S. Carter, "Moody's Rates Garda World's New Senior Secured Notes B1," *Moody's*, https://www.moodys.com/research/Moodys-rates-Garda-Worlds-new-senior-secured-notes-B1--PR_417388

19 Dion Bate and Donald S. Carter, "Moody's Downgrades Garda's Senior Secured Instruments to B2," *Moody's*, https://www.moodys.com/research/Moodys-downgrades-Gardas-senior-secured-instruments-to-B2-and-affirms--PR_462184

20 "Fitch Rates Garda World Security Corp's $700MM TLB 'BB+'/'RR1'," *Fitch Ratings*, https://www.fitchratings.com/research/corporate-finance/fitch-rates-garda-world-security-corp-700mm-tlb-bb-rr1-02-02-2022

21 "GardaWorld Announces the Acquisition of Global Leader ARCA," news release, August 24, 2022, https://www.garda.com/press-release/gardaworld-announces-the-acquisition-of-global-leader-arca

22 Palantir Technologies Inc., "Palantir and Crisis24, A GardaWorld Company, Announce New Partnership to Revolutionize Security and Risk Management for the 21st Century," news release, December 9, 2022, https://www.prnewswire.com/news-releases/palantir-and-crisis24-a-gardaworld-company-announce-new-partnership-to-revolutionize-security-and-risk-management-for-the-21st-century-301698938.html

23 GardaWorld, "GardaWorld International Protective Services Receives ISO 18788:2015 Across Entire Operations," March 7, 2016, https://www.garda.com/blog/gardaworld-international-protective-services-receives-iso-187882015-across-entire-operations

24 Hyder, *Business Council of Canada Podcast*.

25 "Fondation S. Crétier," accessed November 19, 2022, https://fondationcretier.org/en/

CHAPTER 15

Steve Jones
Up Tempo

After injuries cut short Steve Jones' (Steve) hope of becoming an NFL football player, he entered the business world with the goal of obtaining great success. After a brief career in sales and management for two Fortune 500 firms, he was well on his way to that goal. He began his security service industry career as an executive with Universal Protection Service (Universal) in 1996, a small security company with $12 million in sales based in Orange County, California. At Universal, he met Brian Cescolini (Brian), who was managing the company for the founder-owners. In just over 20 years, Steve and Brian would transform Universal into the world's largest global security services company. While we highlight Steve Jones' legendary career in this chapter, we also note the extraordinary role that Brian played in the meteoric rise of Universal.

Steve and Brian revamped what had been a stagnant company, improved service levels, grew sales organically, and began building a team to expand geographically. Steve and Brian struck a deal in 1998 with the owners of Universal to purchase equity in the company if they met certain conditions by 2007. They exceeded the conditions and would purchase the entire company with funding from a private equity group. Once fully in control, Steve utilized leverage to pursue an aggressive acquisition strategy. This was coupled with consistently strong organic growth based on building relationships through quality service. Steve took calculated risks, with Brian by his side. While others might easily consider Steve's approach highly risky, he was always confident that his strategies and abilities would prevail if faced with any adverse event.

In 2016, as chief executive officer of the company, and with the backing of several of the world's largest private equity companies, Steve merged Universal with AlliedBarton to create Allied Universal and become the largest security services company in North America, with revenues of $4.5 billion (Figure 15.1).[1] In 2021, Allied Universal acquired London-based global security company G4S, creating the world's largest security services company. As global chairman and chief executive officer of Allied

DOI: 10.4324/9781003285564-21

The Impact of the Allied Barton/Universal Merger on Security Guard Companies

Keith Oringer - May 30, 2016

Creating a Mega-Company

Founded in 1965 as a janitorial company serving Southern California, Universal expanded into the Security Industry in 1969 with the formation of Universal Protection Service. Under the leadership of the current CEO, the company has grown from $12 million in revenue to more than $2.5 billion and has acquired more than three dozen companies in the last four years.

In 2004, Allied Security acquired Barton Protective to form AlliedBarton Security. The acquisition made AlliedBarton the largest American-owned contract security services company in the United States. The company currently has an annual revenue of $2.0 billion.

The AlliedBarton/Universal merger is expected to generate a revenue representing $4.5 billion, making it the largest in North America and the 3rd largest in the world behind G4S and Securitas. Prosegur & AlliedUniversal will have equivalent revenues.

Overtaking National Market Share

AlliedUniversal will service all of North America and will be in a position to procure any customer within the U.S. and Canada. Having consolidated to become the largest company of its kind in the U.S., AlliedUniversal is well-placed to secure some of the largest national accounts and overtake the market share of other national firms.

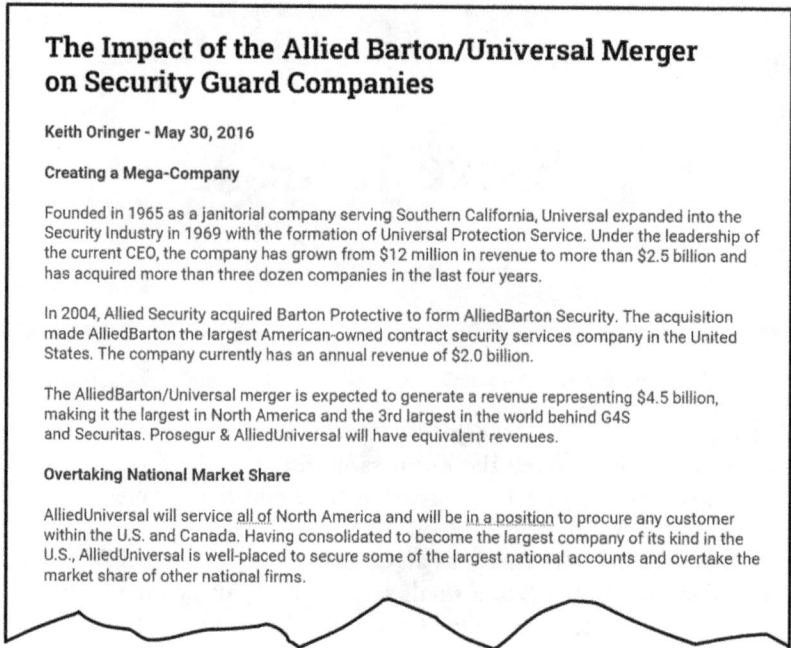

FIGURE 15.1   One intrepid industry writer penned this analysis at the time of the merger.

Universal, Steve Jones presides over the seventh largest employer in the world with over 800,000 employees and revenue in excess of $20 billion.[2]

Steve likes to use sports metaphors to describe aspects of the business world. His 2018 autobiography is titled *No Off Season: The Constant Pursuit of More*, where "off season" refers to periods during the year when a professional sport is not officially being played. We have chosen to title this chapter "Up Tempo," which is a football term used for a no-huddle, hurry-up offense. This offensive strategy is designed to use the speed of play together with prepared and ad hoc plays to catch a defense off balance. Steve plays fast and hard in business and life, as will be illustrated in this chapter. Yet there is also a side to him that is deeply caring for those around him (Figure 15.2).

EARLY LIFE AND MENTORS

Steve's autobiography provides much insight into his formative years. He was born in 1969 in Livermore, California, a blue-collar town about an hour outside of San Francisco. He spent the first 11 years

FIGURE 15.2   Steve believes in a hands-on approach, leading by example.

of his childhood there. His parents were hardworking, and the family lived comfortably but not luxuriously. His father, Steve Sr., was a very good athlete, having played football for Alabama under legendary Coach Bear Bryant. Steve Sr. signed a contract to play professional baseball for the Pittsburgh Pirates organization, but his sports career was cut short when he was drafted for the Vietnam War. In Livermore, Steve Sr. was employed as a delivery driver for Aramark, the large industrial services company. Steve's grandfather was a tough, career Army man and World War II vet who survived the attack on Pearl Harbor. According to Steve, sports was likely the outlet the Jones men needed to release their "latent militaristic instincts." He noted that he obtained his toughness and love of sports from his father, and kindness from his mother, a homemaker who had an earlier career as a flight attendant for TWA.

Steve's intense desire to succeed and to work hard was evident early on. When Steve was seven, his father dropped him off with a shoeshine kit on a street corner in Livermore, where Steve was determined to outdo his father by earning more money than his father had in his early life. Steve's father had told him how he had shined shoes for Army soldiers during his years growing up on various military bases. Steve hustled to shine as many shoes as he could and was convinced he had earned more than his father did when accounting for inflation.[3]

Steve said of sports that it taught him the value of discipline and hard work, and the importance of preparation.

> In sports you train and prepare for the next game, and in business you prepare for your next sales call or meeting. Sports also teach you how to grind, how to compete, how to win graciously and how to lose; and the lessons from losing are sometimes more important, as you can look back and learn from your loss. You can learn how to come back from a loss, and what you can do better the next time.[4]

When Steve was 11 the family moved to the Southern California city of Irvine. Steve Sr. had been promoted to a general manager position after his hard work caught the attention of his bosses at Aramark. In Irvine, "the middle-class kid was thrown into an upper class world," and it was through sports that Steve found his place as the new kid in town. Of significance for Steve at the time was the mentoring provided to him by a friend's father, Dave Roberson. Steve described Roberson as exuding class and an easy confidence. Roberson had made a fortune in the insurance business and took an interest in Steve. He assisted Steve financially by giving him odd jobs, so Steve could earn money and keep up with the rich kids in town. Steve said he learned more from Roberson than he did getting his MBA.

> [M]ore than anything, Roberson taught me the importance of a mentor, not only the advantage of having others to offer experienced guidance and counseling, but also the benefits to be gained on the other side of that equation, in offering advice to and taking care of others.[5]

A Real-World Struggle

Steve attended junior college and then received a scholarship to play football at California Polytechnic State University in San Luis Obispo (Cal Poly). Though Steve Sr. thought he should study physical education, Dave Roberson convinced Steve to study political science. Steve's hope of playing professional football suffered a setback after he sustained a severe neck injury on the field. In excruciating detail, Steve described in his memoir being forced by his coach to play through pain, after nearly suffering a broken neck. The injury proved too much, and with his football scholarship pulled, Steve struggled financially to graduate. The experience taught him about "real-world" struggles and that hardship was no excuse not to find new opportunities. He had put in the work in sports and at school, and as his business career unfolded he concluded that "opportunities abound for those willing to put in the work and take the risks."[6]

Fortune 500 Job Experience

After graduation, Steve considered going to law school, but was unsure whether his heart was in it. The prosperous businessman father of a girl-friend convinced Steve to follow his passion and do something he loved. The businessman, who owned the Del Taco restaurant chain, showed Steve that a business career can be more rewarding than a career in law. Steve took a sales position at Aramark's industrial uniform division. As a leading salesman, within two and a half years Steve was promoted to run regional sales for Southern California.

At the time, Steve received a call from his former junior college coach, inviting him to try out for the World Football League. Steve spoke to his father about the opportunity, but his father told him that dreams of glory are just that, and that Steve had gotten a degree and a great job, and that he was "on track to something bigger than the NFL." Steve declined the football opportunity and continued to build on his business career; after three years at Aramark, he took a job with BFI (Browning Ferris) Waste Services, the second-largest trash company in the world, as a district sales and marketing manager for their Southern California market.

Listening to colleagues who had sold their businesses to BFI, Steve learned an ownership interest was the best way to take advantage of opportunities in the business world. To enhance his business knowledge, he attended the University of the Redlands at night and on weekends to earn an MBA in business, while still working at BFI. Armed with the advanced degree and a desire to become an owner, Steve began a career in the security services industry at Universal Protection Service (Universal), an Orange County–based company with sales of about $12 million.[7]

A METEORIC SECURITY CAREER BEGINS

Everything about Steve's career moved at warp speed. From 1996 when Steve first started at Universal, until the end of 1999 when he convinced Brian Cescolini to partner with him and buy the company, he was in constant motion.

The move to Universal was for Steve a calculated risk. Leaving the comfort of BFI, a Fortune 500 company, to run a "fixer upper" in the security industry was both a challenge and an opportunity. It was part of what Steve viewed as a series of interconnected risks that offer opportunity and reward. The company founders were "still running the company with the same pen and pad methods that they used when they started thirty-four years earlier." There was no sales team, and growth had stagnated.[8]

On his first day on the job at Universal, Steve met Brian Cescolini, who was running the company for its owners, having risen through the ranks after starting as a security guard. On that first day, Brian took Steve to the company's largest customer, the Irvine Company, a prominent real estate company. Steve and Brian were stunned when an Irvine Company property manager informed them that Irvine was cancelling the contract with Universal. Steve convinced the property manager to allow him 30 days to fix the problem. He listened to all the complaints and established a relationship with the managers at Irvine, which enabled him to stay on top of the details. With attention to detail, Steve knew that Universal would be able to bring its service level up to and above any standards set by the customer. Because of Steve's strong belief in the importance of building relationships, Irvine became one of Universal's major and long-standing customers.

In spite of their reluctance to make changes, Steve convinced the owners at Universal to allow him to hire a salesperson. Steve also led the overhaul and modernization of operating systems, including hiring and scheduling systems. He brought a hustle mentality to the firm. The plan was working and within three years sales had doubled to $24 million. At the company Christmas party in 1999, only Steve and Brian knew of the owners' plan to sell the company. Steve convinced Brian to join him in a plan to buy a 40 percent interest in Universal. The plan required that they build Universal into a $60 million company within seven years. If they met this goal the owners would sell their 40 percent stake. If they did not, Brian and Steve would forgo $1.5 million due to the owners sold at the time. The owners agreed to the plan, and Brian and Steve took over operational control.

Steve now felt the freedom to build and take care of his own team. Steve and Brian borrowed $1 million, which they needed to pay the owners, and began a grind to get business, first throughout Southern California and then Northern California. The pair built the reputation of the company through quality service, and they hired and inspired a committed, driven sales and operations team. Everyone was grinding, and Steve built relationships with many real estate companies, including the property managers for the Transamerica Building in Southern California. The company picked up business in many large office buildings, including Los Angeles' famous Century City, and the 75-story Library Tower building.[9]

Steve knew the importance of developing a great team early on. For Steve, having a strong team—one that is taken care of by management at all levels of a company—is critical to the success of an enterprise. To this day, the slogan "Take Care of Your Team" is proudly displayed at corporate headquarters.[10]

Quick Action after the 9/11 Attacks

By the time the 9/11 terror attacks took place, Universal had a large base of business in the Class A office vertical in Southern California. Immediately after the attacks, Steve picked up business at the iconic Transamerica Pyramid building in San Francisco, capitalizing on the reputation of the company and its strong relationship with Transamerica's managers in Southern California. Steve and Brian initiated additional building security measures at their serviced properties. These included bag checks, car scans in the parking garages, and a heightened interface by the guards for anyone entering buildings. Steve developed a two-hour PowerPoint presentation on best practices in building security with input from the FBI and made presentations throughout California and the Southwest. By 2002, sales had doubled again to $48 million. Two years later, Steve and Brian had grown Universal to over $60 million, reaching the threshold to obtain a 40 percent stake in the company three years ahead of time.[11]

Calculated Risks to Attain National Status

By 2007 the goal to achieve $60 million in revenues had already been surpassed; Universal had grown to just over $150 million in revenues. The company made its first acquisition, San Francisco-based Ligouri and Associates, which had about $12 million in revenue, in order to solidify their presence in that market. Steve was looking to make additional acquisitions and purchase Universal, but the financial crisis had taken its toll on one of their two lenders, the Guarantee Bank, which folded. Steve convinced Brian to go along with a deal to obtain financing from Caltius Partners, a mezzanine finance group, at 19 percent interest plus 3 percent equity to purchase the entire company and embark on a more aggressive acquisition program. The terms were difficult, but Steve was confident that it was a calculated risk worth taking. They hired a CFO with acquisition experience, and in 2008 Steve persuaded Steve Claton, then an executive at the multibillion-dollar Irvine Company, to help run Universal, which was now up to $300 million in sales. This was to allow Steve to pursue acquisitions to accelerate growth and bring Universal to the $1 billion level Steve knew from the start that he would achieve.

In 2010, Universal acquired four more companies for $22 million, expanding its presence in Arizona and Texas and growing revenue by

$60 million.[12] That was followed by the 2011 strategic acquisition of SFI. On October 24, 2011, Universal announced that it had acquired Security Forces, Inc. (SFI) and their electronic security systems company, SFI Electronics, Inc. (SFIE). SFI had been in the business of providing security guard services since 1949 and in 2011 employed over 3,500 security professionals through 31 offices throughout the southeastern United States. A news release announcing the acquisition read, "Steve Jones, co-CEO and chief operating officer of Universal Services of America said this acquisition is truly transformational and grants us the ability to provide true coast to coast service to our clients." Headquartered in Santa Ana, California, the company was now the sixth largest security company in the United States and the fourth largest U.S.-owned security organization, with offices throughout Alabama, Arizona, California, Colorado, Delaware, Florida, Georgia, Louisiana, Maryland, North Carolina, South Carolina, Tennessee, Texas, Virginia, and Washington.[13]

Advancing with Integrated Security

In 2013, Universal acquired Thrive Technology. The move would be a precursor to expanding efforts by Universal to bolster physical security capabilities in order to provide a total security solutions program to customers.

Steve said Universal would incorporate Thrive's state-of-the-art technology in deploying remote video and using analytics to manage that video across the United States.

> The future of security is really a total security solution, and that means the security provider has to provide [human] guards as well as technology to solve customers' problems. In the past, people looked to video after a crime to determine how many criminals to seek, while hoping for a clear enough picture to produce a description. Ideally, now we're able to prevent things from happening.[14]

ENTERING THE NEW YORK MARKET

Steve now had his eye on expansion to the large and lucrative New York City market. Caltius had advised Steve that they had exceeded their internal loan limit with Universal, so he struck a deal with the Partners Group, an investor in their original mezzanine financing, again for financing at a 19 percent interest rate. Revenues were now about $700 million.[15]

On January 2, 2013, Universal announced that they had acquired the security officer services division of T&M Protection Resources, LLC. This would enable Universal's security force to service its clients throughout the entire United States and make Universal a major player in the Northeast and the state of New York. Brian, chairman and co-CEO, said

> New York is a major market that we have long aspired to be in. We plan to enhance and invest resources and services into the region, with the goal of bringing a fresh approach not seen in the marketplace in many years.

The company was now the fifth largest U.S.-based security services company.[16]

A Prized Acquisition

Steve twice attempted to buy AlliedBarton, but by 2015 two attempts ended in no deal. He compiled a list of acquisition targets; at the top of the list was Guardsmark. Guardsmark was "such a special company that over time absolutely everyone in the industry had tried buying it at one time or another…The company was headed by Ira Lipman [Chapter 4], who was personally every bit the legend that his company was." It took Steve a lot of effort and meetings over three months to convince Ira to sell to Universal.[17]

With the acquisition Universal was neck and neck with AlliedBarton as the largest U.S.-based security services company. Steve said that being the largest American-owned guard firm will be a "real differentiator" for Universal in the U.S. market. Guardsmark had more than 125 offices in 400 cities in the United States, Canada, Puerto Rico, and the United Kingdom. In addition to guard services, Guardsmark offered risk assessments, executive protection, investigations, and background checks. Universal was operating in 100 U.S. cities, and the combined company would employ 60,000. Guardsmark chief executive officer Ira Lipman joined the Universal board of directors as vice chairman. Steve also announced that Universal had a new majority shareholder, as former majority owner Partners Group had agreed to sell its controlling interest in Universal to Warburg Pincus, a global private equity firm. Universal and Partners Group would remain large shareholders in the business. He noted that Universal competitors "Securitas and G4S are foreign-owned, and AlliedBarton recently announced that it's selling to a French company."[18]

The supercharged growth for Universal would accelerate over the next six years. The size and pace of its growth has never been matched in the history of the security services industry. With resolve, and the backing of some of the world's leading private equity companies, Universal would soon make major acquisitions that would propel the company to become the largest security company in the world.

Universal Merges with AlliedBarton

On August 1, 2016, one year to the day that Warburg Pincus became the majority owner of Universal, it was announced that Universal and AlliedBarton had merged. The merger created the world's third largest security company, Allied Universal. The combined company would have approximately 140,000 employees and $4.5 billion in revenues. Allied Universal would maintain headquarters in Santa Ana, California, and Conshohocken, Pennsylvania. Steve Jones was named chief executive officer, and AlliedBarton's Bill Whitmore (Chapter 8) was named chairman.[19]

The merger of two of the largest U.S. security companies created a major force in the U.S. security market. In terms of size and quality of business, Allied Universal was positioned to challenge the two largest companies: Securitas and G4S. With strong financial backing, and a roster of customers that rivaled any security company, the growth trajectory of Allied Universal would continue on a staggering level. Within a few months of the Allied Universal merger, the company announced that it was acquiring two well-known regional companies: New York-based FJC security, and Waltham, Massachusetts, and New York-based Apollo International. Author Michael Hymanson recalled a meeting at the New York chapter of ASIS where the buzz around the room was about which company might be next on the list for Allied Universal. One executive from a recently acquired regional firm stated that "every company is on the radar, no matter how big the company." Less than two years later, the company Michael worked for would be acquired.

The Acquisition Spree Continues

In October 2018, Allied Universal acquired U.S. Security Associates, the fourth largest security company operating in the United States. With U.S. Security's revenues in excess of $1.5 billion and with over 50,000 employees, "Allied Universal was now an organization with annual revenues of approximately $7 billion and over 200,000 security professionals." The acquisition increased Allied Universal's national presence and customer service capabilities, enhanced Allied Universal's presence in Canada, and expanded its footprint to Central and Latin America, and the United Kingdom. The acquisition also added consulting and investigations, and event staffing services.[20]

In a two-and-a-half-year-period prior to what would be the company's largest purchase ever, Allied Universal purchased not only U.S. Security Associates but also more than a dozen other security and security technology companies. Also, during this time, private equity group fund Caisse de Depot et Placement du Quebec (CDPQ) became a major shareholder, making CDPQ and Warburg Pincus Allied Universal's largest shareholders.[21]

Evidencing the continued importance the company placed on integrated solutions, Allied Universal acquired Securadyne Systems, which specialized in integrated security solutions by offering security consulting, design, engineering, and installation. Steve noted that

> Our new acquisition of Securadyne Systems supports our long-term strategy to become the leader in the security technology market. As security needs change and evolve, Allied Universal will offer clients cutting-edge technology and service that will help make their security programs more effective and efficient to better protect their employees and assets.

The company tech platform to build out global capabilities was rebranded as Allied Universal Technology Services, and headquartered in Dallas, Texas.[22]

ALLIED UNIVERSAL BECOMES THE WORLD'S LARGEST SECURITY COMPANY

On April 5, 2021, Allied Universal announced it had completed the acquisition of G4S, to become the world's largest security services company. Allied Universal became the third largest employer in North America and the seventh largest employer in the world, with over 800,000 employees, and more than $18 billion in revenue. With the acquisition, Allied Universal would transform its largely North American footprint to include the 85-country presence that G4S had. Steve said, "This is truly a very significant moment in Allied Universal's history. Our vision is not only to be the best security company but to be the best corporate services partner in a world of evolving risk."[23]

The acquisition marked the end of a battle for G4S that had begun on September 30, 2020, when GardaWorld (Garda) launched an approximately $4 billion unsolicited takeover for G4S. The offer was rejected, and Allied Universal would later make a conditional offer for a reported $4.4 billion. Bloomberg reported on December 2, 2020, that "GardaWorld increased its hostile offer for G4S to $4.9 billion, unless G4S received a firm bid from someone else... But on December 8, the G4S board, according to Bloomberg, unanimously agreed to a $5.3 billion cash offer by Allied Universal." Since Garda had not declared their offer as necessarily final, an auction scenario was set by the London Exchange, but when Garda did raise its bid for G4S, the accepted $5.3 billion offer by Allied Universal seemed likely to prevail.[24] Allied Universal would prevail and acquired G4S.

Steve said that the acquisition got Allied Universal to global scale immediately, rather than by going one acquisition after another, which would have taken another ten years. "The plan is to grow to $25 billion in annual sales by 2026. We're not slowing down." The company would focus on integrating G4S to incorporate Allied Universal's systems, branding, and culture to boost margins in an industry with traditionally low profit and high turnover, and placing an emphasis on guards using the latest technology.[25]

TESTAMENTS

Justin Nagy, former President—Central Region at Allied Universal, commented on working for Steve at Allied Universal:

> "Steve Jones is a visionary leader whose remarkable journey in the security industry has left an indelible mark on the entire industry. I had the privilege of working closely with Steve for over a decade, during which I witnessed his unwavering dedication, exceptional work ethic, and unrelenting commitment to success.
>
> When I first joined the company, it was a modest, regional player in the US. Under Steve's dynamic leadership, I saw the organization undergo a profound transformation. He possesses a unique ability to not only dream big but to execute his vision with precision and determination. His relentless pursuit of excellence propelled Allied Universal to unparalleled heights, ultimately becoming the leader in global safety and security.
>
> Steve's leadership style is characterized by his focus on assembling a team of extraordinary individuals. He understood that the key to sustained success lay in cultivating a group of strong leaders who shared his passion for excellence. His team consistently raised the bar and refused to accept mediocrity or failure

as options. Steve's leadership was a beacon of inspiration, challenging us to constantly strive for improvement and achieve the extraordinary.

Steve's career and impact on the security industry exemplify the power of unwavering dedication and a commitment to excellence. His exceptional journey serves as an inspiration to the entire security industry, reminding us that with hard work, vision, and a team mentality, there are no limits to what can be achieved. Steve Jones is a true pioneer and a driving force behind the success of Allied Universal, and I am honored to have been a part of his remarkable journey."

During our interview with John Harford, Vice President of Corporate Development at Allied Universal, he provided succinct remarks on Steve.

I am privileged to work with Steve. He was familiar with me prior to Allied Universal's acquisition of U.S. Security, as we competed in acquiring other security companies. Steve has an incredible work ethic. He is a hands-on leader who is competitive and loyal to his associates. He is all about the customer and providing a quality service.

INTERVIEW WITH STEVE JONES

During our November 6, 2023, interview with Steve, he provided simple, yet compelling, answers to a variety of questions. When asked what were the most challenging business crises that he faced during his security career, and how he handled them, he noted three macro events. He cited September 11, 2001, as the first major event.

It caught everyone by surprise by its magnitude and type as an act of terrorism that shook the world. We were able to separate ourselves from the competition, and lead from the front. We provided free consulting services and hardened our customer security posture. We conducted extensive terrorism preparedness training...The global financial crisis also posed a grave threat to our business, as our bank went under. We used a line of credit and were able to manage, but it put the business in great peril.... Then COVID-19. We wondered if everyone was going to shut down. There were logistical issues getting safety equipment, masks, and sanitizers by the hundreds of thousands. We had to deal with new methods to train and hire staff.

Steve said that significant changes in the security industry include the increased use of technology to enhance service and also through its application internally in the business. It's not just "observe and report" but now a matter of intelligence gathering to detect and prevent. He also noted that "private security is more a supplement to police than ever before. Police are understaffed," and we fill a need and are "an extension." He said the rise of social media has also had a great effect on how security must operate.

Regarding managing a wide-spread, diverse, and extremely large company, Steve said,

> it starts with our values, one set of values. We focus on core deliverables. Employee and customer retention along with profitability are keys for us. We have a very strong management team, and as a leader you can actually make a difference.

He said you must have "sustainable processes." Finally, in "every market we operate in, we are still a local business."

With the G4S acquisition, Steve noted that it was particularly challenging because "it occurred during COVID, and we couldn't travel. Due diligence was difficult to do not in person." The acquisition of a public company meant that customers were getting information fast, and this posed another challenge. Further, he noted that operating in over 95 countries, "we had to deal with time zone differences and difficulty handling communications."

Steve said he enjoys the business and loves to compete. From the start. he has remained "focused and gets up every day being passionate about being the world's leading service company." He handles the intricacy and stress in overseeing one of the world's largest companies by having "a great leadership team."

The key for entrepreneurs entering the business, he says, is "to be well capitalized. You need to learn the business: sales, operations, HR, risk management. Licensing and insurance is getting more complex. So, focus on a niche and bring value to customers." Plus, you need to "work hard and be a grinder. Have desire and passion, be prepared to fail, reinvent yourself, learn, adapt, and be committed" (Figure 15.3).

Lastly, Steve noted that "the prospects for the business are unlimited." Echoing the comments of other legends, Steve said, "safety and security are basic needs. The world recognizes their importance, and that fact has created great opportunities. It's not just technology; there will always be a need for security people."

FIGURE 15.3 Steve keynoting the Orange County Business Journal's Excellence in Entrepreneurship Awards in March 2023, an award which he himself received back in 2020.

LEGACY

With no feeling in his arms and fearing that his neck had been broken from a violent football collision with a 300-pound player, Steve still followed the orders of his coach and remained in the game in the pursuit of his football career. He finished his junior year at Cal Poly playing football, but by his senior year the injuries and surgeries had taken their toll. Not able to play in his senior year, his football scholarship was pulled, and he struggled financially to continue his education, but he made it through. Steve learned the value of caring for his team, and he soon found a new excitement in closing business deals and obtaining ownership of a company. With the unanticipated approval of the father he admired, he subsequently passed on an opportunity to resume a quest to be an NFL player, and he built a security services empire that today exceeds $20 billion in revenues (Figure 15.4). He is a man of courage and strength, a leader who pushes ahead with great energy, focused on a dream and a goal. He is also a skilled businessman.

In his autobiography, in interviews and podcasts, Steve provides much business advice using terms familiar to sports enthusiasts on how

Global Revenue of Allied Universal
2015–2022

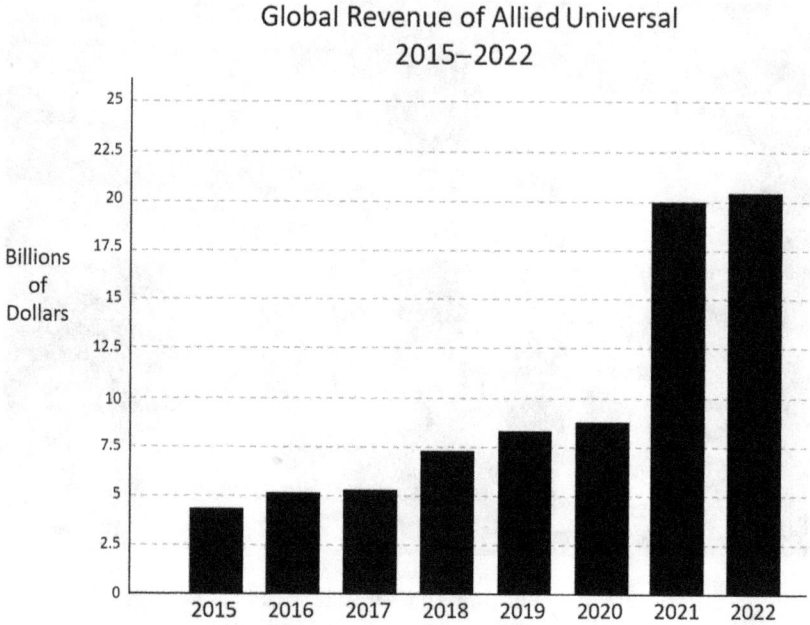

FIGURE 15.4   Global revenue for Allied Universal for 2015 through 2022.

to succeed in business. He said that in both business and in sports you learn discipline, how to prepare for the game or for a business meeting or sales call. In business and in sport you grind and learn how to win and how to lose; and in losing you can learn how you can do things better the next time around.[26]

The importance of family is not lost on Steve. In the conclusion of his autobiography, he advises the reader that the book is "about life" and "life is the game." He wrote, "take every snap and play absolutely every down like the entire game depends on it, because in a way it does."[27] The book's dedication reads,

> Like everything else that I do, this book is for my sons, Carter and Caden. May you have the vision to dream big, the dedication to have those dreams come true, and the courage to drive beyond even your greatest successes so that you can dream something bigger even still.[28]

Steve practices what he preaches, to "be the best you." He is still going strong, continuing his up-tempo approach to business and life (Figure 15.5).

FIGURE 15.5   A current photo of Steve.

NOTES

1   Wendel SE, "AlliedBarton and Universal Services of America Finalize Merger, Creating the Leading Security Services Company in North America," news release, August 1, 2016, https://www.prnewswire. com/news-releases/alliedbarton-and-universal-services-of-america- finalize-merger-creating-the-leading-security-services-company-in- north-america-300306813.html

2   "Meet Our People," accessed November 1, 2022, https://www.aus. com/our-people

3   Steve Jones, *No Off Season: The Constant Pursuit of More* (Charleston, SC: ForbesBooks, 2018), 1–10.

4   Brad Formsma, *The Wow Factor*, podcast audio, How to Establish a Clear Vision for the Future of Your Company, with Steve Jones, https://www.thewowfactorpodcast.com/show-notes/steve-jones- global-chairman-amp-ceo-of-allied-universal-episode-101

5   Jones, *No Off Season: The Constant Pursuit of More*, 11–34.

6   Jones, *No Off Season: The Constant Pursuit of More*, 34–66.

7   Jones, *No Off Season: The Constant Pursuit of More*, 67–93.

8   Jones, *No Off Season: The Constant Pursuit of More*, 91–9.
9   Jones, *No Off Season: The Constant Pursuit of More*, 101–32.
10 Formsma, *The Wow Factor*.
11 Jones, *No Off Season: The Constant Pursuit of More*, 132–48.
12 Jones, *No Off Season: The Constant Pursuit of More*, 149–73.
13 Universal Services of America, "Universal Protection Service Acquires Security Forces, Inc.," news release, October 24, 2011, https://www.prnewswire.com/news-releases/universal-protection-service-acquires-security-forces-inc-132431803.html
14 Leah Hoenen, "Universal Acquires THRIVE Intelligence," *Security Systems News*, December 3, 2013, https://www.securitysystems news.com/article/universal-acquires-thrive-intelligence
15 Jones, *No Off Season: The Constant Pursuit of More*, 150–79.
16 Universal Protection Service, "Universal Protection Service Acquires the Security Officer Services Division of T & M Protection Resources, LLC," news release, January 2, 2013, https://www.prnewswire.com/news-releases/universal-protection-service-acquires-the-security-officer-services-division-of-tm-protection-resources-llc-185431472.html
17 Jones, *No Off Season: The Constant Pursuit of More*, 190–92.
18 Martha Entwhistle, "Universal Buys Guardsmark to form Largest US-Owned Guard Firm," *Security Systems News*, July 29, 2015, https://www.securitysystemsnews.com/article/universal-buys-guardsmark-form-largest-us-owned-guard-firm
19 Wendel SE, "AlliedBarton and Universal Services of America Finalize Merger, Creating the Leading Security Services Company in North America."
20 Wendel SE, "Allied Universal Completes Acquisition of U.S. Security Associates for Approximately $1 Billion," news release, October 26, 2018, https://www.globenewswire.com/news-release/2018/10/26/1627970/0/en/WENDEL-Allied-Universal-completes-acquisition-of-U-S-Security-Associates-for-approximately-1-billion.html
21 Allied Universal, "Allied Universal Acquires G4S plc; Creating a Global Integrated Security Services Leader," news release, April 5, 2021, https://www.aus.com/press-releases/allied-universal-acquires-g4s-plc-creating-global-integrated-security-services
22 Allied Universal, "Allied Universal Acquires Securadyne Systems to Offer Highly Advanced Technology Solutions and Systems Integration Capabilites Throughout the Nation," news release, April 8, 2019, https://www.aus.com/press-releases/allied-universal-acquires-securadyne-systems-offer-highly-advanced-technology
23 Allied Universal, "Allied Universal Acquires G4S plc; Creating a Global Integrated Security Services Leader."

24 Keith Oringer, "The Battle for G4S Reaches a $5.3B Conclusion," *The Security Advisor*, Winter 2021.

25 Peter J. Brennan, "Steve Jones: Strength in Numbers," *Orange County Business Journal*, May 24, 2021, https://www.aus.com/sites/default/files/2021-08/OCBJSteveJonesFeature052421.pdf

26 Formsma, *The Wow Factor*.

27 Jones, *No Off Season: The Constant Pursuit of More*, 227.

28 Steve Jones, "Dedication," in *No Off Season: The Constant Pursuit of More* (Charleston, SC: ForbesBooks, 2018).

PART VI

Conclusions

Dynamic People, Companies, and Times

Looking back on the leaders in the security services industry, we can see that each one has had a unique impact, due to their personal style of interaction, the way they made use of the resources and skills they had available, the risks they assumed while building their company, their ability to read and to forecast the needs of potential customers, or all of the above. The legends, their companies, and the contexts in which they plied their trade all have been dynamic. Part VI summarizes the attributes, skills, and values that made each legend and company successful, and indicates several possible directions that future leaders in the industry may want to consider as they develop their careers and mentor others.

Chapter 16 includes a brief summary of the legends' tenures and the evolution of their affiliated companies. We provide a few examples from their biographies to demonstrate what we feel were their critical success factors. These include both personal characteristics and professional choices. An overarching theme here is that all resources—formal education, informally honed talents, business connections, family friends, religious grounding, one's own hard luck or good luck—can be brought to bear on leadership formation.

Chapter 17 contains information on the growing demand for security services in today's environment. As businesses, public utilities, data storage facilities, agricultural operations, and government entities of all sizes grapple with security threats that seem to morph daily, the next

DOI: 10.4324/9781003285564-22

generation of leaders in the security services industry will have to be just as dynamic as the legends that came before them. There's no other way, if they are to get out in front of the terrorists, ransomware, and the criminals who exploit security weak spots. The book concludes with opportunities for entrepreneurs and security managers, including a brief guide to starting and managing a contract security service.

CHAPTER 16

Forward Momentum

Each legend profiled in this book traveled a unique path to success in the security services industry. Their destination was forged by their experiences. They had the skill and fortitude to lead and manage during good as well as challenging times. None were infallible; however, one can't deny they had talent and an enviable ability to direct their energies toward achieving their goals. In this chapter we'll take some time to connect the dynamic lives of the industry's leaders with the companies they headed, and we'll quickly review how those companies evolved into today's biggest names in security services. Then we'll reflect on what we can learn from the legends about how to confront and rise to challenges in order to succeed. To frame the discussion, we offer this quote from entrepreneurship expert Alex Charfen:

> For entrepreneurs, success can be summed up in a simple phrase: forward momentum. We are either moving forward or we're dying. Success is a function of three vitally important things that create that much needed momentum: We have to understand where we've been, we have to know where we are going, and we should know what our current opportunities are [...] Hone your strengths and you will become world class.[1]

WHAT HAPPENED TO THE LEGENDS AND THEIR COMPANIES

The history of the security services industry is full of mergers and acquisitions, and as a result over time some of the legends' companies were acquired and became divisions of, or were otherwise absorbed into, larger companies that operate today. In the summary, table, and timeline

DOI: 10.4324/9781003285564-23

provided (Figure 16.1 and Table 16.1), we offer a broad-stroke picture of the evolution of the companies and what has happened to each of the legends.

Allan Pinkerton (Pinkerton's): Allan founded the Pinkerton Agency in 1850 and worked there until he passed away in 1884. Successive generations managed the firm until 1967, when the company went public. In 1982 the conglomerate American Brands purchased the company. It was sold to CPP and Tom Wathen in 1988. The company went public once again in 1991, then was acquired by Securitas in 1999.

William J. Burns (Burns International): William founded the Burns agency in 1909, and retired in 1924. He passed away in 1932. Successive generations of the family managed the company until 1981, and in 1982 the company was acquired by Borg-Warner Corporation. In 1993 Burns along with Wells Fargo was spun-off as a public company called Borg-Warner Security. In 2000, operating as Burns International, it was acquired by Securitas.

George R. Wackenhut (The Wackenhut Corp.): The company that George started in 1955, which became the Wackenhut Corp. went public in 1966. George retained majority shareholder status until the company was sold in 2002 to publicly held Group 4 Falck. George passed away in 2004.

Ira Lipman (Guardsmark): The company that Ira founded in 1960 went public in 1970 for 9 years, then remained private until 2015, when Ira sold the company to privately held Universal Protective. Ira served as advisor to Universal, then Allied Universal before he passed away in 2019.

Thomas W. Wathen (CPP and Pinkerton): Tom worked for CPP starting in 1965. He bought the company soon after and then CPP acquired Pinkerton in 1988. Pinkerton went public in 1991. Tom was chief executive and then chairman at Pinkerton's until it was sold to Securitas in 1999. Tom passed away in 2016.

Charles R. "Chuck" Schneider (Wells Fargo, Burns, U.S. Security): Chuck worked for Baker Industries, a division of Borg-Warner, from 1978 to 1993. The company owned Wells Fargo Security and then Burns starting in 1982. Chuck left Borg-Warner Security in 1993 and cofounded U.S. Security Associates with Ken Oringer. U.S. Security had several equity investors, the last being

Goldman Sachs Capital Partners which bought majority control in 2011. He remained at U.S. Security as chairman until it was purchased by Allied Universal in 2018.

Kenneth W. Oringer (Wells Fargo, Burns, U.S. Security): Ken also worked for Baker Industries, a division of Borg-Warner, from 1978 to 1993. He left Borg-Warner Security in 1993 and cofounded U.S. Security Associates with Chuck Schneider. He remained at U.S. Security as chief financial officer and executive vice president until he retired in 2014. Ken passed away on September 28, 2022.

William C. "Bill" Whitmore Jr. (SpectaGuard, Allied, AlliedBarton, and Allied Universal): Bill started with SpectaGuard in 1981. In 2000 it acquired and operated as Allied Security until 2004, when it acquired Barton Protective and operated as AlliedBarton. The company remained privately held with majority ownership from MacAndrews and Forbes, then Blackstone, and finally with Wendel, a global investment company. In 2016 AlliedBarton merged with Universal to form Allied Universal. Bill retired as Chairman by 2018.

Albert J. "Al" Berger (CPP, SpectaGuard, Allied, AlliedBarton): Al was a longtime board member at CPP, but his legendary security career was centered around his time as president of Pinkerton from 1990 to 1994, and his tenure as chief executive officer and chairman at SpectaGuard and Allied Security from 1998 to 2003. His security career ended in 2006, as a director at AlliedBarton.

Jørgen Philip-Sørensen (Group 4, Group 4 Falck & Group 4 Securicor): Jørgen began working in 1955 for security companies owned by his father. Group 4 Securitas was demerged from Securitas by his father, and be privately owned by Jørgen until 2000, when it merged with publicly held Falck to form Group 4 Falck. It then merged with Securicor in 2004 to form Group 4 Securicor. Jorgen retired as chairman in 2006. Group 4 Securicor was renamed G4S in 2007. Jørgen passed away in 2010.

Lars Nørby Johansen (Falck, Group 4 Falck & Group 4 Securicor): Lars started with Falck in 1988. In 2000 publicly held Falck merged with Group 4 to form Group 4 Falck, then merged with Securicor in 2004 to form Group 4 Securicor. Lars left Group 4 Securicor in 2005, but stayed with Falck after it demerged from Group 4 Falck in 2004. He remained as chairman at Falck until he retired in 2014.

Thomas Berglund (Securitas): Thomas started with Securitas in 1988. He was chief executive officer at Securitas from 1993 until 2007. Securitas is a public company that has had global investment company AB Latour as a major shareholder since 1985. Securitas became publicly held in 1991.

Helena Revoredo Gut (Prosegur): Since 1997 Helena has been a director and since 2004 chairman at Prosegur. Her husband Herberto Gut founded Prosegur in 1976, but passed away in 1997. Prosegur has been family controlled since its inception and became publicly traded in 1992.

Stephan Crétier (GardaWorld): Stephan founded the company in 1995. The company went public in 1998; then went private with equity backing in 2012 from Apax. The company recapitalized with private equity financing from Rhone Capital in 2017; and then with BC Partners in 2019. At the time of this writing, Stephan remains chief executive officer at GardaWorld.

Steve Jones (Universal Protective and Allied Universal): Steve began at Universal in 1996. He became the company owner with Brian Cescolini in 2009 through private equity financing by Caltius Partners. In 2015, Warburg Pincus became majority owner of Universal. In 2016, Universal merged with AlliedBarton to form Allied Universal. With the backing of global investment companies Warburg and CDPQ, Allied Universal acquired G4S in 2021. Steve remains chief executive officer at Allied Universal.

One thing we would highlight in the data given above is that, while many of the companies that the legends founded or led were acquired or merged with another company, none of the legends were forced to sell their company. Companies were sold or acquired because some legends monetized their businesses or retired, or because financial firms with a controlling interest decided to merge or sell the firm. In the case of executive legends, retirement from the industry was largely contingent on a board of directors deciding to move in another direction. In those cases the legends' record of success is not in dispute.

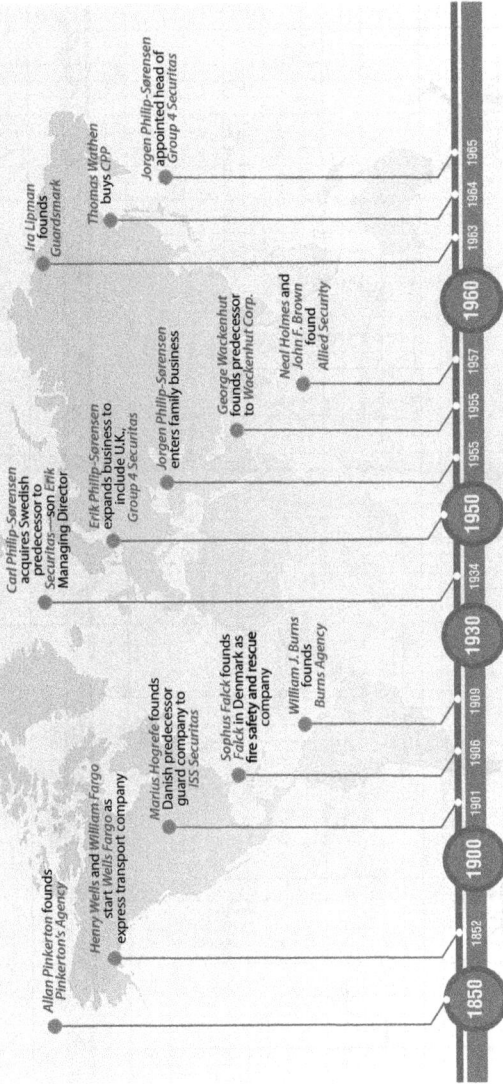

FIGURE 16.1   Legends timeline and comparison, compiled by the authors.

(Figure created by Maureen G. Nowak.)

Timeline: *Legends and their Associated Companies*

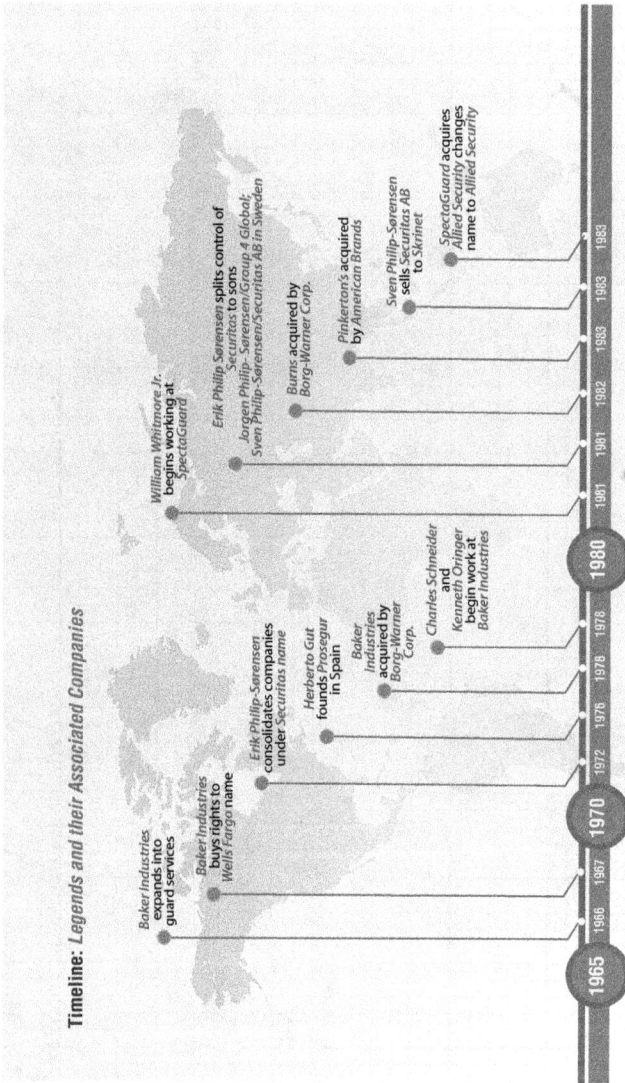

FIGURE 16.1 (Continued) Legends timeline and comparison, compiled by the authors.

(Figure created by Maureen G. Nowak.)

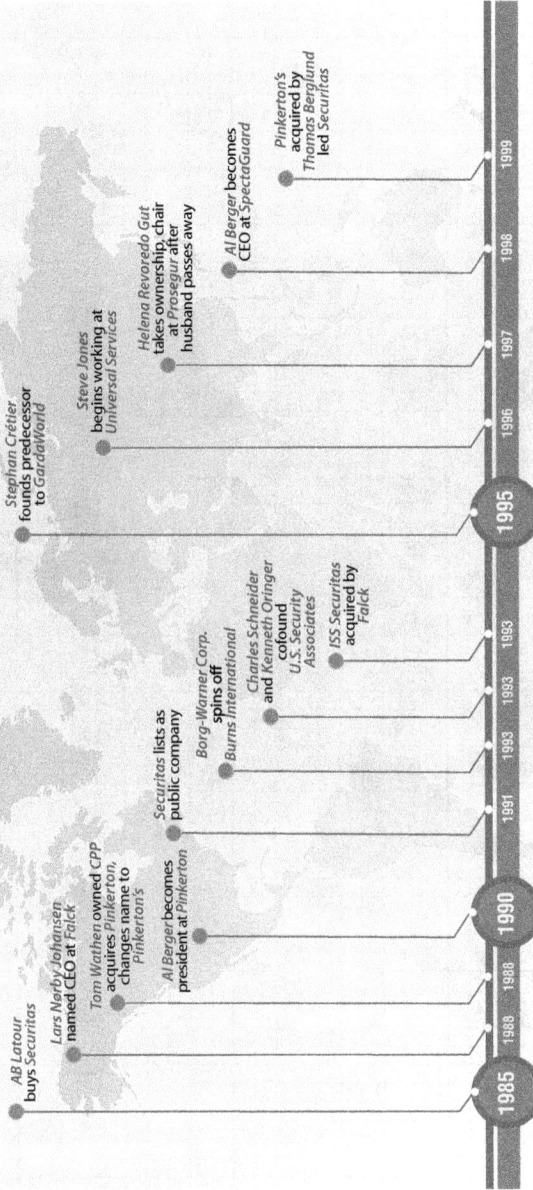

Timeline: *Legends and their Associated Companies*

AB Latour buys Securitas

Lars Nørby Johansen named CEO at Falck

Tom Wathen owned CPP acquires Pinkerton, changes name to Pinkerton's

Al Berger becomes president at Pinkerton

Securitas lists as public company

Borg-Warner Corp. spins off Burns International

Charles Schneider and Kenneth Oringer cofound U.S. Security Associates

ISS Securitas acquired by Falck

Stephan Crétier founds predecessor to GardaWorld

Steve Jones begins working at Universal Services

Helena Revoredo Gut takes ownership, chair at Prosegur after husband passes away

Al Berger becomes CEO at SpectaGuard

Pinkerton's acquired by Thomas Berglund led Securitas

1985   1988   1988   1990   1991   1993   1993   1993   1995   1996   1997   1998   1999

FIGURE 16.1   (Continued)   Legends timeline and comparison, compiled by the authors.

(Figure created by Maureen G. Nowak.)

Timeline: *Legends and their Associated Companies*

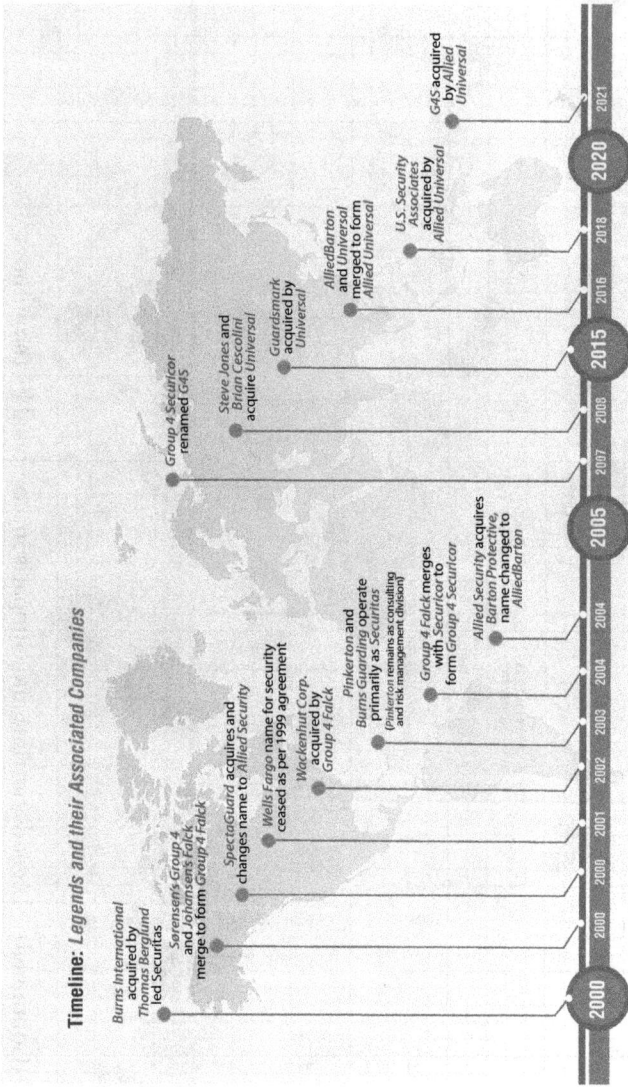

FIGURE 16.1 (Continued) Legends timeline and comparison, compiled by the authors.

(Figure created by Maureen G. Nowak.)

TABLE 16.1 Legends Lifespan and Years in Industry

Legend	Position	Company (Last Successor)	D.O.B./Death	Years In Industry
Part I				
Allan Pinkerton	Founder, President, Chairman	Pinkerton[a] (Securitas)[b]	1819/1884	<1850–1884
William J. Burns	Founder, President, Chairman	Burns[c] (Securitas)	1861/1932	<1884–1924
Part II				
George R. Wackenhut	Founder, CEO, Chairman	Wackenhut[d] (Allied Universal)[e]	1919/2004	1954–2002
Ira A. Lipman	Founder, President, Chairman	Guardsmark[f] (Allied Universal)	1940/2019	1960–2015
Thomas W. Wathen	CEO, Chairman	CPP, CPP-Pinkerton[g], Pinkerton (Securitas)	1929/2016	1963–1999
Part III				
Charles R. Schneider	CEO	Wells Fargo[h] & Burns (Securitas)	1940	1978–2018
	Cofounder, CEO, Chairman	U.S. Security Associates[i] (Allied Universal)		
Kenneth W. Oringer	CFO	Wells Fargo & Burns (Securitas)	1931/2022	1978–2014
	Cofounder, CFO	U.S. Security Associates (Allied Universal)		

(Continued)

TABLE 16.1 (Continued)

Legend	Position	Company (Last Successor)	D.O.B./Death	Years In Industry
William C. Whitmore	President, COO	SpectaGuard, Allied-SpectaGuard, Allied Security[j]	1952	1981–2020
	CEO, Chairman	Allied Security, AlliedBarton[k] (Allied Universal)		
	Chairman	Allied Universal		
Albert J. Berger	President, Vice-Chairman	Pinkerton	1936	1975–2006
	CEO, Chairman	SpectaGuard, Allied-SpectaGuard, Allied Security		
	Chairman	AlliedBarton		
Part IV				
Jorgen Philip-Sørensen	CEO, Chairman	Group 4 Securitas[l]	1937/2010	1955–2006
	Chairman	Group 4 Falck, Group 4 Securicor[m] (Allied Universal)		

Lars Nørby Johansen	CEO, Chairman	Falck	1949	1988–2005
	CEO	Group 4 Falck, Group 4 Securicor (Allied Universal)		1988–2007
Thomas F. Berglund	President, CEO	Securitas	1952	
Part V				
Helena R. Delvecchio	President, Director, Chairman	Prosegur[n]	1947	1997–present
Stephan Crétier	Founder, President, CEO	GardaWorld Security[o]	1963	1995–present
Steve Jones	CEO, Chairman, Global Chair	Universal Protection Service, Allied Universal[p]	1969	1996–present

[a] Founded in the 1850s, Pinkerton's was acquired by American Brands in 1982 and then by CPP (note g) in 1988. It was subsequently acquired by Securitas in 1999.

[b] Founded in 1934 by Carl Julius Philip-Sørensen as AB Hälsingborgs Nattvakt (Helsingborgs Nightwatch); in 1972, operated under SecuritasAB name in Sweden.

[c] Founded in 1909 as William J. Burns Agency. In 1913 changed name to Burns International Detective Agency. Operated as Burns Security and was acquired by Baker Industries division of Borg Warner in 1982. It became publicly traded as part of Borg-Warner Security in 1993, changed name to Burns International in 1999. Acquired by Securitas in 2000.

[d] Founded in 1955 as Special Agent Investigators and Special Agent Guard Services, renamed Wackenhut Corp. in 1959, it was sold to Group 4 Falck in 2002. It became owned by Group 4 Securicor as a result of the merger of Group 4 and Securicor in 2004 (renamed G4S in 2007). It became owned by Allied Universal as a result of the 2021 acquisition of G4S by Allied Universal.

[e] Formed from the 2016 merger of AlliedBarton Security and Universal Protection Service.

[f] Founded in 1963, Guardsmark was acquired by Universal Protection Service in 2015, and became owned by Allied Universal as a result of the 2016 merger of AlliedBarton and Universal Services.

[g] Founded in 1947, and bought by Wathen in 1964, CPP acquired Pinkerton in 1988 from American Brands (see note a), operated briefly as CPP-Pinkerton before changing name to Pinkerton's. Acquired by Securitas in 1999.

(Continued)

TABLE 16.1 (Continued)

[h] Wells Fargo Security, Alarm and Armored Car & Pony Express Courier were owned by Baker Industries, which was acquired by Borg Warner Corp. in 1978. Wells Fargo Armored was sold to Loomis in 1997, and renamed Loomis, Fargo. The rights to use the name Wells Fargo (and Pony Express) for the alarm and security guard divisions was sold in 1999 to Wells Fargo Bank by Borg Warner Security (later Burns International) and use of name discontinued in 2001 subsequent to the sale of Burns International to Securitas in 2000 (note 2).

[i] Founded in 1993. Sold to Allied Universal in 2018.

[j] Founded in the 1950s, SpectaGuard acquired Allied Security in 1998, briefly operated as Allied-SpectaGuard then changed name to Allied Security. Allied Security became AlliedBarton in 2004 when it acquired Barton Protective Services. Became Allied Universal in 2016 when AlliedBarton merged with Universal Protection Service.

[k] See note h above.

[l] Established as a division of Securitas AB in 1968, and split from Securitas AB in 1981.

[m] Group 4 Falck was formed when Group 4 Securitas merged with Falck. Group 4 Falck was renamed Group 4 Securicor after it acquired Securicor in 2004. Group 4 Securicor was renamed G4S in 2007. G4S was acquired by Allied Universal in 2021.

[n] Founded in 1976 by Herberto Gut Beltramo (late husband of Helena Revoredo Delvecchio).

[o] Founded in 1995 as Trans-Quebec Security, renamed Trans-Canada Security in 1998. Purchased Garda Security in 1999 and became GardaWorld Security Corp.

[p] Universal Protection Service was founded in 1965 and became Allied Universal when merged with AlliedBarton in 2016.

PAST EXPERIENCES FORMED STRONG LEADERS

The legends came from varied backgrounds and times, but each had the tools to succeed. Many of the legends had the good fortune of an early life marked by the support of family and mentors. Most gave credit to the values that one or more of their parents taught them; all gave credit to the education they were afforded or pursued. While it was advantageous for many of the legends to have parental or mentor support, in some cases it was the hardships and experiences in early life that created a resolve to overcome adversity. Certainly Allan Pinkerton had an early life unlike any other legend. His was a life that started in abject poverty; he had to flee to another country to escape from possible prosecution for political and union activities. Yet he had the fortitude to overcome adversity and a vision of where hard work effectively applied could lead him. He founded Pinkerton's and his status as a pioneer in the industry is cemented in history.

The legends came to the security service industry in varied ways. They brought with them a vision, a will, acquired and innate skills to succeed. Each worked hard and adapted to changing times and circumstances.

William Burns' father was elected police commissioner. From early on, William developed a fascination for law enforcement that was uniquely informed by details about the work he learned while his father was engage in law enforcement. William had great skills as a detective and used his prowess to build his reputation and later also built his business on that foundation. Ira Lipman and Jørgen Philip-Sørensen came from families with a history in the security services industry in different parts of the world. They followed their own paths from there to success in the industry. Ira started his company from scratch. Guardsmark was shaped and built from his own vision of what a great company should be. Jørgen had to start from the bottom but his fierce competitive spirit and will to succeed took him to areas where others did not go. He was a tireless, self-educated, and inspired leader.

Other legends, including George Wackenhut, Tom Wathen, and Bill Whitmore, had early careers in law enforcement; when they saw that there was opportunity in the contract security services industry they seized it. They all worked hard to build relationships and used their leadership and management skill to build major companies.

Other legends came to security services from other industries. Chuck Schneider and Ken Oringer were executives in other industries before being hired at the same security company; they used their prior education and business experience to succeed as executives in the security industry and later used that knowledge and experience to together, build a company of their own. Lars Nørby Johansen and Thomas Berglund were executives with earlier careers in education and government. They applied their acquired knowledge, skills, and intelligence to propel their respective security companies. Steve Jones had an early desire to become a professional football player, but injury and then early experiences gave him the vision to pursue ownership and a career in the security industry. Stephan Crétier saw his parents struggle and after realizing that being an umpire was not leading to financial independence he achieved success by applying his talents to building GardaWorld. Not to be overlooked, Helena Revoredo Gut faced a decision to carry on the success of her late husband in the security industry, sell, or do something else; she used the tools and lessons acquired through her early experiences and career to succeed as she carried the torch at Prosegur.

SHARED ATTRIBUTES, TRAITS, AND VALUES PROMOTED SUCCESS

The legends shared many personal attributes, traits, and values that were essential to their success. These included the following:

- Working hard
- Having a vision for where to apply their hard work, life experiences, and education
- Persevering through various hardships and adversity
- Pursuing education, formal and informal, to develop business and interpersonal skills
- Developing and guarding their reputation
- Recognizing and seizing opportunities
- Having the confidence to take risks, leave comfort zones, and change paths or careers
- Wielding authority wisely
- Delegating and empowering, but setting standards and communicating them well
- Building businesses through salesmanship, team building, company quality, and brand
- Inspiring by example
- Listening but acting decisively
- Innovating
- Not resting on prior success
- Operating their businesses with integrity

While we hope all of the aforementioned qualities became evident through the life stories of the legends, we wanted to list them together here, so that readers could more easily reflect on and synthesize the information. Are any of the aforementioned qualities particular strengths for you? Are some of them characteristics you would especially like to develop? We invite you to take a few moments and think about opportunities you might have in your life right now to do that. Maybe there's a mentor or coach who can help you develop certain skills, or perhaps there's a situation at work or in your personal life that you can approach with more intention.

UNIQUE PERSONALITIES, LEADERSHIP, AND MANAGEMENT STYLES

While the legends shared attributes, traits, and values, they all developed unique personalities, leadership and management styles that were formed as they navigated through life and business. We provide a few examples:

George Wackenhut had a meticulous father, and he was in turn meticulous. At The Wackenhut Corporation, the security officers and managers were required to maintain a distinctive appearance. The uniforms in which his security officers were attired were fashioned to evoke authority. George was a powerful person, physically and mentally. His company projected strength and order and obtained customers that required tight security, such as nuclear facilities and private prisons. George wanted to be in control and he never relinquished majority ownership of the shares of his company. His tenure ended when he decided to sell the company.

Ira Lipman witnessed racism as a student in Arkansas during the desegregation battle in the South and built Guardsmark to be committed to equality. They paid their employees well, trained them extensively, and required staff to perform according to strict standards. Each employee was encouraged and expected to do what was best to protect the company and its customers. The company earned a reputation in the industry for providing a very high-quality service. Ira insisted that the company price services accordingly and did not waiver from his vision of having the best company in the business. The company had an enviable roster of customers. Ira sacrificed growth for quality, and he did not need to answer to a board because he was the majority owner of the company. His tenure ended when he decided to sell Guardsmark.

Thomas Berglund was a chief executive officer at Securitas. He was a hired executive, not an owner, and reported to a board of directors. While the board set policy, the complexion and direction taken at Securitas took on many of the characteristics of his personality and leadership style. His parents taught him that success was best measured by lifting others. He implemented a strategy of training managers extensively so that they could manage business at the local lever rather than from a corporate headquarters. Managers were empowered to make decisions at the local level based on carefully developed company guidance. He directed the large-scale expansion of Securitas into North America with the acquisitions of

Pinkerton's and Burns. The Securitas brand under Berglund became so strong, that the venerable Pinkerton and Burns names were consolidated under the Securitas brand, although Pinkerton's survived as the risk and consulting division of the company. Because he was an executive and not the controlling owner, however, his tenure was determined by the Securitas board of directors.

Lars Nørby Johansen was another chief executive who reported to a board of directors. Lars was a brilliant student and then a lecturer. He changed careers and proved that he could translate the theoretical into practice. First, despite resistance from unions and employees, he obtained buy-in at Falck to convert what had been a struggling family-owned business into a profitable public company by communicating and executing strategies that restored profitability. He then built a global security power at Falck. He did not control ownership, and his tenure at Group 4 Securicor was abruptly ended. However, he remained for many years as chairman of the board at Falck, which survives as a large and respected fire safety, rescue, and assistance company.

From this discussion we hope you take away a certain curiosity about patterns. What values do you see others carry over from their upbringing or life circumstances into their leadership styles? Have you ever had a manager you thought was too caught up in the details and wasn't very effective as a result? Or maybe you've had a manager who was very good at asking for details and using them to inform their decision-making. If you share an obsession with details or some other deep value like those we've mentioned earlier, take a few minutes and think about the patterns in your life. Where do your core values come from? How can you shape them into success factors? If you've already tasted success with a skill like getting buy-in from others, how might you share that with others or amplify it in your career?

LUCK, FATE, AND ENHANCING YOUR CHANCE OF SUCCESS

While these shared attributes and traits were elemental to their success, the stories of the security services legends also illustrate ways that luck and fate can play a role in one's success. An outcome is never assured, because things happen in different ways, good or bad, for everyone. While your destiny is in large part determined by the path you take, along the way fate, a good break or some luck can play a part in your success. Some examples:

Allan Pinkerton stumbled upon a counterfeit bootleg operation. He solved the case, and that propelled his legendary career in security and investigations as founder and leader of Pinkerton's.

William Burns became fascinated with law enforcement after his father was elected as a local police commissioner. Burns solved local cases, became a celebrated detective, director of the FBI, and founded a successful security company that bore his name.

Chuck Schneider and Ken Oringer were in the right place and time when they were tipped off that a company which would be a perfect platform company for them to start a business was about to be sold. That company owner took a liking to them; they bought the company with private equity funding and proceeded to build U.S. Security Associates.

Al Berger, at the time a chemical industry executive, met Tom Wathen at a business club, and Tom asked Al to be on the board of directors at CPP Security. It would lead to a full-time legendary career for Al years later with CPP-Pinkerton and then SpectaGuard and Allied Security.

Stephan Crétier was a part-time store detective. He was recruited for a job in the security services industry and built GardaWorld into a global security company.

Have you ever found yourself in just the right place at the right time? Maybe a topic you know a lot about came up in a casual conversation, and the exact right person to ask you a key question on the topic did so. Is the kind of luck illustrated by the legends mentioned earlier always mere happenstance? Or are there techniques we can use to shape our lives in such a way that fate more frequently hands us what we want or need to be successful? Important factors in increasing your chance of success include putting yourself in the right place, developing the ability to see and seize opportunities, and then taking a risk on a chosen venture. Most importantly, perhaps, is to develop a mindset of learning from failures and setbacks. As Paul Schoemaker of the Wharton School notes,

- Opportunities are all around us, but we may focus so intently on a specific few that we miss a hundred others. Once you have put yourself in a better environment, physically or mentally, try to become a keener observer. Sometimes luck may actually knock loudly on your door, but most opportunities will not be presented on a gold platter.

- Most people seek identity and acceptance in familiar and well-defined groups, so moving into different worlds is not always comfortable. But there are clear advantages to spreading out and allowing yourself to be vulnerable.

- Setbacks early in life, such as moving around, losing a parent early, or getting fired from your first job, can build inner strength.[2]

Along those same lines, "By increasing the chance of a favorable outcome, you can make your own luck," says David J. Hand in an article for the science publication *Nautilus*. "The key to all this is to give chance the opportunity to produce an outcome in your favor: to give yourself a chance of getting lucky." If you don't open a business, or take risks to expand into a new line of business, or spread your business geographically, you will not put yourself in position to own or expand a business. Louis Pasteur said, "Chance favors the prepared mind"; in other words,

> [Make] sure you are able to recognize and grasp opportunities when they arise.... But when Pasteur commented on a prepared mind, he didn't just mean keep trying until you succeeded. He also meant something deeper: that he was *ready* to see an opportunity when it arose, and to see the links and relationships that others wouldn't notice.[3]
>
> It is up to you to prepare for success. Give yourself as many opportunities as you can, and once you recognize an opportunity seize it, embrace it, and move forward.

NOTES

1   Alex Charfen, "How to Clarify the Meaning of Success," *The Business Journals*, April 14, 2017, https://www.bizjournals.com/bizjournals/how-to/growth-strategies/2017/04/how-to-clarify-the-meaning-of-success.html

2   Paul J. H. Schoemaker, "Forget Dumb Luck—Try Smart Luck: Strategies to Get Lady Fortune on Your Side," *Management and Business Review*, Spring 2021, https://mbrjournal.com/2021/10/27/forget-dumb-luck-try-smart-luck-strategies-to-get-lady-fortune-on-your-side/

3   David J. Hand, "The Deceptions of Luck," *Nautilus*, January 9, 2017, https://nautil.us/the-deceptions-of-luck-236362/

CHAPTER 17

Opportunities for Future Leaders in the Security Services Industry

The security services industry is more vital than ever. Its story in the United States begins with the detective agencies founded by Allen Pinkerton and William Burns, which evolved into the first large security guard companies. In Europe, local night watch companies led to the formation of several global security companies. After World War II, the transition to postwar rebuilding in Europe, the baby boom in the United States, and the resumption and expansion of commercial economic activity globally all contributed to an increased use of security services worldwide. New companies, large and small, began competing for a share of contract security, alarm, and cash-in-transit business, as people and businesses increasingly demanded protective services and products. From a multitude of companies rose the premier companies that our legends founded or transformed (Figure 17.1). In this chapter, we will look at the continued growth of the industry, and how various factors such as increased integration of technologically advanced systems are creating opportunities for entrepreneurs who can become the new industry legends. We will also discuss opportunities in security management.

FACTORS IN THE GROWTH OF THE SECURITY INDUSTRY

Security is playing an increasingly important and evident role in everyday life; a broad range of services are deployed across commercial and residential properties, at schools, healthcare facilities, public and private events and venues, institutions, and government. Over the past several decades "globalization has intensified the movement of people, goods and services across the world, bringing to many not only greater prosperity but also heightened risks of smuggling, theft, drug trafficking,

DOI: 10.4324/9781003285564-24

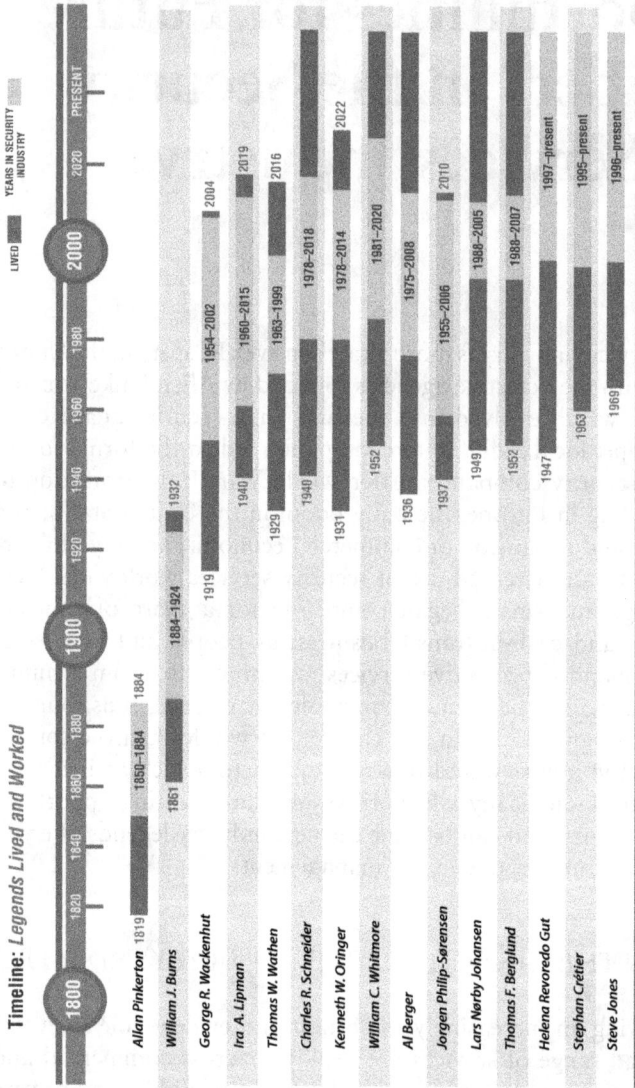

Timeline: *Legends Lived and Worked*

LIVED ▮   YEARS IN SECURITY INDUSTRY ▨

Allan Pinkerton	1819
William J. Burns	1861 · 1850–1884 · 1884
George R. Wackenhut	1919 · 1932
Ira A. Lipman	1940 · 1954–2002 · 2004
Thomas W. Wathen	1929 · 1960–2015 · 2019
Charles R. Schneider	1940 · 1963–1999 · 2016
Kenneth W. Oringer	1931 · 1978–2018
William C. Whitmore	1952 · 1978–2014 · 2022
Al Berger	1936 · 1981–2020
Jorgen Philip-Sørensen	1937 · 1975–2008 · 2010
Lars Norby Johansen	1949 · 1955–2006
Thomas F. Berglund	1952 · 1988–2005
Helena Revoredo Gut	1947 · 1988–2007
Stephan Crétier	1963 · 1997–present
Steve Jones	1969 · 1995–present · 1996–present

FIGURE 17.1   Snapshot of Legends timelines of when they lived and worked, compiled by the authors.

(Figure created by Maureen G. Nowak.)

counterfeiting, illegal entry, disruption to global supply networks, and so on." Other factors in the growth of the security industry include the proliferation of crime, real and perceived, and the desire to prevent it, along with an increased fear of terrorist acts and an increase in the magnitude of terrorism's consequences.[1]

After 9/11, in the United States the Homeland Security Act of 2002 resulted in the creation of the Department of Homeland Security, which merged 22 federal security agencies with a mandate to establish a safe and secure homeland.

> Within a few years following 9/11, every state government and the District of Columbia established an entity to find ways to protect communities from terrorist risks [...] the net effect of DHS was to channel billions of dollars for security products, services, systems, and research throughout the nation.

With increased government investment, private industry and other sectors also recognized that the lack of security could lead to physical loss and costly litigation. They discovered that

> [V]iolent and property crime that could occur within or near a facility or property can be deterred by the presence of security personnel, the installation and functioning of an alarm and closed circuit/Internet Protocol television (CC/IPTV) system, and good security design [...] The presence of trained security personnel and state-of-the-art systems makes employees, vendors, and visitors feel safer at the workplace. Organizations often are required to provide security services and systems because their property and casualty liability insurance coverage – or other specific insurance policies—mandate certain minimum protective measures.

Laws and government regulations have also mandated that security services be implemented in specific industries, notably banking, defense, and transportation and for critical infrastructure.[2] Cyberattacks have created an entire sub-segment of the security industry. There has also been a continuing shift toward outsourcing security services from corporations and, in some cases, from government to private companies, thereby increasing the share of the market for private security.

INVESTMENTS IN TECHNOLOGY ACCELERATE

Traditional contract and physical security services, which include armed and unarmed uniformed and plainclothes security officers, cash-in-transit, alarm systems, cameras, access control devices, mobile patrol, and consulting and investigative services, are increasingly being integrated with developing technologies, to make these services more efficient in meeting many types of security risks. Remote monitoring is taking the place of some patrol functions to reduce workforce costs and improve surveillance capabilities while being used in concert with mobile response. Artificial intelligence is being used to identify risk by analyzing video in real time. Biometrics is being used to speed up and improve access control. Drones and, to a lesser extent, robots are being used to replace surveillance activities traditionally performed by human labor. More sophisticated methods of processing cash and other financial transactions are being implemented. Each technology is improving the effectiveness and efficiency of security programs. The effect of COVID on the cost and availability of labor has also intensified the need for technological solutions to standard guarding. In a tight labor economy security vendors and consumers are changing their approach to security. Security companies and corporate departments are using a variety of more sophisticated recruitment, hiring, and training methods to attract and retain employees, while consumers of security are seeking ways to reduce workforce but not dilute security. According to the website Statista, in 2022,

> the information security products and services market was fore-cast to exceed $172 billion, up from $150 billion in 2021... Analysts have suggested that security trends are being shaped by new markets, such as big data or the internet of things (IoT). One impact of this has been the shift towards managed security services, resulting in an overall growth of the security appliances market.[3]

The global security leaders, Allied Universal, Securitas, Garda and Prosegur, are expanding their technology components. To do this, some are taking the approach of buying other companies that have strong tech-nology assets. For example, on July 22, 2022, Securitas announced the $3.2 billion purchase of Stanley Security, an acquisition unprecedented in size and scope. Securitas said

> this transformational acquisition makes us a strong provider of tech-enabled security solutions and a leading partner to our clients on a global scale. With our combined client proposition and our strong sales structure, we expect to deliver higher, more profitable growth than before. Going forward, approximately 50 percent of our profit contribution will be generated through high-margin technology and solutions sales.[4]

Securitas notes that

> in developed markets, such as the US and Western Europe, the growth potential lies in offering a full range of security services, including technology, that can be bundled into customized solutions. Global security service revenues are expected to grow annually and reach $263 billion in 2024, of which the security systems integration market is expected to account for $12 billion.

China is viewed as a major market for growth.[5]

OPPORTUNITIES FOR ENTREPRENEURS

In successive eras, new legends in the security service industry surfaced, having seen an opportunity to profit by meeting the demands of a growing base of customers that were looking for solutions to different challenges in changing times. Opportunities for the next legends will be in building security services that combine traditional contract guard services with new technology. Still, both stand-alone contract guard services and security technology companies each can also thrive on their own, so long as the provider is able to meet increasingly sophisticated demands of buyers for services and products to counteract the many threats to assets of all kinds.

While the values, attributes, traits, leadership, and management skills that were the backbone of the legends' success are timeless, the legends of tomorrow will need to apply those elements to more sophisticated buyers in a complex social and business environment. Thus, some of tomorrow's security services legends will get their start by inventing a new, transformational technology. Others will need to be excellent analysts and salespeople who are comfortable in tech-adjacent roles, as their main task will be making the case for organizations to integrate a new tool into their existing portfolio. The good news is that starting a security or service business need not be capital-intensive, and there is a low barrier to enter the industry. By comparison, the cash-in-transit business requires more capital and is dominated by well-capitalized and established businesses with distinct advantages over a startup. Below we offer some guiding thoughts for starting and building a security service company, grounded both in the legends' success and in current business literature.

Build from a Base and Leverage Relationships

While Pinkerton, Burns, Wackenhut, Lipman, and Crétier built their companies from scratch, the other legends either acquired a platform company as a model to springboard growth, or exponentially expanded an existing company. Whether the legends started from scratch or grew major companies, they all leveraged relationships and were skilled sales and marketers.

The amount of capital and financing at your disposal will determine whether you need to start from scratch or can begin by acquiring a platform company. For those entrepreneurs with no platform company or a modest one, the start will likely occur from a local presence, often bolstered by business relationships developed from prior industry or law enforcement experience. With a platform company you must maintain existing relationships and build out from there.

Have a Vision, a Plan and Execute

You must have a vision and develop a plan for your business. The legends developed plans for their companies and were flexible as they adapted to changing situations and circumstances. The legends understood what the market needed, and they executed their plans well by operating efficiently. With a plan in place and an understanding of the market, your business can only succeed if you can obtain, and then retain, customers. As you build your reputation and the company brand, additional customers will follow. In addition, a well-designed and -executed sales and marketing program has proven to be a key to success. Recruiting good sales and operations people will be critical as you concentrate on growing a well-managed business. In addition to sales, marketing, and operation management skills, today in most places entrepreneurs must be cognizant of licensing and operating regulations and obtain insurance to protect the company.

Manage Risk

In the security business you help manage risk for your customers, but you must also manage your own risk. The importance of providing security in a world rife with crime and violence provides opportunity, but also requires that the security service owner manage risks inherent in the service. The prevalence of torts against security companies makes operating a security company perilous. Successful security company owners understand the extent of risk in the industry and how to minimize those risks. General liability, employee practices, and statutory worker's compensation insurance are all necessary to cap your exposure to lawsuits that can arise from providing services.

Since the cost of insurance must be factored into your pricing, operating a company that has a low rate of claims is extremely important, especially when you begin building a company. Steps to minimize claims and the risk to your business include taking care of the type of customers you serve. Protecting a facility that has been subject to crime will increase the likelihood of your company being exposed to claims. Signing contracts that expose the company to liability is risky, and many customers will try to transfer risk to the security company through contract language whereby you will be held liable for damages or tort defense whether you are at fault or not. Obtain legal assistance or get some guidance from your insurers when necessary. Like the legends, you must have knowledge to successfully navigate what will be a near-endless stream of obstacles, from both outside factors and from claims within your company.

There is also social and regulatory risk in the industry. There are reputational and compliance risks, including "risks related to working conditions, occupational health and safety, ethical business standards and security practices." You must price contracts to provide "for a level of return commensurate with the risks and the anticipated work involved."[6]

Watch Your Cash Flow and Do Not Depend on Any One Customer

Some of the legends faced precarious situations when a part of their business failed, or when general economic circumstances removed sources of financing. The amount of leverage you employ may jeopardize your company, and it is incumbent not to rely on any one source for financing. To enjoy ongoing profits and protect against default, it is necessary to price your service to be competitive, but do not price it so low that you cannot be profitable. Keep your receivables as low as possible so your cash flow is good. Check the creditworthiness of your customers since defaults can put you out of business; do not rely on one or a few large customers where a loss of their business will severely impact your business.

Gain Traction, Expand, and Lead the Team

Once you gain traction in a local area, expansion can occur geographically, through acquisition, and, if beneficial, an expansion of service lines. Consulting and investigations, risk management, and outsourcing technology to customers are low-capital service lines to consider as they can broaden your appeal in the marketplace.

Most of the legends were able to grow their companies rapidly because they acquired additional companies, merged with other companies, and operated from many offices. There are many companies operating in the security industry that will compete with you for acquisitions;

however, if you can develop a good operating track record, your ability to access capital will improve and enable you to acquire or merge with other companies. Some owners find that acquiring companies is more cost-effective than opening new branches. This is something that you will have to determine based on a careful analysis of the options available to you at a particular time.

Developing a larger business will require building a team. Choose your team wisely and provide them with opportunity. Keeping your team motivated is important in any venture. All the legends took great care in building their business around people that shared their vision for the company and had the competencies to keep pace with the growth. Building a larger business is not for the faint of heart. It will require courage and confidence to take chances, and a lot of hard work. The legends stories taught us that perseverance will be required to succeed, as there will be both personal and business setbacks and hurdles to overcome. As the business grows it will be important to delegate and empower your managers so that you can concentrate on fine-tuning the business plans and building the company standing in the industry as well as with financial investors and markets. The legends all believed that the key to the security business is people, and while the concept may be simple, the management of many people is complex. The legends were all able to manage large groups of people because they had interpersonal skills and inspired those around them.

MANAGEMENT OPPORTUNITIES IN THE SECURITY INDUSTRY

Not everyone wants to be an entrepreneur. For those looking for opportunities to earn a good income, the increasing use of technology in business and industry offers opportunities in mid-level and executive-level security management. "In the past, many CEOs didn't want to know anything about security, and now they are far more interested and tend to view security executives as consultants or trusted advisors." Because the pace of change in the industry is so rapid, there is increasing demand for security managers to meet challenges for both customers of security companies and internally within companies and organizations.[7]

Within companies and organizations, managers at various levels and within various departments are being called on not just to advise on or enforce security policies but also to create a "culture of security."[8] The task of creating a culture of security within an organization usually falls to management and involves a lot of HR and training functions as well as cultivating excellence in IT and cybersecurity. Security directors have an important role in company culture. Wayne Hendricks, managing director and head of global security at the Macquarie Group in Australia, stated, "We are more than just security professionals, we are risk leaders. We are change leaders. We are brand ambassadors. We are culture carriers. The values that we push out directly correlates to your brand and to your reputation."[9]

SECURITY REMAINS A VITAL SERVICE IN A CHALLENGING ENVIRONMENT

The legends profiled in this book were, or still are, at the forefront of an industry experiencing rapid change and continued growth. They have employed millions of security officers and agents, protecting billions of dollars of property, and countless individuals. They developed systems so that their large-scale companies could better screen, train, and supervise their employees and operations. Their companies were in large part successful because they managed risks effectively. They overcame incidents that caused harm to their reputation and finances and brought challenges from competitors. While serious incidents include abuse of authority by security officers and managers, these incidents must be measured against the sheer total of the services rendered and number of security officers and managers employed.

In 1970, the Rand Corporation began a 16-month investigation of "private police" in the United States. The lead investigators who authored the report, James S. Kakalik and Sorrel Wildhorn, were lawyers trained as policy analysts; their task was to "assess private security businesses and personnel with an eye to how private security might be a concern of public policy." Their observations of private security practices concentrated on guard and investigative services. The report "cited weak pre-employment screening, high turnover in the industry, poor hourly compensation, and a lack of meaningful licensing standards"; however, they concluded, "Times have changed. Much evidence indicates that security practices have improved and considerable advancement in the industry occurred, though at a measured, slow rate."[10] Yet, as Lars Nørby Johansen and other legends interviewed said, too many customers still view security services as a commodity, and security service leaders need to do a better job to convince buyers that providing this vital service necessitates more professionalism, higher standards, better paid security officers, and commensurate increased rates for security providers. Security legends will continue to confront these issues, and there are economic realities to be sure; but advances in technology are offsetting some of the increased labor costs while improving the overall effectiveness of the line officer. There is also something to be said about entry-level security jobs offering unskilled workers a means to start in the industry, get training, and seek to advance their careers. New legends are encouraged to further professionalize the industry and promote equality and opportunity for employees, for success is best measured in how leaders contribute to the entirety of their enterprise.

Local as well as international organizations devoted to the professionalism of the industry, notably ASIS International, have proliferated and developed standards for the industry. Despite the efforts of security professionals and regulators there still exists a regulatory patchwork in the United States, Europe, and elsewhere. It has often been the threat of, and increase in, torts relating to the conduct of security companies and their employees that has necessitated the resolve of companies to better train and supervise security officers and managers. The best leaders and companies value the importance of customer service, while providing a safe environment for customers. Training staff in interpersonal conduct and the rule of law in the conduct of security work has been increasingly a focus of successful security companies. Security technology notwithstanding, the business remains a people's business. Consumers are also expecting and demanding more from security providers, with professionalism expected.

As the need for security increases and evolves, tomorrow's leaders and legends will succeed by having the vision and will to provide increasingly professionalized services that are anchored by better trained and managed security officers and managers able to utilize more sophisticated technologies. The challenges will be great, but the tools to provide security will continue to evolve. Tomorrow's leaders will likely come from ever more diverse backgrounds. It is our hope that readers of this book now have a firmer grounding in the industry's backstory and are inspired to play a key role in moving the industry forward and achieving individual as well as collective success.

NOTES

1   Barrie Stevens, *The Security Economy*, 2004, 18, https://www.oecd. org/futures/16692437.pdf

2   Robert McCrie, *Security Operations Management*, 3rd edn (Butterworth-Heinemann, 2016), 44–50.

3   Justina Alexandra Sava, "Security & Surveillance Technology—Statistics & Facts," December 12, 2022, https://www.statista.com/ topics/2646/security-and-surveillance-technology/

4   Securitas AB, "Securitas Has Completed the Acquisition of Stanley Security," news release, July 22, 2022, https://www.securitas.com/ en/news/regulatory-press-releases/securitas-has-completed-the-acquisition-of-stanley-security/

5   Securitas AB, "Securitas Has Completed the Acquisition of Stanley Security."

6   Prosegur, *Bond Prospectus*, 30 March 2022, 6–8, https://ise-prodnr-eu-west-1-data-integration.s3-eu-west-1.amazonaws.com/202204/ee4c2f83-4fbf-4e74-b48d-48108f76063a.PDF

7   Kevin E. Peterson and Joe Roberts, *The State of Security Management: A Baseline Phenomenological and Empirical Study*, ASIS Foundation (Alexandria, VA, 2022), 27, 34.

8   Steve Thomas, "How to Build a Culture of Security," November 20, 2020, https://www.securitymagazine.com/articles/93980-how-to-build-a-culture-of-security

9   Peterson and Roberts, *The State of Security Management: A Baseline Phenomenological and Empirical Study*, 54.

10 McCrie, *Security Operations Management*, 3rd edn, 43.

Bibliography

"A Man the Guard Firms Love to Hate." *Time*, March 9, 1992. http://content.time.com/time/subscriber/article/0,33009,975007,00.html

"A Remarkable Detective; Work of the Late George Henry Bangs. Some of the Principal Cases Which He Successfully Conducted and the Thieves Whom He Captured." *New York Times*, September 15, 1883, 8.

ABM Industries. *Annual Report 2005*. (2006). https://stocklight.com/stocks/us/services/nyse-abm/abm-industries/annual-reports/nyse-abm-2006-10K-06719417.pdf

"About Erik Philip-Sorensen." accessed September 24, 2022, https://www.epss.se/om-erik-philip-sorensen/

"About Us: History." accessed March 14, 2022, https://www.security-ligue.org/about-us/history

Adams, Graham. "Burns, William John." In *American National Biography*, edited by John A. Garraty and Mark C. Canes: Oxford University Press, 1999.

Akerheim, Maria. "Securitas CEO Plans to Resign; Unit Taken Off Block as Net Falls." *The Wall Street Journal*, August 11, 2006. https://www.wsj.com/articles/SB115526199836632975

"Allan Pinkerton." National Park Service, Updated July 31, 2020, https://www.nps.gov/people/allan-pinkerton.htm

"Allan Pinkerton's Death; the Career of the Great Detective Ended. Dying from the Result of an Accident—Winning Fame and Fortune from a Modest Beginning." *New York Times*, July 2, 1884. https://www.nytimes.com/1884/07/02/archives/allan-pinkertons-death-the-career-of-the-great-detective-endeddying.html

Allied Security Holdings LLC. *Annual Report 2006*. (2007). https://www.sec.gov/Archives/edgar/data/1301566/000095013607002252/file1.htm

Allied Security Holdings LLC. *Annual Report 2007*. (2008). https://www.sec.gov/Archives/edgar/data/1301566/000095013608001365/file1.htm

Allied Security Holdings LLC. *Registration Statement*. (September 20, 2004). https://www.sec.gov/Archives/edgar/data/1301573/000095013604003024/file001.htm

Allied Universal. "Allied Universal Acquires G4S Plc; Creating a Global Integrated Security Services Leader." *News Release*, April 5, 2021, https://www.aus.com/press-releases/allied-universal-acquires-g4s-plc-creating-global-integrated-security-services

Allied Universal. "Allied Universal Acquires Securadyne Systems to Offer Highly Advanced Technology Solutions and Systems Integration Capabilities Throughout the Nation." *News Release*, April 8, 2019, https://www.aus.com/press-releases/allied-universal-acquires-securadyne-systems-offer-highly-advanced-technology

"AlliedBarton's Bill Whitmore to Be Honored by Nasco at ASIS 2012." (September 7, 2012). https://www.securityinfowatch.com/security-executives/protective-operations-guard-services/news/10775718/alliedbarton-president-and-ceo-bill-whitmore-to-receive-nascos-edgar-b-watson-award

Allison, Rebecca. "G4: A History of Blunders." *The Guardian*, August 15, 2003. https://www.theguardian.com/uk/2003/aug/15/immigration.immigrationandpublicservices

"Alumni Wall of Fame." accessed February 28, 2022, https://www.upperdarbysd.org/site/Default.aspx?PageID=4665

"An Armored Queen Who Ranks among the Most Powerful Women in Spain." (July 21, 2022). https://puntobiz.com.ar/actualidad/una-reina-blindada-que-rankea-entre-las-mujeres-mas-poderosas-de-espana-202272113440

Anderson, George A. "Prisons for Profit: Some Ethical and Practical Problems." *America: The Jesuit Review*, November 18, 2000. https://www.americamagazine.org/issue/389/article/prisons-profit

Armed "Armed-Guard Company to Stop Using Wells Fargo's Name". (May 5, 1999). https://www.americanbanker.com/news/armed-guard-company-to-stop-using-wells-fargos-name

Baker Industries. *Annual Report 1985*. (1986).

Barrier, Michael. "Tom Wathen's Security Blanket." (1990/2004). https://indexarticles.com/business/nations-business/tom-wathens-security-blanket/

Bate, Dion, and Donald S. Carter. "Moody's Downgrades Garda's Senior Secured Instruments to B2." *News Release*, February 3, 2022, https://www.moodys.com/research/Moodys-downgrades-Gardas-senior-secured-instruments-to-B2-and-affirms--PR_462184

Bayot, Jennifer. "George Wackenhut, 85, Dies; Founded Elite Security Firm." *New York Times*, January 8, 2005. https://www.nytimes.com/2005/01/08/business/george-wackenhut-85-dies-founded-elite-security-firm.html

Behar, Richard. "Ode to Whistleblowers: Ira Lipman (1940–2019), from Civil Rights to the Security Industry." *Forbes*, November 21, 2019. https://www.forbes.com/sites/richardbehar/2019/11/21/

ode-to-whistleblowers-ira-lipman-1940-2019-from-civil-rights-to-the-security-industry/

"Belle Ackerman Lipman." *Commercial Appeal* (Memphis, TN), August 19, 2009. https://www.legacy.com/us/obituaries/commercialappeal/name/belle-lipman-obituary?id=14828060

Bennett, Elizabeth. "Growth's Secure for Spectaguard." *Philadelphia Business Journal*, May 29, 2000. https://www.bizjournals.com/philadelphia/stories/2000/05/29/smallb1.html

"Biography of Ira A. Lipman." n.d. https://iraalipman.com/biography_of_ira_a_lipman/

"Blackstone to Sell AlliedBarton to Wendel." *News Release*, June 30, 2015, https://www.blackstone.com/news/press/blackstone-to-sell-alliedbarton-to-wendel/

Black, Lisa. "James J. Gavin, Jr.: 1922–2007." *Chicago Tribune*, March 6, 2007.

Bloomberg News. "Expanding in Us, Falck Buys Wackenhut Security." *New York Times*, March 9, 2002. https://www.nytimes.com/2002/03/09/business/company-news-expanding-in-us-falck-buys-wackenhut-security.html

"Borg-Warner Security Corp., a Chicago-Based Supplier." *Chicago Tribune*, February 3, 1994. https://www.chicagotribune.com/1994/02/03/borg-warner-security-corp-a-chicago-based-supplier/

"Borg-Warner." *New York Times*, April 28, 1982. https://www.nytimes.com/1982/04/28/business/borg-warner.html

Bray, Chad. "Wendel Agrees to Acquire AlliedBarton Security for $1.67 Billion." *New York Times*, June 30, 2015. https://www.nytimes.com/2015/07/01/business/dealbook/wendel-agrees-to-acquire-alliedbarton-security-for-1-67-billion.html

"Breaking into Prisons." *Group 4 Securitas (International) Magazine*, January 1991.

Brennan, Peter J. "Steve Jones: Strength in Numbers." *Orange County Business Journal*, May 24, 2021. https://www.aus.com/sites/default/files/2021-08/OCBJSteveJonesFeature052421.pdf

"Brown Named President, CEO." (April 21, 1994). https://www.upi.com/Archives/1994/04/21/Brown-named-Pinkerton-president-CEO/6584766900800/

Bunting, Elaine. "Farewell to a Great Sailing Fan." (January 19, 2010). https://www.yachtingworld.com/blogs/elaine-bunting/farewell-to-a-great-sailing-fan-9361

"Burns Adds $50,000 to Bomb Rewards...Requires Exclusive Clues." *New York Times*, November 23, 1920. https://www.nytimes.com/1920/11/23/archives/burns-adds-50000-to-bomb-rewards-brings-total-offers-for-wall.html

"Burns Security Services Elects Grandson of Founder as Chief." *New York Times*, May 4, 1978, D8. https://www.nytimes.com/1978/05/04/archives/people-and-business-burns-security-services-elects-grandson-of.html

Caesar, Gene. *Incredible Detective: The Biography of William J. Burns*. Englewood Cliffs, NJ: Prentice-Hall, 1968.

Castles by the Sea Real Estate. n.d. "Tyecliffe Estate Coral Gables" (Brochure). Vero Beach, Florida.

Chance, Sue. "Allan Pinkerton: A Psychobiographical Sketch." *American Imago* 42, no. 2 (1985): 131–142.

Charfen, Alex. "How to Clarify the Meaning of Success." (April 14, 2017). https://www.bizjournals.com/bizjournals/how-to/growth-strategies/2017/04/how-to-clarify-the-meaning-of-success.html

Clark, Justin. "Outlaws, Pinkertons, and Vigilantes: The Reno Gang and Its Enemies." *Hoosier State Chronicles*, November 30, 2017. https://blog.newspapers.library.in.gov/reno-gang/

Cohen, Ariel. "Ukraine Crisis Highlights Security Needs of Civilian Nuclear Power." *Forbes*, December 16, 2022. https://www.forbes.com/sites/arielcohen/2022/12/16/ensuring-the-security-lof-civilian-nuclear-power/

Cole, Robert J. "Borg-Warner Seeks Baker Industries." *New York Times*, November 8, 1977. https://www.nytimes.com.1977/11/08/archives/borgwarner-seeks-baker-industries-diversified-industrial-company.html

Cole, Robert J. "Merrill Unit to Acquire Borg." *New York Times*, April 13, 1987. https://www.nytimes.com/1987/04/13/business/merrill-unit-to-acquire-borg.html

"College of Arts and Sciences Distinguished Alumni Award: Thomas W. Wathen." 1990, https://honorsandawards.iu.edu/awards/honoree/5010.html

Command Security Corporation. *Securities Deregistration Statement*. (February 22, 2019). https://www.sec.gov/Archives/edgar/data/864509/000149315219002443/forms-8pos.htm

"Commencement Speech at Dean Close School, 26 May 2007." http://www.jpsmemorial.co.uk/dean-close-commemoration-2007/

"Comments Concerning the Anti-Pinkerton Act B-139965." (March 16, 1980). https://www.gao.gov/assets/b-139965.pdf

Commission of the European Communities. *Merger Procedure Article 6(1)(B) Decision: Group 4 Falk/Securicor*. (May 28, 2004). https://ec.europa.eu/competition/mergers/cases/decisions/m3396_en.pdf

"Companies Report Earnings." *New York Times*, March 4, 1978, 33. https://www.nytimes.com/1978/03/04/archives/companies-report-earnings.html

"Company News: Allied Security to Be Bought by Investment Firm." *New York Times* January 18, 2003. https://www.nytimes.com/2003/01/18/business/company-news-allied-security-to-be-bought-by-investment-firm.html

"Company News: Figgie International Sells Its Advance Security Unit." *New York Times*, February 26, 1994. https://www.nytimes.com/1994/02/26/business/company-news-figgie-international-sells-its-advance-security-unit.html

"Company News: Spectaguard Says It Has Acquired Allied Security." *New York Times*, March 3, 2000. https://www.nytimes.com/2000/03/03/business/company-news-spectaguard-says-it-has-acquired-allied-security.html

Conroy, Paul. "The New Guard." *The Age*, March 27, 1998. https://www.theage.com.au/

Copenhagen Business School Center for Corporate Governance. *Annual Report 2017*. (2018). https://www.cbs.dk/files/cbs.dk/ccg_annual_report_2017_0.pdf

"CPP Security Completes Acquisition of Pinkerton's." *Los Angeles Times*, January 26, 1988. https://www.latimes.com/archives/la-xpm-1988-01-26-fi-38676-story.html

Cuff, Daniel F., and Dee Wedemeyer. "Protection Never Dull to Head of Borg Unit." *New York Times*, September 29, 1986. https://www.nytimes.com/1986/09/29/business/business-people-protection-never-dull-to-head-of-borg-unit.html

"The Daily Diary of President Gerald R. Ford." July 1, 1975 President's Daily Diary Collection, Box 76, https://www.fordlibrarymuseum.gov/library/document/0036/pdd750721.pdf

"Director Profiles." 2022, https://www.prosegur.com/accionistas-inversores/gobierno-corporativo/consejos-adm-com-delegadas/perfiles-consejeros

"Discover Our Social Commitment." accessed March 6, 2023, https://www.fundacionprosegur.com/en/

DiStephano, Joseph N. "AlliedBarton Security Merging to Form Industry Giant." *The Philadelphia Inquirer*, May 4, 2016. https://www.inquirer.com/philly/business/20160504_AlliedBarton_Security_merging_to_form_industry_giant.html&outputType=app-web-view

Drexel University College of Computing and Informatics. Dean's Executive Advisory Committee. accessed August 15, 2023. https://drexel.edu/cci/about/deans-executive-advisory-council/

Ed Snider Youth Hockey & Education. *Snider Hockey 2017 Impact Report*. (2018). http://sniderhockey.org/assets/documents/partials/core_buttongroup/T1YQg.pdf

Entwhistle, Martha. "Universal Buys Guardsmark to Form Largest US-Owned Guard Firm." *Security Systems News*, July 29, 2015.

https://www.securitysystemsnews.com/article/universal-buys-guardsmark-form-largest-us-owned-guard-firm

"Erik Philip-Sorensen (1909–2001)." accessed September 24, 2022, https://www.loomis.com/en/about-loomis/history/founder-erik-philip-sorensen

"Falck Buys $1.1b Group 4". (May 2, 2000). https://money.cnn.com/2000/05/02/europe/falck/

"Family Address Given on 26 February, 2010 in Worcester, UK." n.d. http://www.jpsmemorial.co.uk/address-mark-philip-sorensen/

"FBI Files on Wackenhut and Alyeska Pipeline, 1992-1993." n.d. https://documents2.theblackvault.com/documents/fbifiles/fbi/wackenhut-fbi2.pdf

Feder, Barnaby J. "Chairman of Pinkerton's Adds to His Responsibilities." *New York Times*, April 14, 1992, D5. https://www.nytimes.com/1992/04/14/business/business-people-chairman-of-pinkerton-s-adds-to-his-responsibilities.html

Feder, Barnaby J. "Securitas of Sweden to Acquire Pinkerton's in $384 Million Deal." *New York Times*, February 23, 1999, C6. https://www.nytimes.com/1999/02/23/business/securitas-of-sweden-to-acquire-pinkerton-s-in-384-million-deal.html

Fetonti, Bob. "William J. Burns, America's Sherlock Holmes, Vol. 3.3." *Briarcliff Manor-Scarborough Historical Society*, October 31, 2020. https://www.briarcliffhistory.org/the-briarcliff-notebook/william-j-burns-americas-sherlock-holmes

"Financial Information." accessed March 12, 2022, https://academedia.se/investerare/finansiell-information/

"Fitch Rates Garda World Security Corp's $700mm Tlb 'Bb+'/'Rr1'." *News Release*, February 2, 2022, https://www.fitchratings.com/research/corporate-finance/fitch-rates-garda-world-security-corp-700mm-tlb-bb-rr1-02-02-2022

"Fondation S. Crétier." accessed November 19, 2022, https://fondation cretier.org/en/

Font, Consuelo. "Helena Revoredo: The Millionaire Leader of Prosegur Prepares for Retirement." *El Mundo*, February 22, 2020. https://www.elmundo.es/loc/famosos/2020/02/22/5e3c2e6721efa0597c8b468b.html

Formsma, Brad. n.d. *The Wow Factor*. Podcast audio. How to Establish a Clear Vision for the Future of Your Company, with Steve Jones. https://www.thewowfactorpodcast.com/show-notes/steve-jones-global-chairman-amp-ceo-of-allied-universal-episode-101

"Foundation for Entrepreneurship: History." n.d. https://ffefonden.dk/om-fonden/

Fradkin, Philip L. *Stagecoach: Wells Fargo and the American West*. New York: Free Press, 2003.

"G4S History." accessed April 15, 2022, https://www.g4s.com/who-we-are/our-history

G4S. *Annual Report 2004*. (2005). https://www.g4s.com/-/media/g4s/global/files/annual-reports/ara_2004.ashx

G4S. *Annual Report 2005*. (2006). https://www.g4s.com/-/media/g4s/global/files/annual-reports/ara_2005.ashx

G4S. *Listing Particulars on the Proposed Merger of the Security Business of Group 4 Falck A/S with Securicor PLC*. (June 2004). https://www.g4s.com/-/media/g4s/corporate/files/financial-presentations/fa-040604-listing_particulars_final_document.ashx

"Garda Takes over Kroll Security International." (December 7, 2006). https://www.upi.com/Defense-News/2006/12/07/Garda-takes-over-Kroll-Security-Intl/24111165513089/

Garda World Security Corporation. "Completion of Gardaworld Recapitalization for C$5.2 Billion." *News Release*, October 30, 2019, https://www.garda.com/press-release/completion-of-gardaworld-recapitalization-for-c52-billion-0

"Garda World Security Buys Vance International." (November 28, 2005). https://www.securityinfowatch.com/security-executives/protective-operations-guard-services/press-release/10592411/securityinfowatchcom-garda-world-security-buys-vance-international

"Gardaworld Announces the Acquisition of Global Leader Arca." *News Release*, August 24, 2022, https://www.garda.com/press-release/gardaworld-announces-the-acquisition-of-global-leader-arca

"Gardaworld, a Success Story." accessed November 14, 2022, https://www.garda.com/about-us/gardaworld-a-success-story

GardaWorld. "Gardaworld International Protective Services Receives ISO 18788:2015 across Entire Operations." (March 7, 2016). https://www.garda.com/blog/gardaworld-international-protective-services-receives-iso-187882015-across-entire-operations

"Goldman Sachs Merchant Banking Acquires U.S. Security Associates." *News Release*, August 3, 2011, https://mergr.com/goldman-sachs-merchant-banking-acquires-u.s.-security-associates

Goldstein, Alan. "Plant Protection Service Blossoms: 4th Largest Security Firm in U.S. Seeks to Shake Industry's Shabby Image." *Los Angeles Times*, June 17, 1986. https://www.latimes.com/archives/la-xpm-1986-06-17-fi-11813-story.html

"The Great Pennsylvania Execution." *New York Tribune*, June 21, 1877. https://guides.loc.gov/chronicling-america-molly-maguires/selected-articles

Griffin, Joel. "Leadership's Role in Preventing Workplace Violence." (February 29, 2012). https://www.securityinfowatch.com/security-executives/protective-operations-guard-services/article/10635378/

alliedbarton-president-and-ceo-bill-whitmore-shares-his-insights-on-workplace-violence-prevention-in-webinar

Gruber, William. "Borg-Warner Executive Gets Wish to Leave." *Chicago Tribune*, November 19, 1993. https://www.chicagotribune.com/1993/11/19/borg-warner-exec-gets-wish-to-leave/

Gruber, William. "Borg-Warner Revamps Control of Subsidiary." *Chicago Tribune*, Chicago, Illinois, May 5, 1992, 42.

"Guardsmark Honors Top Performers of Fiscal Year 2014." *News Release*, August 28, 2014, https://www.prnewswire.com/news-releases/guardsmark-honors-top-performers-of-fiscal-year-2014-273084081.html

"Guide to the Church League of America Collection of the Research Files of the Wackenhut Corporation, 1931–1973." Tamiment Library and Robert F. Wagner Labor Archives, Updated April 20, 2018, http://dlib.nyu.edu/findingaids/html/tamwag/tam_148/dscaspace_ref11.html

Gustafsson, Anna-Karin, and Peter Kerckhofs. *Representativeness of the European Social Partner Organisations: Private Security Sector*. (Dublin, Ireland: 2019). https://www.eurofound.europa.eu/publications/report/2019/representativeness-of-the-european-social-partner-organisations-private-security-sector

Hand, David J. "The Deceptions of Luck." *Nautilus*, January 9, 2017. https://nautil.us/the-deceptions-of-luck-236362/

Harrison, Scott. "From the Archives: Aftermath of the 1910 Los Angeles Times Bombing." *Los Angeles Times*, October 2, 2018. https://www.latimes.com/visuals/photography/la-me-fw-archives-aftermath-of-the-1910-los-angeles-times-bombing-20180925-htmlstory.html

"Herberto Gut Beltramo." In *Real Academia de la Historia, Diccionario Biográfico electrónico*, 2018. https://dbe.rah.es/biografias/25990/herberto-gut-beltramo

"Herberto Gut, President and Founder of Prosegur, Dies in an Accident." *El País*, June 2, 1997. https://elpais.com/diario/1997/06/02/economia/865202407_850215.html

Hertig, Chris. "Today in Security History: The Death of William J. Burns, American Detective." (April 14, 2021). https://www.asisonline.org/security-management-magazine/latest-news/today-in-security/2021/april/death-of-william-j-burns-american-detective/

Hertig, Chris. "Today in Security History: The Wall Street Bombing." *Today in Security*. https://www.asisonline.org/security-management-magazine/latest-news/today-in-security/2020/september/security-history-wall-street-bombing/

"History." n.d. https://www.constellis.com/who-we-are/history/

Hoenen, Leah. "Universal Acquires THRIVE Intelligence." (December 3, 2013). https://www.securitysystemsnews.com/article/universal-acquires-thrive-intelligence

Holliday, J. S. "Foreword." In *Stagecoach: Wells Fargo and the American West*. New York: Free Press, 2003.

Horan, James D. *The Pinkertons: The Detective Dynasty That Made History*. New York: Crown Publishers, 1967.

"How a Childhood Ambition Changed Lars's Life." (February 28, 2004). https://www.thisismoney.co.uk/money/news/article-1513533/How-a-childhood-ambition-changed-Lars-life.html

"How Bill Whitmore Secured the Future of AlliedBarton Security Services by Emphasizing Culture and Strategy." (November 1, 2011). https://sbnonline.com/article/how-bill-whitmore-secured-the-future-of-alliedbarton-security-services-by-emphasizing-culture-and-strategy/

Hunt, William R. *America's Sherlock Holmes: The Legacy of William Burns*. Guilford, CT: Lyons Press, 2019.

Hyder, Goldy. *Business Council of Canada Podcast*. Podcast audio. Stephan Crétier, Founder, Chairman and CEO of GardaWorld. https://thebusinesscouncil.ca/publication/stephan-cretier/

IFSECGlobal. "Group 4 Falck Confirms Merger Deal with Securicor Security." (March 8, 2004). https://www.ifsecglobal.com/mergers-and-acquisitions/group-4-falck-confirms-merger-deal-with-securicor-security/

"Important Events in Our History." n.d. https://www.securitas.com/en/about-us/our-history/timeline/

"In Memoriam: Don W. Walker, CPP." (October 18, 2022). https://www.asisonline.org/publications--resources/news/blog/in-memoriam-don-w-walker-cpp/

"Integrated Security Services." *Group 4 Securitas (International) Magazine*, May 1992, 17–18.

Johnston, Les. *The Rebirth of Private Policing*. London: Routledge, 1992. doi: https://doi.org/10.4324/9780203977071

Jones, Steve. "Dedication." In *No Off Season: The Constant Pursuit of More*. Charleston, SC: ForbesBooks, 2018a.

Jones, Steve. *No Off Season: The Constant Pursuit of More*. Charleston, SC: ForbesBooks, 2018b.

"Jorgen Philip-Sorensen." Obituary", *The Times*, February 19, 2010. http://www.jpsmemorial.co.uk/the-times-obituary/

Kandell, Jonathan. "Baron Thyssen-Bornemisza, Industrialist Who Built Fabled Art Collection, Dies at 81." *New York Times*, April 28, 2002. https://www.nytimes.com/2002/04/28/nyregion/baron-thyssen-bornemisza-industrialist-who-built-fabled-art-collection-dies-81.html

Kemp, Kathryn W. ""The Dictograph Hears All": An Example of Surveillance Technology in the Progressive Era." *Journal of the Gilded Age and Progressive Era* 6, no. 4 (2007): 409–430. https://www.jstor.org/stable/25144496

Kenworthy, Tom. "Alaska Oil Pipeline Company and Security Criticized." *Washington Post*, July 24, 1992. https://www.washingtonpost. com/archive/politics/1992/07/24/alaska-oil-pipeline-company-and-security-firm-criticized/

Kerr-Jarrett, Peter. "A Family Affair." *Broward Palm Beach New Times*, May 23, 2002. https://www.browardpalmbeach.com/ news/a-family-affair-6322360?showFullText=true

"Key Events in Labor History: 1892 Homestead Strike." n.d. https://aflcio. org/about/history/labor-history-events/1892-homestead-strike

Ko, Louis, and Donald S. Carter. "Moody's Rates Garda World's New Senior Secured Notes B1." *News Release*, January 23 2020, https:// www.moodys.com/research/Moodys-rates-Garda-Worlds-new-senior-secured-notes-B1--PR_417388

Krebs, Andrew, and Miranda Buckheit. "Who's the Man Behind the Chair? An Interview with Chuck Schneider of the Service Enterprise Engineering Board." *Penn State College of Engineering Industrial and Manufacturing Engineering (IME) Newsletter*, 2019, 6–9. https://www.ime.psu.edu/assets/magazine/2019.pdf

Kyriakodis, Harry. "From Click to Clink: A History of Mug Shots in the Quaker City." *Hidden City: Exploring Philadelphia's Urban Landscape*. https://hiddencityphila.org/2018/09/from-click-to-clink-a-history-of-mug-shots-in-the-quaker-city/

"The Labor Strikes in the Anthacite Coal Regions in This State." *Somerset Herald* (Somerset, PA), March 3, 1875. https://guides.loc.gov/ chronicling-america-molly-maguires/selected-articles

"Lars Johansen—Group 4 Securicor PLC (Interview)." (January 10, 2005). https://www.twst.com/interview/lars-johansen-group-4-securicor-plc

"Lars Nørby Johansen to Retire as Falck Chairman and Be Replaced by Thorleif Krarup." (March 20, 2014). https://www.mynewsdesk.com/ falckglobal/news/lars-noerby-johansen-to-retire-as-falck-chairman-and-be-replaced-by-thorleif-krarup-294657

Lekvall, Per, Ronald J. Gibson, Jesper Lau Hansen, Carsten Lønfeldt, Manne Airaksinen, Tom Berglund, Tom von Weymarn, et al. *The Nordic Model of Corporate Governance*. (2014). https://papers. ssrn.com/sol3/papers.cfm?abstract_id=2534331

LeTellier, Val. "The Next ESRM Revolution." *Security Management*, ASIS International, Alexandria, VA, March/April 2022.

Lewin, Tamar. "Pinkerton's Is Being Acquired." *New York Times*, December 8, 1982, D. https://www.nytimes.com/1982/12/08/ business/pinkerton-s-is-being-acquired.html

Lilleør, Kathrine. *Life and Management: Lars Nørby Johansen*. Bianco Luno, 2011.

Lipman, Ira. "The Model Private Security Industry." Paper presented at the Beijing International Security Forum, September 20, 2006. https://iraalipman.com/model-private-security-industry-september-20-2006/

"Little Rock School Desegregation." In *Martin Luther King, Jr. Encyclopedia*, Stanford University Martin Luther King, Jr. Research and Education Institute. https://kinginstitute.stanford.edu/encyclopedia/little-rock-school-desegregation

MacKeith, Bill. "Private Companies That Run Detention Centers in the UK." *Melting Pot Europa*, February 23, 2005. https://www.meltingpot.org/2005/02/private-companies-that-run-detention-centres-in-the-uk/

Mahon, Rianne. "Rescaling Social Reproduction: Child Care in Toronto/Canada and Stockholm/Sweden." *International Journal of Urban and Regional Research* 29, no. 2 (2005): 341–457. https://doi.org/10.1111/j.1468-2427.2005.00588.x

"Mark Lipman, 88, Investigator Who Founded a Private Agency." *New York Times*, May 25, 1995. https://www.nytimes.com/1994/05/25/obituaries/mark-lipman-88-investigator-who-founded-a-private-agency.html

McCrie, Robert. "Allan Pinkerton (August 25, 1819–July 1, 1884): Founder of the Security Services Industry." *Journal of Applied Security Research* 5, no. 4 (2010): 543–552. https://doi.org/10.1080/19361610.2010.510127

McCrie, Robert. *Security Operations Management*, 3rd edn. Oxford, UK/Waltham, MA, USA: Butterworth-Heinemann, 2016.

McGinty, Jon. "Allan Pinkerton: America's First Private Eye." *Northwest Quarterly*, December 12, 2014. https://oldnorthwestterritory.northwestquarterly.com/2014/12/12/allan-pinkerton-americas-first-private-eye/

Medearis, John. "Pinkerton's Going Public to Ease Debt." *Los Angeles Times*, February 20, 1990. https://www.latimes.com/archives/la-xpm-1990-02-20-fi-969-story.html

"Meet Our Founder." accessed October 29, 2022, https://sniderhockey.org/about/

"Meet Our People." accessed November 1, 2022, https://www.aus.com/our-people

"Meet Our Team." accessed November 24, 2022, http://jandrinvestment.com/the-team/

Metz, Robert. "Borg-Warner's Smoke Detector." *New York Times*, December 29, 1978. https://www.nytimes.com/1978/12/29/archives/market-place-borgwarners-smoke-detector.html

Miller, James P. "Burns Agrees to Be Purchased by Rival Security-Services Firm." *Chicago Tribune*, August 4, 2000. https://www.chicagotribune.com/news/ct-xpm-2000-08-04-0008040352-story.html

Minahan, John. *The Quiet American: A Biography of George R. Wackenhut.* Westport, Connecticut: International Publishing Group, 1994.

"The Molly Maguire Murder Trial." *The Columbian* (Bloomberg, PA), May 26, 1876. https://guides.loc.gov/chronicling-america-molly-maguires/selected-articles

"Moody's Assigns Ratings to AB Merger Sub (Allied Security)." *News Release*, August 5, 2008, https://www.moodys.com/research/Moodys-assigns-ratings-to-AB-Merger-Sub-Allied-Security--PR_160507

"Muhammad Ali Quotes." n.d. https://www.goodreads.com/quotes/200873-don-t-count-the-days-make-the-days-count

Mulvad, Nils. "Unclear Exit from G4S by Two Danish Business People." (January 10, 2020). https://privatesecurity.network/stories/unclear-exit-from-g4s-by-two-danish-business-people/

"Non-Pinkerton Gets High Company Post." *New York Times*, August 8, 1967, Business & Finance. https://www.nytimes.com/1967/08/08/archives/nonpinkerton-gets-high-company-post.html

O'Connor, Matt. "Buyout." *Chicago Tribune*, April 14, 1987. https://www.nytimes.com/1987/04/13/business/merrill-unit-to-acquire-borg.html

Oringer, Keith. "The Battle for G4S Reaches a $5.3b Conclusion." *The Security Advisor*, Winter 2021. https://securityproadvisors.com/security-advisor-magazine-winter-2021/

Oticon Foundation. "Changes to the Board of William Demant Holding A/S " *News Release*, February 23, 2017, https://attachment.news.eu.nasdaq.com/a4844bb15dc5931e9a442fed7f9d1b8e8

"Our History." accessed March 12, 2022, https://academedia.se/om-academedia/historia/

"Our History." n.d. https://www.securitas.com/en/about-us/our-history/the-1980s-and-1990s/

"Our Story." n.d. https://pinkerton.com/our-story/history

Palantir Technologies Inc. "Palantir and Crisis24, a Gardaworld Company, Announce New Partnership to Revolutionize Security and Risk Management for the 21st Century." *News Release*, December 9, 2022, https://www.prnewswire.com/news-releases/palantir-and-crisis24-a-gardaworld-company-announce-new-partnership-to-revolutionize-security-and-risk-management-for-the-21st-century-301698938.html

Parfomak, Paul W. *Guarding America: Security Guards and U.S. Critical Infrastructure Protection.* (2004). https://digital.library.unt.edu/ark:/67531/metadc809152/

Parrish, Michael. "Oil Pipeline Operators Settle with Critic Who Said They Spied on Him." *The Los Angeles Times*, December 21, 1993.

https://www.latimes.com/archives/la-xpm-1993-12-21-fi-4236-story.html

Peltz, James F. "He's Buying Security's Holy Grail: CPP's Owner Feels Special Responsibility to Enhance Reputation of Pinkerton's." *Los Angeles Times*, December 22, 1987. https://www.latimes.com/archives/la-xpm-1987-12-22-fi-30463-story.html?_amp=true

"People: The Key to Business. An Interview with Helena Revoredo." *IESE Alumni Magazine*, September 2009, 73–74. https://media.iese.edu/research/pdfs/E114.pdf

Peterson, Kevin E., and Joe Roberts. *The State of Security Management: A Baseline Phenomenological and Empirical Study.* (Alexandria, VA: ASIS Foundation, 2022).

Petruno, Tom. "Investors Cast Watchful Eye on Initial Pinkerton Offering." *Los Angeles Times*, March 28, 1990. https://www.latimes.com/archives/la-xpm-1990-03-28-fi-352-story.html

Philip-Sørensen, Jørgen. "Chairman's Column." *Group 4 Securitas (International) Magazine*, August 1991.

"Pinkerton Force Is Family Affair; Founder's Great-Grandson Heads Private Police." *New York Times*, August 16, 1964. https://www.nytimes.com/1964/08/16/archives/pinkerton-force-is-family-affair-founders-creatgrandson-heads.html

"Pinkerton's National Detective Agency Records, 1853–1999: Finding Aid Scope and Content Note." Library of Congress, Updated May 2021, https://findingaids.loc.gov/db/search/xq/searchMfer02.xq?_id=loc.mss.eadmss.ms003007&_faSection=overview&_faSubsection=scopecontent&_dmdid=d13497e25

Pinkerton's Inc. *Annual Report 1998.* (1999). https://www.sec.gov/Archives/edgar/data/78666/0000898430-99-001129.txt

Pitts, Gordon. "Stephan Cretier: The New Wonder Boy." *The Globe and Mail*, July 1, 2007. https://www.theglobeandmail.com/report-on-business/stephen-cretier-the-new-wonder-boy/article1077809/

Potts, Mark. "Borg-Warner Succeeds by Breaking the Cycle." *Washington Post*, April 1, 1982. https://www.washingtonpost.com/archive/business/1982/08/01/borg-warner-succeeds-by-breaking-the-cycles/ec94caba-ce9c-4a86-8e01-23a9410559e7/

"Preservation Demolition of the Tyecliffe Castle, by Allison's Adam and Eve." *News Release*, January 25, 2008, https://www.prweb.com/pdfdownload/651811.pdf

Proceedings of the Thirty-Sixth Annual Convention of the American Bankers' Association. Los Angeles, CA, 1910.

"Profile: Helena Revoredo." Accessed November 16, 2022. https://www.forbes.com/profile/helena-revoredo/?sh=551a1acd15e5

Prosegur Compañía de Seguridad S.A. and Subsidiaries. *Consolidated Annual Accounts and Directors' Report for the Year Ended 31 December 2021*. (2022). https://www.prosegur.com/dam/jcr:843276ef-0dc9-4b88-8b8e-c6b01142fead/Cons%20%20%202021.pdf

Prosegur Compañía de Seguridad S.A. and Subsidiaries. *Consolidated Annual Accounts and Directors' Report for the Year Ended 31 December 2022*. (2023). https://www.prosegur.com/dam/jcr:aca7fe46-4919-47aa-95e8-e1dbd6f51c32/Conso%202022.pdf

Prosegur Compañía de Seguridad S.A. *Annual Report 2009*. (2010). Pajaritos, Madrid.

Prosegur Compañía de Seguridad S.A. *Bond Prospectus*. (March 30 2022a). https://ise-prodnr-eu-west-1-data-integration.s3-eu-west-1.amazonaws.com/202204/ee4c2f83-4fbf-4e74-b48d-48108f76063a.PDF

Prosegur Compañía de Seguridad S.A. *Note Issue Prospectus*. (March 30, 2022b). https://ise-prodnr-eu-west-1-data-integration.s3-eu-west-1.amazonaws.com/202204/ee4c2f83-4fbf-4e74-b48d-48108f76063a.PDF

"Prosegur and Best Security Industries Announcement." 2019, https://www.prosegur-eas.com/Prosegur-and-BSI-Announcement

"Protecting Embassies in India." *Group 4 Securitas (International) Magazine*, January 1992.

Provost, Claire. "The Industry of Inequality: Why the World Is Obsessed with Private Security." *The Guardian*, May 12, 2017. https://www.theguardian.com/inequality/2017/may/12/industry-of-inequality-why-world-is-obsessed-with-private-security

Pyrillis, Rita. "AlliedBarton's Bill Whitmore: A Higher Calling for Security." (March 24, 2014). https://www.chieflearningofficer.com/2014/03/24/alliedbartons-bill-whitmore-a-higher-calling-for-security/

Raab, Selwyn. "Private Guards: Now a Growing, Troubled Industry." *New York Times*, January 12, 1978, B20. https://www.nytimes.com/1978/01/12/archives/new-jersey-pages-private-guards-a-growing-troubled-industry-private.html

Rafalko, Frank J. "The Civil War: Lack of a Centralized Direction." In *A Counterintelligence Reader: American Revolution to World War II, Volume 1*. Homeland Security Digital Library. Washington, DC: National Counterintelligence Center, 2001.

"Raymond Burns, Former Chairman of Burns Security Agency, Was 91." *New York Times*, July 8, 1977. https://www.nytimes.com/1977/07/08/archives/raymond-burns-former-chairman-of-burns-security-agency-was-91.html

Reckert, Clare M. "Indian Head Cites an 11% Profit Rise." *New York Times*, December 24, 1969. https://www.nytimes.com/1969/12/24/

archives/indian-head-cites-an-11-profit-rise-sales-show-18-advance-in-the.html

"Remembering Belle Ackerman Lipman." *Congressional Record* Vol 155, Issue 131 (September 16, 2009), https://www.govinfo.gov/content/pkg/CREC-2009-09-16/pdf/CREC-2009-09-16-pt1-PgS9428-3.pdf

"Rest in Peace, Ira Lipman (1940–2019), Guardsmark Founder/CEO and Nasco Co-Founder." (September 17, 2019). https://www.nasco.org/rest-in-peace-ira-lipman-1940-2019/

Rettman, Andrew. "Private Guards Outnumber Policemen in Seven EU Countries." *EU Observer*, December 14, 2010. https://euobserver.com/justice/31501

Rita, Abrahamsen, Michael C. Williams. *Security Beyond the State: Private Security in International Politics*. New York: Cambridge University Press 2011.

"Robert A. Pinkerton, Chairman of Detective Agency, Is Dead." *New York Times*, October 12, 1967. https://www.nytimes.com/1967/10/12/archives/robert-a-pinkerton-chairman-of-detective-agency-is-dead.html

Roberts, Sam. "Ira Lipman, Security Man Who Spoke out for Air Safety, Dies at 78." *New York Times*, September 27, 2019. https://www.nytimes.com/2019/09/27/business/ira-lipman-dead.html

Sava, Justina Alexandra. "Security & Surveillance Technology--Statistics & Facts." (December 12, 2022). https://www.statista.com/topics/2646/security-and-surveillance-technology/

Schmidt, Waldemar. "Memorial Information: Nils Jorgen Philip-Sorensen." (February 3, 2010a). http://www.jpsmemorial.co.uk/journal/2010/2/3/tribute-by-waldemar-schmidt-english-danish.html

Schmidt, Waldemar. The Phillip-Sorensen Family's Unnoticed Influence on the Global Security Services Industry [PowerPoint Presentation]. Crans Montana, Switzerland, 2010b.

Schneider, Keith. "Industry Critics Were Target of Pipeline Owner's Inquiry." *New York Times*, November 6, 1991. https://www.nytimes.com/1991/11/06/us/industry-critics-were-target-of-pipeline-owner-s-inquiry.html

Schoemaker, Paul J. H. "Forget Dumb Luck--Try Smart Luck: Strategies to Get Lady Fortune on Your Side." *Management and Business Review*, Spring 2021. https://mbrjournal.com/2021/10/27/forget-dumb-luck-try-smart-luck-strategies-to-get-lady-fortune-on-your-side/

Schoenrock, Todd Brady. "ISO 9000: 2000 Gives Competitive Edge." *Quality Progress*, Milwaukee, WI, May, 2002, 107.

Schudel, Matt. "George Wackenhut Dies." *Washington Post*, January 7, 2005. https://www.washingtonpost.com/archive/local/2005/01/07/george-wackenhut-dies/49ba2b1f-ee06-4426-9717-7fb3cd75b1a0/

Securitas AB. "Securitas Ab Full Year Report January–December 2021." *News Release*, February 8, 2022a, https://www.securitas.com/en/news/regulatory-press-releases/securitas-ab-full-year-report-januarydecember-2021/

Securitas AB. "Securitas Has Completed the Acquisition of Stanley Security." *News Release*, July 22, 2022b, https://www.securitas.com/en/news/regulatory-press-releases/securitas-has-completed-the-acquisition-of-stanley-security/

Securitas AB. *Annual Report 1999*. (2000). https://www.securitas.com/en/newsroom/press-releases_list/annual-report-1999/

Securitas AB. *Annual Report 2001*. (2002). https://www.securitas.com/en/newsroom/press-releases_list/annual-report-2001/

Securitas AB. *Annual Report 2006*. (2007). https://www.securitas.com/en/newsroom/press-releases_list/annual-report-2006/

Securitas AB. *Annual Report 2021*. (2022c). https://www.securitas.com/en/news/regulatory-press-releases/securitas-ab-full-year-report-januarydecember-2021/

Securitas.Com Group Management, Magnus Ahlqvist, President and CEO of Securitas AB, https://www.securitas.com/en/about-us/group-management/magnus-ahlqvist/

Shabong, Yadarisa. "UK's G4S Rejects 2.95 Billion Pound Offer from Canadian Security Firm Gardaworld." (September 14, 2020). https://www.reuters.com/article/uk-gardaworld-m-a-g4s-idUKKBN2651P4

Silcoff, Sean. "Rebounding Garda Back in Acquisition Mode." *The Globe and Mail*, August 28, 2012. https://www.theglobeandmail.com/report-on-business/rebounding-garda-back-in-acquisition-mode/article4506404/

Sims, Brian. "Two's Company." (March 4, 2005). https://www.building.co.uk/twos-company/3047516.article

Singer, Penny. "Generations: Keeping It in the Family." *New York Times*, June 8, 1986. https://www.nytimes.com/1986/06/08/nyregion/generations-keeping-it-in-the-family.html

Singer, Penny. "Leased-Employee Concept Rides Again." *New York Times*, March 12, 1995, WC 13. https://www.nytimes.com/1995/03/12/nyregion/leased-employee-concept-rides-again.html

Stavro, Barry. "Buyer Seeks to Pay Off Detective Agency's Debt." *Los Angeles Times*, December 11, 1988. https://www.latimes.com/archives/la-xpm-1988-12-11-fi-313-story.html

Stemman, Roy. "Celebrating an Impressive Career." *G4S International*, June 2006. http://www.jpsmemorial.co.uk/jps-g4s-retirement-article/

"Stephan Crétier: Founder, Chairman, President and Chief Executive Officer," accessed November 14, 2022, https://www.garda.com/about-us/stephan-cretier

Stevens, Barrie. *The Security Economy.* (2004). https://www.oecd.org/futures/16692437.pdf

"Still Sore." *Forbes*, April 1, 2022, 2022. https://www.forbes.com/global/2002/0401/024sidebar.html

Strom, Kevin, Marcus Berzofsky, Bonnie Shook-Sa, Kelle Barrick, Crystal Daye, Nicole Horstmann, and Susan Kinsey. *The Private Security Industry: A Review of the Definitions, Available Data Sources, and Paths Moving Forward.* Bureau of Justice Statistics (2010). https://www.ojp.gov/pdffiles1/bjs/grants/232781.pdf

Tatom, Oliver. "Oregon Land Fraud Trials (1904–1910)." In *Oregon Encyclopedia*, March 17, 2018. https://www.oregonencyclopedia.org/articles/oregon_land_fraud_trials_1904_1910_/#.YiKUruj MJhE

Taylor, Alan. "The Riots That Followed the Assassination of Martin Luther King." *The Atlantic*, April 3, 2018. https://www.theatlantic.com/photo/2018/04/the-riots-that-followed-the-assassination-of-martin-luther-king-jr/557159/

"The Teapot Dome Trials: 1926–30." n.d. https://law.jrank.org/pages/2878/Teapot-Dome-Trials-1926-30.html

The Freedonia Group. *Global Security Services.* (2022).

The Wackenhut Corp. *Annual Report 2001.* (2002a). https://www.sec.gov/Archives/edgar/data/104030/000095014402002003/g74165e10-k405.txt

The Wackenhut Corp. *Proxy Statement and Notice of Special Meeting to Approve and Adopt Merger Agreement.* (April 9, 2002b). https://www.sec.gov/Archives/edgar/data/104030/000095014402003675/g74655ddefm14a.htm#011

"Thomas William 'Tom' Wathen, 1929–2016." *Santa Barbara News Press*, June 27, 2016. https://www.legacy.com/us/obituaries/newspress/name/thomas-wathen-obituary?id=7383634

Thomas, Steve. "How to Build a Culture of Security." (November 20, 2020). https://www.securitymagazine.com/articles/93980-how-to-build-a-culture-of-security

"Today in History--August 25: The Pinkertons." Library of Congress, 2021, https://www.loc.gov/item/today-in-history/august-25/

"Tributes Paid to Pioneer of the Security Industry." *Evesham Journal*, January 28, 2010. https://www.eveshamjournal.co.uk/news/4877338.tributes-paid-to-pioneer-of-the-security-industry/

U.S. Bureau of Labor Statistics. *Occupational Employment and Wage Statistics.* (2021). https://www.bls.gov/oes/tables.htm

U.S. Security Associates, Inc. Two Decades of Success (2013).

"Uncle Sam Teaching Detectives How to Detect." *New York Herald*, November 27, 1921. https://www.loc.gov/resource/sn83045774/1921-11-27/ed-1/?sp=80

Universal Protection Service. "Universal Protection Service Acquires the Security Officer Services Division of T & M Protection Resources, LLC." *News Release*, January 2, 2013a, https://www.prnewswire.com/news-releases/universal-protection-service-acquires-the-security-officer-services-division-of-tm-protection-resources-llc-185431472.htmlc

Universal Protection Service. "Universal Protection Service Acquires the Security Officer Services Division of T&M Protection Resources, LLC." *News Release*, January 2, 2013b, https://www.prnewswire.com/news-releases/universal-protection-service-acquires-the-security-officer-services-division-of-tm-protection-resources-llc-185431472.html

Universal Services of America. "Universal Protection Service Acquires Security Forces, Inc." *News Release*, October 24, 2011, https://www.prnewswire.com/news-releases/universal-protection-service-acquires-security-forces-inc-132431803.html

"Unsung Heroes: First Female Detective Kate Warne." Updated March 27, 2020, https://pinkerton.com/our-insights/blog/unsung-heroes-first-female-detective-kate-warne

"W. Sherman Burns Is Dead at 86; a Pioneer in Industrial Security." n.d. *New York Times*. https://www.nytimes.com/1978/01/07/archives/w--sherman-burns-is-dead-at-86-a-pioneer-in-industrial-security.html

Wackenhut Corrections Corporation. *Proxy Statement and Notice of Annual Meeting of Shareholders*. (March 16, 2001). http://media.corporate-ir.net/media_files/irol/91/91331/pdf/WHC2001_Proxy.pdf

Wackenhut Corrections Corporation. *Securities Prospectus*. (August 6, 2003). https://www.sec.gov/Archives/edgar/data/923796/000095014403009400/g83842sv4.htm

Waldemar Schmidt, Gordon Adler, Els van Weering. *Winning at Service: Lessons from Service Leaders*. Chichester, UK: John Wiley & Sons Ltd., 2003.

"Wall Street Bombing 1920." n.d. https://www.fbi.gov/history/famous-cases/wall-street-bombing-1920

Walton, Geri. "Allan Pinkerton: Great American Detective and Spy." (January 17, 2020). https://www.geriwalton.com/allan-pinkerton-great-american-detective-and-spy/

"Wells Fargo Stories." n.d. https://stories.wf.com/category/living-our-values/history/

Welton, Benjamin. "The Man Arthur Conan Doyle Called 'America's Sherlock Holmes'." *The Atlantic*, November 30, 2013. https://www.theatlantic.com/entertainment/archive/2013/11/the-man-arthur-conan-doyle-called-americas-sherlock-holmes/281618/

Wendel SE. "Allied Universal Completes Acquisition of U.S. Security Associates for Approximately $1 Billion." *News Release*, October 26, 2018a, https://www.globenewswire.com/news-release/2018/10/26/1627970/0/en/WENDEL-Allied-Universal-completes-acquisition-of-U-S-Security-Associates-for-pproximately-1-billion.html

Wendel SE. "Allied Universal to Buy U.S. Security Associates." *News Release*, July 16, 2018b, https://www.reuters.com/article/us-allieduniversal-m-a-wendel/allied-universal-to-buy-u-s-security-associates-for-1-billion

Wendel SE. "AlliedBarton and Universal Services of America Finalize Merger, Creating the Leading Security Services Company in North America." *News Release*, August 1, 2016a, https://www.prnewswire.com/news-releases/alliedbarton-and-universal-services-of-america-finalize-merger-creating-the-leading-security-services-company-in-north-america-300306813.html

Wendel SE. "AlliedBarton and Universal Services of America Finalize Merger, Creating the Leading Security Services Company in North America." *News Release*, August 1, 2016b, https://www.prnewswire.com/news-releases/alliedbarton-and-universal-services-of-america-finalize-merger-creating-the-leading-security-services-company-in-north-america-300306813.html

Whitmore, Bill. "Milestones and Rewards." *New York Times*, December 15, 2012. https://www.nytimes.com/2012/12/16/jobs/alliedbartons-ceo-on-milestones-and-rewards.html

Wiedrich, Robert. "Disarming Security Guards." *Chicago Tribune*, May 31, 1988. https://www.chicagotribune.com/news/ct-xpm-1988-05-31-8801030646-story.html

"William J. Burns to Tell of Experiences at Union Tonight at 8." *The Harvard Crimson*, March 24, 1922. https://www.thecrimson.com/article/1922/3/24/william-j-burns-to-tell-of/

"William J. Burns, August 22, 1921–June 14, 1924." n.d. https://www.fbi.gov/history/directors/william-j-burns

"William Whitmore Sr., 1926–2019." *The Times Herald* (Norristown, PA), June 28, 2019. https://www.legacy.com/us/obituaries/timesherald/name/william-whitmore-obituary?id=12452232

"Wind Point Partners Sells U.S. Security Associates." *News Release*, July 29, 2011, https://www.wppartners.com/overview/ussa-sale

Index

Pages in *italics* refer to figures, pages in **bold** refer to tables, and pages followed by n refer to notes.

A

ABA, *see* American Bankers
    Association (ABA)
ABM Industries, 156n9
AcadeMedia, 213
Acquisition Corp., 133
Adams, Graham, 45n1
Adler, Gordon, 207n13, 224n7
Advance Security Engineering, 117,
    135, 137
Ahlqvist, Magnus, 227
Air Products Corporation, 58
Akerheim, Maria, 225n19
Alaska oil industry, 63
Al Berger, *see* Berger, Albert J.
Allen, E. J., 15
AlliedBarton Security Services, 6,
    103–104, 144, 150, 271, 287
  attracts high-profile investors,
    150–152, *153*
  Universal merges with, 272
  with Universal Services of America,
    153
Allied Security, 6, 104, 144, 149–150,
    156n7, 157n14, 159,
    163–164, *164*, 287
Allied SpectraGuard, *148*, 148–149
Allied Universal, 7, 140–141, 144,
    154–155, 227–228, 275,
    287–288
  acquired G4S, 263–264, *264*
  global revenue for, *278*
  Securadyne Systems acquisition,
    273
  U.S. Security Associates
    acquisition, 272
  world's largest security company,
    273–274

Allison, Rebecca, 191n34
Altschul, Kenneth, 57–58
Alyeska, 63–64
American Bankers Association (ABA),
    36, 42–44
American Brands Inc., 25, 94
American Protective Services, 217
American Society for Training and
    Development (ASTD), 120
American Stock Exchange, *61*, 95
Ammarell, John, 58–59
Anderson, George A., 70n29
Anti-Pinkerton Act (1893), 21, 23–24
Antonelli, James "Jim", 82
Apax Funds, 257
ARCA, 255
Arthur Young, 128
artificial intelligence, 306
ASIS Certified Protection Professional
    certification (CPP)®, 78
ASIS International, 312
ASSA Swedish lock company, 213
Assurandor-Societetet, 194
Atlanta Constitution, 39
Atomic Energy Commission, 161
Auerbach, Carol, 168

B

Baker Industries, 6, 130, 286–287
  Borg-Warner acquires, 112–114
  Chuck career at, 111–115
  Ken's career at, 126, 130–134,
    131, *134*
Baker, Malcolm, 112, 114
Baker Protective Services, 142
Baker, Solomon, 131
Baltica, 195
Baltimore Plot, 18

Bangs, George H., 15, *17*, 18, 23
Barcelona company, 222, *223–224*
Barrier, Michael, 100n6
Barton Protective Services, 150
Bate, Dion, 261n19
Bauman, Marty, 130
Bayot, Jennifer, 69n18
Bednarz, Edward J., 25
Behar, Richard, 87n20
Bell, Bessie Blanche, 54
Bell Security, 138
Bennett, Elizabeth, 157n11
Bere, James, 114
Berger, Albert J., 6, 95–96, 98,
        103–105, *146*, 146–147,
        150, 153, 287, 301
  chemical industry, 161–162
  at CPP, 159
  early life and education, 159–161
  legacy and charitable work,
    167–169
  military service, 161–162
  in security services industry
    Allied Security, 163–164, *164*
    at CPP and Pinkerton,
      162–163
    Gryphon Partners, 163–164
    MAFCO, 164–165, *165*
    meeting, 162
    mission focused management,
      166–167
    SpectaGuard, 163–164, *164*
Berger, Carol, 146, *168*
Berger, Samuel J., 159
Berglund, Thomas F., 6, 98, 171–172,
    288, 297, 299
  early life and education, 210–211
  government service to private
    industry, 211–213
  at Securitas, 209–210, *210*,
    213–214
    in integrity, vigilance, and
      helpfulness, *214*, 214–216
    leading worldwide, 216–220
    reflections on career, 220–222,
      221, *223–224*
Berliner & Marx company, 161
Bernstein, Alan, *55*, *199*

Best Security Industries, 236
BFI (Browning Ferris) Waste Services,
    267
Bill, *see* Whitmore, William C. Jr.
biometrics, 306
Black, Lisa, 143n2
Bolo (be on the lookout) Program,
    259
Borg-Warner Corporation, 6, 20, 25,
      43, 107, 126, 130, 286–287
  acquired Globe Security, 133
  Baker Industries, 112–113
  Burns International Security,
    113–114
  departure from, 115
  Ken at, 131–133
  Protective Services Group,
    114–115
Bray, Chad, 157n21
Brazilian cruzeiros (BRZ), 129
Brennan, Peter J., 281n25
Brian, *see* Cescolini, Brian
Brockway, William, 33–34
Brooklyn Navy Yard, 109
Brown, Denis R., 96, 135, 216
Brown, Denman, 141
Brown, John, 15
Brown, Larry, 57
Buckheit, Miranda, 125n21
Buckles, Nick, 200
Buckman, David, 154
Bunting, Elaine, 191n27
Bureau of Investigation, 40–42, *41*,
    57–58
  criminal history records, 78
  former agents, 81
Burns and Sheridan Agency, 36
Burns, D. Bruce, 42
Burns International, 6, 43, 103–104,
    113–114, 216–218, 286–287
Burns, Michael, 31–32
Burns, Raymond J., 42
Burns, William J., 1, 5, 20, 49, 286,
    297, 301, 303
  dynasty, 42
    Borg-Warner, acquisition by, 43
    King, George E. B., 43
    legacy, 43–45, *44*

early life and career
  Brockway counterfeiting ring,
    breaking, 33–34
  Burns and Heney, corruption
    cases, 35
  conversation and confessions, 33
  land fraud investigations, 34–35
  theatrical talent and curiosity
    about people, 31–32
International Detective Agency
  Inc., 32
namesake agency, 36
  Bureau of Investigation, 40–42,
    41
  Leo Frank case (1913), 38–39
  Los Angeles Times bombing
    (1910), 36–38, 37–38
  Teapot Dome, 40–42
  Wall Street bombing (1920), 39,
    39–40
Burns, William S., 42
Bush, George W., 155
Business Risk International (BRI), 98

C
Caesar, Gene, 45n2
Caisse de Depot et Placement du
    Quebec (CDPQ), 273
California Plant Protection (CPP),
    5–6, 25, 159, 166, 286–287,
    301
  Berger, Albert J., 95–96, 162–163
  organic growth, 94
  Tom at, 91–92
  understanding risk profiles, 92–93,
    93
Caltius Partners, 269
Canadian Air Transport Security
    Authority (CATSA), 251
Carnegie, Andrew, 24
Carter, Donald S., 261n18–261n19
Carter Goble Associates, 182
cash-in-transit services, 219, 251, 254
Center for Corporate Governance
    (CCG), 205
Central High School in Little Rock,
    73–74, 74

Certified Public Accountant (CPA), 128
Cescolini, Brian, 263, 267–268
Chambers, William, 23
Chancellor, John, 73
Chance, Sue, 30n46
Charfen, Alex, 302n1
Chicago Musical Instruments, 111
Chief Learning Officer®, 152
Chiles, Lawton, 54
Christofferson, Peter, 195
Chuck, see Schneider, Charles R.
Church League of America, 62
Cipher, S.A., 235
Clark, Justin, 28n15
Coating Composites, 162
Cognisa, 138
Cole, Robert, 124n3, 125n12, 143n7,
    46n30
Colin, Samuel, 147
Colin Service Systems, 147
Command Security, 236
Copenhagen Stock Exchange, 193,
    196
Correctional Services division, 60, 64
correction system security, 185
COVID-19 pandemic, 236–237, 254,
    275–276, 306
CPP, see California Plant Protection
    (CPP)
Crétier, Stephan, 6, 227–288, 298, 301
  early life, in Canada, 244–245
    baseball experience, 245–246,
      246
    transition to security industry,
      246–247
  focused and inspired leader,
    257–258
  GardaWorld Security Corporation,
    247–249, 248
    Crisis24 division, 255–256
    financial crisis of 2008, 249
    for G4S, 254
    as global security company,
      256–260
    private growth, 250–251, 252
    strong from pandemic, 254–256
    in U.S. presence, 251, 253, 253

service and awards, 258–260
Cuff, Daniel F., 124n4
culture of security, 310
Curtiss-Wright Corporation, 161
Custom Protection division, 55
Custom Protection Officer® program, 60
Custom Security Services, 75–76
cyberattacks, 305
Cybersecurity Services, 235

D
The Daily Trainer (2008), 119
Dallas-based Tidel Engineering (Tidel), 255
Dare to Be Great, 151
Daugherty, Harry M., 40–41
David, C.L., 177
Delphi Automotive Systems, 96–97
Derosier, Mark, 168
Derosier, Virginia Ginny, 168
Det Danske Rengorings Selskab (DDRS), 177
Diamond, Robert M., 147
DiStephano, Joseph N., 156n4
diversification, at Wackenhut Company, 59–60, 61
Douglas, Gustaf, 213
Dow Chemical Company, 161
drones, 306
DuBois, Edward, 57–58

E
EAA, see Experimental Aircraft Association (EAA)
Edgar B. Watson Award, 155
Ed Snider Youth Hockey and Education Organization, 155, 158n27
Effective Security, Inc., 146–147, 163, 168
Eighty Exemplary Ethics Statements, 84
Electronic Site Inspection System (2013), 119
Endesa, 239, 240
endowments, 83
Enterprise Risk Security, 236

Enterprise Security Manager (2003), 119
Enterprise Security Risk Management (ESRM), 5
Entwhistle, Martha, 280n18
Ericsson, Lars Magnus, 178
ESRM, see Enterprise Security Risk Management (ESRM)
European Union (EU), private security sector, 4
Experimental Aircraft Association (EAA), 99
Exum, John D., 110, 114

F
Fair Credit Reporting Act, 62
Falck company, 1, 172, 195–196, 196, 287, 300
   leadership, 197
   safety business, 206
Falck Holding A/S, 193, 200
Falck Redningskorps (Rescue Corps) A/S, 193
Falck, Sophus, 172, 204
Fall, Albert, 41–42
FBI, see Bureau of Investigation
fear factor, 5–6
Feder, Barnaby J., 100n4–100n5, 101n20, 143n10
Feinberg, Mortimer J., 164
Fetonti, Bob, 125n9
Figgie, Harry E. Jr., 117, 136
Figgie, Henry, 135
Figgie International, 117, 135, 136
Filiatrault, Jean-Michel, 257
First Security, 217
Flabob Airport, 99
Florida Power and Light (FPL), 58–59
Font, Consuelo, 242n3
Ford, Gerald, 114, 125n10
Fordham Law, 127
Formsma, Brad, 279n4
Fortune 500, 79, 154, 267
Foundation for Entrepreneurship, 205
Fradkin, Philip L., 28n17
Franklin, Benjamin, 23
Frick, Henry, 24
Fugitive Slave Law (1850), 15

G

G4S, *see* Group 4 Securicor (G4S)
Galleani, Luigi, 40
GardaWorld Aviation Services, 251
GardaWorld Cash Services, 251
GardaWorld Security Corporation, 6,
    227, 247–249, *248*, 273–
    274, 288, 298, 301
  Crisis24 division, 255–256
  financial crisis of 2008, 249
  for G4S, 254
  as global security company, 256–260
  private growth, 250–251, *252*
  strong from pandemic, 254–256
  in U.S. presence, 251, 253, *253*
Gate Master (2007), 119
Gavin, James J., 114, 128, 129, 131,
    132
General Electric (GE) plant, 52
General Motors (GM), 96
Gibson Guitars (Gibson), 111
Glenn, John, 110
Global Entry cards, 80
Global Solutions Limited (GSL), 200
GlobeNewswire, 125n20
Globe Security, 133–134
Golder, Thoma, Cressey, Rauner
    (GTCR), *116*, 116–117, 135,
    136
Golding, Mike, 184
Goldman Sachs, 137, 140
Goldman Sachs Capital Partners, 121,
    121
Goldstein, Alan, 100n7
Gottesman company, 130
Gowen, Franklin, 21
Grant, Ulysses S., 40
Great Depression, 51, 126
Greif, Lloyd, 94
Griffin, Joel, 157n24
Group 4 Falck, 6, 64–65, *65*, *66*, 171,
    186, 193, 197, 287
  Securicor, 200–201
  Wackenhut Corporation, *198*,
    198–200, *199*
Group 4 International Correction
    Services BV, 182
Group 4 Magazine, 180–181

Group 4 Securicor (G4S), 6, 175, 178,
    193, 197, 204, 254, 272–
    274, 276, 287, 300
  facing obstacles, 185–186
  Group 4 Falck and, 200–201
  Lars exits, 202–204
  Philip-Sørensen building, 180–184,
    181–183
  security and technology
    integration, 184–185
  sponsorship, 184
  subsequent acquisition, 186
Group 4 Total Security, 180
Gruber, William, 125n13, 125n14
Gryphon Partners, 104, 159, 163–164
GTCR, *see* Golder, Thoma, Cressey,
    Rauner (GTCR)
Guardsmark, 5, 71, 72, 75–76, 271,
    286, 299
  events shape, 79–81, *80*
  family faces adversity, 81–82
  founding of, 76–77
  moves on, 82
  reflections, on legendary career,
    84–86, *85*
  setting high professional standards,
    77–78
Gubel S.A., 229
Gustafsson, Anna-Karin, 7n9
Gut, Christian, 227, 228, 229, *230*,
    231, 235–239
Gut, Helena Revoredo, 6, 227, 228,
    229, *230*, 288, 298
  early life and education, 232–233
  at Madrid Stock Exchange, 229, *230*
  Prosegur, 234
    civic, charitable, and
      professional endeavors,
      239–241
    expansion to U.S. market, 236
    global expansion and resilience,
      235–239
    navigating loss, recession, and
      pandemic, 236–238
    in Spain, 233–234
    successful family enterprise,
      238–239
Gut, Herberto, 229, 233, 234

H
Hamel, Charles, 64
Hammond, John, 111, 114
Hand, David J., 302, 302n3
Harding, Warren G., 40
Harford, John, 142, 275
Harris, Cal, 55
Harrison, Scott, 45n12
Harvard Business School, 111, 166
Harvey, Alton, 118
Hazen, William P., 34
HCC Industries, 166
Helena, see Gut, Helena Revoredo
Hendricks, Wayne, 310
Heney, Francis J., 35
Hennessey, Enid, 109, 109
Hennessey, James L., 109
Henry, R.A., 77
Herberto, see Gut, Herberto
Hertig, Chris, 45n14, 46n18, 46n24
Hire Our Heroes program, 152
Hirshhorn Museum, 259
Hitchcock, Ethan, 34
Hoenen, Leah, 280n14
Hogan, Frances, 49
Hogrefe, Marius, 172
Holliday, J. S., 28n18
Homeland Security Act of 2002, 305
Homestead Acts, 34
Homestead strikes, 23–24
Horan, James D., 27n2
House Interior Committee, 63, 64
Hudson, David, 183
Huling, Cyrus, 33
humanitarianism, 83
Hunt, William R., 45n6
Hyder, Goldy, 261n3
Hymanson, Michael, 104, 120, 123,
        142, 272

I
IFSEC Global, 207n23
Indian Head, Inc., 129–131
"In Safe Hands", 136
Instant Alert Equipment Monitoring
        (2010), 119
International Advisory Board (IAB),
        240

International Detective Agency Inc.,
        32
International Organization for
        Standardization (ISO), 120
International Security Ligue, 216, 227
Investment AB Latour, 213
Irvine Company, 268, 269
Isaacson, Molly, 159
ISS Securitas, 172, 175, 193, 195, 196,
        204

J
Johann, Ruth, 54–55
Johansen, Lars Nørby, 6, 65, 171,
        173, 186, 193, 221, 287,
        297, 300, 311
    early life, 193–194
    exits Group 4 Securicor, 202–204
    Falck's security company, 195–196,
        196
    going public and acquisitions,
        196–197
    Group 4 Falck
        Securicor, 200–201
        Wackenhut Corporation, 198,
        198–200, 199
    legacy, 204–206, 206
    merging firms, with Philip-
        Sørensen, 197–198
    private sector, leaving academia for,
        194–195
John, J., 36–37
Johns Hopkins University, 56
Johnston, Les, 7n1
Jones, Steve, 6, 147, 227, 288, 298
    Allied Universal, 263–264, 264,
        273–274
    career, 267–269
        after 9/11 terror attacks, 269
        with integrated security, 270
        risks, to attain national status,
        269–270
    early life and mentors, 264–266
        Fortune 500 job experience, 267
        real-world struggle, 266–267
    hands-on approach, 265
    interview with, 275–276, 277
    legacy, 277–278, 279

New York City market, 270–271
    prized acquisition, 271–272
    Universal merges with
        AlliedBarton, 272–273
    testaments, 274–275
    Universal Protection Service, 263
Joseph Bancroft Company, 129
Julius, Carl, 172

K
Kakalik, James S., 311
Kandell, Jonathan, 143n4
Karandakir, Ashish, 257
Kelly, Barbara, 79
Kemp, Kathryn W., 45n13
Ken, see Oringer, Kenneth W.
Kennedy, Weldon, 82, 86
Kentucky Fried Children, 212
Kenworthy, Tom, 70n25
Kerckhofs, Peter, 7n9
Kerr-Jarrett, Peter, 70n32
King, George E. B., 43
King, Martin Luther, 73, 79
Kirk, Claude R. Jr., 61, 62
Ko, Louis, 261n18
Korean War, 127, 161
Krebs, Andrew, 125n21
Kyriakodis, Harry, 29n24

L
land fraud investigations, 34–35
large-scale terrorist attacks, 5
Lars, see Johansen, Lars Nørby
laws and government regulations, 305
legends character attributes, 7, 285
    attributes, traits, and values,
        298–299
    lifespan and years in industry,
        293–296
    past experiences, formed strong
        leaders, 297–298
    personalities, leadership, and
        management styles, 299–300
    success, 300–302
    and their companies, 285–288
    timelines, 290–292, 304
Leo Frank case (1913), 38–40

LeTellier, Val, 46n33
Levin, Carl, 75
Levine, Murray, 66
Lewin, Tamar, 29n41
Liberal Party, 211
Library of Congress, 14, 22
Library of Congress Administrative
    File, 14
Ligouri and Associates, 269
Lilleor, Kathrine, 206n4
Lincoln, Abraham, 14, 15, 16, 18
Lindgren, Astrid, 212
Lipman, Barbara, 81
Lipman, Belle, 71, 72, 75, 86n8–86n9
Lipman, Chick, 71
Lipman, Gus, 73–75, 77, 79, 81, 82,
    86n2
Lipman, Ira A., 5, 71, 100, 271, 286,
    297, 299
    authored books and articles, 83–84
    awards and honors, 83
    early life and career, 71–73
        at Central High School in Little
            Rock, 73–74, 74
        Custom Security Services, 75–76
        foundational values, 75
    endowments, 83
    Guardsmark, 71, 72
        events, 79–81, 80
        family faces adversity, 81–82
        founding of, 76–77
        moves on, 82
        reflections, on legendary career,
            84–86, 85
        setting high professional
            standards, 77–78
    humanitarianism, 83
    philanthropy, humanitarian, and
        industry awards legacy, 82–83
Lipman, Mark, 71–73, 75, 81, 86n4
Little Rock Nine, 73, 74
Little Rock School Desegregation,
    86n6
Loomis, 218, 219
Los Angeles Olympics, 93, 93
Los Angeles Times bombing (1910),
    36–38, 37, 38

M

MacAndrews & Forbes Holdings
    Inc. (MAFCO), 149, 150,
    164–165
MacKeith, Bill, 207n22
Madrid Stock Exchange, 229, *230*,
    231
MAFCO, *see* MacAndrews & Forbes
    Holdings Inc. (MAFCO)
Mahon, Rianne, 224n4
Majtenyi, Gabor, *182*
Mark Lipman Services, 72, 76, 81
The Martin Company, 58
Mattel Corporation, 91
McClellan, George B., 14, 15
McClernand, John A., *16*
McCrie, Robert D., 28n5, 29n22, 77,
    94, 95, 138, 312n2
McDonald, Joseph, 57
McFarland, Harry, 142
McGinty, Jon, 28n10, 29n23, 29n25
McKenna, James, 22
McNamara, James B., 37
McParland, James P., 14, 22
McQueen, Isabella, 12
Medearis, John, 101n15
Merrill Lynch Capital Partners, 133
Merz, Harry, 54
Metz, Robert, 124n5
Miller, George, 63, 64
Miller, James P., 46n31
Million Swedish Krona (MSEK), 209,
    219–220
Minahan, John, 68n1
Minnesota Multiphasic Personality
    Inventory (MMPI), 78
Molly Maguires, 21–23, *22*
Montgomery, Robert, 33
Montreal Economic Institute, 259
Montreal Museum of Fine Arts, 259,
    259
Moody's Investor Services, 254–255
Mulvad, Nils, 207n9
Murray Guard acquisition, 138
Murray, Roger Jr., 138

N

Nagy, Justin, 274
National Accounts program, 118

National Advisory Committee for
    Foundations, Inc., 168
National Association of Security
    Companies (NASCO), 78,
    155
National Retail Dry Goods
    Association, 36
Nelson, D.D., 77
Nelson-Henry Award, 77
New York City market, 270–271
    prized acquisition, 271–272
    Universal merges with
        AlliedBarton, 272–273
Nils Karlsson-Pyssling, 212
Noa, 110
*No Off Season: The Constant Pursuit
    of More* (Jones), 264
Nørby Committee, 205
NVD, 197
NYA, 253

O

Oasis Outsourcing, 60
O'Connor, Matt, 143n6
Older, Freemont, 35
Olympic Torch Tower, 93, *93*
"One Group, Three Businesses"
    model, 235
operational leadership, 96
organic growth, at Wackenhut
    Company, 59–60, *61*
Oringer, Cecile, 130, *131*
Oringer, Keith, 116, 281n24
Oringer, Kenneth W., 6, 103–105, 107,
    112, 115–117, 286–287,
    297, 301
    Baker Industries, career at, 126,
        130–134, *131*, *134*
    early life and career, 126–127
        accounting, tax, and finance,
            128
        financial acumen, 128–130
        law degree, military service, and
            marriage, 127–128
    graduation picture, *127*
    reflections on career, 141–143
    team up with Chuck, 132–133
    U.S. Security Associates, 134–136,
        136, *137*

acquisitions and investors,
 136–140, *139*, **139–140**
Allied Universal, acquisition by,
 140–141
Goldman Sachs, 140
Oticon Foundation, 206n6, 207n7

P
Palantir Technologies Inc., 262n22
Pan-American Investigation Service,
 Inc., 142
Paragon Systems, 221
Parrish, Michael, 70n26
Partners Group, 270, 271
Pasteur, Louis, 302
Past-Positive (1998), 119
Pearl Harbor, *52–53*, *53*, 265
Pedersen, Nels, 204
Peltz, James F., 100n3
Penn Mutual Insurance Company, 51
Penn State University, 124, *124*
Pennsylvania coal fields, violence in,
 21–23
Perelman, Ronald O., 149, *165*, 167
Perform & Transform, 238
Peterson, Kevin E., 7n11, 313n7
Petruno, Tom, 30n43
Phagan, Mary, 38
Philip-Sørensen, Carl Julius, 177
Philip-Sørensen, Erik, 172, *175*, *176*,
 177–178, 190n10
Philip-Sørensen, Jørgen (JPS), 6,
 171–172, *175*, *176*, 197,
 199, 202, 204, 287, 297
 early life, 178–179
 facing obstacles, 185–186
 family rift, 180
 Group 4 building services, 180–
  185, *181–183*
 legacy, 186–190, *187*, *188*
 mergers and acquisitions, 186
 in security and cleaning industry, 177
 security business, learning,
  179–180
Philip-Sørensen, Mark, 188–190
Pinkerton, Allan, 1, 5, 6, 36, 49, 94,
 286, 297, 300, 303
 agency
  express companies, *19*, 19–20

hiring talented agents and
  managers, 15, *16*, *17*, 18
 Library of Congress
  Administrative File on, 14
 National Detective Agency, 14
 Reno Gang, 18–19
 service, during Civil War, 15
Anti-Pinkerton Act (1893), 23–24
business innovations, 20–21
Code of ethics, 20
debt, refinanced, 95
dynasty, 24–25
early life and career, *12*, 12–13
General Motors, 96
Homestead strikes, 23–24
later life, 21
 death and company succession,
  23
 Molly Maguires, 21–23, *22*
leadership and management skills,
 11
legacy, 25, *26*, 27
logo, *13*
Manhattan corporate
  headquarters, 95
ownership changes, 25
Rogues' Gallery, 21
secret service, 15
Securitas acquires, 97, 98
security services dynasty, 11
shareholders, 97
Pinkerton Detective Agency, 24
Pinkerton, Joan, *12*
Pinkerton, Robert A., 24, 25, 29n39
Pinkerton's Inc., 4, 25, 96, 97, 100n2,
 162–163, 166, 172, 216–
 218, 286
Pinkerton, William, *12*
Pittmetal Company, 232
Pitts, Gordon, 260n1
Plant Protection, 179
Plough, Abe, 77
Pony Express, 20, 103
Post-Positive (1995), 119
*Potential: Workplace Violence
 Prevention and Your
 Organizational Success* (Bill),
 155
Potts, Mark, 125n8

P.R. Hoffman Company, 111
Private Security Officer Employment
    Authorization Act, 78
Professional Security Bureau (PSB),
    149, 165
Prosegur, 6, 133, 227, 228, 229, *231*,
    232, 232, 234, 288, 298,
    313n6
  civic, charitable, and professional
    endeavors, 239–241
  expansion to U.S. market, 236
  global expansion and resilience,
    235–239
  Helena steps up to run, 234
  navigating loss, recession, and
    pandemic, 236–238
  in Spain, 233–234
  successful family enterprise,
    238–239
Provost, Claire, 7n2
Pyrillis, Rita, 156n1
Pysslingen, 212–213

Q
Queen Elizabeth II Diamond Jubilee
    Medal, *259, 260*

R
Raab, Selwyn, 112, 124n1
Rabena, Ron, *148*
Rafalko, Frank J., 28n11
Ramos, Jerold, 152
Rand Corporation, 311
Rathblott, Paul L., 133
RCA Corporation, 91
Reckert, Clare M., 143n3
Red Box Alert (2011), 119
Reed, Mark, 141
remote monitoring, 306
Reno Gang, 18–19
Responsive Management (2000), 119
Ressler, Anne Marie, 33
Revoredo, Helena, 227
Reynolds, Tim, 117
Rick, *see* Wackenhut, Richard R.
Right of Privacy Act, 62
Roberson, Dave, 266
Roberts, Joe, 313n7

Roberts, Sam, 86n1
Rogues' Gallery, 21
Roosevelt, Theodore, *35*
Roy, George M., *35*
Ruef, Abraham, *35*

S
Sabatino, Tony, 221
SAFETY Act, 120
Sanders, Gary A., *199*
Sapse, Marcel, 138
Sava, Justina Alexandra, 312n3
Scandinavian business model, 172
Schering-Plough, 77
Schmidt, Waldemar, 172, 190n3, *196*,
    203–204, 207n13, 224n7,
    225n12
Schneider, Charles R., 6, 103, 104,
    126, 286–287, 297, 301
  Baker Industries, security career at,
    111–115
  career, reflections on, 122–124,
    123, 124
  early life and education, 107–111,
    109
  at International Security Ligue
    Meeting, 107, *108*
  Ken team up with, 132–133
  U.S. Security Associates, 116–117
    acquired, *121*, 121–122
    employee morale and company
    growth, 120–121
    innovative programs, 119–120
Schneider, Chuck, 137
Schneider, Keith, 70n27
Schoemaker, Paul J. H., 301, 302n2
Schoenrock, Todd Brady, 69n15
Schörling, Melker, 213
Schudel, Matt, 69n22
Scott, Henry, 38–39
Seacurity, 99
Second Industrial Revolution, 44–45
Securitas AB, 4, 6, 180, 227, 272, 288,
    299–300, 306–307, 312n4
  Berglund's career at, 209–210, *210*,
    213–214, 220–222, *221*,
    223–224
  global presence and size of, 172

in integrity, vigilance, and
    helpfulness, *214*, 214–216
leading worldwide, 216–220
logo, 178
Pinkerton's Inc., 11, 25, 97, 135
Securitas Executive Training (SET),
    222
Securitas model, 215, 217
Securitas Toolbox, 222
Securities and Exchange Commission,
    149
Security Bureau, Inc., 142
Security Direct, 220
Security Forces, Inc. (SFI), 270
Security Information Systems (2012),
    119
Security Services Corporation, 58
security services industry
    in challenging environment,
        311–312
    growth of, 3–5, 303, 305
    investments, in technology
        accelerate, 305–307
    management opportunities in,
        310–311
    opportunities, for entrepreneurs,
        307
        base and leverage relationships,
            307–308
        cash flow, 309
        gain traction, expand and lead
            team, 309–310
        risk management, 308–309
        vision, plan and execute, 308
    understanding, 2–3
Security Systems, Inc., *165*
Segura, Tony, 161
Service Employees International
    Union (SEIU), 218
service enterprise engineering (SEE)
    program, 124
Seward, William H., 15
SFI Electronics, Inc. (SFIE), 270
Shabong, Yadarisa, 261n17
Sheridan, William, 36
Silcoff, Sean, 261n13
Sims, Brian, 208n29
Sinclair, Harry, 41, 42

Singer, Penny, 156n8
Skagen 2004 Trust, 201
Skrinet, 180
Smith, Jay, *57*
Smith, Marshall, 130
Social Democrat Party, 212
Special Agent Security Guards, Inc.,
    58
SpectaGuard, 6, 103–104, 144–148,
    153, 159, 163–164, *164*,
    167, 287
Spreckler, Rudolph, 35
Staffing Services, 60
Stanley Security, 220
Stanton, William, 57–58
Stavro, Barry, 101n14
*Stealing: How America's Employees
    Are Stealing Their
    Companies Blind* (Lipman),
    81
Stemman, Roy, 191n16
Stéphan Crétier Foundation, 258–259,
    260
Stephens, Inc., 79
Stephens, Jack, 79
Stern, Andy, 218
Steve, *see* Jones, Steve
Stevens, Barrie, 312n1
Stockholm Exchange, 213
Stockholm School of Economics, 211
storm clouds, 94
    Berger, Albert J., 95–96
    challenging acquisition, 94–95
    General Motors, 96
    operational leadership, 96
Strom, Kevin, 7n4
Stumpp, Dorothy M., 88
Sustainable Development Goals, 240
Swedish Employer's Confederation
    (SAF), 212
Swedish Management Group, 212
Swedish Nattvakt, 178
Swedish Securitas, 175
System 4 International BV, 185

T
Tatom, Oliver, 45n8
Taylor, Alan, 87n18

Teapot Dome, 40–42
TenBroek, James, *116*
Textron Inc., 129
Thoma, Carl, *116*
Thomas, Steve, 313n8
Thompson, C.W. Bud, 57
Thornbury, Frederick, *55*
Thrive Technology, 270
Thyssen, Baron, 130
Thyssen-Bornemisza Group, 130
T&M Protection Resources, LLC, 271
Tom, *see* Wathen, Thomas W.
Tour-Positive (2004), 119
Trahey, Bridget, 31
TransCanada, 259
Transportation Security
      Administration, 80
Trauscht, Donald C., 115
Tyecliffe, 63

U
Ullsten, Ola, *212*
Ulrich, Charles, 32–34
uniformed security guard service, 93
United American Security LLC (UAS),
      251
United Guarding Company, 177
Universal Protection Service, 6, 82,
      156n10, 228, 263, 280n16, 288
   with AlliedBarton, 271–272
   SFI, 270
   Steve's career at, 267–269
Universal Services of America, 153
USA Link (2003), 119
USA Training Academy (2005), 119
USA Visitor Management System
      (2007), 119
U.S. market, expansion to, 236
U.S. Private Guard Contractor Key
      Operating Statistics (2003),
      139–140
U.S. Secret Service, 33–34, 36
U.S. Security Associates, 6, 103–105,
      107, 112, 126, 132, 142,
      286–287
   Allied Universal acquired, 272
   Chuck and Ken founded, 116–117,
      134–136, *136–137*

   acquired, *121*, 121–122
   acquisitions and investors,
      136–140, *139*, **139–140**
   Allied Universal, 140–141
   employee morale and company
      growth, 120–121
   Goldman Sachs, 140
   innovative programs, 119–120
   operating efficiency, 117–118
   right partners, right people, 118
   systems implementation, 117–118

V
van Weering, Els, 207n13, 224n7
Viewpoint, 236
Vimy Foundation, 259

W
Wackenhut Corrections Corporation
      (WCC), 6, 49, *51*, 53, *54*, *55*,
      57, 186, 286, 299
   becomes industry power, 58–59
   controversy and notoriety, 61–64, *62*
   Group 4 Falck, 64–65, *65–66*,
      198–200
   organic growth and diversification
      at, *59–60*, *61*
Wackenhut, George R., 5, 49, *55*, 199,
      286, 297, 299
   career at FBI, 57–58
   early life, 49–52
   legacy, 66–67, *67–68*
   military service, pearl harbor, and
      marriage, 52–56, *53–55*
   teacher and coach, 56–57
   The Wackenhut Corporation, 58–59
   controversy and notoriety,
      61–64, *62*
   Group 4 Falck, 64–65, *65–66*
   organic growth and
      diversification at, 59–60, *61*
Wackenhut, Richard R., 49, *50–51*,
      52, *54*, 55, *55*, 58, 63–66,
      65–68, 95
Wackenhut, Ruth, *55*, 56, *56*, 57, 60,
      63, 66, 199
Wackenhut Services, Inc., 59–60
Wackenhut, William Henry, 49

Walker, Donald W., 97–98, 101n19
Wall Street bombing (1920), *39*,
        39–40
Walmart, 73, 79
Walton, Geri, 27n4
Walton, Sam, 73
Warne, Kate, 15, *17*, 18
Wathen, Susie, 88–90, *90*, 94–95, 100
Wathen, Thomas W., 5, 25, 105, 135,
        162, 286, 297, 301
    in Air Force, 88, *89*
    CPP, 92
        organic growth, 94
        understanding risk profiles,
            92–93, *93*
    early life, 88–90, *90*
        aerospace and security, passion
            for, 91
        West Coast businesses, 91–92
    legacy, 97–100, *99*
    storm clouds, 94
        Berger, Albert J., 95–96
        challenging acquisition, 94–95
        General Motors, 96
        operational leadership, 96
    winds of change, 96–97
Wathen, William H. "Jack", 88–89
WCC, *see* Wackenhut Corrections
        Corporation (WCC)
Weather Watch (2009), 119
Wells Fargo, 6, 103, 107, 112–113,
        115, 126, 133, 142, 218,
        286–287
Wells Fargo Express, *19*, 20
Welton, Benjamin, 45n4, 46n16
Wendel SE, 152–153, 156, 157n22,
        279n1, 280n19–280n20

Wesleyville High School, 108
Wharton School of Business, 81
Wheeler, Burton K., 41
Whelan Security, 251
Whitmore, Jeanie, *146*
Whitmore, William C. Jr., 6, 103–105,
        146, 156n2, 163, *164*, 287,
        297
    AlliedBarton Security Services,
        150–153, *153*
    Allied SpectraGuard, *148*,
        148–149
    early life and career, 144–145, *145*
    leads Allied Security, 149–150
    legacy, 153–156
    SpectaGuard, 144, 146–148
    Universal Services of America, 153
Wiedrich, Robert, 87n22
Wildhorn, Sorrel, 311
Wilkie, John, 34
Winberg, Håkan, 214
Wind Point Partners, 117, 121, *121*,
        136–137
Winners Circle, 120
Witco Company, 161
World Aware, 253
World Class Customer Service, 120
World Trade Center (1993), 81
Wright-Patterson Air Force
        Base, 91

Y
Yoxall, Patricia, 133

Z
Zirilli, Marie, *66*
Zoley, George, *54*

For Product Safety Concerns and Information please contact our EU
representative GPSR@taylorandfrancis.com
Taylor & Francis Verlag GmbH, Kaufingerstraße 24, 80331 München, Germany

9 781032 259048